The Husserl Dictionary

Continuum Philosophy Dictionaries

The *Continuum Philosophy Dictionaries* offer clear and accessible guides to the work of some of the more challenging thinkers in the history of philosophy. A-Z entries provide clear definitions of key terminology, synopses of key works, and details of each thinker's major themes, ideas and philosophical influences. The *Dictionaries* are the ideal resource for anyone reading or studying these key philosophers.

Titles available in the series:

The Gadamer Dictionary
Chris Lawn and Niall Keane

The Hegel Dictionary
Glenn Alexander Magee

The Marx Dictionary
Ian Fraser and Lawrence Wilde

The Sartre Dictionary
Gary Cox

Also available from Continuum:

Husserl: A Guide for the Perplexed
Matheson Russell

The Husserl Dictionary

Dermot Moran and Joseph Cohen

Continuum Philosophy Dictionaries

continuum

Continuum International Publishing Group

The Tower Building	80 Maiden Lane
11 York Road	Suite 704
London SE1 7NX	New York NY 10038

www.continuumbooks.com

British Library Cataloguing-in-Publication Data
A catalogue record for this book is available from the British Library.

ISBN: HB: 978-1-8470-6462-2
PB: 978-1-8470-6463-9

Library of Congress Cataloging-in-Publication Data
Moran, Dermot.
The Husserl dictionary / Dermot Moran and Joseph Cohen.
p. cm. -- (Continuum philosophy dictionaries)
Includes bibliographical references and index.
ISBN 978-1-84706-463-9 (pbk. : alk. paper) -- ISBN 978-1-84706-462-2 (hardcover : alk. paper) -- ISBN 978-1-4411-1244-6 (ebook pdf : alk. paper) -- ISBN 978-1-4411-1648-2 (ebook epub : alk. paper) 1. Husserl, Edmund, 1859-1938--Dictionaries. I. Cohen, Joseph D., 1971- II. Title. III. Series.

B3279.H93Z88 2012
193--dc23
2011034819

Typeset by Fakenham Prepress Solutions, Fakenham, Norfolk NR21 8NN
Printed and bound in India

Contents

Acknowledgements

We are very grateful to the Philosophy Editor at Continuum, Sarah Campbell, and to David Avital, for their patience and encouragement. We would also like to thank Rasmus Thybo Jensen and Ignacio de los Reyes Melero for their assistance on several entries and for their general philosophical advice. We are deeply grateful to the many Husserl scholars who have commented on individual entries. In particular, we would like to thank Jocelyn Benoist, Steve Crowell, Françoise Dastur, Nicolas de Warren, John Drummond, Lester Embree, Sara Heinämaa, Burt Hopkins, Hanne Jacobs, Sebastian Luft, Tom Nenon, Andrea Staiti, Thomas Vongehr and Dan Zahavi, for discussion of matters Husserlian. Of course, in addition to being a work of reference, a dictionary is also a work of interpretation and, as authors, we must bear full responsibility for the interpretations offered here. We also gratefully acknowledge the Irish Research Council for Humanities and Social Sciences (IRCHSS) for their support for the 2008–2010 research project 'Phenomenology of Consciousness and Subjectivity' (PI: Dermot Moran) under whose auspices the research and writing of this book was carried out.

Introduction

The aim of this *Husserl Dictionary* is to provide, in a single volume, clear, concise and, at the same time, philosophically informative, brief definitions and explanations (in an A to Z) of Edmund Husserl's key technical terms. We have also included information on Husserl's major publications, as well as brief biographical entries on the main philosophers who either influenced him or were influenced by him. As far as possible, Husserl's key concepts are explained in non-technical terms and the main instances of their occurrence in his published works are recorded.

Husserl was an innovative thinker and was something of a magpie in the way in which he gathered his terms together. He sometimes invented terms (e.g. 'the neutrality modification', *die Neutralitätsmodifikation*; 'sensings', *Empfindisse*) or ran existing terms together to make new terms (e.g. 'self-thinker', *Selbstdenker*). He borrowed terms from the philosophical tradition (essence, matter, form, transcendental, soul), including classical Greek thought, e.g. *doxa, eidos, epochē, hyle, morphē, noesis, noema, telos, theoria*), as well as Latin philosophy (*a priori, alter ego, cogito, cogitatio, cogitatum, ego, sum*). He adapted terms from psychology (e.g. 'outer perception', 'inner perception', 'ideation') or other sciences (e.g. 'attitude', 'worldview') or invested everyday terms with new technical meanings (e.g. 'adumbration', 'horizon', 'world'). He took up and adopted in a unique manner terms that were in use in the philosophical circles of his day (e.g., 'facticity', *Faktizität*; 'lived experience', *Erlebnis*; 'life-world', *Lebenswelt*; 'empathy', *Einfühlung*; 'intersubjectivity', *Intersubjektivität*). Sometimes, Husserl borrows terms directly from Descartes, Hume (e.g. 'matters of fact'), or Kant ('manifold', 'receptivity', 'synthesis', 'transcendental ego'). But, even with all his inventions and borrowings, the outcome is uniquely Husserl's own and his thinking is expressed in a unique and identifiable style of expression.

As with other major philosophers such as Aristotle or Hegel, Husserl's technical terms belong within a web of mutual interconnecting meanings. It is often therefore impossible to explain one term without invoking another related or contrasting technical term. As far as possible, this *Husserl Dictionary* endeavors to present Husserl's technical vocabulary by connecting the key terms with one another in a transparent and systematic way. Husserl himself aimed at – although manifestly never attained – systematicity and his thought often proceeded by making more refined distinctions within existing contrasting terms or replacing standard distinctions with new ways of understanding the problem. Of course, Husserl's thought was also constantly evolving through his career and certain terminological distinction are only found in the earlier writings or, again, emerge only in the later work (e.g. 'life-world'). Husserl often became dissatisfied with his earlier conceptions and attempts at clarification, and sometimes remarks that the new concept expresses what he really tried to say with the older concept (thus 'eidetic intuition' replaces 'ideation' in *Ideas* I, although the term does continue to appear in later writings). To address this difficulty, the *Husserl Dictionary* has tried as far as possible to indicate to which period a term belongs and whether Husserl later abandoned it or altered its meaning. We have also tried to give a canonical instance or location in a published text to help situate the concept. Finally, Husserl's thought moved relentlessly on, and although he continually revisited and revised earlier manuscripts, he was also impatient with the editing process and even abandoned manuscripts that were almost ready for publication. One consequence of this is that Husserl often introduces new distinctions or terms in the middle of analysis that do not appear to be employed in later drafts. Moreover, Husserl is not always consistent with his terminology and it is often a matter of interpretation as what exactly he meant. For example, he uses the term *Vergegenwärtigung*, translated as 'representation' or as 'presentification' or 'presentiation' (to distinguish it from 'presentation' (*Vorstellung*)), which in everyday German suggests the process of 'calling to mind', 'visualizing' or 'conjuring up an image in one's mind', to characterize quite a number of processes – including not just imagining, but remembering and also empty intending – which are to be contrasted with the full presence of the intended object in a genuine 'presenting' or 'presencing' (*Gegenwärtigung*). Here, some familiarity with Husserl's overall theory of intuiting is needed to understand fully what is at stake. In our entries, therefore, we have tried to flesh out the philosophical significance of these terms for Husserl. As far as possible, and as befits a dictionary, we have tried to give as sound and conservative a reading as possible but there are undoubtedly interpretations of terms with which the experts will disagree. Compiling a dictionary opens up, to paraphrase Husserl, a set of infinite tasks. It can never be finished; new clarifications are called for and new connections constantly manifest themselves. We have tried as best we can to present a solid and reliable guide to Husserl's main terms. We are confident that the *Dictionary* can be of assistance of students struggling to understand Husserl's often dense and challenging texts but we also hope, given that we have ventured to offer our own original interpretation of Husserlian terms, that it will be of interest to more advanced readers of Husserl.

Edmund Husserl (1859–1938), founder of the philosophical method known as *phenomenology* (the descriptive science of experience and its objects in the manner in which they are experienced), became one of the most influential philosophers of the twentieth century and undoubtedly *the* most influential philosopher in the European Continental tradition (strongly influencing Martin Heidegger, Alfred Schütz, Emmanuel Levinas, Jean-Paul Sartre, Maurice Merleau-Ponty and Jacques Derrida, among many others). Over a long and active research and teaching career he elaborated on the meaning of phenomenology, initially as a method for clarifying central concepts in logic and epistemology, but gradually expanded as a fully fledged transcendental philosophy and even transcendental idealism.

Edmund Husserl was born into a middle-class, Jewish family (his father owned a draper's store) in Prossnitz, Moravia (now Prostejov in the Czech Republic), on 8 April 1859. He studied mathematics and physics at the universities of Leipzig and Berlin (where he was deeply influenced by the mathematician Carl Weierstrass, (1815–1897)), before moving to the University of Vienna, where he completed his doctorate in mathematics in 1882. Following a brief period as Weierstrass' assistant and a term of compulsory military service in the army, Husserl went back to Vienna, on the recommendation of his friend and philosophy student Thomas Masaryk to study philosophy with Franz Brentano from 1884 to 1886. On Brentano's recommendation, Husserl then went to the University of Halle to study under the direction of Brentano's most senior student, Carl Stumpf (1848–1936), completing his *Habilitation* thesis, *On the Concept of Number. Psychological Analyses* in 1887.

Husserl remained in Halle as a lowly, unsalaried lecturer or *Privatdozent* from 1887 until 1901, the unhappiest years of his life, as he later confessed. In 1891 he published his first book, *Philosophy of Arithmetic*, whose opening chapters contained a revised version of his 1887 *Habilitation* thesis.[1] *Philosophy of Arithmetic* is an essay in descriptive psychology. It analyses the psychological operations necessary to generate the concept of number. It was planned as the first of two books but the second was never published. In 1894 Husserl's *Philosophy of Arithmetic* was reviewed critically by the German mathematician and logician Gottlob Frege who pointed out the *psychologism* latent in Husserl's approach to arithmetic, i.e. that Husserl was assuming that logical inference really was a matter of certain psychological operations. It was to be another 10 years before Husserl published his immense two-volume *Logical Investigations* (1900/1901).[2]

Husserl first announced his new phenomenological approach in his *Logical Investigations*. The first volume, *Prologomena to Pure Logic*, appeared separately in 1900, and contains a long and detailed critique of psychologism, with Husserl freely admitting that he now sides with Frege on this matter. This volume was well received in Germany and was reviewed by Paul Natorp and other well-known German philosophers. Natorp reviewed the *Prolegomena* favourably in *Kant-Studien* in 1901, portraying Husserl as broadening the essentially Kantian inquiry into the necessary conditions of the possibility of experience

In the First Edition of the Second Volume (itself published in two parts) of this work, Husserl took over an existing philosophical term 'phenomenology' (*Phänomenologie*) – a term already in use in Germany philosophy since Lambert, Kant and Hegel, but given new currency by Husserl's teacher Franz Brentano – to characterize his new approach to the conditions of the possibility of knowledge in general. Husserl initially conceived of phenomenology as a kind of descriptive psychology, clarifying the essential terms (perception, judgement, and so on) employed by psychology and that underpinned the sciences, especially logic. As Husserl wrote in the Introduction to his *Logical Investigations*:

> *Pure* phenomenology represents a field of neutral researches,
> in which several sciences have their roots. It is, on the one
> hand, ancillary to *psychology* conceived as an *empirical sci-
> ence*. Proceeding in purely intuitive fashion, it analyses and

describes in their essential generality – in the specific guise of a phenomenology of thought and knowledge – the experiences of presentation, judgement and knowledge, experiences which, treated as classes of real events in the natural context of zoological reality, receive a scientific probing at the hands of empirical psychology. Phenomenology, on the other hand, lays bare the 'sources' from which the basic concepts and ideal laws of *pure* logic 'flow', and back to which they must once more be traced, so as to give them all the 'clearness and distinctness' needed for an understanding, and for an epistemological critique, of pure logic. (LU Introduction § 1, **I**, p. 166; Hua XIX/1 6–7).

According to Husserl, the logician is not interested in mental acts as such, but only in the objective meanings to which the mental acts are directed and in their formal regulation and implications; the phenomenologist, by way of contrast, is concerned with the essential structures of cognitive acts and their essential correlation to the objects apprehended by those acts. It is in this Introduction to *Logical Investigations* Volume Two that Husserl utters the famous sentence, 'we must go back to the things themselves' (*Wir wollen auf die 'Sachen selbst' zurückgehen*, LU Intro. § 2, **I**, p. 168; Hua XIX/1 10), an expression that would quickly become the clarion cry of the new phenomenology indicating the bypassing of sterile philosophical disputes and a turn to the concrete issues.

Husserl initially characterized phenomenology ambiguously as either a parallel discipline to *epistemology* or 'the critique of knowledge' (*Erkenntniskritik*) or even as a more radical grounding of epistemology, that sought to *clarify* the essences of acts of cognition in their most general sense. In analyzing knowledge, Husserl wanted to do justice both to the necessary *ideality* (that is: self-identity and independence of space and time) of the truths known in cognition (e.g. the Pythagorean theorem; or the statement $2 + 2 = 4$), and to the essential contribution of the knowing acts of the subject. Looking back in 1925, Husserl described the aim of the *Logical Investigations* as follows:

In the year 1900–01 appeared my *Logical Investigations* which were the results of my ten year long efforts to clarify the

Idea of pure Logic by going back to the sense-bestowing or
cognitive achievements being effected in the complex of lived
experiences of logical thinking.[3]

Husserl himself regarded his *Logical Investigations* as his 'breakthrough
work, not so much an end as a beginning' (*Werk des Durchbruchs, und
somit nicht ein Ende, sondern ein Anfang,* LU Foreword to 2nd Edition,
I, p. 3; Hua XVIII 8). Soon after its publication, around 1902/1903,
Husserl began to distance his phenomenology from descriptive psychology,
which he felt was too much in thrall to empirical psychology. Husserl
now claimed that transcendental phenomenology as a science of pure
essential possibilities of knowing was entirely distinct from psychology
in all forms, including descriptive psychology (which he now treats as a
branch of empirical psychology). Psychology was a factual science that
studied the mental acts of human beings and other animals understood as
belonging to nature. Phenomenology, in contrast, was to be a pure a priori
science of essential necessities, finding essential laws governing cognition,
knowledge and the whole of the life of consciousness. This led to Husserl's
lifelong struggle against *naturalism* and the naturalistic misconstrual of
consciousness (as expressed for instance in his 1910/1911 essay 'Philosophy
as a Rigorous Science'). In later years, he would again return to the issue of
the relationship between a phenomenological psychology of the essential
structures of consciousness and his transcendental phenomenology, which
located all sense formations in the achievements of the transcendental
ego. For the mature Husserl, every insight of phenomenological psychology
would have its parallel in the domain of transcendental phenomenology.

The publication of the *Logical Investigations* enabled Husserl to move
from Halle to Göttingen University, at that time a renowned centre
of mathematics under David Hilbert (1862–1943). During his years at
Göttingen (1901–1916) Husserl began to attract both German and international students to pursue the practice and theory of phenomenology.
However, Husserl still managed only two publications between 1901 and
1916: an important long essay, 'Philosophy as a Rigorous Science', commissioned by Heinrich Rickert for his new journal *Logos* in 1910/1911,[4] in
which Husserl outlined his opposition to all forms of naturalism and historicism; and a major book, *Ideas pertaining to a Pure Phenomenology and
to a Phenomenological Philosophy*[5] (hereafter *Ideas* I), published in 1913

in his own newly founded *Yearbook for Philosophy and Phenomenological Research*, which offered an entirely new way of entering into phenomenology. Many of Husserl's earlier students (including Edith Stein, Moritz Geiger and Roman Ingarden) were shocked by the idealist turn of *Ideas* I and wanted to return phenomenology's commitment to realism.

In 1916 Husserl took up the chair of philosophy, vacated by neo-Kantian Heinrich Rickert, at the University of Freiburg, which he held until his retirement in 1928. However, in these years he published almost nothing, apart from an article on the renewal of philosophy in a Japanese journal *Kaizo*, a short article on the Buddha, and a truncated version of his lectures on time, *On the Consciousness of Internal Time* (1928), edited by his successor to the Freiburg Chair, Martin Heidegger.[6] Following his retirement and more or less to the end of his life, however, Husserl was extremely active, giving lectures in Germany, Holland and France in the late 1920s. He also published *Formal and Transcendental Logic* in 1929,[7] a book meant to offer an update on his thinking about logic, and the French version of his Paris lectures, *Méditations cartésiennes*, in 1931, translated by Gabrielle Peiffer and Emmanuel Levinas.[8] In his mature works from *Ideas* I, notably the *Cartesian Meditations* (1931), Husserl presented his approach as a radicalization of Descartes' project that sought to return knowledge to a foundation in the certainty of subjective experience (*cogito ergo sum*).

Following the National Socialist seizure of power in Germany in January 1933, Husserl and his family suffered under the increasingly severe anti-Semitic laws enacted from 1933 onwards, leading to the suspension of his emeritus rights and in 1935 to the withdrawal of his German citizenship. Meanwhile, he continued to live in Freiburg, forced to wear the yellow star, mostly shunned by his former colleagues, apart from his loyal assistant Eugen Fink (1905–1975) and his former student Ludwig Landgrebe (1902–1991), who was then professor in Prague. In his later years, Husserl prepared his extensive research manuscripts for publication, but he also managed to write with new vigour against the crisis of the age, producing work of astonishing scope and originality, namely the *Crisis of European Sciences*, developed in lectures in Vienna and Prague, and published in article form in a new journal, *Philosophia*, in Belgrade in 1936 (publication in Germany being denied him).[9] After a period of illness beginning in 1937, Husserl died in Freiburg in 1938. His last work, *Erfahrung und Urteil* (*Experience and Judgment*) appeared posthumously, with the extensive editorial involvement of Ludwig Landgrebe, in 1938 but due to the outbreak of war was not distributed until after 1945.[10] In the summer of 1938, Father Herman Leo von Breda, a young Franciscan priest and philosopher reading at the time for the Doctorate in Philosophy at the Catholic University of Leuven, visited the University of Freiburg in order to complete his doctoral research on phenomenology and, having met with Husserl's widow Malvine and his former assistant Eugen Fink, discovered that Husserl's legacy, more than 40,000 manuscripts, was in danger. Rightly fearing they would be entirely destroyed by the Nazi regime, Father von Breda took it on himself to rescue the totality of these manuscripts and bring them to safety at the Catholic University of Leuven. This highly courageous act was accomplished with the help of Fink and Landgrebe, both of whom were also attributed the responsibility of editing the manuscripts in Leuven, as well as with the assistance of then Belgian Prime Minister, Paul-Henri Spaak. The manuscripts constitute the basis of Husserl's Complete Works, the *Husserliana* edition, edited in Leuven. These manuscripts are now kept at the Husserl Archives there. There are further archives in Freiburg, Cologne, Paris and in New York (New School for Social Research), where important research and editorial work on Husserl's *Nachlass* continues to be carried out.

Over the course of the twentieth century Husserl's phenomenology influenced a large and diverse group of European philosophers, including Martin Heidegger, Alfred Schutz, Aron Gurwitch, Hans-George Gadamer, Jean-Paul Sartre, Maurice Merleau-Ponty, Paul Ricoeur, Jacques Derrida, Emmanuel Levinas, and Jan Patočka, to name but some. His thinking stimulated reactions from the Frankfurt School, especially Max Horkheimer, who regarded Husserl's philosophy as 'traditional theory' to which he opposed his own new 'critical theory', and Theodor Adorno, who criticized Husserl's epistemology, while Husserl's notion of the life-world was – through the mediation of Alfred Schutz – influential on Jürgen Habermas. Husserl's work continues to act as a stimulus for philosophy in France, for example in the work of Michel Henry and Jean-Luc Marion. Husserl continues to be an influential philosopher not just in terms of phenomenology and the postphenomenological traditions of contemporary European philosophy, but in relation to philosophy of mind, cognitive science, formal ontology and philosophy of logic and mathematics. In recent years, there has been a strong revival of interest in Husserl among analytic philosophers, especially those – such as Michael Dummett – interested in the origins of analytic philosophy and in Husserl's understanding of sense, reference and intentionality. Here Husserl's interaction with Frege is a matter of particular interest. Husserl's conception of intentionality continues to attract interest in contemporary philosophy of mind, with its renewed attention to consciousness, perception, embodiment and the relation to other subjects (intersubjectivity), e.g. in the work of Kevin Mulligan, Peter Simons, Barry Smith, David Woodruff Smith, among many others. Husserl's attempts at a formal ontology have been greatly developed during the twentieth century, and his philosophy of mathematics continues to provoke discussion. There is no doubt that Husserl has joined the list of great perennial philosophers and his work will continue to endure and stimulate creative thinking into the twenty-first century.

Husserl was a brilliant, original philosopher, a restless thinker whose thought never stopped evolving. His research work, like that of Wittgenstein, was always in progress, underway with frequent changes of mind. He called himself a perpetual beginner and he was constantly revising his views. But Husserl was also a deeply traditional German academic professor who wrote in a somewhat stilted, pedantic and heavily technical style, embedded with many terminological innovations. For these reasons it is difficult – without substantial help – to read a Husserl text and understand it. There is, therefore, an indisputable need for a *Husserl Dictionary* for non-specialists and philosophy students wanting to understand Husserl's phenomenology. In preparing this dictionary, we are fortunate to have had the opportunity to consult other dictionaries and guides to translation. We make particular mention here of Dorion Cairns' *Guide for Translating Husserl*, John J. Drummond's *Historical Dictionary of Husserl's Philosophy*, Jacques English's *Le Vocabulaire de Husserl* and Hans-Helmut Gander's *Husserl-Lexikon*.[11]

Dermot Moran and Joseph Cohen
University College Dublin
May 2011

Notes

1 Edmund Husserl, *Philosophie der Arithmetik. Mit ergänzenden Texten (1890–1901)*, hrsg. Lothar Eley, *Husserliana* Volume XII (The Hague: Nijhoff, 1970), trans. Dallas Willard, *Philosophy of Arithmetic. Psychological and Logical Investigations*, Husserl Collected Works vol. X (Dordrecht: Kluwer, 2003). Hereafter 'PA' with page number of the

English translation followed by the *Husserliana* (= 'Hua') volume and pagination of German edition.

2   See Edmund Husserl, *Logische Untersuchungen*. Erster Band: *Prolegomena zur reinen Logik*. Text der 1. und der 2. Auflage. hrsg. E. Holenstein *Husserliana* Volume XVIII (The Hague: Nijhoff, 1975) and *Logische Untersuchungen*. Zweiter Band: *Untersuchungen zur Phänomenologie und Theorie der Erkenntnis*. In zwei Bänden. hrsg. Ursula Panzer. *Husserliana* Volume XIX (Dordrecht: Kluwer, 1984), translated John Findlay, revised by Dermot Moran, edited with a new Introduction by Dermot Moran and new Preface by Michael Dummett, two volumes (London and New York: Routledge, 2001). Hereafter 'LU' with volume number (indicated in bold as **I** or **II**) and page number of English translation followed by the *Husserliana* (= 'Hua') volume and pagination of German edition.

3   Husserl, 'Task and Significance of the *Logical Investigations*', text taken from Husserl's 1925 lectures on *Phänomenologische Psychologie*, Hua IX (The Hague: Nijhoff, 1962), p. 20, trans. John Scanlon, *Phenomenological Psychology. Lectures, Summer Semester 1925* (The Hague: Nijhoff, 1977), p. 14. Hereafter '*Phen. Psych.*', with page number of the English translation followed by the *Husserliana* (= 'Hua') volume and pagination of German edition.

4   E. Husserl, 'Philosophie als strenge Wissenschaft', *Logos* 1 (1911), pp. 289–341, now collected in Husserl, *Aufsätze und Vorträge 1911–1921*, Hrsg. H.R. Sepp und Thomas Nenon, Hua XXV (Dordrecht: Kluwer, 1986), pp. 3–62, trans. 'Philosophy as Rigorous Science' by Marcus Brainard, *New Yearbook for Phenomenology and Phenomenological Philosophy* 2 (2002), pp. 249–95.'

5   The critical edition is published in *Husserliana* Vol. III/1 as *Ideen zu einer reinen Phänomenologie und phänomenologischen Philosophie. Erstes Buch: Allgemeine Einführung in die reine Phänomenologie 1. Halbband: Text der 1–3. Auflage*, hrsg. Karl Schuhmann (The Hague: Nijhoff, 1977), trans. by F. Kersten as *Ideas pertaining to a Pure Phenomenology and to a Phenomenological Philosophy, First Book* (Dordrecht: Kluwer, 1983). Hereafter '*Ideas* I' followed by page number of English translation and *Husserliana* volume number and pagination of German.

6   E. Husserl, *Zur Phänomenologie des inneren Zeitbewusstseins*

(1893–1917), hrsg. R. Boehm, Hua X (The Hague: Nijhoff, 1966, 2nd edn, 1969), trans. J.B. Brough, *On the Phenomenology of the Consciousness of Internal Time*, Husserl Collected Works IV (Dordrecht: Kluwer, 1990). Husserl expressed dissatisfaction with Heidegger's edition of these time lectures more or less from their publication.

7 Now *Husserliana* Vol. XVII: Edmund Husserl, *Formale und transzendentale Logik. Versuch einer Kritik der logischen Vernunft. Mit ergänzenden Texten*, hrsg. Paul Janssen (The Hague: Nijhoff, 1974), trans. by D. Cairns as *Formal and Transcendental Logic* (The Hague: Nijhoff, 1969).

8 E. Husserl, *Méditations cartésiennes: introduction à la phénoménologie*, trans. G. Peiffer and E. Levinas (Paris: Almand Colin, 1931). The German text was not published until 1950 as *Cartesianische Meditationen und Pariser Vorträge*, hrsg. Stephan Strasser, *Husserliana* I (The Hague: Nijhoff, 1950), trans. D. Cairns as *Cartesian Meditations. An Introduction to Phenomenology* (Dordrecht: Kluwer, 1993).

9 Edmund Husserl, *Die Krisis der europäischen Wissenschaften und die transzendentale Phänomenologie. Eine Einleitung in die phänomenologische Philosophie*, hrsg. W. Biemel, *Husserliana* VI (The Hague: Nijhoff, 1962), trans. David Carr as *The Crisis of European Sciences and Transcendental Phenomenology. An Introduction to Phenomenological Philosophy* (Evanston, IL: Northwestern University Press, 1970). Hereafter '*Crisis*' with page number of the English translation followed by the *Husserliana* volume and pagination of German edition.

10 E. Husserl, *Erfahrung und Urteil: Untersuchungen der Genealogie der Logik*, hrsg. L. Landgrebe, (Hamburg: Meiner, 1999), trans. James S. Churchill and Karl Ameriks as *Experience and Judgment. Investigations in a Genealogy of Logic* (Evanston, IL: Northwestern University Press, 1973).

11 Dorion Cairns, *Guide for Translating Husserl* (The Hague: Nijhoff, 1973); John J. Drummond, *Historical Dictionary of Husserl's Philosophy* (Lanham, MD: Scarecrow Press, 2008); Jacques English, *Le Vocabulaire de Husserl* (Paris: Editions Ellipses, 2004); Hans-Helmuth Gander, ed., *Husserl-Lexikon* (Darmstadt: Wissenschaftliche Buchgesellschaft, 2010). See also Helmuth Wetter, ed., *Wörterbuch der phänomenologischen Begriffe* (Hamburg: Felix Meiner, 2005).

Chronology: Husserl's Life and Works

1859 8 April	Born in Prossnitz, Moravia into a middle-class family of assimilated non-religious Jews. His father Adolf Abraham (1827–1884) owned a draper's store.
1865–1868	Attended local school in Prossnitz.
1868–1869	Attended Leopoldstädtes Realgymnasium in Vienna.
1869	Entered Deutsches Staatsgymnasium in Olmütz.
1876 30 June	Graduated from Deutsches Staatsgymnasium in Olmütz.
1876–1878	Studied astronomy, physics and mathematics at University of Leipzig. Some philosophy lectures from Wilhelm Wundt (1832–1920). Met philosophy student, Thomas Masaryk (1850–1937), who became a lifelong friend.
1878–1881	Studied mathematics with Karl Weierstrass (1815–1897) and Leopold Kronecker (1823–1891); philosophy lectures from Friedrich Paulsen (1846–1908) and Johann Eduard Erdmann (1805–1892) at the University of Berlin.
1881–1882	Studied mathematics at the University of Vienna.
1882 October	Submits his Doctorate thesis in mathematics entitled *Contributions to the Theory of the Calculus of Variations*, supervised by Leopold Königsberger (1837–1921), a disciple of Weierstrass.

1883–1884	Military service.
1884 April	Father dies.
1884–1886	On the recommendation of his friend Thomas Masaryk, Husserl studies philosophy with Franz Brentano in University of Vienna.
1884–1885	Attended Brentano's lecture course *Elementary Logic and its Necessary Reform.*
1886 26 April	Husserl baptized in the Lutheran church in Vienna.
1886–1887	Studies philosophy and psychology with Carl Stumpf in the University of Halle.
1887	Publication of *Habilitation* thesis, *On the Concept of Number. Psychological Analyses*, supervised by Carl Stumpf. Mathematician Georg Cantor (1845–1918) was a member of the examination committee.
1887 6 August	Husserl married Malvine Charlotte Steinschneider, a Jew who also converted to Christianity.
1887–1901	*Privatdozent* at the University of Halle.
1891	Publication of *Philosophy of Arithmetic. Psychological and Logical Investigations.*
1891	Corresponds with Gottlob Frege on logical problems.
1892 29 April	Daughter Elizabeth (Elli) born in Halle.
1893 22 December	Son Gerhart born in Halle.
1894	Frege reviews Husserl's *Philosophy of Arithmetic.* Husserl publishes article 'Psychological Studies in the Elements of Logic'.
1895 18 October	Son Wolfgang born in Halle.
1896	Unpublished review of Twardowski's 1894 book, *On the Content and Object of Presentations.*

1900   Publication of *Logical Investigations*. Volume One. *Prolegomena to Pure Logic*.

1901   Publication of *Logical Investigations*. Volume Two. *Investigations concerning the Phenomenology and the Theory of Knowledge* (published in two parts: Investigations One to Five in Part One; Investigation Six in Part Two).

1901   Meets Max Scheler.

1901 September   Appointed professor at University of Göttingen where David Hilbert is Professor of Mathematics and supportive of Husserl.

1902   Johannes Daubert (1877–1947), a student of Lipps, visits Husserl in Göttingen.

1903   Husserl publishes article 'Report on German Writings in Logic From the Years 1895–1899'.

1904   Husserl visits the psychologist Theodor Lipps in Munich and gives talk. Writes first draft of unfinished essays *Intentional Objects*.

1904–1905   Husserl lectures on internal time consciousness at Göttingen.

1905   Meeting with Wilhelm Dilthey in Berlin. Hilbert recommends Husserl for promotion, and the Ministry is ready to agree but the Göttingen Philosophy Faculty rejects his application on the grounds that his work lacks scientific merit. On vacation at Seefeld, near Innsbrück, Austria, writes manuscript in which the term 'phenomenological reduction' is used for first time.

1906–1907   Lectures on *Logic and the Theory of Knowledge* (published posthumously).

1907 March–April   Husserl delivers five lectures in Göttingen, *The Idea of*

	Phenomenology (published posthumously). Lectures on *Thing and Space* (published posthumously).
1908	*Lectures on the Theory of Meaning* (published posthumously).
1910/1911	Publication of 'Philosophy as a Rigorous Science' in Rickert's new journal *Logos*.
1910–11	Lectures on *Fundamental Problems of Phenomenology* (published posthumously).
1912	Establishment of the *Yearbook for Philosophy and Phenomenological Philosophy* with co-editors, Scheler, Reinach, Geiger and Pfänder. First drafts of manuscript that later became known as *Ideas* II.
1913	Publications of *Ideas Pertaining to a Pure Phenomenology and Phenomenological Philosophy* (*Ideas* I) in Volume One of the *Yearbook*. Second Revised Edition of *Logical Investigations* published.
1914	Outbreak of Great War. Husserl's sons drafted and his daughter volunteers for a field hospital.
1915	Son Wolfgang injured in the Great War.
1916 8 March	Son Wolfgang killed in Verdun.
1916 1 April	Husserl appointed to the Chair of Philosophy in Freiburg as successor to Heinrich Rickert. Meets Martin Heidegger who has just completed his Habilitation thesis.
1916–1918	Edith Stein employed as Husserl's assistant.
1917	Lectures on Fichte and the Idea of Humanity. Reinach killed on the Western front. Death of Franz Brentano. Lectures on *Nature and Spirit*.
1918	End of Great War.
1922 6–12 June	Visits London to give four lectures entitled 'The

Phenomenological Method and Phenomenological Philosophy'.

1923   Publication of article 'Renewal' in Japanese journal *Kaizo*. Contributes two more articles.

1923–1924   Lectures on *First Philosophy* (published posthumously).

1924   Lecture 'Kant and the Idea of Transcendental Philosophy' in Freiburg on occasion of 200th birthday of Kant.

1925   Delivers lecture course 'Phenomenological Psychology' (published posthumously).

1927   Publication of Heidegger, *Being and Time*. Cooperated with Heidegger in writing article on 'Phenomenology' for 14th Edition of *Encyclopedia Britannica*.

1928 31 March   Husserl retires from Freiburg University.

April   Delivers two lectures in Amsterdam on Phenomenology and Psychology. Publication of *Lectures on Internal Time Consciousness* edited by Heidegger.

1929 23–25 February   Delivers two lectures in Paris in the Descartes Amphitheatre of the Sorbonne, invited by the German Institute of the Sorbonne. In attendance were Emmanuel Levinas, Lucien Lévy-Bruhl, Jean Cavaillès, Jean Héring, Alexandre Koyré, Gabriel Marcel, and, possibly, Maurice Merleau-Ponty. Publication of *Formal and Transcendental Logic*.

1930   Publication of English translation by W.R. Boyce Gibson of Husserl's *Ideas* I. Husserl contributes an Afterword; German text published in *Yearbook*.

1931   Publication of French translation of *Cartesian Meditations* edited by Emmanuel Levinas and Gabrielle Peiffer.

1931	Delivers lecture 'Phenomenology and Anthropology' to Kant Society, Frankfurt. Further lectures in Berlin and Halle to large audiences.
1933 January	National Socialists come to power in Germany.
1933 6 April	Suspended from university due to National Socialist laws against non-Aryans in the civil service.
1934	Invited to VIIIth International Congress of Philosophy in Prague.
1935 7–10 May	Delivers Vienna lecture.
1935 November	Delivers lectures in Prague. During his Prague visit, on 18 November, Husserl also addressed the Brentano Society, and, on the invitation of Roman Jakobson, the *Cercle linguistique de Prague*.
1936	Publication of the first two parts of the planned
1937 January	*Crisis of European Sciences* in Belgrade in the journal *Philosophia*.
1937	Husserl forced to leave his house in Lorettorstrasse, Freiburg. From August becomes ill.
1938 27 April	Husserl dies. No one from the Freiburg Philosophy Faculty, except Gerhard Ritter, attended his funeral. Another Freiburg professor, Walter Eucken, an economist, also attended. Heidegger later explained he was sick in bed.
1938 15 August	A young Belgian Franciscan priest, Father Hermann Leo Van Breda, who had just completed his licentiate in philosophy in the Catholic University of Leuven, arrived in Freiburg intending to conduct doctoral research on Husserl. Meets Malvine Husserl and Eugen Fink and arranges for Husserl Archives to be moved to Leuven.

1938	*Experience and Judgment* prepared and published by Ludwig Landbrege.
1939 April	Husserl Archives open in Leuven. Merleau-Ponty one of the first to visit.
1950	First volume of *Husserliana* published. To date 40 volumes have appeared.

Abbreviations

APS	Husserl, *Analysen zur passiven Synthesis*, Hua XI (*Analyses Concerning Passive and Active Synthesis*, trans. A. J. Steinbock)
Briefwechsel	Husserl, *Briefwechsel*, ed. K. and E. Schuhmann, *Husserliana Dokumente*, Vol. 3, 10 vols
Chronik	*Husserl-Chronik*, ed. K. Schuhmann
CM	Husserl, *Cartesianische Meditationen*, Hua 1 (*Cartesian Meditations*, trans. D. Cairns)
Crisis	Husserl, *Die Krisis der europäischen Wissenschaften und die Transzendentale Phänomenologie*, Hua VI (*The Crisis of European Sciences*, trans. D. Carr)
DP	Brentano, *Deskriptive Psychologie*, ed. R. Chisholm and W. Baumgartner (*Descriptive Psychology*, trans. B. Müller)
DR	Husserl, *Ding und Raum*, Hua XVI (*Thing and Space: Lectures of 1907*, trans. R. Rojcewicz)
EB	*Encyclopaedia Brittanica* Article, Hua IX (*Psychological and Transcendental Phenomenology*, trans. T. Sheehan and R. E. Palmer)
ELE	Husserl, *Einleitung in die Logik und Erkenntnistheorie: Vorlesungen 1906/1907*, Hua XXIV (*Introduction to Logic and Theory of Knowledge*, trans. Claire Ortiz Hill)
EP I	Husserl, *Erste Philosophie (1923/1924)*, Erster Teil: *Kritische Ideengeschichte*, Hua VII (*First Philosophy* I)
EP II	Husserl, *Erste Philosophie (1923/24)*. Zweiter Teil: *Theorie der phänomenologischen Reduktion*, Hua VIII (*First Philosophy* II)

EU	Husserl, *Erfahrung und Urteil*, Hrsg. L. Landgrebe (*Experience and Judgment*, trans. J. Churchill and K. Ameriks)
EW	Husserl, *Early Writings in the Philosophy of Logic and Mathematics*, Collected Works Vol. V, trans. D. Willard
Fichte Lectures	Husserl, 'Fichtes Menschheitsideal. Drei Vorlesungen,' *Aufsätze und Vorträge (1911–1921)*, Hua XXV 267–93, trans. James G. Hart, 'Fichte's Ideal of Humanity [Three Lectures],' *Husserl Studies* 12 (1995), pp. 111–33.
FTL	Husserl, *Formale und transzendentale Logik*, Hua XVII (*Formal and Transcendental Logic*, trans. D. Cairns)
GPP	Husserl, *Grundprobleme der Phänomenologie* (*Fundamental Problems of Phenomenology* lectures 1910–11, trans. Ingo Farin and James G. Hart)
HSW	Husserl, *Shorter Works,* trans. and ed. Frederick Elliston and Peter McCormick.
Hua	*Husserliana*, Springer Publishers, 1950–
Ideas I	Husserl, *Ideen zu einer reinen Phänomenologie und phänomenologischen Philosophie*. Erstes Buch (*Ideas pertaining to a Pure Phenomenology and to a Phenomenological Philosophy, First Book*, trans. F. Kersten)
Ideas II	Husserl, *Ideen zu einer reinen Phänomenologie und phänomenologischen Philosophie*. Zweites Buch: *Phänomenologische Untersuchungen zur Konstitution*, Hua IV (*Ideas pertaining to a Pure Phenomenology and to a Phenomenological Philosophy, Second Book*, trans. R. Rojcewicz and A. Schuwer)
Ideas III	Husserl, *Ideen zu einer reinen Phänomenologie und phänomenologischen Philosophie*. Drittes Buch: *Die Phänomenologie und die Fundamente der Wissenschaften* (*Ideas pertaining to a Pure Phenomenology and to a Phenomenological*

	Philosophy, Third Book, trans. T. E. Klein and W.E. Pohl)
ILI	Husserl, 'Entwurf einer 'Vorrede' zu den *Logischen Untersuchungen* (1913)', Hrsg. Eugen Fink, *Tijdschrift voor Filosofie* Vol. 1 No. 1 and No. 2 (May 1939), pp. 319–39 (*Draft Introduction to Logical Investigations*, ed. Fink., trans. P. J. Bossert and C.H. Peters); Hua XX/1 272–29
Intersubjektivität	Husserl, *Zur Phänomenologie der Intersubjektivität. Texte aus dem Nachlass*, Hua XIII, XIV and XV
IP	Husserl, *Die Idee der Phänomenologie*, Hua II (*Idea of Phenomenology*, trans. L. Hardy)
LU	Husserl, *Logische Untersuchungen*, Hua XVIII, XIX/1 and XIX/2 (*Logical Investigations*, trans. J. N. Findlay, ed. D. Moran, Routledge 2001)
LV	*Londoner Vorträge*, Hua XXXV
PA	Husserl, *Philosophie der Arithmetik*, Hua XII (*Philosophy of Arithmetic*, trans. Dallas Willard)
PES	Brentano, *Psychologie vom empirischen Standpunkt*, 3 vols. Hamburg: Felix Meiner Verlag, 1973 (*Psychology from an Empirical Standpoint*, trans. A. C. Rancurello, D. B. Terrell and L. L. McAlister)
Phen. Psych.	Husserl, *Phänomenologische Psychologie. Vorlesungen Sommersemester 1925*, Hua IX (*Phenomenological Psychology*, trans. J. Scanlon)
PP	Merleau-Ponty, *Phénoménologie de la perception* (Paris: Gallimard, 1945), (*Phenomenology of Perception* trans. C. Smith, London: Routledge & Kegan Paul, 1962). 'PP' followed by page number of English translation; then, pagination of French edition
Prol.	Husserl, *Prolegomena, Logische Untersuchungen* (*Prolegomena, Logical Investigations*, trans. J. N. Findlay)
PRS	Husserl, *Philosophie als strenge Wissenschaft*, Hua XXV (*Philosophy as Rigorous Science*, trans. Marcus Brainard, *The New Yearbook for Phenomenology*

	and *Phenomenological Philosophy*, 2 (2002): 249–95)
PV	*Pariser Vorträge*, Hua I (*Paris Lectures*, trans. P. Koestenbaum)
Rezension	Frege's Review of Husserl's *Philosophy of Arithmetic*
SZ	Heidegger, *Sein und Zeit* (*Being and Time*, trans. J. Macquarrie and E. Robinson)
Trans. Phen.	Husserl, *Psychological and Transcendental Phenomenology and the Confrontation with Heidegger (1927–1931)*, ed. Palmer and Sheehan
Wiss.	Bolzano, *Wissenschaftslehre* (*Theory of Science*, trans. R. George)
ZB	Husserl, *Zur Phänomenologie des inneren Zeitbewusstseins (1893–1917)*, Hua X (*On the Phenomenology of the Consciousness of Internal Time*, trans. J. Brough)

In general, citations from Husserl will give the *Husserliana* volume number and page numbers and the section number (where available). In the case of *Ideas* I, the German pagination will be that of the original published edition of 1913, printed in the margin of the *Husserliana* edition. For the English translation of Husserl's *Logical Investigations*, the revised edition of Findlay's translation (London and New York: Routledge, 2000) will be used with Volumes One and Two indicated by **I** and **II** respectively, followed by section and page number.

—A—

Absolute being (*absolutes Sein*)   See also **consciousness, immanence, transcendence, transcendental idealism**

Husserl frequently characterizes the realm of transcendental **consciousness** as the domain of 'absolute being' (*Ideas* I § 76) and also contrasts transcendent being understood as relative with immanent being understood as absolute (*Ideas* I § 44). Elsewhere he writes: 'My consciousness is absolute being and each consciousness is absolute being' (Hua XIII 6). 'Absolute' in this context, means primarily 'non-relative', i.e. not relating to anything else, but it also has the connotations of final, complete, and independent. All other forms of being are *relative to* and *dependent on* the absolute being of transcendental consciousness. This is often regarded as the central claim of Husserl's **transcendental idealism**. According to Husserl, each kind of being has its own mode of **givenness**, which is determined **a priori** (*Ideas* I § 78). Absolute being (which is also characterized by Husserl as **immanence**) is opposed to transcendent being which is regarded as dependent on consciousness. Transcendent entities are given through manifesting sides or **adumbrations** and hiding others, whereas absolute being is given as it is in itself without **adumbrations**. Its *esse* is *percipi*; its being is its being perceived. Absolute being is completely self-disclosing whereas transcendent being contains dimensions of hiddenness. The **phenomenological reduction** aims to disclose the realm of absolute being. In the reduction, the world is considered as a **phenomenon**, it is grasped as depending on consciousness (Hua XXXIX 668). Husserl rejects the idea that transcendent being, for instance, the being of things in nature can ever be absolute: 'The absolute being of a nature, a being that is substantial in and old sense, is unthinkable' (Hua XXXV 279).

Absolute consciousness (*absolutes Bewusstsein*) See also **consciousness, time-consciousness**
Around 1907 Husserl came to postulate an 'absolute' or 'primal consciousness' (*Urbewusstsein*, Hua X 119) as a temporalizing consciousness that is not itself temporal but constitutes everything temporal. This absolute consciousness is the basic level of consciousness; it is 'originary consciousness' (*Urbewusstsein*). **Consciousness** as such is **absolute being** to which everything else has to be related. Absolute consciousness contains the past, present and future, all included within it.

Absolute givenness (*absolute Gegebenheit*) See also ***cogito*, evidence, givenness**
In ***The Idea of Phenomenology*** (1907) and elsewhere Husserl claims that **phenomenology** is seeking a form of **evidence** or self-givenness which is absolute, apodictic and adequate. Phenomenology is seeking 'absolute givenness' according to Husserl's ***The Idea of Phenomenology*** (IP, p. 24; Hua II 31). This is contrasted with evidence that is relative, doubtful or inadequate. Science, according to Husserl, cannot be satisfied with anything less than 'absolute givenness' although the mature Husserl recognized that this was an ideal. For him, the Cartesian ***cogito*** is a paradigm of absolute givenness. Phenomenology claims – against various forms of empiricism that want to restrict what is given to the realm of sensibility – that there are myriad forms of genuine **givenness**, and that for instance, numbers or **states of affairs** or ideal entities are intuited with just as much givenness as physical objects are given in **perception**, albeit that the mode of givenness differs in each case.

Absolute grounding (*absolute Begründung, letzte Begründung*) See also **absolute being, absolute givenness, first philosophy, foundation, foundationalism, phenomenology, science**
Husserl always claims that phenomenology is an absolutely grounded science. This position is often described as **foundationalism**. Husserl's characterization of phenomenology as **first philosophy** (following **Descartes** and ultimately Aristotle) expresses this commitment to seeking absolute or final foundations. Inspired by Descartes, Husserl sees the task of **phenomenology** as that of securing absolute or ultimate grounding or foundation for scientific knowledge in all its forms. Husserl maintains that

each individual **science** begins from a set of presuppositions that science itself simply assumes and does not interrogate (thus the biological sciences begin from the fact of the existence of organisms). It is phenomenology's task to clarify the presuppositions underlying the positive sciences and to provide a grounding for them. Phenomenology has to be absolutely grounded or, indeed, 'self-grounding' in order to provide an adequate grounding for every other form of knowledge including all the sciences (Hua VII 168–9). The sciences of the individual regions of being have to be grounded relative to constituting consciousness. Phenomenology investigates the realm of **consciousness** as providing an absolute grounding of the **world** in its essentially different ways of being given.

Abstraction   See also *epochē,* ideation, intuition

In the **Logical Investigations**, Husserl criticizes traditional empiricist accounts of abstraction that attempt to deny the genuine reality of universal, ideal objects (e.g. a triangle in general). In particular, Husserl criticizes Locke's and **Berkeley**'s accounts of abstraction as a kind of 'selective attention' (LU II § 13), whereby one attribute or property (a real **part**) of the object is separated off and attended to without reference to the whole **object** (e.g. we can think of the head of the horse separate from the horse). For Husserl, the empiricist account presumes that an object as a complex or collection of ideas. This is not genuine abstraction according to Husserl. He proposes a phenomenologically informed theory of abstraction that acknowledges the unique character of the abstracted entity that he calls a '**species**' (a universal) which has a special kind of identity distinct from that of an individual. To think of 'red' is not to think of a particular shade or **nuance** of red. Intending the species is essentially different in kind from intending the individual *qua* individual. Positively speaking, abstracting is not a separating at all, rather it is a 'viewing' (*Schauung*), a 'beholding' of the species as something independently meant and referred to, if not independently existing. In intending the species and the individual, the same concrete object (*das Konkretum*) is given, with the same sense **contents** interpreted in exactly the same way (LU II § 1), but we *mean* 'red' in general not the individual colour 'red' of the house, the species not the individual. In the act of individual **reference**, we intend this thing or property or part of the thing, whereas in the specific act we intend the species as such, that is, we intend not the thing or a property understood in the here and now, but rather the 'content' (*Inhalt*), the 'idea' (*Idee*), that is 'red' as opposed to the individual 'red moment' (LU II § 1). As Husserl adds in the Second Edition (referring forward to LU VI), this act of intending the species ('the specific act') is a *founded* (*fundierte*) act, involving a new 'mode of apprehension' (*Auffassungsweise*), which sets the species before us as a general object. Grasping the species is a higher order act founded on the grasp of a sensuous particular but different in categorial kind from that grasp of the individual (LU II § 26). Species are grasped as the dependent contents of certain mental acts. However, in the Second Edition (1913), Husserl modifies the view that we grasp the species through abstraction and instead claims that we have an act of **ideation**, an essential intuiting of the species themselves (see EU § 88). In later writings, he drops the term 'ideational abstraction' and prefers to talk simply of **intuition**: 'seeing an essence is also precisely intuition' (*Ideas* I § 3). In *Ideas* I § 3, Husserl will say that he now prefers the term 'originary giving essential intuition' (*originärgebende Wesenserschauung*) to indicate that these essential intuitions are not given purely in acts of theoretical thinking. In general, Husserl thinks certain parts of a whole are real parts and some are 'abstract' in the sense that they cannot be considered apart from the whole to which they belong. In his later writing, Husserl speaks of certain kinds of **epochē** as being 'abstractive', e.g. the attempt think away all social predicates (CM § 44). Husserl also sees the approach of modern mathematical sciences as abstracting from every property which is not quantifiable.

Accomplishment (*Leistung*)   See **achievement**

Achievement (*Leistung*)   See also **constitution, intentionality, subjectivity, transcendental ego**
Husserl very frequently uses the German term *Leistungen* (plural of *Leistung*), translated as 'accomplishments', 'achievements', 'performances', 'results') to characterize the products of knowing **subjects** when they engage in **intentional acts** involved in the **constitution** of intentional objects of all kinds (including natural and cultural objects and the **world** itself). For Husserl, not just every object but the whole culturally experienced **world** is an 'achievement' of what he terms 'anonymous' or '**functioning subjectivity**'. All sense and being is an achievement of the intentional activity of the **transcendental ego**. By *achievement* Husserl means not just the

outcome or result but also the constitutive process itself. **Consciousness** is intentionally directed at objects that are grasped as certain sense forma- tions. These meanings are the result of certain a priori regulated structures of consciousness. Husserl claims Brentano, who rediscovered **intention- ality**, never appreciated its full significance as a 'complex of achievements' (FTL § 97).

Act (*Akt*) See also **content, intentionality, lived experience, matter**
Husserl follows the nineteenth-century psychologists, including **Brentano** and **Meinong**, in referring to conscious processes as *acts*. Brentano and others stressed that they did not intend this to mean that every **mental process** or state involves deliberate *action* on the part of the subject. An act is Husserl's general name for a psychological process, a mental occurrence, an episode of consciousness, or indeed some ideal component part of a conscious experience. It can also refer to a specific **part** or element of the experience, namely that element being directed to an object and contains an object. In the Fifth Logical Investigation, Husserl stresses that act should not be understood as having the connotation of an activity, a deliberately willed act. Sometimes he uses the term 'state' (*Zustand*). Typical *acts* include: fearing, hoping, imagining, judging, perceiving, remembering, and so on. Acts can be very complex and can include moments of self-reflection. Conscious acts, states, processes or **achievements** are the outcome of some kind of **synthesis** of a subjective activity and an objective or content component. Husserl speaks of **mental processes** or **lived experiences** (*Erlebnisse*) as having different **act characters** or **act qualities**, e.g. they are acts of fearing, hoping, perceiving, promising, remembering, and so on. Correlated with the act quality is a specific content or in Husserl's terminology, **matter** (the object seen, the promise made, the matter remembered and so on, see Husserl Fifth Logical Investigation § 22). Act quality and matter make up two different **moment**s (non-independent parts) of intentional experiences. In Ideas I, Husserl recognizes the subject or **ego** as the source of acts. As Husserl puts it, the ego *lives through* the act. Certain acts are characterized by Husserl as being 'originary giving acts' also called 'presentive acts' (see *Ideas* I § 19).

Act quality See also **act, lived experience, matter**
Husserl speaks generally of conscious states and processes as **acts**. Acts are distinguished by having diverse **act characters** or **act qualities**, e.g. they

are specific acts of fearing, hoping, perceiving, promising, remembering, and so on, each with its own **matter**. As he writes: 'the general act-character, which stamps an act as merely presentative, judgemental, emotional, desiderative, etc.' (LU V § 20). When an intentional act is performed a certain instance of an act type (act character) is correlated with a specific act **matter** (the object seen, the promise made, the matter remembered and so on), see Husserl's Fifth Logical Investigation § 22. Act quality and matter make up two different **moment**s (non-independent **parts**) of the whole intentional **lived experience**. The matter fixes the object that is intended by the act, and the act quality is an abstract, dependent part of the whole act, which cannot be thought without its matter (LU V § 20). The act, however, consists of much more than the combination of act quality and matter; indeed two acts with identical matter and quality can still differ in **intentional essence**.

Active and passive genesis (*aktive und passive Genesis*)   See also genetic phenomenology, passivity, synthesis

Husserl understands by 'genesis' (literally: 'coming to be') the laws-like processes whereby some experienced thing comes to be constituted with the particular sense it has. Active and passive processes are generally found together, but should be distinguished. In **Cartesian Meditations** § 38, Husserl distinguishes between active and passive genesis. Active genesis involves the **ego** explicitly, whereas passive genesis is a kind of meaning connecting that takes place without the active engagement of the ego and things have the character of already being formed in a particular sense formation. Husserl speaks in this context of 'preconstitution'. *Passive* genesis names those processes which give the world its pregiven, stable and harmonious character. It also gives the objects encountered in the world their sense character that is encountered as fully formed by active perceiving etc. The genetic constitution of the ego involves problems such as the constitution of **time consciousness** and the phenomenology of **association**. For Husserl, **association** is the universal principle of passive genesis. An inquiry into genesis attempts to identify those intentional structures that allow a world to appear in a harmonious and stable manner (CM §38). One law of passive genesis, for instance, is that every experience becomes a trace in retention and does not vanish completely (see APS, p. 114; XI 72). In Kantian terms (which Husserl invokes), the transcendental aesthetic (the structuring of sensuous experience in spatial and temporal terms) has to do with a passive genesis, while the transcendental logic (concerned with judgement and categorical forms) has to be with active genesis. The production of ideal objects (as in geometry), for instance, is a matter of active genesis (see APS, p. 631; XI 341). From around 1917 onward, Husserl contrasts static and **genetic phenomenology**. Whereas the static phenomenology focuses on the necessary structural relationships between objects and acts, genetic phenomenology attempts to clarify the evolution or genesis of this constitution, i.e. the different levels that are at stake within the constitution within the constitution of different objectivities. In *Formal and Transcendental Logic* and *Experience and Judgment,* Husserl expores genetic constitution of logical sphere of judgement. *Passive genesis* has to be distinguished from **passive synthesis** (see **passivity**).

Adumbration, profile (*Abschattung, Aspekt, Profil*) See also appearance, material thing in space

The adumbration (*Abschattung*) or 'profile' is the side or 'aspect' through which a material object presents itself to the perceiver. When Husserl offers an analysis of the perception of physical objects in space for instance, he emphasizes that it belongs to the essence of such objects to always reveal themselves in 'profiles' or 'adumbrations' (*Abschattungen, Ideas* I § 3) or 'perspectival aspects' (*Aspekte*, CM § 61). A table can only be *seen* from one point of view, one position, and so on. In fact, every material thing unveils itself in endless spatial profiles. Husserl speaks of a 'manifold of adumbrations' (*Abschattungsmannigfaltigkeit, Ideas* I 41). Every sensory modality is given in profiles. The same object can present itself in different ways (I can *see* you in the street or *hear* you, e.g. on the telephone). One profile is visual and one is aural yet both are profiles of the *same* thing. Strictly speaking, the thing itself is never seen but appears across the endless series of appearances (see *Crisis* § 47). No act of perceiving a physical object can present all sides at once, or all perspectives. Even God, for Husserl, can only grasp a physical thing in profiles (*Ideas* I § 149). There is therefore no 'God's eye' view possible because such an a-perspectival view would contradict the essence of the object's self-revealing. Husserl frequently announces this insight as having the status of an **a priori eidetic law**: 'even the most intuitively vivid and rich presentation of a real thing must be in principle one-sided and incomplete' (LU IV § 3, **II**, p. 52; Hua XIX/1 307). Not even God can alter this eidetic truth, Husserl frequently attests (see Hua XVI 65).

According to Husserl, moreover, it is neither an accident nor purely a feature of human constitution that a spatial thing can only appear in profiles (*Ideas* I § 42), it belongs to the **essence** of the spatial object itself. For Husserl, a **lived experience**, a *cogitatio*, e.g. an act intending, hoping, fearing, and so on, does not appear in adumbrations, but gives itself as it is, its *esse* is *percipi*, it is as it is perceived.

Alien world (*die fremde Welt, die Fremdwelt*)   See also **historicity, homeworld, horizon, normality, other, world**

The mature Husserl distinguishes various intentional contexts or **horizons** in which our experiences appear. Human life takes place primarily in a familiar world, which Husserl often calls the 'near-world' (*Nahwelt*), e.g. in the *Crisis*. He distinguishes the familiar world from strange or alien or foreign worlds that appear unfamiliar. There are horizons of familiarity and unfamiliarity in all experience. The extreme limit is the completely unfamiliar or alien world in which customs and traditions are alien, strange, foreign. Husserl considers various cases, including someone transported from one cultural situation to a completely foreign one. One has a sense that their traditions are not ours, yet there is also recognition that their behavior, activities and so on constitute a tradition, a culture with values, and an overall **world**.

Allure, stimulus (*Reiz*)   See also **drive, instinct**

Husserl uses the term *Reiz* meaning 'allure' or 'stimulus' (originally found in nineteenth-century psychologists who referred to the stimulation of the nervous system) to refer to the kind of attraction that things of a certain similar kind exercise on **consciousness** so that its attention is awakened and its interest is drawn towards them (see APS § 32; *Ideas* II § 50). The intentional meaning of stimulus is a new sense relative to the mechanistic understanding of stimulus in psychology. Allure or stimulus is a matter of **motivation** rather than **causation** (*Ideas* II § 55). According to Husserl, it is as if the sensory field itself exerts a force on consciousness and this gives consciousness a tendency to draw its attention towards that field. A birdsong may become prominent among several street noises and draw us in with its affective allure. According to the laws of the **passivity**, something affects us when it emerges on a field with an affective strength (*Kraft*). For Husserl, it is a matter of complete contingency whether some people are attracted to particular shades of colour or enjoy or dislike certain sounds. There is a kind of facticity operating at the pre-reflective level of experience where people find themselves passively being affected and their interest awakened, e.g. hearing a sudden loud noise. Homogeneity and heterogeneity (contrast) define this framework according to which something enters into our horizon and awakens new unities of sense (see **Experience and Judgment** § 17). Different ways of following this first impact on consciousness define different types of act, from the passive noticing to explicit attention towards the objects or its properties. I am initially stimulated and then I can be awakened to act (the room's stale air stimulates me to open the window, *Ideas* II § 55).

Alter ego (*alter ego*)   See also **ego, other experience**
The Latin term *alter ego* literally means 'the other ego' and is used by the mature Husserl especially in the **Cartesian Meditations** and elsewhere to describe the experience of another **ego** or **subject** based on the projection of one's own experiences of oneself as an ego. The challenge in experiencing other egos is to grasp them precisely as 'other' and not just as **modifications** of oneself (see CM § 42).

Analogical or analogizing apperception (*analogische Apperzeption* or *analogisierende Auffassung*)   See also **animate body, apperception, empathy, intuition, lived body, pairing**
Husserl uses the phrase 'analogical' or 'analogizing apperception' to express the manner in which I experience another subject as a source of conscious subjectivity akin to myself (see CM § 50). I have original, primordial experience of myself but I also can have a 'non-original' yet genuine experience of the inner conscious life of another **subject** (human or animal). Others are not presented directly in the manner in which I experience myself but are *appresented* on the basis of an analogy with my own experience. For instance, I see other people's living bodies as also possessing the character of 'I can', i.e. abilities to move, to feel, and so on. I apperceive the other person's body as *sensitive*. In this way, we do not perceive mere **physical bodies** (*Körper*) but **lived bodies** (*Leib*), guided by a **consciousness**. Husserl denies apperception involves reasoning, inference, or hypothesis formation; for him this apperception is a species of direct intuition although it does not present the other's experiences in **self-experience,** *in propria persona*. Analogical apperception is involved in

empathy and the understanding of other's expressions, speech, and bodily movements. The grasping of analogy is based on **empathy**. It is possible to extend imaginatively the degree of analogical apperception so that, for instance, inanimate objects could be imagined to have inner lives.

Analyticity   See also **apriori**

Husserl defines analyticity in the Third Logical Investigation, §§11–12 where he contrasts analytic and synthetic a priori propositions in terms of the contrast between formal and material regions. In Kant, analytic propositions are defined as true in virtue of their terms (e.g. every triangle has three angles), or the predicate is contained in the subject, whereas in synthetic propositions some extra piece of information (e.g. the triangle is three metres high) is given by the predicate which is not found in the subject. **Kant** famously postulated not just analytic a priori and synthetic a posteriori statements but also synthetic a posteriori statements. Husserl regards his position as a clarification and improvement on Kant's distinction. In the Third Logical Investigation, Husserl distinguishes *analytic laws* and *analytically necessary propositions*. Analytic laws are 'unconditionally universal propositions' that make no reference to existence and include only purely formal concepts with no material content. They are purely formal statements e.g. If A stands in some relation to B then B also stands in some relation to A. or 'the existence of a whole W implies the existence of its parts (A, B, C)'. In analytic laws any terms referring to material regions can be replaced by the concept of an 'empty something' without change of its truth value. Analytically necessary propositions he sees as 'specifications' or instantiations of these analytic laws, which include concepts with a certain material content, e.g. if the house exists then its roof exists; or there cannot be a king without subjects (LU III § 11). The truth of these statements is independent of the content of the concepts they contain. As a result analytically necessary propositions can be completely formalized as their content is irrelevant to their truth. In other words, the truth of analytic statements is given by their logical form, although Husserl does not put it this way. **Synthetic a priori** statements are statements that contain a material content falling under one of the domains of material ontology and whose truth is grounded in the specific nature of the contents. These include: 'this red is different from that green' or 'a colour cannot exist without something coloured'. Husserl's reasoning is that the concept of colour is 'absolute' and non-relative and hence the concept of something coloured does not belong to the concept of colour. To say that every colour requires something coloured is therefore a synthetic a priori statement. As a result, synthetic propositions cannot be formalized (i.e. their contents cannot be replaced by an empty something in general). In his **Formal and Transcendental Logic**, Husserl discusses analytic consequence and analytic contradiction in terms of invariant logical form arrived at through **eidetic variation**.

Animate body   See **lived body**

Annihilation of the world (*Weltvernichtung*)   See also **absolute being, idealism, world**
In *Ideas* I § 49 and in many of his writings on transcendental idealism (e.g. *Husserliana* volume XXXVI), Husserl discusses the thought experiment of the 'annihilation of the world' (*Weltvernichtung*). According to Husserl, performance of the **phenomenological reduction** leads one to realize that **consciousness** has primacy over objective being. It is possible to imagine the flow or stream of worldly experience being entirely disrupted to the point where all is chaos, but, it is impossible at the same time to think away pure consciousness. If the entire experience of the harmonious flow of the **world** were disrupted so that it became a meaningless chaos, the experience of the **ego** would be profoundly modified and altered, but it would still exist, even if its flow of temporal experience was chaotic. On this basis, Husserl concludes that pure **consciousness** is absolute and independent of all objective being. This statement by Husserl has been very controversial and was seen by **Roman Ingarden** and others as an assertion of the metaphysical idealist claims of the mind dependence of reality. Husserl is not saying that consciousness survives the non-existence of the world but that consciousness and its flow of experiences still makes sense in a coherent way even if its experiences are no longer coherent.

Anthropologism   (*Anthropologismus*)   See   also   **psychologism, relativism**
For Husserl, *anthropologism* is a species of psychologism and hence **relativism**. In the *Prolegomena* § 36 to the **Logical Investigations**, Husserl accuses **Kant** and certain neo-Kantians of being guilty of anthropologism when they understand logical laws as constraints governing the

human mind rather than as purely formal **a priori** truths. *Anthropologism* maintains that truth is relative to the human species and, hence without humans, there would be no truth. Husserl understands Kant's account of knowledge as a kind of anthropologism in this sense. He accuses Kant of misunderstanding the subjective domain as if it were something natural, and hence of construing the a priori as if it were an essential part of the human species (*Prol.* § 38). But Husserl maintains this is a contradiction, since 'there is no truth' would then be true. Truth as such does not depend on any facts, including facts of human nature. The Law of Non Contradiction is not merely a law governing the species *homo sapiens*. If there were no minds to think them the logical laws would still hold, though as ideal possibilities unfulfilled in actuality (*Prol.* § 39). Furthermore one should not confuse a *true judgement*, one made in conformity with truth, with the *truth* of the judgement, the objective true content of the judgement (*Prol.* § 36). For Husserl, logic emerges from considering the essential necessary relations between basic concepts:

> Anyone can see from my statements up to this point that for
> me the pure truths of logic are all the ideal laws which have
> their whole foundation in the 'sense' (*Sinn*), the 'essence'
> (*Wesen*) or the 'content' (*Inhalt*) of the concepts of Truth,
> Proposition, Object, Property, Relation, Combination, Law,
> Fact, etc. (LU *Prol.* § 37)

Anthropology (*Anthropologie*)   See also **anthropologism**

Husserl understands anthropology in several senses. For him it is both a natural biophysical science of human beings (see *Ideas* II, p. 150; Hua IV 142; or Hua XIII 481–3) and a human science (See Hua XV, Text Nr. 30, pp. 480–507, *Universal human science as an anthropology* ...). The latter (sometimes called 'intentional anthropology'), which is developed mainly in his later works, is a universal science of humanity, the science focused on human beings living in their **surrounding world** or *Umwelt* (see Hua XXXIX 204). In this sense, Husserl thinks that anthropological knowledge embraces human relationships linked to the world, the universality of human aspirations, values and actions, etc. (see Hua XV 480). Husserl maintained that anthropology could be used as a clue for transcendental phenomenology: 'We must come to understand, on ultimate transcendental grounds, why psychology – or anthropology, if you wish – is in fact not just a positive science along with the natural sciences, but rather has an *intrinsic affinity* with philosophy, with transcendental philosophy' (Hua XXVII 181). Husserl's anthropology influenced Hellmut Plessner and others.

Apodicticity (*Apodiktizität*)   See also **evidence**
Apodicticity is considered by Husserl to be the highest level of **evidence** or **self-evidence** (*Evidenz*). The term 'apodicticity' from the Greek meaning 'capable of being demonstrated' has a long history in philosophy. The term is usually applied to judgements that are necessarily true, e.g. mathematical conclusions. In Aristotelian logic, apodictic judgements are contrasted with probable reasoning as found in dialectics. Aristotle speaks of 'demonstrative science' (*epistēmē apodeiktikē*) in the *Posterior Analytics*. The concept of apodicticity is used by **Descartes**, Kant and Leibniz. Apodictic insights are necessary, indubitable and infallible. Kant distinguishes three kinds of judgements: assertorical, problematic and apodictic judgements (*The Critique of Pure Reason* B100/A75). For Husserl, apodicticity characterizes the mode of **givenness** of the object in **consciousness**. Apodicticity means that there is no conceivable way in which the piece of knowledge could be false. In *Ideas* I § 6 Husserl speaks of the consciousness of a necessary eidetic insight as an 'apodictic consciousness'. For Husserl, the contrary or non-being of an apodictic truth cannot be even imagined (CM § 6). The mere fact that a law is universally binding (e.g. the laws of nature) does not yet mean that it is necessary. Husserl thinks Kant is mistaken to associate necessity with universality. For Husserl, necessity has to be the logical requirement that it cannot be otherwise. Husserl's goal of apodicticity is often expressed by him in Cartesian terms but he rejects the view that evident science has to have the form of a deduction. While Husserl tended to identify adequacy and apodicticity in his earlier works, he distinguishes them in **Cartesian Meditations** § 6. Adequate evidences are not necessarily apodictic. Phenomenology seeks not only the adequacy but the highest level of evidence: reach universal laws that cannot be denied. In his *Crisis* (p. 340; Hua VI 275), Husserl even speaks of leading 'a life of apodicticity' by which he means a life guided by judgements that are based on phenomenologically purified insights secured by evidence.

Apophantic logic (*apophantische Logik*)   See also **judgement, logic**
Apophantic logic is the logic of **judgements** or propositions as opposed to

the logic of terms. Husserl contrasts apophantics with **formal ontology**. Formal ontology is concerned with the kinds of possible object whereas apophantics is concerned with the range of possible judgements.

Apophantics   See also **apophantic logic, judgement**

In some respects, his account of logic is quite traditional, being centred on the notion of judgement or assertion (Greek: *apophansis*) and hence is, following Aristotle, characterized as 'apophantic logic' (see LU IV § 14 II 72; Hua XIX/1 344; see also ELE § 18 Hua XXIV 71), although his detailed account of judgements goes far beyond Aristotle. Husserl always insisted on the judgement or proposition as the highest category in logic and specifically the apophantic form 'S is P', the copulative judgement, as the absolutely fundamental form. Similarly, he took the Law of Non-Contradiction to be one of the absolutely basic ideal laws. One of his innovations is his view that formal logic in the sense of the science of the forms of implication needed to be complemented with a pure formal grammar specifying the rules for meaningfulness in the most general terms, offering an 'anatomy and morphology of propositions' strictly in regard to their sense (ELE § 18 Hua XXIV 71). Formal apophantics, which is concerned with truth and falsity as articulated in judgement, builds on this formal grammar. Before something is true or false, it must meet minimum conditions of coherence and meaningfulness as *a possible truth*, that is, as a possible *piece of knowledge*. Husserl always draws a distinction between the mere elaboration of consistent rules (rules of a game) and the specification of the possible forms of judgements understood as items of genuine knowledge (see FTL § 33; EJ § 3). In FTL and elsewhere, Husserl refers to the unity of formal logic and mathematics as 'objective logic'.

Appearance   (*Erscheinung, Apparenz*)   See   also   **adumbration, phenomenon**

Husserl speaks about the **phenomena** of experience as *appearances* (*Erscheinungen, Crisis* § 2; *Apparenzen*, CM § 61). He does not accept the Kantian account of appearances as dependent on a thing-in-itself lying behind appearances. Neither is Husserl a phenomenalist who thinks that the world consists solely in appearances without underlying substances. Husserl speaks of 'appearances' to mean everything that is manifest to a conscious subject or subjects. He distinguishes between 'what appears'

and the 'mode of appearance' (*Erscheinungsmodi*, *Erscheinungsweise*, e.g.
Crisis § 23). Usually, it is things and situations that are manifest and their
mode of appearance or their 'appearing' is veiled (see LU V § 2 where
Husserl comments on the equivocation in the word 'appearance' to mean
the appearing process as well as the thing that appears. In the Second
Logical Investigation, he accuses **Hume** of confusing the two). Normally,
our attention is on the things that appear and not on the sequence of
appearances (see *Crisis* § 28). Phenomenology aims to make the mode of
appearance itself manifest. Wherever there is appearing so also there is
being, Husserl says (Hua VIII 47). Modern natural science sought to exclude
what were considered to be the 'subjective-relative appearances' (*Crisis* §
9). At *Crisis* § 47, Husserl says that appearances are always experienced as
appearances of some thing. In fact the thing as such is never experienced
except as what remains stable across the open-ended infinity of experiences of it. Appearance is always a kind of **givenness** and there is also
the 'to whom' it is given. In the transcendental **reduction**, the **world**
is reduced to **phenomena**, i.e. to appearances. A physical thing has an
infinite number of possible appearances as it is always given in adumbrations. The concept of 'appearance' is fundamental to phenomenology.
Phenomenology's fundamental presupposition is that one cannot claim to
have **knowledge** until one has returned or reverted to the conditions in
which the object of knowledge appears. The task of phenomenology is to
decipher the very conditions of the constitution of the objects of knowledge
for **consciousness** before these objects appear to the subject as already
constituted. This means that phenomenology focuses on the explication of
the modality by which *appearance itself appears*. Phenomenology operates
according to a double function: it operates at once on the appearance of
the object *and* on that which allows for that appearance to appear. This
double function, inscribed in the very unity of appearance, opens the field
of Husserl's phenomenological project: to reveal the intentional character
of consciousness itself, that is, to expose the projective movement of
consciousness towards that which it is not but which nonetheless appears
to it. In this sense, phenomenology proceeds from the '**sense bestowal**' or
'donation of meaning' (*Sinngebung*) to that which appears to consciousness
– donation whose fundamental truth lies in the fact that, contrarily to the
certainty of the natural attitude of consciousness, it remains retracted from
the constituted appearance – in such a manner that appearance is then

reconverted into a **being** (*Seiendes*) for consciousness. The double function of appearance is thus characterized, most particularly in the inaugural Freiburg Lecture of 1917, as the *'appearing of appearance'* and as *'that which appears in appearance'*, each modality corresponding to the double *factum* of consciousness: the constituting act of consciousness and the constituted world received by consciousness. Accordingly, the phenomenological project depends on this fundamental distinction between that which appears to consciousness, also defined by Husserl as the 'givens' (*Gegebenheiten*) whose indubitable 'value' emerges from that they are absolutely evident in the real immanence of the subject's lived states, and the act by which consciousness constitutes the horizon of intentionality necessary for these givens to be given as appearing appearances to consciousness itself. This fundamental distinction within appearance itself becomes the very field in which the phenomenological investigation will be forwarded. First, 'modifications' (*Verwandlungen*) that continuously affect the appearances themselves must be explicated. These modifications of appearances are categorized according to three modes: perception, imagination, and 'predication or signification'. The recognition of these three modes constitutes what Husserl labels the 'genealogical analysis of appearance'. The role of this genealogical analysis in the general economy of the phenomenological investigation is to explicate and isolate, by level of intentionality, the manner in which appearances are actively constituted by consciousness. In other words, the recognition of 'perception', 'imagination' and 'signification' as acts of consciousness constituting appearances serves as the first step towards the phenomenological explication of the *noesis* and *noema* couple which, according to Husserl, typifies, at the highest level of **intentionality**, the manner in which appearances are for consciousness teleologically allied one to the other and thus in which manner they form a systematic configuration (*Gestaltung*) from which invariable and *a priori* *eidetic* laws can be derived. Second, and consequently, the 'ontological reality' of appearances for consciousness will be typified. The 'ontological reality' of appearances will be deduced – and this point of deduction constitutes the completion of the 'phenomenological reduction' – by their being mapped onto a *mathesis universalis* (according to the retrieval of the Leibnizian proposition) in which their constitutive layers of intentionality will be explicated and clarified for consciousness. In this sense, appearances will be integrated into a signified development of intentionality. Hence, phenomenology, as the science whose task it is to explicate the conditions of the three primary modalities of intentionality – 'perception', 'imagination' and 'signification' – by linking these to the higher intentional order of a transcendental foundation as ontology, aims at deploying the ensemble of eidetic laws which regulate all the 'lived states' of consciousness, that is, seeks to explicate the rapport or relation between consciousness and its ideal and/or real phenomenon by demonstrating that appearances are always constituted by the intentional act of consciousness who, in return, receives these as simple 'givens'.

Apperception (*Apperzeption, Vergegenwärtigung*) See also **appresentation, presentification**
For Husserl, an apperception (*Apperzeption*) always presupposes and is founded on a **perception** (see CM § 55). To *apperceive* means to grasp something over and above what is actually perceived. Apperceptions accompany and form part of perceptions. The term 'apperception' is used by **Descartes, Kant** and Leibniz. In **Brentano**, an apperception is *founded* on a perception. In perception, there is a direct experience of the self-givenness of the object. In apperception, there is a sense that the object is mediated through something else that is presented immediately. For instance, in all perception of a physical object, direct perception is of the facing side of the object, the hidden sides of the object are *apperceived* or *appresented* in an empty manner. Perception involves a horizon of sense that is co-intended and appresented. In his *Passive Synthesis* lectures, Husserl defines apperception as 'a consciousness of having something that is not present in the original' (APS, 367; Hua XI 234). Apperception involves a certain awareness of properties, profiles, horizons that are not sensuously given in the perceiving itself, e.g. if I am in a room, I am aware not only of the objects that are inside the room, but also of the building in which I am. This connection between presence and absence is crucial for phenomenology. There are not only apperceptions of the things and the world but also of the self and others. Our interests, customs, convictions, judgements, etc. are grasped 'apperceptively' (*Crisis*, § 59). Husserl employs the term 'presentiation' or 'presentification' (*Vergegenwärtigung*) to cover a huge range of experiences including memories, fantasies, anticipations, awareness of the hidden side of a physical object, and so on: 'There are different levels of apperception corresponding to different layers of objective

sense' (CM § 50, 111; Hua I 141). Husserl says that an apperception does not involve inference (CM § 51). For Husserl, seeing another living body as a subject or cogito is a typical example of an **apperception**.

Apprehension (*Auffassung*)   See also **content, interpretation**

Apprehension (*Auffassung*) refers to the manner in which consciousness apprehends, grasps or registers a particular experience. Husserl even says in *Ideas* II § 10 that 'apprehension' (*Auf-fassung*) is a part of 'grasping' (*Er-fassung*). When one hears a violin playing a particular note, the note is apprehended as a certain kind of sensuous **datum** in a certain manner. Husserl frequently distinguishes (as in LU) between the *apprehension* as an act and the apprehensional content (*Auffassungsinhalt*) and talks of an apprehension-content schema. He applied this schema even to **time consciousness**, although it is not clear what kind of '**content**' (*Inhalt*) pertains to a temporal experience considered just as a time apprehension.

Appresentation (*Appräsentation*)   See also **apperception, memory, presentation**

Appresentation is a kind of co-presenting that is founded on a **presentation** (*Präsentation*, *Vorstellung*, *Gegenwärtigung*) where something is directly given in the flesh, as it were. According to Husserl every appresentation presupposes a core of presentation (see CM § 55). Every **perception** simultaneously presents and appresents. It appresents the empty **horizons** around the direct perception. When I perceive someone's living **body**, I perceive it as a living organism but I apperceive it as *someone else's* living body. Husserl tends to use the term 'appresention' as synonymous with 'apperception' or indeed with '**presentification**'.

Apriori (*a priori*)   See also **apriority**

The term 'a priori' is made up of two Latin words (the preposition 'a' meaning 'from' and the adjective 'prior' meaning 'behind;') but it is sometimes written as one word 'apriori' and means 'from before, from what is prior' and is usually contrasted with 'a posteriori' (from afterwards, from what comes after). In philosophy, the term is usually applied to characterize the nature of knowledge and in particular the sources of knowledge. A priori knowledge is knowledge drawn from the resources of the intellect itself, whereas a posteriori knowledge is knowledge that comes after or consequent on experience. Rationalist philosophers including **Descartes** held that certain truths are knowable a priori, e.g. 'every effect has a cause' or 'the whole is greater than the part'. These truths are known by definition, without recourse to experience. They are often termed 'analytic' truths. **Kant** defined an analytic statement as one in which the predicate was 'contained' in the subject, e.g. the very idea of a triangle 'contains' the idea of three angles; or the concept of 'bachelor' contains the idea of 'unmarried'. Kant introduced a new complexity into the notion of the a priori when he claimed that there was *synthetic apriori* knowledge, e.g. that in several areas of knowledge, such as arithmetic and geometry, statements could be a priori and yet add to our knowledge. Thus, for Kant, '7 + 5 = 12' is an a priori synthetic truth. Similarly, Kant argued that a statement such as 'every event has a cause' is something that goes beyond the domain of the purely analytic apriori and belongs to the synthetic apriori, in that it adds to our knowledge of 'event' that it be something that of necessity is caused while at the same time it is a truth that is independent of experience. According to Kant, universality and necessity are marks of the a priori. Husserl accepts Kant's view that university and necessity are features of the a priori but he believes the realm of the a priori needs much closer examination. In fact, for Husserl, philosophy involves the exploration of the a priori. He writes in the *Logical Investigations*:

> The a priori … is, at least in its primitive forms, obvious, even trivial, but its systematic demonstration, theoretical pursuit and phenomenological clarification remains of supreme scientific and philosophical interest, and is by no means easy. (LU IV § 14, **II**, p. 73; Hua XIX/1 345)

For Husserl, pure logic is an a priori analytic science (Hua XXVI § 1, 4) consisting of 'truisms', 'tautologies' or propositions that are self-evident (*Selbstverständlichkeiten*). It is concerned with purely formal concepts, as Husserl writes:

> [F]or me the pure laws of logic are all the ideal laws which have their whole foundation in the 'sense', the 'essence' or the 'content' of the concepts of Truth, Proposition, Object, Property, Relation, Combination, Law, Fact, etc. (LU, *Prol.* § 37, **I** 82; Hua XVIII 129)

Pure logic covers the whole domain of the formal a priori (as opposed to the material a priori domain explained in LU III), including mathematics and may be more accurately described as '**formal ontology**' (a phrase not used in the First Edition of the *Logical Investigations*). Besides pure logic, Husserl also believes that all domains of knowledge contain an a priori part relative to the kind of subject matter involved. This is what he calls, in the Third Logical Investigation, the *material* as opposed to the *formal* a priori. Husserl believes his distinction between the *formal* and the *material* a priori is a more accurate and exact way of characterizing what Kant called synthetic and analytic a priori. The Third Logical Investigation § 11 defends synthetic a priori propositions, influenced by Husserl's understanding of Hume's relations of ideas, Leibniz's truths of reason, and Kant's analytic truths. Husserl distinguishes between formal ontology, which studies 'empty' or what Husserl calls 'pure' categorial forms such as unity, object, relation, plurality, whole, part, number, and so on, and *material ontologies*, which have concepts with genuine content (LU III § 11), e.g. house, tree, colour, tone, space, etc. On this basis, he distinguishes between **formal** and **material a priori**. As Husserl says:

> [N]ature with all its thing-like contents certainly also has its *a priori*, whose systematic elaboration and development is still the unperformed task of an ontology of nature. (LU III § 25, **II** 43; Hua XIX/1 297)

That colour as such depends on extension involves necessity and universality and hence the proposition expressing it is a priori. Contrariwise, it is *synthetic* and not analytic. This leads Husserl to formulate a new account of analyticity (LU III § 12), which he claims purifies Kant's account of what Husserl understands to be psychologistic tendencies. Analytic a priori truths are tautologies, where the terms of the proposition express 'correlatives', i.e. concepts that mutually entail each other (e.g. there cannot be a father without children; no whole without parts, etc.). Formal analytic statements are absolutely universal and contain only formal categories. They are without existential commitment; their truth is independent of their content. *Synthetic* a priori statements, by way of contrast, involve contents that are not correlative concepts (e.g. Husserl claims the concept of 'colour' is not relative to extension). He writes:

> Though colour is 'unthinkable' without something coloured,
> the existence of the latter, and more accurately that of a
> space, is not 'analytically' founded on the notion of colour.
> (LU III § 11, **II**, p. 20)

Every material *specification* of a necessary law is, for Husserl, a priori synthetic (LU III § 12). Husserl speaks of these material a priori truths as 'essential truths' or 'essential laws' that have universal validity and are do not posit factual existence (see *Ideas* I § 5). Husserl distinguishes between purely eidetic laws that make no presumption of existence, e.g. 'all material things are extended', and laws having unrestricted generality that involve the presumption of existence, e.g. all laws of nature such as 'all bodies are heavy' (*Ideas* I § 6).

The term *a priori* in Husserl undergoes a profound shift away from Kant. In fact, Husserl – contrarily to the Kantian heritage of this word – speaks first of an *objective a priori*. Husserl, in this sense, interprets objectivity as the place where the *a priori* is exercised. All appearing objects can appear only according to *a priori laws* of essence that govern the totality of the relations linking together particular givens in experience to the whole of experience. In order to grasp what Husserl properly means by the notion of an *objective a priori*, one must begin with the general theory of the relation between the parts and the whole as sketched in the Chapter I of the *Philosophy of Arithmetic*. Certainly in this text, Husserl does not yet refer to the *objective a priori* to designate the connection between the parts and the whole since the primary question is the reconstitution of the steps in the process by which intentionality has moved from the lower level of the concrete givens in experience, the *concreta*, to the superior level of their *abstracta*. At this time, however, Husserl does not evoke the possibility of **laws of essence** but rather focuses, in order to grasp the difference between the lower level, the *concreta*, and the superior level, the *abstracta*, on the very description of **intentionality** and its modality. Husserl focuses thus on the modality of intentionality in order to deploy its inherent functioning. In the **Logical Investigations** (1901), this description will be completed by recourse to the notion of **ideation**. In the Third Logical Investigation, entitled *On the Theory of Wholes and Parts*, Husserl evokes the notion of the *a priori* in order to define the modes of this relation founded in the idea of the object. Husserl's perspective is here to reveal an 'ideal essence', which can mark the signification of an 'objective lawfulness' by which and in which it becomes possible for the subject to separate and dissociate two ontological spheres, the one in which the object can be grasped as an analytic proposition and the one in which the object can be comprehended as a synthetic proposition. This possibility of distinguishing between the *analytic* and the *synthetic* is taken up in Chapter I of Section I of the *Ideas* I. Husserl here, however, does not simply reassert the opposition between a material ontology and a formal ontology, but specifies precisely that these logical analyses have not yet introduced the phenomenological perspective. In this sense, the entire Husserlian project will now seek to pass from the domain of 'facts' to that of 'essences' and thus require that the idea of a pure phenomenology must be developed which will be defined as a 'science of essences' rather than as an *a priori* appropriation of factuality. Book I of the *Ideas* I will categorically reject the thesis according to which the phenomenological reduction, exposed and explicated in Section II, leads to a *subjective a priori*. Rather, as *Ideas* I § 36 specifically states it, what is capital for phenomenology – contrarily to psychology – are the lived experiences considered only in function of their 'pure essence' in which what is *a priori* is already included and inherent in and within their essence. Hence, the unique preoccupation, for Husserl, is to reveal the possibility of disengaging all transcendent objectivity by returning, as it is stated in § 46, to the appropriation of 'being as consciousness'. This, however, signifies that another problematic will soon appear, one where Husserl will have to call onto the necessity of an *a priori organization* in order to grasp the foundation between perception *and* symbolic representations (image and sign), that is, an *a priori organization* which will and can take into account their eidetic difference. Hence, in Section VI of the *Ideas* I, Husserl will search for a purely *a priori* theory capable of grasping the ensemble of the foundational relations that constitute the rapport between perception and symbolic representations by image and sign. In this sense, for Husserl, the phenomenological reduction will always possess an *a priori* foundational character in which all constitution will necessarily presuppose an *a priori* without which no synthetic unity of a world would ever be possible.

Apriority (*Apriorität*)   See also **apriori**

In *Phenomenological Psychology* § 4, Husserl characterizes the apriority of **descriptive psychology** as focused on the universal, necessary truths without which subjective life would be impossible.

Association (*Assoziation*)   See also **Hume, pairing, passivity**
Husserl discusses 'association' in a number of his works, especially in ***Ideas II*** (see § 32), *Passive Synthesis*, **Cartesian Meditations** (see CM § 39), and ***Experience and Judgment*** (see EU § 16). He defines association as the 'lawful regularity of immanent genesis that constantly belongs to consciousness in general' (APS § 26). According to Husserl, the true nature of association can only be understood in terms of an essential or eidetic law of **consciousness** rather than an empirical law. Indeed, 'association is a fundamental concept belonging to transcendental phenomenology' (CM § 39). For Husserl, 'associative genesis' dominates the sphere of pregiven, passive experience (EU § 16, p. 74). Husserl is critical of **Hume** for seeing association as a matter of empirical, inductive, mechanical, psychological laws, rather than a matter of eidetic necessity. Husserl is critical of empirical psychology for its understanding of association as a kind of psychophysical causality, and for limiting association to the appearing together of similar clusters of sense data. By the same token, Husserl credits **Kant** with recognizing that causality is an a priori **synthesis** of association. Association is actually the name for a rich set of procedures at different strata of conscious life from the level of time consciousness, the sensory level, the level of the unity of the object, memory, to the levels of judgement and the unity of ego. For instance, time consciousness is possible only through a kind of associative synthesis between **retention, protention** and the **now phase**. Something present recalls something past. Perception can evoke memory and so on. This association is omnipresent in psychic life and experienced passively. The concept of **world** itself emerges from an associative synthesis that occurs at the passive level. The understanding of consciousness as such can be uncovered through a genetic phenomenology of association. The main sense of association is that of 'something reminds one of something else' (EU §16). Association is a principle of passive genesis in CM § 39. Association is never mechanical, for Husserl, it is a matter of intentionality, according to which different aspects of meaning are drawn together into synthetic unities. In ***Logical Investigations***, Husserl discusses 'associative connections' between similars (LU II § 34) and the general notion of 'association' is discussed at LU I § 4 where association is explained as a connection

between two psychic experiences being forced on the experiencer; it is not just the co-presence of these experiences in consciousness. There is a 'felt mutual belongingness' between experiences. There are lower and higher levels of association. Husserl talks about different kind of synthesis – synthesis of identification and also similarity. The recognition of something as a 'unity' within the flowing life of **consciousness** is realized through association, e.g. to the similarity grasped between the contents offered in different moments. Certain contents simply have a qualitative similarity with one another, as for instance, the colour areas in a carpet shade off into one another and give one a sense of the unity of the carpet. Without an awareness of the similarities highlighted by association it would be impossible to constitute the identity of things in a stable way. Association proceeds passively; one experience in consciousness is linked to another, and so on.

Attitude (*Einstellung*)   See also **natural attitude, naturalistic attitude, personalistic attitude, theoretical attitude, transcendental attitude, worldview**

Husserl borrows the term 'attitude' (*Einstellung*) from nineteenth-century psychology, where it is used to mean 'mindset', to refer very broadly to the overall ' view', 'outlook' or 'stance' of consciousness towards the world. The neo-Kantians already had the notion of a 'standpoint' from which objects can be viewed. Every object is constituted through a particular subjective accomplishment that requires a specific standpoint. Thus art approaches objects from one perspective and science from another. In general, the neo-Kantians considered science to be a value-free standpoint; whereas ethics necessarily involves attention to value. In the *Vienna Lecture*, Husserl defines an attitude as a style of life: 'a habitually fixed style of willing life comprising directions of the will or interests that are prescribed by this style, comprising the ultimate ends, the cultural accomplishments whose total style is thereby determined' (*Crisis*, p. 280; Hua VI 326). Attitudes are adopted for particular purposes and are essentially teleological, although the natural attitude has a certain hold on humans and cannot be said to be freely adopted unlike the scientific attitude. According to Husserl, it is an essential attribute of conscious subjectivity that it can freely adopt different attitudes or approaches towards the world, e.g. the **theoretical attitude**, the psychological attitude, the mathematical attitude, the aesthetic attitude, the scientific attitude, and so on. Attitudes can be changed (*Einstellungwechsel*) or altered or switched (*Einstellungänderung*) and there is a certain layering or stratification of attitudes, e.g. the scientific attitude is actually a version of the natural attitude in that science has an attitude of realism and belief towards the objects it studies. All motivation, willing, knowing and acting takes place within an overall attitude that is guided by specific interests. Primarily and most of the time, humans are in the **natural attitude**, characterized by having directedness towards the world in a 'general positing' and with an overall belief in the reality of things and of the world. In Ideas II, Husserl says that the **personalistic attitude** according to which we interpret human beings as persons subject or amenable to reasons is actually more basic that the natural attitude. The natural attitude can evolve into the narrower **naturalistic attitude**. Generally speaking, Husserl discusses attitudes in terms of certain contrasting pairs, e.g. natural versus phenomenological attitude, naturalistic versus personalistic, practical versus theoretical, evaluative versus disengaged, and so on. In his *Vienna Lecture*, Husserl contrasts the theoretical attitude discovered by ancient Greek philosophers with the mythic-religious attitude, a practical attitude towards the world. It is an essential feature of **consciousness** that alterations or changes in attitude can be brought about freely. It is possible to undergo a complete reorientation of attitude and the **phenomenological *epoché*** is a special form of this change of attitude that is necessary in order to enter the phenomenological attitude. Husserl speaks of the 'natural-scientific attitude' and the 'naturalistic attitude' (in *Ideas* II) and acknowledges that there are also 'evaluative and practical attitudes'. An attitude is an all encompassing stance towards objects whereas a **worldview** has a more existential connotation and suggests a way of living in relation to the world.

Avenarius, Richard (1843–1896) Avenarius was an exponent of empirio-criticism and positivism and regarded as one of the philosophers who influenced the Vienna Circle. His anti-materialist views were criticized by Lenin. Avenarius completed his PhD in Leipzig with a dissertation on Spinoza's pantheism in 1868 and, after his *Habilitation* in 1876, he taught at Leipzig and then Zurich. He advocated a scientific philosophy that eschewed both metaphysics and materialism and was grounded in experience. His main works are: *Philosophy as Thinking of the World* (*Philosophie als Denken der Welt gemäß dem Prinzip des kleinsten Kraftmaßes. Prolegomena zu einer Kritik der reinen Erfahrung*, 1888, 2nd edn, 1903); *Critique of Pure Experience*

(*Kritik der reinen Erfahrung*, 2 volumes, 1888–1890); and *The Human Concept of the World* (*Der menschliche Weltbegriff*, Leipzig, 1891). Avenarius advocated a return to the prescientific world of immediate experience as the basis on which to construct the scientific conception of the world. He wanted to determine the nature of the 'natural concept of the world' (*natürlicher Weltbegriff*) which expressed human experiencing and knowing prior to explicit scientific theorizing and indeed prior to the split between physical and psychical that emerged in modern science and philosophy. Avenarius deeply influenced Husserl's conception of the life-world and is discussed by Husserl in his *Basic Problems of Phenomenology* lectures (1910–1911).

Axiology (*Axiologie*)   See also **ethics, value**
Axiology means 'pertaining to the sphere of **values**', and is normally used as a synonym for 'theory of value'. Values here mean anything that is an object of enjoyment, admiration, dislike, beauty, ugliness, use, and so on. Axiology therefore, includes **ethics** and aesthetics, but, in Husserl, it can also include religious veneration, reverence, etc. In *Ideas* I, *Ideas* II and elsewhere, Husserl often contrasts the **theoretical attitude** with the practical and axiological attitudes. Axiology covers the sphere of acts of valuing, pleasing, displeasing, and all other attitudes that belong to the affective sphere (*Ideas* II § 4). To be entranced by a blue sky is not simply an attitude founded on seeing a blue sky but a wholly new attitude of living in the enjoyment of the blueness of the sky. We are living through the performance of a new attitude which takes its own specific object, what Husserl calls a **value**. Art works for Husserl, are apprehended with aesthetic or 'axiological' intuition (*Ideas* II § 4). This is distinct from a theoretical contemplation of an art object.

—**B**—

Being (*Sein, Seiendes*)   See also **absolute being, being in itself, consciousness**
Husserl often refers to the realm of 'being' (*Sein*) or 'the being' (*Seiendes*,

das Seiende), or 'all that is' (*alles Seiende*, *Crisis* § 48), 'the whole of being' (*All des Seienden*, *Crisis* § 12) to refer to that at which **intentionality** aims. Philosophy is defined as the 'science of the whole of being' (*Crisis* § 3; see also VI 26). He often speaks of the 'being sense' (*Seinssinn*) of constituted entities, and speaks of the realm of 'being and validity' (*Sein und Geltung*). Husserl develops an account of ontology divided into two branches: **formal ontology** and **material ontology. Heidegger** praised Husserl for reviving ontology. In Husserl's transcendental idealism, all being gets its **sense** and validity in relation to the **transcendental ego**.

Being in itself', 'in-itself-ness' (*Ansichsein*)   See also **consciousness**
For Husserl, ideal entities or **idealities** have a 'being in themselves' independent of their being known. He also speaks of the 'being in itself' of the world (see *Crisis* § 9) which is the way the world is conceived in modern mathematical sciences. Besides 'real' or 'actual' existent things in the world, such as stones, horses, and even conscious episodes (temporal slices of thinking), with their causal powers and interactions, that there is another domain of objecthood, which contains such 'ideal' (later: 'irreal') objectivities as the 'Pythagorean theorem' or 'the number 4' which must be understood as abstract individuals (unities) of a peculiar kind. These ideal objects, moreover, are *not* psychological entities or parts thereof. Husserl recognizes both the in-it-selfness of certain ideal objectivities (of the arithmetic and pure logic) and the historical and intersubjective experience in which they are given. Husserl wants to understand such 'Platonic entities' without metaphysical considerations (see *Experience and Judgment* § 87).

Belief (*Glaube, doxa*)   See also **conviction, *doxa*, doxic modality**
Belief is a **'doxic modality'** that can be altered freely into doubt, uncertainty, incredulity, and so on. Perception involves an implicit belief in the existence of what is perceived. Our perceptions have the character of certainty. Husserl stresses that our 'fundamental belief' or 'basic belief' (*Urglaube*) concerning the existence and actuality of the world is given by **perception**. He contrasts belief (Greek: *doxa*) with knowledge (*Erkenntnis, episteme*). The **natural attitude** is fundamentally an attitude of unquestioned belief in the world. Beliefs are lived experiences of a temporal nature but they can settle down into **convictions**.

Berkeley, George (1685–1753)   See also **empiricism, idealism**

Irish philosopher and Church of Ireland bishop, empiricist, immaterialist, and subjective idealist, author of *New Theory of Vision* (1709) and *A Treatise concerning the Principles of Human Knowledge* (1710). Husserl criticizes Berkeley's representationalist theory of abstraction in the Second Logical Investigation § 29. In later writings, he distances his own transcendental idealism from the Berkeley's empirical or subjective idealism (see *Cartesian Meditations*, Hua I 192). The mature Husserl was an admirer of Berkeley, calling him 'one of the radical and, in fact, most genial philosophers of modernity' in *Erste Philosophie* I (Hua VII 149), a 'groundbreaker' (*Bahnbrecher*) in epistemology, who developed the first 'immanent – albeit naturalistic – theory' of the constitution of the material world (VII 150). He commends Berkeley for re-establishing the 'right of natural experience' (VII 150), and insisting that perception is based neither on supposition nor deduction. In *Erste Philosophie*, as in *Crisis* § 23, Husserl presents Berkeley as offering a 'sensationalist critique of knowledge' (Hua VI 89), reducing all perceived bodies to 'complexes of **sense data**' (*Komplex von Empfindungsdaten*) that can only be inferentially linked to other sense data. For Husserl, Berkeley, no more than other empiricists, has no answer to the main challenge to such an empiricist account of **knowledge**, namely: how our fluctuating sensations can account for the experience of the object as identically the *same* (Hua VII 151).

Binswanger, Ludwig (1881–1966)   Ludwig Binswanger was born in Switzerland and studied medicine at the universities of Lausanne, Heidelberg and Zurich. He studied with Bleuler and completed his doctorate with Carl Gustav Jung in Zurich in 1907. Through Jung he met Freud in Vienna and they become close friends. In 1911, his father died and Ludwig Biswanger subsequently inherited the "Bellevue Sanatorium", in Kreutzlingen, Switzerland, which was founded in 1857 by his grandfather, also a medical doctor. This clinic treated many famous patients including Freud's 'Anna O' and the art historian Aby Warburg, who later founded the Warburg Institute and was in the clinic from 1921–24. Binswanger was interested in developing phenomenology for application to psychiatry. He was interested in the approach of Karl Jaspers. He was particularly interested in Husserl and Heidegger and gave a lecture 'On Phenomenology' in 1922. He developed an analysis of human existence (Dasein) that emphasized the importance of being-with others ('being-with') and the meaningfulness of the individual's symptoms in relation to their history and their own interpretation. He saw his approach as a 'phenomenological anthropology', later renamed as Daseinsanalysis. Husserl visited the clinic in 1923 while on holidays in the region and expressed his admiration for Binswanger's work. Binswanger was a friend of Erwin Straus and influenced philosophers such as Maurice Merleau-Ponty and Michel Foucault.

Body (*Körper*)   See also **lived body or animate body (*Leib*)**

The term 'body' (*Körper*) is used by Husserl primarily to refer to the physical body which occupies space and is subject to causal laws. He used the term *Leib* (**lived body** or animate body, see *Ideas* II § 18) to refer to the body as a living organic entity. The body is constituted as a physical thing like other physical things; it is affected by gravity, causality, has the character of weight, impenetrability, having 'parts outside of parts', and so on. This is the body understood as belonging to nature and as the subject matter of the natural sciences, especially physics. But as an animate body that I possess, the lived body (*Leib*) is also a living centre of my experience. Curiously, the body is experienced not as identical with the **ego** but rather as something which is 'mine'. It is normally experienced as something over and against the ego (*Ideas* II § 54). The lived body is experienced as a bearer of **sensations** (*Ideas* II § 36) and as an organ of my **will** (§ 38). It is the vehicle of my 'I can's. In particular, the lived body is the **zero point of orientation** from which all directions get their sense. Husserl claims the body is present in all our perceptual experience and is involved in all other conscious functions (*Ideas* II § 39). In ordinary life, the body is not experienced as a centre of resistance but can become like that if I am tired or the body is injured, I am limping for instance.

Bolzano, Bernard (1781–1848)   See also **propositions in themselves, theory of science**

Bernard Bolzano was a contemporary of G. W. F. Hegel, a Catholic priest, professor of philosophy, political liberal, mathematician and logician. He was born in Prague in 1781 and studied philosophy (1796–9) and theology (1800–1804) there, graduating with a thesis on the foundations of mathematics. He was ordained a priest in 1805 and served as professor of religion in Prague from 1805 until 1819, when he was dismissed from his professorship by imperial decree. From 1820 to 1830 he retired to Techobuz where he worked on his main book, *Wissenschaftslehre (Theory of Science)*, published in four volumes in 1837. He also published a four-volume work on religion, *Textbook of the Science of Religion*, in 1834. Subsequently, he dedicated himself to mathematical problems but died in 1848 before completing his research. Due to his suspect religious heterodoxy and radical political liberalism, Bolzano remained in relative obscurity, and indeed, was forbidden to teach or to publish. Husserl was partly responsible for his revival. The mathematician **Carl Weierstrass** originally introduced Husserl to Bolzano's work on infinite sets, as found in his *Paradoxes of the Infinite*, originally published posthumously in 1851. Brentano introduced Husserl to Bolzano's *Theory of Science*. In his 1913 Draft Preface to the Revised *Logical Investigations*, Husserl discusses the influence of Bolzano (see E. Husserl, *Introduction to the Logical Investigations*, ed. E. Fink, trans. P. J. Bossert and C. H. Peters (The Hague: Nijhoff, 1975, p. 37)). Husserl adopted Bolzano's notions of a '**theory of science**' and his conception of 'pure logic' (see Husserl, *Prolegomena* § 61). Husserl never abandoned the Bolzano-inspired vision of mature science as a coherent intermeshing system of theoretical truths, 'truths-in-themselves' (*Wahrheiten an sich*) and '**propositions in themselves**' (*Sätze an sich*).

Bracketing (*Einklammerung*)   See also *epochē*, reduction

In *Ideas* I § 31, Husserl introduces the phenomenological **epochē** as a kind of bracketing, parenthesizing, putting into suspension, various assumptions associated with the **natural attitude**, especially the bracketing or exclusion of any assumptions drawn from the natural sciences. Husserl speaks of suspending or bracketing the basic belief in the existence of the world, the **general thesis** of the **natural attitude**. The image of bracketing presumably comes from mathematics, where the expression within the brackets can be kept separate from the operations going on outside the brackets. Bracketing is not a negation, but rather like putting something in quarantine, a putting out of use, a 'switching off' of the activity of the thing. No 'use' should be put of the belief that is bracketed. Under the **epochē**, Husserl attempts to put into brackets those assertions about the world that have to do with the natural attitude. Bracketing helps uncover the pure **ego** and its **acts**. In the bracketing, attention shifts from the object to the manner in which the object is apprehended by consciousness.

Brentano, Franz (1838–1917) See also descriptive psychology, inexistence, intentionality

Franz Brentano (1838–1917) was born in Marienberg-am-Rhein, Germany, in 1838 into a wealthy, aristocratic Catholic family that originally had come from Italy. Soon after his birth, the family moved to Aschaffenburg, Germany, where he attended school. In 1856 he enrolled in the University of Munich, and then studied theology at the University of Würzburg. He transferred to Berlin to study with the Aristotle scholar, Friedrich August Trendelenburg (1802–1872). Desiring to specialize in medieval philosophy, Brentano moved to Münster to study with the Thomist Franz Jacob Clemens (1815–1862). He submitted his doctoral thesis, *On the Several Senses of Being in Aristotle*, to the University of Tübingen. This work, published in 1862, and dedicated to Trendelenburg, and was, much later in 1907, to be **Martin Heidegger**'s first introduction to philosophy and to the meaning of being. In 1862 Brentano entered the Dominican house in Graz, but he soon left to become a seminarian in Munich. He was ordained a priest in 1864. In 1866 he completed his *Habilitation* at the University of Würzburg with a thesis entitled *The Psychology of Aristotle, In Particular His Doctrine of the Active Intellect*. Brentano then became *Privatdozent* at the University of Würzburg. In 1873 he resigned from the priesthood. In 1874, partly due to the support of Hermann Lotze, Brentano was appointed professor at the University of Vienna. In May 1874 he published the first edition of *Psychology from an Empirical Standpoint*, an attempt to delimit a scientific, empirical, but non-physiological, *psychology*. Brentano quickly attracted another circle of brilliant students at the University of Vienna, including **Meinong**, Husserl, Freud, Höfler, Twardowski, Ehrenfels, Masaryk and Kraus. He was forced to resign the chair in 1880 due to his marriage. He continued teaching as a non-salaried lecturer until his retirement in 1895. He then left Austria and eventually settled in Italy. Following the entrance of Italy into the Great War he moved to Switzerland in 1915 where he died in 1917. He left behind a large number of unpublished manuscripts, including lectures on the history of philosophy. Many of his works were also edited by his pupils. Husserl's friend, Thomas Masaryk, who had completed his doctorate under Brentano in 1876 recommended Brentano's lectures to

Husserl. Husserl spent two years (1884–6) studying with Brentano and he gratefully acknowledged Brentano's influence throughout his subsequent career. Having completed his doctorate in pure mathematics, Husserl was inspired by Brentano's conception of philosophy as an exact science, by his programme for the reform of logic, and by his conception of **descriptive psychology**. Brentano believed that psychology, through inner perception with evidence, could secure certain knowledge and identify universal laws governing the psychic realm. These laws included the following: every mental state is either a presentation or depends on a presentation. Brentano characterized these universal psychological laws as 'a priori' and 'apodictic'. Brentano's classified mental acts into three 'fundamental classes', namely: '**presentations**' (*Vorstellungen*), '**judgements**' (*Urteile*), and the 'phenomena of love and hate'. The term 'presentation' refers to that part of any mental process that brings something before the mind: 'We speak of a presentation whenever something appears to us' (PES, p. 198). A presentation in general is an act of mental seeing or mental entertaining of an individual object or concept, or even of a complex relation as in the entertaining of a state of affairs. In *Psychology from an Empirical Standpoint*, Brentano proposes ***intentionality*** as the essential characteriztic of psychic states. Every presentation is *of* something. In *Psychology from the Empirical Standpoint*, Brentano states:

> Every mental phenomenon is characterized by what the Scholastics of the Middle Ages called the intentional (or mental) inexistence of an object [die *intentionale (auch wohl mentale) Inexistenz eines Gegenstandes*], and what we might call, though not wholly unambiguously, reference to a content, direction towards an object (which is not here to be understood as meaning a thing) [*die Beziehung auf einen Inhalt, die Richtung auf ein Objekt (worunter hier nicht eine Realität zu verstehen ist)*] or immanent objectivity (*oder die immanente Gegenständlichkeit*). Every mental phenomenon includes something as object within itself, although they do not all do so in the same way. In presentation something is presented, in judgement something is affirmed or denied, in love loved, in hate hated, in desire desired and so on (PES 88).

—C—

Cantor, Georg (1845–1918) Cantor was a German mathematician, student of **Weierstrass** and close friend and colleague of Husserl at the University of Halle. He was a member of Husserl's dissertation committee. Cantor was one of the founders of set theory and also developed ways of handling transfinite numbers. Cantor and Husserl were among the first mathematicians to take **Frege** seriously.

Cardinal number (*Anzahl*) See also *Philosophy of Arithmetic*
In general, cardinal numbers distinguish quantities, whereas ordinal numbers distinguish the order of the items' numbers. For Husserl, cardinal number is a finite, natural number. Husserl believed we had an 'authentic' **intuition** of the lower cardinal numbers (up to around 12) and thereafter such numbers could only be understood symbolically.

Carnap, Rudolf (1891–1970) Rudolf Carnap was a German philosopher, logical positivist and member of the Vienna Circle. From 1910–14 he studied physics at the University of Jena but attended the lectures of Frege (on mathematical logic) and Bruno Bauch (on Kant). After the Great War he studied physics in Freiburg and then returned to Jena to complete his thesis 'Space' (*Der Raum*) published in *Kant Studien* (1922). Carnap attended Husserl's seminars in 1924–5, when he was living near Freiburg and assembling the material that would become *The Logical Construction of the World* (1928). Carnap became associated with the Vienna Circle after he moved to take up a position in Vienna in 1926, introduced to **Moritz Schlick** through his friend Hans Reichenbach. In 1929 Carnap, along with Hans Hahn and Otto Neurath wrote the *Manifesto of the Vienna Circle*, which aimed at propagating a 'scientific conception of the world' [*wissenschaftliche Weltauffassung*] in opposition to traditional metaphysical and theological worldviews. This manifesto suggested that the survival of metaphysical outlooks could be explained by psychoanalysis or by sociological investigation, but most advanced was the 'clarification of the logical origins of metaphysical aberration, especially through the works of Russell and Wittgenstein'. Carnap was deeply disturbed by Martin Heidegger's inaugural lecture, 'What is Metaphysics?' delivered at the

University of Freiburg in July 1929. His reply, entitled 'On the Overcoming of Metaphysics through the Logical Analysis of Language', appeared in the new journal of the logical positivists, *Erkenntnis* (Volume 2) in 1931. Carnap's essay was actually a programmatic manifesto against traditional metaphysics involving the supposed demonstration of the meaningless of metaphysical claims based on a 'logical analysis' of meaning. In this essay, Carnap criticized many kinds of traditional metaphysics. In 'Overcoming Metaphysics', Carnap argues that there is a fault in human language that admits sentences (both meaningful and meaningless) that possess the same 'grammatical form'. Carnap suggests that sentences in Heidegger's 1929 essay – Carnap places Heidegger in 'the metaphysical school' – such as 'The Nothing nothings'(*Das Nichts selbst nichtet*) bear a superficial grammatical resemblance to acceptable sentences such as 'The rain rains'. But this sentence is misleading because 'nothing' cannot function like a normal noun. Indeed, the journal *Erkenntnis* had been explicitly founded by Carnap and Reichenbach to preach the logical positivist message and explicitly advocate 'scientific philosophy'. Carnap's essay has been seen as effectively unmasking Heidegger's nonsense (literally). In contrast with his contempt for Heidegger, Carnap had respect for Husserl and even invokes Husserl's **epochē** approvingly in his *Aufbau* Section 64. In speaking about beginning from one's personal experiences (which Carnap, adapting the term 'methodological individualism,' calls 'methodological **solipsism**'), Carnap says that he will suspend belief as to whether the beliefs are actual or not.

Cartesian dualism   See **dualism**

Cartesian ideal of science   See also **Descartes, science**
In the *Cartesian Meditations* §§3–5, Husserl discusses Descartes' ideal of scientific knowledge as absolutely self-grounded knowledge, 'grounded on an absolute foundation and absolutely justified' (CM § 5). Descartes presupposed geometry as meeting the requirement of being an absolutely justified **science**. All other sciences would have to live up to that ideal. For Descartes, that meant that the science must form a deductive system of truths. Husserl wants to retain the guiding ideal of an absolutely self-justifying science of systematic cognitions but refuses to accept any model offered by the existing sciences. For Husserl, the key to self-justifying science is the idea of **evidence**.

Cartesian Meditations (*Méditations cartésiennes,* **1931**)   See also
Cartesian way, Descartes, epochē, transcendental ego
Husserl's *Cartesian Meditations. An Introduction to Phenomenology* was
first published in French in 1931, translated from the German by **Emmanuel
Levinas** and Gabrielle Pfeiffer, with advice from **Alexandre Koyré**. On 23
and 25 February 1929, in Paris, Husserl delivered in German two two-hour
lectures entitled 'Introduction to Transcendental Phenomenology' (later
published as the *Paris Lectures* in *Husserliana* Volume I) at the Descartes
Amphitheatre of the Sorbonne, invited by the German Institute of the
Sorbonne. In attendance were Emmanuel **Levinas**, Lucien **Lévy-Bruhl**, Jean
Cavaillès, Jean Héring, Alexandre **Koyré**, Gabriel Marcel, and, possibly,
at least according to the recollection of Maurice de Gandillac, the 20-year
old Maurice **Merleau-Ponty**. Invited by Jean Héring, Husserl repeated
these lectures in Strasbourg a week later to a smaller invited audience.
The French edition of the *Meditations* was enormously influential, opening
up a new French audience for Husserl. For many years this was the only
significant Husserlian text available in French. But Husserl himself felt he had
run into problems precisely in his account of the constitution of intersubjective experience and held back the German edition for further revisions.
Although a German typescript of the lectures circulated among Husserl's
students, the original manuscript from which Levinas translated got lost. A
revised German version of the text was eventually published in 1950 edited
by Stephan Strasser as *Husserliana* Volume I. Husserl envisaged the Paris
lectures as merely a sketch of the breadth of transcendental life, an introduction to the vast domain of transcendental phenomenology. However,
due to their broad circulation, the *Cartesian Meditations* have taken on
the status of a canonical expression of Husserl's mature transcendental
philosophy. Indeed, Husserl himself held these lectures in high regard and
called them as '*major work – my life's work*' in his letter to Dorion Cairns of
21 March 1930. Husserl deliberately decided to introduce phenomenology
to a French audience through 'France's greatest thinker' and by a revisiting
of Descartes' *Meditations on First Philosophy* (1641) which, for Husserl
aimed at 'a complete reforming of philosophy into a science grounded
on an absolute foundation' (CM § 1). In fact, there is only a very tenuous
effort made to follow the course of Descartes' own *Meditations on First
Philosophy*. Like **Descartes**, Husserl wants to begin in 'absolute poverty',
abandoning all his own convictions. For Husserl, the current situation of the

sciences parallels that of the young Descartes, there is enormous progress in science yet also deep insecurity. The *Cartesian Meditations* is presented by Husserl as an exercise in 'solipsistic philosophizing' (CM § 1). As such, it stands in sharp contrast to the approach to phenomenology through the communal life-world that is to be found in the **Crisis of European Sciences**. Husserl explicitly calls phenomenology a 'neo-Cartesianism' although it explicitly rejects almost all of Descartes' own tenets. Husserl applauds Descartes for abandoning naive objectivism and returning to 'transcendental subjectivism' by beginning with the 'I think', *ego* **cogito**. Descartes, however, failed to make the genuine transcendental turn and fell back into a naive metaphysics. He failed to grasp the genuine sense of transcendental subjectivity (CM § 10). Husserl embraces the Cartesian **epochē**, the 'putting out of action' of all one's previous opinions and convictions. Through the *epochē*, I come to confront my whole worldly life as the outcome of my conscious experiences. Everything in the world is there for me because I accept it, perceive it, think about it, and so on: 'I can enter no world other than the one that gets its acceptance or status in and from me, myself' (CM § 8). The *Cartesian Meditations* introduces new themes such as the reduction to the **sphere of ownness**, and the attempt to explicate the experience of the other in **empathy** (Fifth Meditation). In CM Husserl also talks about **passive synthesis**, **time** as the **horizon** of all experience, and of egos as **monads**. Indeed, he presents the whole of phenomenology as essentially an **egology**. Husserl's assistant **Eugen Fink** sought to develop, with Husserl's encouragement, a *Sixth Cartesian Meditation: The Idea of a Transcendental Theory of Method. With Textual Notations by Edmund Husserl*, which laid down the conditions making it possible to undertake transcendental inquiry in the first place and proposed Husserl's work as a continuation of Kant's transcendental philosophy, with both a 'transcendental aesthetic' and a 'transcendental doctrine of method'. Fink's work takes Husserl's work in a Hegelian and Heideggerian direction.

Cartesian way   See **reduction**

Cassirer, Ernst (1874–1945)   Ernst Cassirer was a neo-Kantian philosopher of the Marburg school who had an immense knowledge of the history of philosophy and wrote pioneering studies of Leibniz, Kant and Renaissance philosophy. He was born in Breslau, Silesia, and studied philosophy and literature at the University of Berlin (1892–5) where he studied with Georg Simmel. He then moved to Marburg to study with Hermann Cohen from 1896 to 1899. He wrote his *Habilitation* in Berlin in 1906 and then became a lecturer there. He became professor at the University of Hamburg in 1919 where he taught until 1933. Being partly Jewish, he was forced to resign. He left Germany for Oxford (1933–5), Gotheburg, Sweden (1935–41) and then Yale University (1941–43) before settling at Columbia University in New York. Cassirer was an expert on Kant and published *Kant's Life and Thought* (1918). He developed his *Philosophy of Symbolic Forms* published in three volumes from 1923 to 1929. Cassirer corresponded with Husserl, debated with **Heidegger** in Davos, Switzerland, in 1929, and argued with Mortiz Schlick about the meaning of relativity theory. Cassirer's two-volume *Problem of Knowledge* (1906/1907) was an important historical and critical study of epistemology that Husserl regularly consulted when discussing the epistemology of modern philosophers such as Locke, **Hume**, or **Kant**. Cassirer had respect for Husserl's phenomenology but regarded his own theory of symbolic forms as superior for handling the nature of meaning and explaining the function of art, literature and culture.

Categorial intuition (*kategoriale Anschauung*) See also **eidetic intuition, fulfilment, intuition, synthesis**
Categorial intuitions are presented in Husserl's Sixth Logical Investigation as complex intentional acts that apprehend states of affairs or objects in combination or in relation in contrast to simple, straightforward acts of sensuous perceiving that apprehend objects or properties in a direct non-mediated way. Categorial intuition, for Husserl, involves a broadening of the traditional concepts of perception and intuition (LU VI § 46). In simple perception, one sees things or their properties, whereas in categorial intuition, one apprehends more complex affairs ('categorial objects') such as things in relation, combination, separation, and so on. These categorial intuitions are given directly in intuition rather than apprehended through reasoning and inference. According to Husserl, when I intuitively grasp a **state of affairs** (*Sachverhalt*), e.g., 'I see *that* the paper is white', rather than a simple seeing of *white paper*, I am experiencing a categorial intuition, a complex intuition that something is the case or that some situation 'holds'. In a judgement of this kind, I intuit *what is going on*, as it were. Here my intuition goes beyond, exceeds or surpasses what

is presented sensuously. I have a fulfilling intuition that meets my intention but what fulfils the intuition is not purely sensuous but has what Husserl calls a 'categorial' dimension. For Husserl, categorial acts are **founded** on the sensory acts of perceiving, but are not *reducible* to them. For Husserl, categorial acts grasp states of affairs and in fact constitute them in the very categorial act itself. It is not the case that I grasp sensuously the components of the judgement and synthesize them using some kind of subjective rules of the understanding, as Kant suggests (according to Husserl's interpretation), rather I apprehend the state of affairs of which the non-sensuous categorial elements are necessary constituents. Categorial intuition involves acts of identification and discrimination, acts of **synthesis**. Suppose we perform the expressive act (i.e. articulate a meaning) such as 'this is a blackbird'. A categorial intuition consists of a certain **synthesis** between the act of meaning expectancy or signification and the act of **fulfilment**. Of course, these acts of synthesis are themselves only grasped by acts of reflection, but the crucial point is that they must be present for a meaning to be understood holistically, to be given as an **objectivity**. Categorial acts are those in which we grasp relations and make identifications of the form 'x is y'. It is through categorial intuition that our grasp of 'is-ness' comes about, that we directly encounter *being* as that which is the case. Husserl's treatment of categorial intuition in the Sixth Logical Investigation inspired **Heidegger** to examine the question of being and how being is given in our experience. Husserl agrees with Kant that being is not a predicate, that is, that the existing situation is not a property of the individual object (the white paper). Saying that something *is* does not give us an intuition of a new property in a manner similar to learning 'something is red'. But this shows for Husserl that assertion of the category of being does not involve grasping a property or the object itself. Neither does it emerge from reflecting on the act of consciousness, as some had thought, rather the categorial structure belongs to the ideal structure of the object, to the objectivity as such. Categorial acts yield up the grasp of the pure categorial concepts, 'if ... then', 'and', 'or' and so on, which have no correlates in the objects of the perceptual acts themselves. Heidegger saw Husserl's discussion of categorial intuition as crucial to his own account of intentionality in terms of the meaning of being. Heidegger himself always pointed to Husserl's discussion of categorial intuition in the Sixth Investigation as providing the most important step in his own quest to understand the 'meaning of being' encountered in **Brentano**'s reading of Aristotle. Furthermore, it was Heidegger who urged Husserl again and again to bring out a revised edition of the Sixth Investigation. Heidegger clearly saw that Husserl depended on, but had not properly analysed, the concept of being present in the bodily fulfilment of sensuous intuitions and in the categorial synthesis expressed by the copula in more complex acts. To this extent, then, Heidegger rightly recognized that Husserl's account called for a further analysis of the being of what is grasped in the intentional act.

Categorical imperative   See also **ethics**

Husserl discusses Kant's categorical imperative in his lectures on ethics (*Husserliana* Vol. XXVIII, *Lectures on Ethics and Value Theory*) which contains the lecture course on ethics and axiology from 1908/09 that Husserl repeated in a slightly changed version in 1911 and 1914. Husserl criticizes Kant's categorical imperative as too formal to decide what is morally good for the will. According to Kant's universalization, an act is morally good if it can be willed universally. Husserl believes that this universality requirement is not enough, it is equivalent to the manner in which formal logic guarantees validity but not truth. It is easy to universalize harmless maxims (look right before crossing the street) but these have no moral value. It is also possible for different imperatives to clash. In order to decide which to follow, one must know more than the mere universalizability of the imperative. In order to decide whether a maxim is ethically significant, we need more than the mere formal criterion of universalizability; we also have to know something about the significance and the value of the aim of the **will**. In his later manuscripts from the first half of the 1920s, love in addition to reason comes to be seen as the fundamental ethical motive. Love, which wells up from the depth of the **person** and the absolute obligation that it generates, individualizes the person and her ethical law.

Causality (*Kausalität*)   See also **motivation, nature, spirit**

Husserl contrasts the domain of **nature** as the domain of causality with the domain of **spirit** where **motivation** provides the essential law. From the naturalistic point of view, the physical world is understood as a spatio-temporal domain of material things regulated by causal laws (see *Crisis* § 61). Natural causality is inseparable from the notion of spatiotemporality (see *Crisis* § 62); indeed the concepts of 'reality' and that of 'causality' are intimately connected (*Phen. Psych.* § 22). Causality in nature, for Husserl, has to be understood in terms of inductive generality. Husserl writes: 'Causality in nature is nothing other than a stable empirical regularity of co-existence and succession' (*Phen. Psych.* § 23, p. 103; Hua IX 134). In the *Crisis*, Husserl says that the method of modern physics, inherited from Galileo, is 'nothing but prediction' extended to infinity' (*Crisis* § 9h, p. 51; VI 51). According to Husserl, causality belongs to the very essence of the notion of a physical thing as understood by the natural sciences (*Ideas* II § 60). Husserl denies, however, that we actually apprehend or experience causation in perception. Husserl was deeply influenced by Hume's understanding of causation in terms of regularity. Hume writes in his *Enquiry Concerning Human Understanding* that the ideas of necessity and causation arises 'entirely from the uniformity observable in the operations of nature, where similar objects are constantly conjoined together, and the mind is determined by custom to infer the one from the appearance of the other'. He goes on to state that 'beyond the constant conjunction of similar objects, and the consequent inference from one to the other, we have no notion of any necessity or connexion'. According to Husserl, Hume had shown that humans naively introduce causality into the world and assume it to be a necessary connection (see *Crisis* § 25). Exact causality is an idealization of modern mathematical science quite different from the typical patterns of succession experienced in the **life-world**. In his letter to the anthropologist Lucien **Lévy-Bruhl** Husserl discusses the notions of causality of primitive peoples.

Certainty (*Gewißheit*)   See also **conviction, doxic modality, possibility**
Certainty is the most simple **doxic modality** (*Doxische Modalität* or *Modalität des Glaubens*, Hua III/1 271), whereby we have a **conviction** about certain facts or situations. This doxical modality can be changed in other types of modality: modalization of certainty (*Modalisierungen der Gewißheit*) into doubt, possibility, negation is possible (***Experience and Judgment*** § 21). Certainty has its grades of 'perfection' or 'completeness' (*Vollkommenheit*) and imperfection or purity (*Reinheit*) and impurity (EU § 77). There is imperfection when different possibilities entry in our horizon and we decide only for one of them. Empirical certainty can be denied (even though we do not find motivations to deny it in the present). Certainty that is based on empirical terrain is always a

presumptive certainty, but we have to distinguish this kind of certainty from the mere 'supposition' (*Vermutung*). While empirical certainty is full motivated, mere supposition considers at the same time contrary reason and possibilities. Certainty about the empirical world is necessarily presumptive, but it does not mean that it is a mere supposition. Our beliefs about the world are full motivated but can be cancelled or corrected. Husserl places apodictic certainty at the highest level. Apodictic judgements grasp true states of affairs and show them in a perfect way. Also, apodictic certainty plays a decisive role in Husserl's method. For him, phenomenology must identify apodictic laws of consciousness or essential structures of subjectivity.

Clarification (*Klärung*)   See also **description, phenomenology**

For Husserl, clarification (*Klärung*) is the central function of philosophy, and is usually contrasted with 'explanation' (*Erklärung*). He uses many different terms: 'uncovering' (*Enthüllung*), 'illuminating' (*Erhellung, Aufhellung*), and 'clarifying' (*Aufklärung, Klarlegung*). For him – as for Brentano and, indeed, later for Wittgenstein – philosophy aims at 'clarification' or 'illumination' (*Klärung, Aufklärung, Klarlegung, Erhellung*). *Clarification* means 'making sense', casting critical light on the achievements of **cognition** (*Erkenntnis*), which Husserl understood in the broadest sense, especially in his later writings, to include the whole human encounter with the **world** as it is carried out in the '**natural attitude**' as well as in scientific practice. Indeed, philosophy itself aims at 'ultimate clarification' (*Letztklärung*) or 'ultimate grounding' (*Letztbegründung*) of the sense of our entire cognitive accomplishment. Clarification, however, must – as with Aristotle – accord with the level of exactness that the subject matter itself allows. The philosophical clarification that Husserl sought involved grasping the essential (or, in his words, 'eidetic') character of the key concepts in any specific epistemic or ontological domain. In his early years Husserl was concerned primarily with *epistemological* clarification, the 'critique of knowledge', 'the elucidation … of the sense and possibility of validly objective knowledge'. For him, clarification could not be piecemeal but had to extend to the interconnecting unity of all the sciences, indeed it had to justify the very theories of science also. In short, philosophy requires a complete '**theory of science**' (*Wissenschaftslehre*) and must be carried out in a rigorously scientific manner:

Above all, philosophy means not irrelevant, speculative mysticism but rather nothing other than the ultimate radicalization
of rigorous science. (*Draft Preface*, p. 30; Fink 123)

In his *Phenomenological Psychology* § 1 lectures, Husserl says that clarification is the same as what **Dilthey** means by the term **understanding**
(*Verstehen*).

Cogitatio   See also **cogitatum**, **cogito**, **ego**, **lived experience**
Husserl uses Descartes' Latin term *cogitatio* (plural *cogitationes*) to refer
broadly not just to an act of thinking, but to any lived experience that is
consciously experienced (see *Crisis* VI 418). Sometimes, Husserl specifically
uses the term *cogitatio* to refer to conscious states as they are apprehended
under the **epochē**, i.e., without attention being paid to their relationship with
the causal objective order of nature. He says that he chose the word *cogitatio*
as a general term for mental acts, since, he says, the Latin term is 'not infected
with the problem of transcendence' (Hua X 346) and can therefore pick
out the lived experience as immanently apprehended. He praises Descartes
for reducing the world to the stream of *cogitationes* (Hua I 8). He criticizes
Descartes, however, for not clearly distinguishing between the **cogito** as
an act of thinking and as the *content* of what is thought (**cogitatum**). Each
cogito has its *cogitatum* (Hua I 13). We are conscious of or 'live through'
our mental acts or episodes – acts of imagining, perceiving, remembering,
willing, and so on. Contrariwise, thoughts are also 'about' objects and have
a certain intentional **content**. They are, in some sense, representations or
'pictures' of things, as Descartes says. Husserl frequently uses the coupling of
ego-*cogitatio*-**cogitatum** (e.g. CM § 21) or *ego-cogito-cogitatum* (Hua I 14).
Husserl writes in *The Basic Problems of Phenomenology* (1911):

> A *cogitatio*, a being conscious, is every kind of sensing,
> presenting, perceiving, remembering, expecting, judging, con-
> cluding, every kind of feeling, desiring, willing, etc. (GPP Hua
> XIII 150, my translation)

Cogitatum   See also **cogitatio, cogito, content ego, lived experience,
noema**
Husserl uses the term *cogitatum* (Latin word, meaning 'that which is

thought'; plural *cogitata*) to refer to the **object** of thought or of conscious attention. If I am looking at the sky, then *the sky* is the *cogitatum* of my intentional act. The *cogitatum* refers not just to the object of thought or perception but also to the manner in which the object is apprehended in the act of perception or thought. The *cogitatum* is only possible through the cogito (Hua I 17). The term is used by Husserl interchangeably with **noema**.

Cogito or Ego cogito   See also **cogitatio, cogitatum, ego,** transcendental subjectivity

Cogito (meaning 'I think') is the first-person singular present tense of the Latin verb *cogitare* ('to think'). Husserl uses the term *cogito* and the phrase *ego cogito* (e.g. Hua I 9) as a shorthand for **Descartes'** famous expression *cogito ergo sum* ('I think, therefore I am'), which appeared in his *Discourse on Method* (1637). Sometimes, Husserl simply refers to the *sum* or 'I am' (*Ich bin,* CM § 11). Husserl generally uses the term *cogito* to express the manner in which the 'I' or 'ego' or **ego pole** is involved in each conscious act or mental process. He distinguishes between *cogito* and **cogitatum** at CM § 14. Husserl uses the term in the phrase *ego-cogitatio-cogitata* (*Crisis* § 50) which means 'I–thinking–what is thought'. Husserl praises Descartes for his breakthrough discovery of the *cogito* (CM § 8) and thereby of **transcendental subjectivity** and the domain of **'transcendental experience'** but criticizes him for reifying the ego as a thinking substance rather than remaining within the transcendental sphere. According to Husserl, the cogito inaugurated a new kind of philosophy overcoming the naive **objectivism** of traditional philosophy (Hua I 5). The *ego cogito*, for Husserl, here agreeing with Descartes, is a model of an apodictically certain truth, with the highest kind of **evidence**, that can provide a **ground** for subsequent scientific truths (Hua I 7). Sometimes, Husserl uses the term *cogito* to mean an individual life of consciousness. Thus he speaks about one *cogito* recognizing through **empathy** another *cogito* as also a living subject of experiences.

Coincidence (*Deckung*)   See also **fulfilment, intention**

Husserl uses the term *Deckung* meaning 'coincidence', 'congruence', 'coinciding', 'covering', to refer to the relation between an **intention** or **signitive act** and its **fulfilment** (especially in the Sixth Logical Investigation § 8, but see also ***Cartesian Meditations*** § 4). When an intending act is fulfilled then there is a coincidence between the intending act and the fulfilling act. If I lose my car keys and am looking for them, then the intentional act is one of looking for *my* car keys. The fulfilling act consists in finding that precise set of car keys. The coincidence comes when I recognize the found car keys as the very ones I was looking for (and not for instance another identical set of car keys that do not belong to me). Husserl may very well have in mind the geometrical notion of coincidence when one figure (perhaps after a rotation) can be laid precisely on top of the other. Complete coincidence is an ideal. More often, intentions may be only partially fulfilled; coincidence may be full or partial (see *Cartesian Meditations* § 51). The experience of the coincidence between the empty intention and its fulfilment has the character of **evidence**, correctness or truth. Husserl speaks of this coincidence as a kind of **synthesis**, i.e. an act performed by or an experience undergone by the intending subject.

Collective combination (*kollective Verbindung*)   See also **multiplicity,** *Philosophy of Arithmetic,* **something**
The term 'collective combination' is introduced by Husserl in his ***Philosophy of Arithmetic*** to express the specific higher order mental act of **synthesis** that grasps a multiplicity of entities as a particular unitary whole or totality: 'that sort of combination which is characteristic of the totality' (PA XII 20). It is a special psychic act of a higher order not part of straightforward everyday experience. It is one kind of experience to see one tree and then another, and quite a different mental experience to see the trees as a *group* of trees. Identifying, selecting and collecting a number of individuals together into a **multiplicity** is a necessary prerequisiteto the special act of counting. The items to be counted must first be isolated (selected out) and their irrelevant properties have to be ignored before they can be enumerated as members of the same set. For the purposes of enumeration, the actual nature of the items contained in the multiplicity is of no importance. One can count the *objects* on one's desk (e.g. pens, papers, computers). Husserl writes:

> It was clear to begin with that the specific nature of the particular objects which are gathered in the form of a multiplicity could contribute nothing to the content of the respective general concept. The only thing that could come into consideration in the formation of these concepts was the *combination*

> of the objects in the unitary representation of their totality. It
> was then a question of a more precise characterization of this
> mode of combination. (PA, p. 67; Hua XII 64)

Husserl felt, the nature of this **synthesis** had been misunderstood by
previous philosophers of mathematics, who all sought to determine it on
the basis of some aspect of **content**. According to Husserl, extrapolating
from **Brentano**'s conception of our awareness of **parts** of a **whole**, the
presentation of a concrete multiplicity is a unity that includes within it
presentations of the specific elements of the multiplicity (Hua XII 20).
In order to apprehend a group as a group and not just as a series of
individuals, I must be able to run through or 'colligate' the items understood
as bare '**somethings**' in the group and unify them together in a special
way. Numbers arise through the 'enumeration of multiplicities' (PA XII 182).

Collectivity   Husserl's name for a collection or 'set' of entities as brought
together by an act of **collective combination**.

Community of monads (*Monadengemeinschaft*)   See also **intersubjectivity, monad, monadology**
The mature Husserl employs the term 'community of **monads**' or 'intermo-
nadic community' (*intermonadologische Gemeinschaft*) – the term 'monad'
is borrowed from Leibniz – for the open-ended collection of transcendental
subjects that, acting together, constitute the **world**, including nature,
history and culture. In CM § 55, he talks about the process of the 'commu-
nalization' (*Vergemeinschaftigung*) of monads and the basis of this is the
constitution of an intersubjectively shared **nature**. When other **persons**
are perceived by the ego as other persons through **empathy**, then a shared
world is at the same time apprehended and a harmonious flow of confirma-
tions of one's experience by the other is experienced. There is an 'intentional
communion' between monads (CM § 56). Husserl calls the open plurality of
the community of monads **transcendental intersubjectivity**.

Concretum (*Konkretum*)   See also **moment, part, whole**
A concretum, for Husserl, is an individual whole. A concretum that has
no abstract parts is called an 'absolute concretum'; see Third Logical
Investigation §17.

Conflict (*Widerstreit*), (*Entäuschung*)   See also **intentionality, noema**

Husserl regularly discusses the perceptual shift or experience of 'conflict' (*Widerstreit*) or 'disagreement' that can take place when the fulfilment on an intention actually fails to fulfil the specific intention. Conflict, for Husserl, is a form of synthesis. The intention is put into relation with the fulfilling object but the object fails to fulfill and instead 'frustrates' or 'disillusions' the intention (see Sixth Logical Investigation § 11). According to Husserl's favourite example, when on a visit to a waxworks museum, one realizes that the 'woman' one supposedly saw is actually a wax figure – a mannequin (*Thing and Space* § 15) – then the original intention (seeing a woman) is set in conflict with the current perception, which frustrates our original intention. Conflict is the opposite of coincidence. Two series of intentions can come into conflict with one another, according to Husserl, only if there is an assumed underlying context which remains the same. When one realizes that the 'person' is actually a wax figure, a new chain of intentional fulfilments is then set in motion but the original intentional object is experienced as nullified.

Conrad-Martius, Hedwig (1888–1966)   See also **realist phenomenology, Stein**

Hedwig Martius was born in Berlin and was one of the first women in Germany to enter university. She initially studied literature in Rostock and in Freiburg before moving to the University of Munich to study with **Theodor Lipps** and **Moritz Geiger**. She later went to study with Husserl at Göttingen in 1911 where she was chair of the Göttingen Philosophical Society. She married the philosopher Theodor Conrad. She became a very close friend of **Edith Stein**, who had a revelation that led to her conversion to Catholicism while staying in the Conrads' house. Her earlier work was in phenomenology, especially on the nature of perception and imagination, and on ontology. Her essay on 'real ontology' was published in Husserl's **Yearbook for Philosophy and Phenomenological Research** in 1923 and she proposed a 'phenomenological ontology' that was quite independent of that developed by **Heidegger** in *Being and Time*. Because she was partly Jewish, she was excluded from an academic career. After the Second World War she became a professor at Munich where she remained. She developed an interest in the philosophy of biology and in cosmology.

Consciousness (*Bewusstsein*) See also **intentionality, life, lived experience, stream of consciousness, time consciousness**

Husserl defines **phenomenology** as the science of the essence of consciousness (*Ideas* I § 34). In *Ideas* I § 33, Husserl says that the term consciousness in the broadest sense includes 'all **mental processes'** (*Erlebnisse*). Consciousness is essentially intentional. Already in the *Logical Investigations*, Husserl discusses briefly different senses of the term 'consciousness'. He finds his first concept of consciousness in psychologists such as **Wilhelm Wundt**, who understand consciousness as the flow of real, individual, empirical conscious experiences or 'events' (*Ereignisse*) that interpenetrate and interweave in the unity of a single consciousness (LU V § 2). On this account, all **acts**, their component **parts**, whether concrete or abstract, are counted as part of the content of consciousness (whether or not they are accessed by a special inner perception). In the Second Edition, he adds a paragraph (XIX/1 357) acknowledging that this approach can be construed in a purely phenomenological manner, if all reference to existence is stripped away. In elaborating on this first conception, Husserl specifically discusses the important and often confused distinction between different kinds of **appearances** (*Erscheinungen*), namely, apprehending the object and apprehending the experience of some aspect of the object (e.g. its colour). There must be a distinction between the appearing experience and the thing that appears (*das erscheinende Objekt*) in (or through) the experience (LU V § 2, XIX/1 359). Clearly this first concept of consciousness can be 'phenomenologically purified' to yield the deeper notion Husserl wants to work with. But he does not address this conception further in the Fifth Investigation. His second concept of consciousness relates to a more traditional philosophical characterization, deriving from **Descartes** and found in **Brentano**, of 'inner consciousness' (*innere Bewusstsein*) and **'inner perception'**, which he acknowledges is more primitive and has priority over the first sense (LU V § 6), but he recognizes that Brentano tended to merge these two concepts. There is an ambiguity between an adequate, self-evident **perception** (one that yields the thing itself) and the more philosophically problematic notion of an inner perception directed at an inner conscious experience and Husserl criticizes Brentano for failing to distinguish between *adequate* perception and *inner* perception (he will return to this discussion in the Appendix to the Sixth Investigation). Husserl does recognize that there is an important notion embedded in the discussion of inner perception, namely the kind of self-givenness of *cogito* experiences, and this pushes Husserl in the direction of the pure **ego** but his remarks on this ego in the First Edition are confused. Already in the First Edition, he recognizes that the ego of the *cogito* cannot be the empirical ego, but, adds in an 'additional note' (*Zusatz*, XIX/1 376) that discussion of the ego is irrelevant here. Husserl clearly had some of the difficulties in untangling the notions of consciousness. In the Second Edition, he excises a whole section (LU V § 7) that had been too Brentanian in tone in that it entertained the possibility of phenomenalism, that things may be no more than bundles of phenomena. His third concept of consciousness is approached in terms of intentional experiences, acts that bring objects to notice, and it is with this concept that he remains for the rest of the Fifth Investigation. But it is not entirely clear how this third category is different from the phenomenologically purified field of the first characterization of consciousness. This third version emerges from consideration of the question: how can being-an-object itself be considered by us objectively (LU V § 8). Husserl is focusing on what he tentatively calls (even in the First Edition) the essential correlation between act and object. It is clear that he believes he still has some work to do on disentangling his own account of intentionality and adequate intuition from the traditional account of inner perception. He returns to these themes in the Appendix to the Sixth Investigation. In later years Husserl emphasizes the complexity of the life of consciousness and the keep role of temporality in the unfolding of conscious **life**. In writings after 1905, Husserl speaks of the flow of consciousness in terms of its fundamental temporal stratum, and he speaks about time as the fundament of all consciousness. In *Ideas* I, he focuses on pure or transcendental consciousness. In later writings, Husserl also focuses attention on unconscious and on the **drives** and instincts that act as a kind of 'underground' motivating consciousness.

Constitution (*Konstitution*) See also **achievement, construction** (*Aufbau*), **correlation, genetic phenomenology, primal establishment, static phenomenology**

'Constitution' (*Konstitution*) is a term commonly used by the neo-Kantians to refer to the manner in which an **object** is formed and given its particular structure and attributes by certain a priori acts of consciousness. According to the neo-Kantian tradition (to which the mature Husserl broadly belongs), objects do not exist simply on their own but receive their particular intelligible structure from the activity of the conscious **subject** apprehending them (see, e.g., *Ideas* I § 83). For Husserl, objects and other classes of entities (divided into various ontological **regions**) do not simply exist but are experienced by consciousness according to pre-delineated sets of acts of consciousness to which they is correlated. 'Every object is constituted in the manner peculiar to consciousness' (*Ideas* I § 149). These acts are closely interrelated (e.g. judging, perceiving, remembering, etc.). The constitution of an object is determined by certain predetermined meaning forms as laid down by the essential nature of the object in question (e.g. a material object can only be perceived in profiles and this process is inexhaustible; *Ideas* I § 149). Everything experienced is constituted in some specific way. In this respect, Husserl speaks of the **a priori correlation** between **noesis** and **noema**. There are different layers of constitution, e.g. a physical thing is constituted at one level as a 'sight thing' (*Sehding*; *Ideas* I § 42), a thing understood according to **causality**, and so on. Even the domain of **'nature'** itself has to be understood as a product of constitution (see *Ideas* II § 49). Constitution is an essential part of Husserl's **transcendental idealism** (see FTL § 98). Hume was the first to grasp this correlation between the objective world and features of subjective inner life (see FTL § 100). Husserl speaks of the constituting subject as giving an object its 'sense and being' (*Sinn und Sein*), or 'sense and validity' (*Sinn und Geltung*). Constitution is an **achievement** of intentional consciousness. Husserl thinks of constitution not so much as an active constructing (*Aufbau*) by the subject and more as a particular manner in which meaning is disclosed. In his *History of the Concept of Time* lectures, **Heidegger** says that constitution should be understood as a manifesting, a letting something be itself. Husserl's assistant **Eugen Fink** also wants to make clear that for Husserl constitution is not 'creation', it is not a 'making', but rather a revealing, an allowing of the object to show itself in a meaningful way, in a way that cannot be articulated by previous philosophy. Constitution can be actively in the sense that the subject actively generates a new meaning (as in artistic creation) but constitution also proceeds passively. There are always already constituted layers of meaning encountered in our experience. Husserl says everything 'worldly' is constituted intersubjectively (XV 45). Each person has to constitute himself or herself as one person *among others*. There is a reciprocal constitution among subjects. Furthermore, **time consciousness** plays an essential role in all constitution.

Constitutive phenomenology   See **static phenomenology**

Construction (*Aufbau*)   See also **constitution**
Husserl uses the term 'structure' or 'construction' (*Aufbau*, literally: 'building up, constructing') occasionally (see *Ideas* I § 116) to refer to the manner in which intentional correlations are built up. **Rudolf Carnap**, who attended Husserl's seminars in the 1920s, refers, in his *Logical Structure of the World*, to the logical 'construction' or 'structure' of the world. For Husserl, there is a contrast between construction and deconstruction (*Abbau*). In *Ideas* I § 18, Husserl speaks of the 'construction' (*Aufbau*) of the idea of phenomenology as a science. **Constitution** includes the idea of reference to an intending consciousness whereas construction suggests the a priori arrangement of elements and parts of conscious experience.

Content (*Gehalt, Inhalt*)   See also **act, intentionality, noema, object**
The term 'content' is used by Brentano and his followers to refer to that which is contained in an act of experiencing (feeling, perceiving, remembering, thinking, etc.). **Brentano** explains content in his *Descriptive Psychology* as follows: 'If one speaks of the content of a presentation, of a judgement or of an emotional relation, one is thinking of what is enclosed in it' (DP, p. 160). The term 'content' goes back to **Kant**, who maintained that intuitions provide the content for conception. For Kant, according to Brentano, 'content' referred to the **matter** as opposed to the form of intuition. In his *Psychology from an Empirical Standpoint*, Brentano equates the 'content' and the '**object**' of an intentional act. When one sees a cat, then 'cat' is the content or object of one's seeing. According to Brentano's threefold classification of mental acts, each class has its own particular kind of content. Thus presentational content, judgeable content, and emotional content have to be distinguished. Brentano's students criticized him for failing to make a distinction between the *content* and the *object* of an intentional act. In 1890, Alois Höfler and Alexius Meinong pointed out in their *Logic* that a distinction must be made between the intra-mental content, on the one hand, and the actual existent thing, on the other. In 1894 another of Brentano's students, **Kasimir Twardowski**, similarly

distinguished between the immanent content and the extra-mental object. Twardowski wrote: 'What is presented *in* a presentation is its content; what is presented *through* a presentation is its object.' The content, according to Twardowski, is purely a vehicle to the real object, something like a Frege sense. The later Brentano sometimes appears to be acknowledging the need to insert a sense between the mind and its object, especially when he talks of a 'mode of presentation' but in fact he repudiates the distinction between content and object in so far as he understands it at all (PES 293). Brentano thought of the content as what is psychologically available for inspection. He acknowledges a certain depth in mental content however, when he distinguishes between the *explicit* and *implicit* content. The explicit content is the whole which is presented. When I see a tree, the tree is the explicit content but the leaves are implicitly the content (DP 160). Unfortunately, Brentano never distinguished between the psychologically apprehended elements, and the logical or ideal components in the content of the act. He is thus never able to distinguish between what belongs to the thought as a mental episode, and what in the thought supports and conveys the meaning, a recurrent problem in the Cartesian tradition. Despite being part of an inner psychological episode, Brentano's content can be communicated. When we hear words spoken, we apprehend the content of the speaker's mind. But since Brentano's content remains resolutely that which is psychologically before the mind, his analysis was to say that the mental content of the speaker evinces in the hearer a mental content that gives notice of the speaker's intentions. Twardowski reproduces this account, which conspicuously fails to demonstrate how private mental contents can be turned into common meanings. As early as 1894, Edmund Husserl, struggling against **psychologism**, recognized the need to distinguish between the 'psychological' or 'real' content (*Gehalt*) and the 'ideal content' (*Inhalt* or *ideales Gehalt*) or 'meaning content' (*Bedeutungsinhalt*), whereby the *psychological* content is individual but the meaning content is not. The ideal content or meaning does not reside, as Brentano thought, in the act as a real, i.e. temporal, component of it. In the Fifth Logical Investigation, Husserl recast his original distinction as a distinction between the *real* and *ideal* contents of the act, and in the second edition of 1913 between the *phenomenological* and the *intentional* content (LU V, § 16). The real content of the act is everything that can be identified in the act including concrete and abstract parts. The objectivity of the meaning must transcend the act that is its vehicle. For Husserl, as for Frege, the thought of an ideal truth, e.g. the Pythagorean theorem, is extra-mental and does not dwell within the mental episode. Everything objective is transcendent and intentionality is simply the name for this astonishing fact. Moreover, for Husserl, as for Twardowski, ordinarily, our intentional acts are directed at or are 'about' the object not the content. Husserl acknowledges that the content of the act can be construed to include the intentional object (Fifth Logical Investigation § 17). It requires a special act of reflection to make the 'content' of an act itself into its object. In his early analyses of **time consciousness**, Husserl attempted to apply the **apprehension-content** schema that he had used for interpreting sensible matter of experience for time consciousness. After 1908, and especially in *Ideas* I, Husserl replaced the ambiguous concept of 'content' with the **noema**.

Conviction (*Überzeugung*)   See also **belief, habit, sedimentation**

Husserl uses the term 'conviction' for judgements that have become sedimented into one's consciousness so that they have the character of **habits** or habitualities. I have a conviction according to Husserl when I become 'thus and so decided' (see CM Hua I 29). There are different levels of conviction. Husserl says that the power of the conviction corresponds with the grade of certainty (*Experience and Judgment*, § 77). Conviction requires an active deciding on the part of the believer and an original taking of a stance, but this becomes incorporated into the ego as a habit.

Correlation (*Korrelation*)   See also **apriori, constitution, noema, noesis, phenomenology**

In his mature philosophy, Husserl speaks of his phenomenology as 'correlational research' (CM § 41, p. 88; Hua I 121). In general, phenomenology explores the a priori correlation between **consciousness** and objectivity. Husserl wants to explore the 'a priori of correlation' between intentional objects and their modes of givenness or manifestation to consciousness, that is, between the **noema** and the **noesis**. In *Ideas* I § 90, Husserl speaks of an intentional 'correlation' between noesis and noema and says there are strict essential laws of correlation. Intentionality, for Husserl, is a doctrine that claims there is an a priori correlation (or structural alignment) between the intended object and the intending act, e.g. a perceived object presents itself in a particular profile to a perceiver. The manner in which the object comes to givenness is a priori structured by the nature or essence of the intending act and there are different forms of correlation depending on the kind of act involved i.e. the perceived object is correlated with **perceiving**, the remembered object with remembering, and so on). Thus in FTL Husserl speaks of 'noetic and noematic multiplicities'. Although Husserl only speaks of 'correlation' in his mature writings, he claims in *Crisis* (§ 48) that the idea occurred to him in 1898 while writing the *Logical Investigations*. The **phenomenological reduction** aims to overcome the naive thinking about the object in the nature attitude as something that simply exists on its own and comes to understand the object as correlated with a specific mode of apprehending it. The perceived object, as intentional correlate of the perception, is distinct from the real object. Husserl also speaks of an essential correlation between constituting and constituted (*Ideas* II § 49).

Crisis of European Sciences and Transcendental Phenomenology (Die Krisis der europäischen Wissenschaften und die transzendentale Phänomenologie. 1936)

Husserl's last work *Crisis of European Sciences and Transcendental Phenomenology* (1936) was a disrupted and ultimately unfinished project. It was written when Husserl was in his seventies, struggling with declining health. The original *Crisis* consists of two articles published in *Philosophia* in Belgrade (as a Jew, Husserl was forbidden to publish in Germany) in 1936 (Sections 1–27 of the present expanded text of *Husserliana* VI), together with material Husserl had prepared for the publisher (now 'Part Three', Sections 28–71), along with a series of related research manuscripts. These were posthumously selected and edited by Walter Biemel and published as *Husserliana* Volume VI, *Die Krisis der europäischen Wissenschaften und die transzendentale Phänomenologie. Eine Einleitung in die phänomenologische Philosophie*, edited by Walter Biemel, in 1954. It has been partially translated by David Carr as Edmund Husserl, *The Crisis of European Sciences and Transcendental Phenomenology. An Introduction to Phenomenological Philosophy* (Evanston, IL: Northwestern University Press, 1970).The *Crisis* is universally recognized as Husserl's most lucidly written, accessible and engaging published work, aimed at the general educated reader as an urgent appeal to address the impending crises of the age. The Biemel edition includes two important essays: the controversial **Vienna Lecture** (1935) – controversial because of its claim that 'Europe' stands as the name for the idea of universal humanity, and for its allegedly ethnocentric remarks about non-European cultures – as well as his influential essay '**The Origin of Geometry'**, the subject of a long and influential commentary by the French philosopher **Jacques Derrida**. Several new themes are introduced in the *Crisis*. The work begins with an analysis of the meaning of the modern revolution in the natural sciences (as exemplified by **Galileo**) involving the **mathematization of nature** and the idealization of space. Husserl goes on to offer his most extensive published discussion of the nature of the '**life-world**' (*Lebenswelt*), as well as explicating the meaning of modern philosophy from **Descartes** to **Kant**, the shift from mythic thought to rationality brought about by philosophy, the peculiar status of **psychology**, the meaning of human temporality and **historicity**, cultural development (the 'shapes of the spiritual world', *Crisis*, p. 7; VI 4) and intercultural understanding, the concept of nationality, internationality and 'supranationality' (*Übernationalität, Crisis*, p. 270; VI 315), the inbuilt teleology of western civilization towards universal rationality and the threats facing it, and so on. At the outset Husserl raises the question as to whether history teaches us nothing but the contingency of human events, a meaningless cycle of progress and disappointment (*Crisis* § 2, p. 7; VI 4–5) or is there meaning and reason in history (*Crisis* § 3, p. 9; VI 7)? To address these pressing questions, Husserl describes a methodological approach of 'questioning back' (*Rückfragen*) that he believes will allow him to penetrate through to the essential meaning at the heart of various forms of historically evolving cultural institution. In previous works, Husserl's main approach to **phenomenology** had employed a more static form of constitutional analysis, examining the 'levels and strata' (*Crisis*, p. 168; VI 170) of meaning involved in the constitution of perceptual or other objects, but not particularly addressing issues of temporal development. This new approach which specifically addresses historical and temporal development is what Husserl calls '**genetic phenomenology**'.

Crisis of foundation (*Grundlagenkrise*)   From early in his career, Husserl was conscious of the 'crisis of foundations' (*Grundlagenkrise*) evident in contemporary mathematics and logic. The physicist and mathematician Hermann Weyl is normally associated with the term *Grundlagenkrise*, but it is often used by Husserl in a broad sense, e.g. in 1934, Hua XXVII 226, to cover a general crisis in the sciences.

Critique of knowledge (*Erkenntniskritik*) See also **epistemology, knowledge**

Husserl frequently speaks of the necessity for a thorough critique of **knowledge**. Husserl believes it is necessary to radicalize the programme of critique begun by **Kant** in his *Critique of Pure Reason*. Husserl presents the critique of knowledge as overcoming the naive view of knowledge in the **natural attitude** (which takes for granted the possibility of knowledge; see *Idea of Phenomenology*, Lecture One). The critique of knowledge has to explicate the possibility of knowledge and to clarify the essence of knowledge. In particular, the critique of knowledge has to clarify the meaning of objectivity. Traditionally, the critique of knowledge began by accepting the validity of scientific knowledge. But a genuinely radical critique of knowledge must also seek to justify its own task.

—D—

Dependency (*Unselbstständigkeit, Abhängigkeit*) See also **formal ontology, foundation, mereology, part, whole**

'Dependency' or more literally 'non-independence' (*Unselbstständigkeit*) is Husserl's term for the a priori logical relation of one thing to another, where that thing A cannot exist without the other thing B, on which it is dependent. Husserl develops relations of dependency in his Third Logical Investigation (see especially § 13 in his discussion of the necessary formal relations between **wholes** and **parts**). In this sense, colour *depends* on extension. There are different kinds of dependency relation that can hold between parts (he distinguishes between *absolute* and *relative* dependence) and Husserl attempted to set out the formal character of these relations in various laws. The relation of dependency or independence also applies to parts in relation to wholes and again to the larger wholes in which those themselves are parts. There are parts that are independent (pieces) and there are parts that cannot exist without the whole on which they depend. These dependent parts are called **moments** by Husserl.

Derrida, Jacques (1930–2004)   Jacques Derrida is the founder of 'deconstruction'. Born in Algiers (Algeria) on 15 July 1930, of Sephardic Jewish
extraction, he entered a *lycée* in 1941, but his family life and school studies
were disrupted by the Second World War, and by restrictions imposed on
Jews by the Vichy government anti-Jewish laws. As all French-Algerian born
Jews, he was enrolled in the Jewish Community School until the end of the
Second World War. After 1945, and eligible to reenter the French lycée,
he began reading Camus, Bergson, Sartre, Nietzsche and Gide. In 1949
he moved to Paris in order to enroll in an *école préparatoire*, a school that
prepared students for university education, at the Lycée Louis-le-Grand.
He entered the *École Normale Supérieure* in 1952. There he studied with
Louis Althusser who became a close friend. He also began attending the
lectures of Michel Foucault and Jean Hyppolite. Initially, he focused on
Husserlian phenomenology and in 1953–4 he prepared his *diplôme d'études
supérieures*, under the direction of Jean Hyppolite and Maurice de Gandillac,
entitled *The Problem of Genesis in Husserl's Philosophy*. In this early work,
Derrida shows himself to be well grounded in Husserl's texts. In this early
student's work (which was not published before 1990), Derrida already
deploys the 'method' of reading which will later be called 'deconstruction'.
Derrida claims Husserl's oppositions (e.g., eidetic/empirical; transcendental/
worldly; pure/impure, genetic/constitutive), in fact, enter in some kind of
'dialectic', and 'contaminate' each another. Derrida translated Husserl's
'Origin of Geometry' and wrote a long introduction to it published in
1962. Derrida also wrote a commentary on Husserl's conception of linguistic
meaning and expression, *Speech and Phenomena* in 1967. In this work,
Derrida offers a 'patient reading' of Husserl's *Logical Investigations*. The main
claim of *Speech and Phenomena* is that Husserl, who proposes a phenomenology of signification in the First Logical Investigation, remains trapped in a
'metaphysics of presence' and thus a logocentrism that privileges the spoken
act of meaning over all other forms of inscription. Phenomenology has clung
to the link between *logos* and *phonè* (SP 15; 14), whereas Derrida seeks
to emphasize the priority of *writing* (écriture), that is the set of signs that
function in the 'eclipse' of the subject who utters or expresses them. Derrida
is thus critical of Husserl's assumption of the presence of meaning in fulfilled
intuition; and he is especially critical of Husserl's retention of Platonic, essen-
tialist elements, and his positing of self-identical ideal meanings. Following
his studies on Husserl's phenomenology and Heidegger's fundamental

ontology, Derrida coined the term 'deconstruction'. This term, which is, first, for Derrida the interpretative translation of both Heidegger's *Destruktion* and Husserl's *Kritische Abbau*, opens to an affirmative strategy which proceeds *to reverse* the traditional oppositions, and consequently the hierarchies, inherited from the history of philosophy. This strategy of reversal also proceeds to the release from the space and the regime of these oppositions by marking, in their very 'systematicity', an 'un-decidability', an 'aporia' that both constitutes and overflows the logic of oppositions. 'Deconstruction' is thus applied, first, to the texts of the philosophical tradition and, second, following the concept of 'general text', to sociopolitical institutions and doctrines. Jacques Derrida's philosophical writings thus span from a rereading of the history of philosophy to the elaboration, through deconstruction, of an idea of justice irreducible to justification, recognition or reconciliation.

Descartes, René (1599–1650)   See also *Cartesian Meditations, cogito, dualism*

French philosopher, mathematician and scientist, founder of modern philosophy, author of the *Discourse on Method* (1637), *Meditations on First Philosophy* (1641) and *The Principles of Philosophy* (1644). Husserl was a great admirer of Descartes for his attempt to set scientific knowledge on a secure foundation through a procedure of radical doubt and a return to what is clearly and distinctly given in intuition. When Husserl delivered his lectures in Paris in 1929, he deliberately modelled them on Descartes's *Meditations* and the work was subsequently published as **Cartesian Meditations**. Husserl's procedure of **epochē** is deliberately modelled on Cartesian doubt. Through his sceptical doubts, Descartes put the very existence of the world in question in a radical way. Husserl refers to Descartes' 'quasi-sceptical *epoché*', but he emphasizes that his phenomenological **epochē** is different from Cartesian doubt (*Ideas* I § 32) in that the actual, historical Cartesian doubt involved the dogmatic denial of the existence of the world. Husserl interprets Descartes as attempting a universal world negation, whereas he himself sought not negation but rather **neutralization** of all existential commitments to the world. The **epochē** puts the natural attitude 'out of action' by suspending it or parenthesizing it. This achieves *a certain annulment of positing*' (*Ideas* I § 32). The positing of our natural attitude remains what it is yet it is effectively corralled or put into brackets. Husserl also credits Descartes with discovering transcendental domain ('epoch-making awakener of the transcendental problematic'; Hua IX 248), in his discovery of the *cogito ergo sum* but he accuses Descartes of failing to capitalize on this discovery and falling back into a naive metaphysics that treated the transcendental ego as just another 'bit' of the world. In his *Paris Lectures*, Husserl characterizes his own approach as 'almost' a 'new Cartesianism' (Hua I 3), one that aims to show that the supposed results of the Cartesian foundation of objective knowledge burst apart at the seams (as he said in *Crisis* § 16). As Husserl would proclaim in 1924 in his Kant lecture, *Ideas* I achieves a new Cartesianism (see also III/1 87):

> [With the *Ideas*] the deepest sense of the Cartesian turn of modern philosophy is, I dare to say, revealed, and the necessity of an absolutely self-enclosed eidetic science of pure consciousness in general is cogently demonstrated – that is, however, in relation to all correlations grounded in the essence of consciousness, to its possible really immanent moments and to its noemata and objectivities intentionally-ideally determined therein. (EP I, p. 12; Hua VII 234)

Strictly speaking, however, Descartes is only 'a precursor of transcendental philosophy' (Hua VII 240); in whom is found the 'seed' (*Keim*, VIII 4; VI 202) of transcendental philosophy. Like Moses, he *saw* the Promised Land, but did not set foot there. Descartes' founding insights must be rethought to recover their true meaning, a meaning to which he himself had been blind. Specifically it was Descartes' *Meditations* and his method of doubt (IX 330) that first made visible transcendental subjectivity by showing up the doubtfulness or possible non-being of the world and at the same time the indubitability of the *cogito* (VIII 80). Husserl also adopts and reinterprets Descartes' criteria of clarity and distinctness as the marks of **evidence**. Descartes operated with a principle that whatever was immune from doubt had the character of certainty. However, he was blind to the need to discover the level of certainty within the ego. Husserl distinguishes between natural certainty and apodictic certainty. No empirical truth can completely ensure against the possible non-being of the world altogether. Transcendental reflection, for Husserl, must go beyond empirical certainty to *apodictic* certainty. He speaks of the 'reduction to the apodictic' (XXXV 98) In this regard, his **epochē** aims to achieve an improvement over

Descartes' methodic doubt. He regards Descartes as having been misled about the apodicticity of the ego as discovered in the doubt. Husserl himself thinks only the ego in its now moment is in fact given apodictically. But of course, strictly speaking, this is also the Cartesian position, when Descartes insists that the 'I am, I exist' is true *'whenever* it is put forward by me and conceived by my mind'. Descartes, of course, illegitimately moved from the certainty of the 'I think' to the givenness of the ego as thinking *substance*. Husserl, by way of contrast, wants to remain within the givenness of I and recognizes that its horizons of past and future are not given apodictically. Indeed, it belongs to transcendental philosophy to offer a critique of the modes of apodicticity (CM § 63). The regress is to the transcendental ego, which is not a substance or a 'thing' understood as a 'real object within the world' (V 146), although quite misleadingly Husserl dubs it as 'absolute'. It is 'subject for the world':

> [T]he Ego (and I am this Ego) that bestows ontological validity
> on the being of the world … the Ego that exists in itself and
> that in itself experiences the world, verifies it, etc. (*Postscript
> to Ideas* I, Hua V 149)

Description (*Beschreibung*)   See also **descriptive psychology, explanation, phenomenology**

For Husserl, **phenomenology** proceeds through exact description (*Beschreibung*) rather than **explanation** (*Erklärung*). In this regard, Husserl is following in the tradition of Brentano's **descriptive psychology**. In *Ideas* I § 60, Husserl characterizes phenomenology as a 'purely descriptive eidetic doctrine of the immanental consciousness formations'. It is not interested in generating theories or importing hypotheses from other fields; neither does it attempt causal explanation. In general, it also seeks to avoid inferences and instead focuses on what is directly given in intuition. Phenomenology aims to describe experience in a non-reductive manner and especially to pay attention to the role of **subjectivity** in the **constitution** of objectivity. Husserl believes the empiricists rightly emphasized description but erroneously allowed prejudices to interfere with the description. Noematic description involves focusing on the objectively meant phenomenon precisely as it is meant and avoiding subjective expressions (see *Ideas* I § 130). Husserl's *Logical Investigations* aims at a descriptive investigation of the lived experiences involved in logical judgements and in the apprehension of ideal objectivities.

Descriptive   psychology   (*deskriptive   oder   beschreibende Psychologie*)   See also **description, genetic psychology**
Brentano and his school (including Stumpf, Meinong, Marty and others) used the term 'descriptive psychology' for the a priori description and classification of mental phenomena. Husserl uses the term also in his early work. Brentano distinguishes 'descriptive psychology' (which he also calls 'psychognosy' or 'descriptive phenomenology') from **genetic psychology**, which aims to explain psychic phenomena in terms of their psychophysical causes and conditions. According to Brentano's conception, descriptive psychology is an *exact a priori* science like mathematics, which is independent of and prior to 'genetic' or 'physiological psychology'. Brentano sought a priori necessary laws governing psychology, e.g. every mental phenomenon is either a presentation or founded on a presentation. For Brentano, 'genetic' or causal explanations should be introduced only after the mental phenomena in question have been correctly described (PES, p. 194). The title of Brentano's University of Vienna lecture course for 1888–9 was 'descriptive psychology or descriptive phenomenology (*Deskriptive Psychologie oder beschreibende Phänomenologie*), later published as *Descriptive Psychology*. In this work, Brentano claimed that consciousness cannot be explained by physico-chemical events and that this represents a confusion of thought. Different orders of inquiry are involved. These lectures were deeply influential on Husserl. In 1894 **Wilhelm Dilthey** wrote a study, *Ideas for a Descriptive and Analytic Psychology*, in which he contrasted descriptive psychology with explanatory psychology. For Dilthey, naturalistic explanatory psychology was atomistic whereas the concrete life of the mind with its domain of inner experience is holistic, a **nexus** (*Zusammenhang*) consisting of internally interwoven states. In his *Phenomenological Psychology* lectures of 1925, Husserl acknowledges Dilthey's breakthrough work for its assault on naturalistic psychology and for its promotion of a 'descriptive and analytic' psychology. In the First Edition of the *Logical Investigations*, Husserl calls his discipline phenomenology or descriptive psychology In the First Edition of the *Logical Investigations* (1901), Husserl characterizes the study in which he is engaged as a form of 'descriptive psychology'. In the Second Edition of the *Logical Investigations* (1913), Husserl emphatically rejects the view that

the phenomenological description of pure consciousness was in any way to be confused with naturalistic psychology. He felt that the characterization of phenomenology as descriptive psychology could be misunderstood as a certain 'psychologizing of the eidetic' (see also *Ideas I*, § 61). In the *Logical Investigations*, phenomenology is proposed as an essentially neutral, presuppositionless science. In the First Edition of the *Logical Investigations*, Husserl tended to move easily between three kinds of philosophical approach, which he tends to equate, namely: 'phenomenology', 'descriptive psychology' and 'epistemology', 'theory of knowledge' or 'critique of knowledge' (*Erkenntnistheorie, Erkenntniskritik*). In the *Selbstanzeige*, or author's announcement, to the Second Volume of the *Investigations*, Husserl says that he is conducting a phenomenological clarification of logical acts of knowledge and not a 'genetic-psychological clarification' (*genetisch-psychologische Erklärung*; Hua XIX/2 779). In his Introduction to the *Investigations*, Husserl explicitly identifies phenomenology with epistemological critique and 'descriptive psychology':

> Phenomenology is descriptive psychology. Epistemological
> criticism is therefore in essence psychology, or at least capable
> of being built on a psychological basis. (LU, Intro., I, p. 176;
> Hua XIX/1 24)

Husserl writes in the First Edition:

> Phenomenology represents a field of neutral researches, in
> which several sciences have their roots. On the one hand, it
> serves as preparatory to *psychology* as an *empirical science*. It
> analyses and describes – in the specific guise of a phenomenol-
> ogy of thinking and knowing – the experiences of presentation,
> judgement and knowledge, experiences which should find their
> genetic clarification, their investigation according to empirical
> lawful connections. (LU, Intro. § 1, I, p. 166; Hua XIX/1 7)

In his *Phenomenological Psychology* lectures § 4, Husserl summarizes the four central characteristics of descriptive psychology as **aprioricity, eidetic intuition** or pure **description**, *intentionality*, and the **transcendental attitude**.

Dilthey, Wilhelm (1833–1911)   See also **descriptive psychology**

Dilthey was born in Germany and studied theology at Heidelberg before moving to Berlin where he studied the work of Schleiermacher. He went on to a career as philosopher in Berlin and exercised an enormous influence in German philosophy. Dilthey began from the distinction in method between the natural and the human sciences. He wanted to provide a critique of historical reason to complement Kant's critique of pure reason. While he was closely interested in understanding history, he wanted to maintain a distance from Hegel. Dilthey was attempting to have a descriptive science of life that took into account facticity, individuality and historicity and for this reason he was later associated with the life philosophy (*Lebensphilosophie*) movement. Understanding history requires looking not so much at causal explanations but at **understanding** (*Verstehen*) the **motivations** of the individuals involved. Especially through his work on Schleiermacher, Dilthey was centrally involved in developing **hermeneutics** as a methodological approach in philosophy and the human sciences. His first important publication was *Introduction to the Human Sciences* (1883), in which he announced his 'critique of the historical reason'. In 1900 he wrote an influential essay 'The Rise of Hermeneutics' on the relevance of hermeneutics for philosophy and history. In 1910 he published his *The Formation of the Historical World in the Human Sciences*, which influenced Husserl's thinking on the personal and cultural world. Dilthey had a huge influence on Hans-George **Gadamer**. Dilthey reviewed Husserl's *Prolegomena* to his *Logical Investigations* favourably and later acknowledged Husserl's influence on his own development of epistemology. Husserl borrowed Dilthey's conception of **lived experience** (*Erlebnis*), the idea of the connectedness of life (*Lebenszusammenhang*) and the idea that human sciences utilize not causation but **motivation**. His account of hermeneutics and the effort to understand life had an enormous influence on Heidegger's early work leading up to *Being and Time*. Husserl was more critical of Dilthey, suspecting him of **historicism** in his **Philosophy as a Rigorous Science (1910–1911)** but in his *Phenomenological Psychology* lectures (1925) he praises Dilthey's *Ideas for a Descriptive and Analytic Psychology* of 1894 for its recognition of the importance of descriptive psychology. Husserl was generally suspicious of a 'philosophy of worldviews' that presents history as a series of self-enclosed and incommsurate 'worlds'. Husserl also thought Dilthey fell prey to the very naturalism he sought to oppose. In his late works, such as **Crisis of European Sciences**, he uses a conception of life as intentional achievement that is reminiscent of Dilthey.

Disillusion, frustration, disappointment (**Enttäuschung**) See also intention

Husserl uses this term 'disillusion', 'disappointment', or 'frustration' (*Enttäuschung*) in his Sixth Logical Investigation § 12 on, to refer to the experience when one's intentional expectation is exploded or falls apart. Disillusion happens when an intention is not fulfilled in the manner expected. If, for instance, we apprehend a figure as a man, then we expect that man to have human movements. But it can happen that, on closer inspection, we realize that the figure is actually a mannequin. Our original expectation is shattered; as Husserl puts it the **noema** has exploded. Another type of disillusion relates to anticipations of those sides or features of things that are not directly manifest. If I see the front side of a red ball, I usually think that the back side is red as well. If I look at the back and I realize that it is not red but green, we can say a 'disillusion' has occurred (*Experience and Judgment*, § 21). The English translation 'frustration' (as in 'my expectation was frustrated') as used by John Findlay is not intended to refer to any emotional element (frustration as an emotional state or feeling) but rather to the cognitive sense of one's assumption being dissipated. The intentional fulfilment is not in harmony or coincidence with the intention.

Disinterested spectator (**der uninteressierte Zuschauer**) In his later works, from the 1920s on (the term does not appear in *Ideas* I), Husserl frequently speaks about the attitude of the 'detached', 'non-participating' spectator or onlooker (*unbeteiligter Zuschauer*, Hua XXXIV 9), or 'disinterested' spectator (*uninteressierter Zuschauer*, Hua XXXIV 11) (see especially CM § 15, *Crisis* § 45, § 69, and *Vienna Lecture*). The disinterested spectator has broken free of the bewitchment of the **natural attitude** with its naive belief in the world and has learned to perform the transcendental **epoché** and to be free of practical engagements and interests and is in a position to understand the natural attitude precisely *as* an **attitude** or stance. The disinterested spectator is able to see the world as the harmonious unfolding of a stream of subjective appearances, in other words, he or she is able to see the world as the outcome of the process of constitution by the transcendental ego. This is called transcendental reflection as opposed to

natural reflection (CM § 15). The uninterested or disinterested spectator or observer is no longer captivated by the fundamental belief in the world or the general thesis of the natural attitude. Husserl's student **Eugen Fink** questions the ontological status of this transcendental spectator in his Sixth Cartesian Meditation. He compares Husserl's theoretical attitude of the non-participating spectator to that of the figures in Plato's Allegory of the Cave who have managed to escape from the cave and see the sunlight and then return to the cave and see it for what it really is.

Doxa (*Doxa*)   See also **belief, epistēmē**

The Greek term '*doxa*' meaning 'belief' or 'opinion' and is used by Husserl to characterize the interrelated network of unquestioned beliefs and assumptions that make up the **natural attitude** and the everyday attitude of prescientific life. Plato contrasted belief (*doxa*) as an opinion that can change with **knowledge (*epistēmē*)** that is certain and secured through justification and **evidence**. Scientific knowledge is founded on our ordinary assumptions in the natural attitude. Thus, for instance, in *Crisis* § 34 (a), Husserl notes that traditional philosophy has a negative or disparaging attitude towards *doxa* (see also *Crisis* § 44). However, Husserl believes it is important to establish a science of our naive everyday beliefs, a science of *doxa*. He also thinks our everyday beliefs have their own kind of validation and justification within the life-world of our practical engagements and interests. In this regard, Husserl's position is close to that articulated by Wittgenstein in *On Certainty* – where certainty is described as a raft floating on a sea of belief. Husserl devotes many analyses to understanding how the world is the universal ground of belief (e.g. *Experience and Judgment* § 7). Passive belief in the world is called by Husserl 'passive *doxa*'. We can establish different grades of *doxic* complexity (from passive levels to active) and different modal variants (see **doxic modalities**).

Doxic modalities (*die doxischen Modalitäten*)   See also **doxa**

'Doxic modalities' is Husserl's term (see *Ideas* I § 117) for basic epistemic states such as being in the state of certainty, doubt, questioning, assuming, actualizing, and so on). There are different doxic position but the **fundamental belief** or *Urdoxa* is perceptual certainty, a kind of naive immediate acceptance of the existence and reality of the objects of perceptual experience. All forms of positing (thetic commitment) involve some kind of doxic modality. Doxic belief consciousness (*doxische Glaubensbewusstsein*) is a simple certainty, which can be modified. The three main variants that Husserl takes in consideration are: negation, possibility and doubt (EU § 21). Simple certainty can be modified by means of new events or disillusions that break the initial concordance. Nevertheless, the lack of concordance in many acts or situations does not cancel the main doxic position, whereby we live a basic belief about the world. This elemental concordance is the background for the partial certainties and their modalities (EU § 7).

Drive (*Trieb*)   See also **allure, instinct, life**

Husserl uses the term 'drive' to refer to the instinctual, unconscious urges (e.g. self-preservation, overcoming hunger, sexual satisfaction, avoidance of pain, of death, realization of desires) that are at the foundation of conscious **life** (see *Ideas* I § 85, in which Husserl acknowledges that drives can have certain sensuous components or moments). In his writings of time consciousness, he sees the act of synthesizing temporal moments into a unified experience as an essentially instinctive action. Similarly, there is an instinct to hold on to and continue the past into the future. The **ego** is also affected in certain ways and is drawn instinctively towards certain things that attract it and is repelled by other things. There is a drive towards the satisfaction of needs. In his later writings, Husserl is aware of the discussion of drives in Freudian psychoanalysis or what he calls 'depth psychology' (see for instance *Crisis* § 71, where he mentions 'instincts and drives'). In many texts related to his **genetic phenomenology**, Husserl raises the problem of drives in order to understand different levels of our consciousness of the world. This led him to raise problems related to the status of the infant and of animal life generally, regarding the first primitive forms of intentionality (*Urintentionalität*). In this sense, he speaks also about 'original instinctivity' (*Urinstinktivität*) as a first way of being open to the 'world' and to the self-subjectivity. Drives are bound to the lived body (*Leib*) in terms of needs that are not primarily consciously apprehended but are lived, e.g. hunger (*Nährungstrieb*) or sexual instinct (*Geschlechtstrieb*). Husserl speaks even about a 'drive intentionality' (*Triebintentionalität* Hua XV, Text Nr. 34), which he characterizes as 'universal'. Feelings are already ways of integrating drives into the conscious life of the ego. Drives can be taken up and lived through in a rational way.

Dualism (*Dualismus*)   See **Descartes, naturalism, objectivism, primary properties, subjective-relative properties**

Dualism is the metaphysical doctrine that the world is divided into two different kinds of entity – material entities and minds. Husserl believes psychophysical dualism is a product of the approach of early modern objectivist mathematical science (see *Crisis* §§ 10–11) to nature that concentrated on the mathematically determinable **primary properties** of things (e.g. extension) and left to one side all '**subjective-relative' properties** (see also *Crisis* § 57). According to modern science, the objective world is a self-enclosed material domain entirely governed by law. This split off the realm of the psychic and the new science of psychology is assigned to study this separated realm. Husserl often speaks of **Cartesian dualism** (*Crisis* § 64) or of dualistic **naturalism**, which treats the psychic (soul, mind) in analogy with nature, as a self-enclosed realm of inner experiences (see *Crisis* § 67).

—E—

Ego (*Ego, Ich*)   See also ***cogito*, ego body, ego pole, intersubjectivity, living present, monad, person, Natorp, subject**

Husserl uses the term 'the ego' (*das Ego*) or the 'I' (*Ich*) both for the first-person 'empirical ego' (***Logical Investigations***), or 'psychological' ego (see CM § 11), which is the **subject** of experiences, and provides identity across experiences, and also for what he terms the 'pure' (*rein*, see *Ideas* I § 57, § 80) or the 'transcendental' ego (*das transzendentale Ego*). In this respect Husserl accepts **Kant**'s distinction between the empirical and the transcendental ego. Husserl usually begins his meditations on the ego in the **natural attitude** with the embodied human self in the world (in *Ideas* I § 29 called 'ego subject'), and then progressively traces the layers of **constitution** of the self, correlated as they are with different **attitudes**. He recognizes that the ego 'in its full concretion' (CM § 33) is not an empty '**ego pole**' (*Ichpol*) sending and attracting conscious 'rays of regard', rather it is a living self identical over time (*Ideas* I § 57), an individual, with its unique sense of self, its history and its finite temporal duration. It lives, has experiences, then dies. Husserl emphasizes the unity and indeed 'infinite multiplicity of possible states and experiences of the "concrete ego"' (CM § 16); the ego is necessary to unite the changing **lived experiences** or *cogitationes*. In this sense, the ego is a **transcendence** in the **immanence** of lived experiences. However, he also recognizes the diverse modalities of the ego. He normally begins from the fully awake conscious ego, but he was also aware of the modalities of sleeping, dreaming, dullness, vitality of the ego, and so on, e.g. the sleeping ego has no temporal awareness and apparently no being 'for itself' yet it has the very capacity to be awakened (XIV 156) and to return to unity with itself. There are periods of dullness and alertness (*Ideas* II § 26). The ego has **drives** and **instincts** (IV 255), it seeks its self-preservation, satisfaction of desires, enjoyment, and so on. Husserl even speaks of a passive domain that is the 'pre-ego' (*Vor-ich*). The ego develops itself through its **habits**. The ego is a dynamic entity for Husserl: 'the ego constitutes itself for itself in, so to speak, the unity of a history' (CM § 37). Yet, while living in time, the ego is also somehow the source of time itself. Each ego has its own **temporalization** (*Zeitigung*), yet it also finds unity in a communal temporalization (XV 576–7). In the First Edition of the ***Logical Investigations***, influenced by Brentano, Husserl pursued a Hume-style investigation of **lived experiences** while expressing scepticism towards the existence of a stable, abiding ego (see the author's note in *Ideas* I § 57). In the Fifth Logical Investigation, he claimed, against **Paul Natorp**, not to be able to find any pure ego in the Kantian sense as a 'primitive, necessary centre of relations' (see Fifth Logical Investigation § 8). Husserl is criticizing Natorp who posits the ego as a subject or centre of relations that has no content and can never be an object and he rejects all efforts to objectify it. However, in an Addendum to the Second Edition, Husserl admits that he had since *found* that pure ego. The discovery of the pure or transcendental ego is related to the process of the transcendental **reduction** (see *Ideas* I § 34) and is discussed in detail in ***Ideas* I** and ***Ideas* II**. In *Ideas* I, Husserl explains the ego as a kind of 'transcendence in immanence' (*Ideas* I § 57), an account that influenced **Sartre**'s 1936 account of the 'transcendence of the ego'. Husserl focuses on the identity of the ego in experiences (see *Ideas* I § 80) and on the activities of the ego in **position taking**, judging, remembering, reflecting, and so on; whereas, in *Ideas* II, he describes the embodied self, with its passive experiencing, habits and so on. The ego as an intentional centre of **sense giving** (*Sinngebung*) is discovered in phenomenological reflection. In *Ideas* I § 80, more or less in agreement with the neo-Kantians, Husserl believes that the ego as discovered in **reflection**, aside from being a centre of unity, is empty of essential components and is undescribable in itself: 'It is pure ego and nothing more.' In *Cartesian Meditations*, he embraces the idea of the **cogito ergo sum** and attempts to reduce all experience to what belongs solely to the **sphere of ownness** of the ego. Each ego has its own unique stream of experiences. He acknowledges that this approach is treating the ego abstractly as if it were on its own, a *solus ipse*. In fact, Husserl sees the ego as always part of a community of other egos or **community of monads**. Strictly speaking, there can never be an ego on its own. Furthermore, the ego is always related to a world that forms its **environment**. The transcendental ego covers 'the universe of the possible forms of lived experience' (CM § 36). The ego actually includes both its 'self-experience' (*Selbsterfahrung*) and its 'other experience' (*Fremderfahrung*), i.e. its encounter with objectivity in general and with other egos. Egos relate to other egos through **empathy**. Husserl never arrived at a final account of the transcendental ego; his thought on it was in constantly flux and grew more complicated. He even spoke of the *self-constitution* of the ego through some kind of passive genesis in **time consciousness**. The nature of the ego's relation to time occupied Husserl in his Bernau manuscripts. As a 'pole' of experiences the ego is strictly speaking not in time but is 'super-temporal' (Hua XXXIII 202).

Ego pole (*Ichpol*)   See also **ego, monad, sphere of ownness**

Ego pole or 'I-pole' (German: *Ichpol*) is a term frequently used by Husserl to express the manner in which the subject or ego is involved in each intentional **act** (see CM § 33). The ego pole is the 'centre' of all actions, passivities, and habitualities of the ego (see CM § 44) and is the source of the identity experienced by a consciousness. Every intentional act has both a **subject** that carries it out and is directed at an object, which is the object pole of the act. Husserl often contrasts the ego pole as the presence of an identical self across the flow of experiences with the full experience of the self in all its concreteness, the self in full concretion, which he also calls **monad** (see CM § 47). The ego pole is often a kind of empty form that makes every experience *mine* in some formal way. Husserl does not intend the notion of the ego pole to have **content**.

Egology (*Egologie*) See also **ego, self-experience, sphere of ownness**
The term 'egology' is used only occasionally by the mature Husserl (see, for
example, *Cartesian Meditations* § 13; the term does not appear in *Ideas* I,
Formal and Transcendental Logic or *Crisis*) for the phenomenological science
that studies the ego and the domain of **self-experience**. Husserl speaks
of egology as a 'transcendental descriptive' science (CM § 16); it is an 'a
priori science of the ego and of everything that can already be found in the
domain of the ego (Hua XXXV 253). In this sense, its problems encompass
the whole of phenomenology. In the ***Cartesian Meditations***, Husserl
proposes a methodological **solipsism** (at CM § 64 he speaks of a '"solipsis-
tically" reduced egology') whereby a sustained effort is made to exclude all
matters extraneous to the ego and its own domain which Husserl calls 'the
sphere of ownness'. A genuine egology also needs to explain how other
egos are apprehended as egos. Egology is usually contrasted by Husserl
with an intersubjective phenomenology (see CM § 13).

Eidetic insight (*Wesensschau*, *Wesenserschauung*) See also **eidetic
variation, eidetics, *eidos*, essence**
Wesensschau, or *Wesenserschauung* (see *Ideas* I § 3) translated as 'eidetic
insight', 'eidetic intuition', or 'essence viewing' or 'eidetic seeing' or 'essence
inspection' is one of Husserl's key technical terms and plays a central role in
Husserl's phenomenological method. Especially in the revised 1913 edition
of the ***Logical Investigations*** (see Introduction to Second Volume § 6;
see also Fifth Logical Investigation § 27) and thereafter, Husserl claims that,
besides seeing particular things and events in sensuous **perception**, we
can *see* **essences** through a non-sensuous **intuition** that is founded on
sensuous perception and is analogous with it. Husserl occasionally calls this
'ideation'. Husserl's critics, e.g. **Moritz Schlick**, claimed that Husserl was
invoking a mystical vision but Husserl denied it was in any way mysterious
although he did think eidetic insight requires trained attention. According
to Husserl, eidetic insight is in fact practised by mathematicians when
they grasp a priori truths such as '2 + 2 = 4'. Eidetic insight is a particular
species of **categorial intuition**. In eidetic seeing, there is a deliberate
'ideating abstraction' from the factual and particular in order to focus on
the universal and necessary. As with Aristotle, the central aim of science for
Husserl is to apprehend ('see') *essences*, and hence he needs to defend the
very possibility of eidetic intuition. As he puts it in *Ideas* I:

The truth is that all human beings see 'ideas,' 'essences,' and
see them, so to speak continuously; they operate with them
in their thinking, they also make eidetic judgments – except
that from their epistemological standpoint they interpret them
away. (*Ideas* I § 22, p. 41; Hua III/1 41)

In order to justify knowledge, the grasp of essence has to be understood, in
part by overcoming inherited epistemological prejudices. Essential intuition
is, therefore, in part concerned with the conceptual conditions under which
purely formal truths, truths depending on meaning alone, are possible. At
the same time, essential intuition or insight also establishes the *existence*
of certain kinds of *object* that owe their existence purely to form, including
numbers, sets, and other mathematical objects. Eidetic intuitions grasp
truths independent from empirical facts. The way to the eidetic intuition is
through variation in free phantasy (*Ideas* I § 70). Seeing essence is the way
to gain access to the a priori (*Phenomenological Psychology* § 9). In order
to have essential insight, it is necessary to practice **eidetic or imaginative
free variation** and also **ideation**. Eidetic insight can begin with a single
phenomenon (real or imaginary does not matter) and proceeds by eidetic
variation and ideation to grasp what is universal and invariant, i.e. essential.
Husserl articulates many different essential insights as universal necessary
laws holding for a particular domain, e.g. everything coloured is extended;
every consciousness has to have an egoic centre, and so on. According
to Husserl every essential insight expresses an unconditional norm for all
possible empirical existence (*Ideas* I § 78).

Eidetic intuition (*Wesensschau*)   See **eidetic insight**

Eidetic variation (*eidetische Variation*) See **imaginative free
variation**

Eidetics (*Eidetik*)   See also **eidetic insight, *eidos*, essence**
Husserl speaks of **phenomenology** as a 'new eidetics' (*Ideas* I § 71). Eidetic
sciences (*Ideas* I § 7) are not concerned with matters of fact or existence,
but are focused on the necessary and essential. There are many different
eidetic sciences, e.g. geometry, 'eidetic psychology' or ontology, all of
which are concerned with essences of a universal character: Husserl writes:

'The essence proves to be that without which an object of a particular kind cannot be thought, i.e., without which the object cannot be intuitively imagined as such. This general essence is the *eidos*, the idea in the Platonic sense, but apprehended in its purity and free from all metaphysical interpretations, therefore taken exactly as it is given to us immediately and intuitively in the vision of the idea which arises in this way.' Phenomenology is an eidetic science because its descriptions are not empirical. Phenomenology is distinguished from the other eidetic sciences by the fact that it does not focus directly on any region of the world but on the consciousness. The role of phenomenology is therefore the eidetic description of those structures that enable the world of our experience. There are different **regions** of essences (all factual sciences are founded in regions of essences) and hence Husserl speaks of a 'regional eidetics' (*Ideas* I § 8), e.g. the region **nature**.

Eidos (*Eidos*)   See also **apriori, eidetic intuition, eidetics, essence**

The Greek word *eidos* means '**essence**' and is employed frequently by Husserl especially from *Ideas* I onward as a 'terminologically unspoiled' word (see *Ideas* I Introduction; Hua III/1 6, and § 2). Husserl also constructs the adjective 'eidetic' (*eidetisch*) to mean 'essential'. Husserl speaks of phenomenology as offering a 'new **eidetics**'. The essence is opposed to the factual instance, e.g. the *triangle* as such, the *straight line* as such, *colour* as such (*Ideas* I § 5). There are essences of material things, of properties, relations, and also essences of mental acts such as perceiving, imagining, remembering, knowing, and so on. The essence is referred to as the thing or property 'in general' (*überhaupt*). Even such abstract ideas as a 'theory' have an essence – *theory as such* (see *Logical Investigations*, *Prol.* § 66b). Husserl claims that the 'essence' or *eidos* is a new object of knowledge that is distinct from the individual entity given in perception or empirical intuition (see *Ideas* I § 3). The essence or *eidos* can be exact or inexact (which Husserl calls 'morphological'). The essences are organized in a hierarchy of generality and specificity (*Ideas* I § 12). There are different regions of essence – nature, consciousness. Pure eidetic sciences include mathematics and logic (*Ideas* I § 8). The *eidos* is apprehended by a **free variation** from the individual instance that may be given in perception, imagination, memory, and so on (see *Ideas* I § 4). Assertions about essence do not involve issues of existence or matter of fact. Husserl says that the correct understanding of the a priori is to understand it as the eidetic.

Emotion (*Gemüt*)   See also **feeling, will**

Husserl categorizes emotions as belonging to the sphere of '**acts**' (LU V § 29). Emotions are positing, objectivating acts (*Ideas* I § 117) that have their own unique composition and structures. **Brentano**'s classification of emotions in his tripartite division of mental acts as belonging to the 'phenomena of love and hate' is discussed briefly by Husserl in the Fifth Logical Investigation. Emotion, for Husserl, involves valuing or evaluation. We experience certain states as welcome or to be avoided, and so on. As such, emotions are not just passive states of the person but involve willing and indeed a degree of self-awareness. Psychologists often distinguish between feeling (*Gefühl*) and emotion. Feelings can be transitory episodes where as emotions are more longlasting. Husserl, however, tends to group emotions as belonging to feeling. For Brentano and Husserl, emotions are intentional acts and are essentially directed at or 'about' something: in love someone is loved, in hate hated, and so on. Emotions and feeling have an embodied aspect; the body is the locus where feeling and emotions are experienced (*Ideas* II § 40). Husserl rejects **emotivism** in ethics, nevertheless, he holds that moral concepts are based on feelings or on emotional or affective consciousness (*Gemütsbewusstsein*).

Emotivism   See also **ethics**

Emotivism (not a term Husserl himself uses) is the view that ethical attitudes are really expressions of emotion. Husserl rejects emotivism in ethics, because, for him, if morality were based on emotions, it would become entirely subjective. Furthermore, feelings are constantly changing therefore they cannot provide a proper foundation for value judgements and for morality.

Empathy (*Einfühlung*)   See also **apperception, intersubjectivity, Lipps, monad, other experience, pairing, presentification, transference, Stein**

Empathy or intropathy (*Einfühlung*), as used in Husserl's phenomenology, means one's personal experience of another's **consciousness** or subjectivity, i.e. the phenomenon of feeling (or thinking) one's way into the first-person, experiential life of another consciousness, mind or spirit (including animal minds). In contemporary analytic philosophy the term 'mind reading' if often used here and considered to be more expansive than empathy, thought to refer primarily to representing emotional states. Husserl, however, used the term *Einfühlung* in a very broad way to refer not merely to emotional but to all cognitive and experiential states of the other. Husserl uses the German *sich einfühlen* which is a reflexive verb that literally means 'to feel one's way into'. The concept of empathy was a focus for discussion among late nineteenth-century German psychologists, e.g. Hugo Münsterberg (1863–1916), Stephan Witasek, Johannes Volkert (1848–1930), Benno Erdmann, Oswald Külpe, and **Alexius Meinong** (in *On Assumptions* § 53–54, in which there is a discussion of empathy in relation to works of art and the employment of 'fantasy feelings') and others. **Wilhelm Dilthey** also regarded empathy as important for understanding the motivation of historical figures. Max **Scheler** continued to use the older term 'sympathy' (*Sympathie*) – although Lipps, Scheler and Husserl also use the terms *Mitgefühl* ('fellow feeling' – following Adam Smith) and *Nachgefühl* ('imitative feeling'). Following the Munich psychologist Theodor **Lipps**, Husserl, **Stein**, and Max Scheler all believed that the philosophical clarification of empathy was central to the philosophical foundation of sociology and the human sciences generally. The philosophical discussion of *sympathy* (later *empathy*) originally emerged in the discussions of British moralists, especially Shaftesbury, Hutcheson, Hume, Adam Smith, Herbert Spencer, and Alexander Bain in the eighteenth century, who postulated affective 'sympathy' as the basis of morality and aesthetic experience. **Hume** defines it in his *Treatise on Human Nature* as 'that propensity we have to sympathize with others, and to receive by communication their inclinations and sentiments, however, different from, or even contrary to our own'. In his research notes from 1905, Husserl employs the term *Einfühlung*, explicitly engaging with Lipps. Husserl was uncomfortable with it as a term, remarking that 'empathy is a false expression' (Hua XIII 335). Empathy refers to one's ability to *grasp* or *comprehend* or *experience* (*erfahren*) the conscious life of another person, their 'stream of experience' (*Erlebnisstrom*), psychic 'states' (*Zustände*), **lived experiences** or 'mental processes' (*Erlebnisse*), and **attitudes**(*Einstellungen*). I constitute someone else as the *alter ego*, as another **ego** (*Ich*), with its own 'centre' and **'ego pole'** (*Ichpol*) of psychic experiences, affections and performances, through empathy. Husserl distinguishes between what is *immediately* (*unmittelbar*) and personally intuited in the first person and what is gained by some kind of 'founded' or 'mediated' intuition. For Husserl, I grasp my own

self-experiences (my conscious stream, my feeling of warmth, my sense of time passing, of standing upright in this space, of it being day time, and so on), everything that belongs to what he calls my '**sphere of ownness**' immediately, at first hand, in the flesh, really there (*selbst da*). I know my own personal experiences in a personal manner, *in propria persona*. There is another dimension of experience, namely, what is gained through some kind of intermediary, or is *founded* on something given directly. According to Husserl, I have an immediate and lived experience of my own body and this is present in all my perceptions of things transcendent to me. Everything outside myself is 'other' in this sense: all material entities, living things, animals, humans, social institutions, and so on. But this problem of the constitution of 'otherness', of the 'not-me' (non-egoic) and of the experience of the region of 'ownness' is extremely difficult to articulate, and in a way covers the whole range of phenomenological problems, the whole range of the spheres of givenness. The standard approach to empathy claims that one grasps others through some kind of analogical 'inference' (Husserl uses the term *Schluss*) based on one's own understanding of one's own psychic states, motivations and actions. Defenders of the inference theory – such as Benno Erdmann – saw empathy as based on a kind of 'hypothesis' (see Husserl, Hua XIII 36). Lipps, Husserl, Scheler and Stein were united in their rejection of 'inference by analogy' (*Analogieschluss*) as an explanation of empathy. Husserl repeatedly states that empathy is not any kind of *inference* (*Schluss*), whether deliberately and calculatively performed, or, even as carried out unconsciously. We do not first experience the body of the other and then infer to a state. Rather, we experience the other's state directly: we see an angry face; we don't see a face and infer anger: Lipps sees empathy as a kind of identification or fusion of oneself with the other, based on 'imitation' (*Nachahmung*) or mimicry of the other's 'expressions' or 'externalizations' (*Ausdrücken*, *Äusserungen*) which are signs of his or her internal life. Lipps speaks of a kind of 'objectivation' whereby my own experiences become objects for me. I can be interested in things, judge them, desire them, and so on, but I can also find myself thinking of things, judging, striving, and so on. This 'self-objectivation' (*Selbstobjectivation*) or *appresentation* is already *Einfühlung*. Through this self-objectivation, my own experiences become objects for me and, so to speak, foreign to me. As we have seen, Lipps employs the term *Einfühlung* for the manner in which I relate to earlier states of my own self, e.g. in the sphere of memory.

Husserl, Scheler, and Stein attack Lipps' view that the basis of empathy is some kind of *imitation* (*Nachahmung*). Scheler argues that we understand from the wagging tail that a dog is happy to see us, but not on the basis that we are able to imitate this behaviour ourselves. Husserl classifies empathy as a kind of **'apperception'** or **'presentification'** or 'presentiation' (*Vergegenwärtigung, Apperception*), i.e., not a **perception** which gives the thing directly *in propria persona*, in the flesh, but a certain kinds of quasi-perceptual awareness 'interwoven' (*verflochten*) with and founded on these perceptions. In his *Passive Synthesis* lectures, Husserl defines it as 'a consciousness of having something that is not present in the original'. Husserl employs the term 'presentiation' or 'presentification' (*Vergegenwärtigung*) to cover a huge range of experiences including memories, fantasies, anticipations, awareness of the hidden side of a physical object, and so on. For Husserl, as for Stein, empathy is an *experience*, by which they mean it is a first-person undergone event with a certain character that is different from that of a mode of inference or reasoning. He criticizes Lipps' notion of a *non-experienced* apprehension of the other as a kind of appresentation (Hua XIII 23) since all apperception is *eo ipso* a kind of experience (*Erfahrungsapperzeption*, XIII 24). But, for all this stress on *Erfahrung*, the particular kind of experience involved in empathy is not cashed out by Husserl. Husserl's basic contrast between what we experience as our own in our own immediate sphere and what we co-experience as other in some sense. Thus in his published text, *Ideas I* § 1 (1913) Husserl had already made a distinction between what is experienced in a *genuine* or *originary* (*eigentlich, originär*) manner – namely, external transcendent things in immediate perception, experience of our own states of consciousness, versus non-originary (*nicht originär*) experiences such as the object given in memory or expectation. In *Ideas I*, for instance, Husserl states that we do not have 'originary experience' (*originäre Erfahrung*) of others in empathy (*Ideas I* § 1, p. 6; Hua III/1 8). Already Husserl characterizes empathy as an 'intuitive, presentive act' (*ein anschauender, gebender Akt*) but not one that presents *originär*. That is, in normal external perception of transcendent things, there is a process whereby the whole is given in a series of profiles and at any one time there is actual perception of one side and a co-presentation in an empty way or an 'appresentation' of the absent other sides. It is a kind of 'co-experiencing', co-perceiving (*Mitwahrnewhmung*) or 'co-presencing'. Empathy is a version of this kind of apperceptive experience of another thing, but it is not exactly the same, as Husserl makes clear. Husserl distinguishes in a perception between the actual moments that are originally given or present themselves in a *Darstellung* in what he calls 'primary originarity' (*primäre Originarität*) and what he calls the 'secondary originarity' of the emptily co-presented other sides of the object that do not actually appear. A projective presentification is filled by a further genuine perception. But the *apperceived* internal life of the other will never become visible by a movement to a new position. This clearly makes off empathy from thing perception (Hua XIV 4–5). The other's inner experience is never given in the mode of its being perceivable. This kind of perceptual verification is excluded a priori (CM § 50, p. 109: Hua I 139). Husserl believes every apperception has its own kind of fulfilment or cancellation and this is not recognized by Lipps. Moreover, its apperceptions are not fulfilled by actual perception. For Husserl then, it is crucial to empathy that is a presentification that, in principle, cannot be verified in the manner in which I verify my own projective experiences or anticipation. Husserl claims that the perception of the other as a subject is founded on another analogizing perception of another's **living body** (*Leib*) as *a living body* to which are attributed sensations, freedom of movement, a separate point of view, different aspects of things as seen from *that* perspective, and so on. In an early account in Hua XIII 21ff (written before 1909 but put together probably 1916), Husserl speaks of the other body as given as an 'analogon of my interiority' (*ein Analogon meiner Innerlichkeit*), a phrase that often recurs in later manuscripts (e.g. Hua XIV 5). My apperception of 'my body' has a kind of absolute primordiality for Husserl. I have an inner sensuous awareness of it. It belongs to my 'interiority' (*Innerlichkeit*, Hua XIV 4). This leads Husserl even to speak of the manner in which my own body is given as 'subjective-objective' (Hua XIV 6). It is not a simple 'in itself'. Husserl later emphasizes the sense in which I am always present to myself within my own sphere of experience. I have furthermore a sense of myself as '**governing**' or 'holding sway' (*waltend*) in this region. According to Husserl, in his 1910/11 course *Fundamental Problems of Phenomenology* § 39 (Hua XIII 189), however, there is no 'canal' (*kein Kanal*) connecting my psychic stream with that of another, one experience cannot be in the 'environment' (*Umgebung*) of another, although (and this is important) they do belong to the same temporal frame. Indeed, this temporal coincidence is an important structural feature of empathy, as Stein will stress. The empathized experience is experienced as being in the same *now* as my own experience. The other experience is given in a presentified 'now' that is identified with my 'now' yet there is no road linking one now with the other. The other now cannot be brought to intuition by me (Hua XIII 190). Yet it is experienced as *actually present*. There is a recognition of a plurality of 'I's, a plurality of **monads** (Hua XIII 192). The other living person, this is grasped not just as a body but perceived immediately as *Leib*. Husserl speaks of some kind of 'apperceptive **transfer**' or 'carrying over' (*Übertragung*; CM § 50) based on **association** or likeness (which raises the question how this differs from Lipps' account). According to Husserl, in empathy I directly apprehend a 'physico-psychic' complex of body and soul, an animate body that has 'introjected' into it an individual psychic life. There must be *similarities* connecting our two bodies that form the basis of an '**analogizing apperception**'. In agreement with Lipps, this is not to be understood as an inference by analogy, since it is not a specifically *thinking* act (CM § 50). There is rather a pointing back to an *Urstiftung*, an act of 'primal instituting', in which something with a similar sense was grasped for the first time. This involves an analogizing transfer. In *Cartesian Meditations* and elsewhere, Husserl emphasizes the element of '**pairing**' (*Paarung*). This is an associative relation between two bodies where the one (myself) is always present and there is a continuous 'primal constituting' going on to the other self (CM § 50):

> Pairing is a *primal form of that passive synthesis* which we designate as 'association,' in contrast to passive synthesis of 'identification'. (CM § 50)

There seems to be a stress here on the actual presence of two consciousnesses together or at least of two living bodies being present to one another. There also an element of imaginative insertion into the life of another. One of the clearest articulations of Husserl's understanding of how it is that I experience the other person is given in Hua XIV text no. 35 (523–34) written in preparation for lectures in 1927 Husserl states the matter simply:

> The perception of another human is original perception in respect of his corporeality; in respect of the alien subjectivity it is first of all empty presentification. (Hua XIV 523, my translation)

Empathy means, for Husserl, the opening of an intentional milieu of inter-subjectivity where other egos exist but cannot be appropriated according to the meaning that is uniquely theirs. The emergence of this term in Husserl's lexicon opened a specific problematic where the 'other' is called to play a fundamental role in the deployment of the phenomenological project. The term of *Einfühlung* is evoked by Husserl in order to enlighten and explain, what he called in § 95 of *Formal Logic and Transcendental Logic* the 'dark corner from haunted by the spectres of solipsism' (FTL, p. 237; XVI 210). It is, however, quite late in Husserl's development when he understood that he needed to reserve an appropriated vocabulary for the problem of the constitution of the other egos by one's own ego. This new vocabulary concerning empathy does not appear the *Philosophy of Arithmetic* or the *Logical Investigations*. It is only in 1905 in a series of reflections concerning the status and extent of individuation that the problem of the 'other' is first posed. The first text in which Husserl addresses this problematic is entitled 'Uniqueness, Spiritual Individuality and Individuality of Objects of Nature' (*Eigenart, geistige Individualität und Individualität der Naturobjekte*, Hua XIII). Here the possible constitution of other egos by one's own ego is presented as a necessary and general thesis for the comprehension of the world. In order to grasp the complexity and the centrality of the question of the other in Husserl's philosophy, one needs only consider the texts published in the first of the three volumes of the *Husserliana* entitled *On the Phenomenology of Intersubjectivity*, which run from 1905 to 1920 (Hua XIII). The question of the other – and thus of intersubjectivity – became very quickly, for Husserl, the question to which all the other problems in phenomenology would be subsequently treated, since it is by and through the question of the other that all intentional developments are inter-related. It is by and through the question of the *other* that phenomenology is opened to all the different fields of objectivity. For the other appears to the ego, first, through the perception of its **body** but precisely *not* as any appearing **object** since the ego cannot appropriate the other as a subjectivity similar to its own and only as if it attributes to it lived states that are never as such given in a direct presentation but only as an '*ap*-presentation'. As we know, this problematic is, of course, explicated in the Fifth Cartesian Meditation. But before the Paris Lecture of 1929 (translated in French language by Levinas and published in 1931), Husserl had already elucidated the problem that arises in the meeting of other intentional egos by inscribing *between* each individual subject and the world a dimension which he will call a 'social ontology' (Hua XIII). Although *Ideas* I § 1 states explicitly that 'apperception by empathy is an intuitive, a presenting act' – which is enough to cancel any suspicion of solipsism in Husserl's first person or phenomenological perspective – it is not enough, since this act is not an 'originary' presenting or donating act, to escape the difficulty that the constitution of the meaning of the other poses. In *Ideas* I Section IV, § 151, Husserl will entertain the possibility of an intersubjective **world** as the correlative of the intersubjective experience. After having entertained this possibility, Husserl will not, however, remain attached to such a vague description. He will state in *Ideas* I § 152: 'Although essentially founded in psychical realities which, for their part, are founded in physical realities, these [intersubjective] communities prove to be novel *objectivities of a higher order*' (*Ideas* I, p. 365; Hua III/1 318). In this sense, it is the very transcendental foundation of phenomenology that is here put into question. Through this problematic of **intersubjectivity**, the very possibility of constituting meaning itself is put in question, including the meaning of other egos and reciprocally of the ego itself as that which remains the 'other' of the other. The entire discussion of intersubjectivity, empathy, and other egos, will be once again reassessed and reformulated in the Fifth Cartesian Meditation. In this reformulation, the concept of empathy will be central. For, in the Fifth Cartesian Meditation, Husserl does not simply consider the question of the other by reference to the phenomenological reduction but, by a type of radicalization of this sphere of intentionality, by demonstrating the necessity for the phenomenological reduction to be supplemented by the movement of an intersubjective mediation where the objective world is constituted *in* and *as* intentionality. The text of the Fifth Cartesian Meditation explicitly marks it as its task, in § 42: reveal and deploy the implicit and explicit intentionality in which and from which the transcendental *ego* announces and confirms the ***alter ego***. And, furthermore, explicate according to which syntheses the meaning of the *alter ego* is formed in and within the *ego*, that is according to which motivations it is confirmed as existing for the *ego*. This task is, for Husserl, a necessary mediation for the constitution of all objectivity. Hence, the phenomenological reduction redirects the ego to itself, to its rapport with its own lived states but only by affirming an auto-a-perception of itself as both spatial and temporal, that is as both constituted by the temporal flux of its lived states and the spatiality of its *Leib* capable of co-existing with a multitude of bodies (*Körper*) and in which the ego is forced to recognize as and in itself a secondary sphere, that is a sphere in itself constituted by the *ego* as the *ego* but which is also given to the *ego* as foreign. It is precisely this sphere in the *ego* and yet foreign to the *ego*. In this sense, and by this foreign sphere in and within the movement of constitution proper to the transcendental *ego*, it is commanded to recognize that it cannot be a *solus ipse* and, furthermore, that there must be a sphere where empathy is always and already at work. Which means, fundamentally, for Husserl: the transcendental ego is always and already constituted and constituting if it evolves in and within intersubjectivity.

Empirical psychology (*empirische Psychologie*)   See also **descriptive psychology**

Husserl always understands empirical psychology as a factual study of the actual mental experiences of humans and other animals. **Brentano**'s *Psychology from an Empirical Standpoint* was not actually a treatise in what is now called empirical psychology, rather it was an essay in a priori descriptive psychology, the a priori description of what is given to **inner perception**. **Wilhelm Wundt** described empirical psychology as physiological psychology. Husserl believes empirical psychology is an inductive science. He also believed that it was not properly grounded but had been set up by analogy with the exact method of the natural sciences. Husserl tends to distinguish between empirical psychology and descriptive psychology or what he later described as eidetic, phenomenological psychology. In fact, he thinks that the latter has to be the guide for the former: 'I am certain that in the not too distant future it will be a common conviction that phenomenology (or eidetic psychology) will be the methodologically foundational science for empirical psychology in the same sense that the material mathematical disciplines (e.g., geometry and phoronomy) are foundational for physics' (*Ideas* I, §79, p. 190). Eidetic phenomenology treats the possible experience and empirical psychology about real experience.

Empiricism (*Empirismus*)   See also **Berkeley, Hume, naturalism, objectivism, scepticism**

For Husserl, empiricism represented 'a radicalism of philosophical practice' (*Ideas* I, § 19), setting itself against all idols of superstition and bad speculative metaphysics. In that sense, Husserl says in *Ideas* I, empiricism 'springs from the most praiseworthy motives', but it carries a conceptual and unexamined baggage (*Ideas* I, § 19). Husserl admired **Berkeley** and **Hume** for their attempt to do detailed work 'from below' and for producing at least a kind of proto-phenomenological analysis of certain concepts. An instance of such empiricist analysis is Locke's suggestion that the concept of solidity has its origin in the experience of resistance. Similarly, in his *New Theory of Vision*, Berkeley explains how the *sense of distance* is achieved in terms of certain immediately felt experiences of the sensory movements of the eyes that act as cues, which, although custom and habit, come to be associated with different distances of the object from the perceiver. In similar vein, Husserl was deeply impressed by Hume's analysis of causation in terms of contiguity and succession, which he interpreted as a diagnosis of the 'subjective genesis' of 'transcendent objectivities' that had been taken for granted as realities independent of subjectivity (see FTL § 100). Although he was an admirer of what was genuine in empiricism, Husserl was a relentless critic of extreme empiricism 'as absurd a theory of knowledge as extreme **scepticism**' (LU *Prol.* § 26 Appendix). Husserl's overall complaint against empiricism was that it misunderstood and incorrectly 'theorized' the very nature of the 'given' on which it depended. Empiricists start from 'unclarified preconceived opinions' (*Ideas* I, § 20). In the *Prolegomena* (1900), Husserl writes:

> Extreme empiricism is as absurd a theory of knowledge as extreme scepticism. It destroys the possibility of the rational justification of mediate knowledge, and so destroys its own possibility as a scientifically proven theory. (LU *Prol.* § 26 I, p. 59; Hua XVIII 94)

Empiricism purports to arrive at general statements yet these are supposedly drawn from 'singular judgements of experience'? It justifies its principles and laws *mediately* through induction, but what principles justify such induction, what principles govern this mediate inference? Empiricists are forced to appeal to 'naive, uncritical, everyday experience' which it then explains in Humean fashion in terms of psychological regularities. Empiricism thus confuses the *psychological origin* of judgements, 'on account of their supposed "naturalness"' (LU, *Prol.* §26, I, p. 60; Hua XVIII A85), with their epistemic *justification*. This ends up as a form of psychologism. Husserl sees

Hume as a 'moderate empiricist' who retained logic and mathematics and gave them a priori justification, but who still thinks mediate inferences have only a *psychological* explanation and no rational justification (LU *Prol.* §26, I, p. 60; Hua XVIII A86). The radical empiricist assumes that the only access to things themselves comes through *immediate* sensory experience. But, for Husserl, natural things do not constitute the whole set of kinds of thing, and thus empiricism at best only reveals things of nature. Already in LU, Husserl argues that empiricism unnecessarily and, quite arbitrarily, restricts the range of possible verification or confirmation of judgements. In the Second Investigation in particular, he attacks the empiricist *psychological* accounts of abstraction and points to their defects in terms of a conceptual analysis of what is required to intuit universals. In general, empiricism has no sense of the normative nature of cognition.

Empty intention (*Leerintention, Leermeinen*)   See also **fulfilment, intuition, signitive intention**

Empty intentions are to be contrasted with the kind of full intentions one experiences in **perception** of a here-and-now present object where the object is given 'with fleshly presence' (*leibhaftig*). Empty intentions intend the object in its intuitive absence, that is, they represent it, or symbolize or 'signal' it (*signitively*) in some empty or token way. In the **Philosophy of Arithmetic**, for instance, Husserl thought that we could bring very small numbers (e.g. '3') fully to **intuition** whereas intuitions of large numbers cannot be genuinely filled and hence are empty or 'inauthentic' presentations. Most speaking and writing invokes the intended objects in an empty way (and since signs are conventional, the manner of representation is arbitrary). When, for instance, I simply repeat the words 'e =mc^2' I cannot be said to be grasping the meaning of this equation in any fulfilled manner. Empty intentions lack the full sensuous presence of the object such as is found in direct perception. In perception, I have a fulfilled intuition of the object from one side but I have empty intuitions of the other sides. Empty intentions are the largest class of intentions and every sensuous perception consists of a mix of full and empty intentions.

Encyclopedia Britannica article 'Phenomenology' (1929)   Husserl was

commissioned to write the article 'Phenomenology' for the 14th edition of the *Encyclopaedia Britannica*. He worked on it from 1927 to 1928. It was eventually published in 1929. In late 1927, Husserl invited **Heidegger** to cooperate in writing the entry. They worked through several drafts together from September 1927 through to February 1928; in all five versions of the article were drafted, but their views diverged radically. In the final submitted version, Husserl had excised much of Heidegger's contribution especially the latter's introductory paragraph locating phenomenology within fundamental ontology. Husserl's German text was translated into English by Christopher V. Salmon. For a long time this article was an important source of Husserl's mature understanding of phenomenology as a transcendental discipline. The article is divided into two parts: 'Phenomenological Psychology' and 'Transcendental Phenomenology'. Part One outlines the development of a pure a priori phenomenological psychology based on intentionality and eidetic reduction. Part Two explains the origins of transcendental philosophy in Descartes and goes on to see the central problem as the transcendental constitution of the **world**. According to Husserl, all possible worlds are relative to the **absolute being** of **consciousness**.

Epistēmē (□πιστήμη) See also *doxa,* **knowledge**
The term *epistēmē* (□πιστήμη) is the Greek word for **knowledge** (*Erkenntnis*) and is used by Husserl to mean justified knowedge in the scientific sense, that is, knowledge that is secured with evidence. He contrasts it with another Greek term *doxa*, which means the entire nexus of prescientific, everyday belief or opinion (see *Crisis* § 44). Husserl uses the German word *Erkenntnis* as equivalent to *episteme* and *Erkenntnistheorie* (theory of knowledge) as equivalent to '**epistemology**'.

Epistemology or theory of knowledge (*Erkenntnistheorie*) See also **cognition, critique of knowledge,** *epistēmē*
From the Greek **epistēmē** ('knowledge' – as opposed to *doxa*, 'belief' or 'opinion'), epistemology is the branch of philosophy that studies the nature of **knowledge**. Husserl uses the term 'theory of knowledge' in continuity with the neo-Kantian tradition to refer to the task of specifying the conditions for the possibility of objective knowledge. In particular, Husserl sees the central problematic of epistemology in Kantian terms as the question how **objectivity** is accomplished in subjective acts of consciousness (see **The Idea of Phenomenology**). **Paul Natorp**, for instance, had a similar approach, and was influential on Husserl while he was writing the

Investigations (see LU V § 8). Husserl did not have a highly developed conception of epistemology in the First Edition, but returned to the subject in his 1906/7 lectures, *Introduction to Logic and Theory of Knowledge*, where he develops the structural relations between the **critique of knowledge**, **formal ontology** and formal **logic**. On this conception, the critique of knowledge is **first philosophy** (Hua XXIV § 31), in the Cartesian sense, which is in a sense prior to metaphysics, since only the proper clarification of the nature of objectivity in general can ground formal ontology and the material ontologies of the sciences. Husserl states a similar view of epistemology in his 1907 lectures, *The Idea of Phenomenology* (Hua II). After 1913, he tended not to portray his work as primarily theory of knowledge. He later regarded his earlier epistemological orientation as missing the true nature of the transcendental turn and therefore leading to form of 'epistemological psychologism' (*der erkenntnistheoretische Psychologismus*, see FTL § 56, p. 152; Hua XVII 160). In the *Crisis* and elsewhere, Husserl sees modern philosophy from **Descartes** to **Kant** as evolving into empiricism and rationalism and missing the true nature of knowedge as an **achievement** of transcendental subjectivity and intersubjectivity.

Epochē (Ἐποχή, *Epoche*)   See also **neutrality modification, phenomenological reduction**

The Greek term *epochē* (Ἐποχή) is used by Husserl (sometimes transliterated in German as *Epoche*, Hua VIII 21) to mean a procedure of **bracketing**, excluding, cancelling, putting out of action certain belief components of our experience. The term was originally found in Greek scepticism. In Greek, the term *epochē* means a 'cessation' or 'suspension of judgement', and was used by the Greek sceptics (such as Arcesilaus) as a way of refraining from making epistemic commitments based on inadequate evidence. The Greek sceptic Pyrrho recommended **epochē** as a way of withholding assent. Husserl often contrasts his way of applying the **epochē** with the sceptical approach which he attributes to **Descartes** in his *Meditations* (see *Ideas* I § 31). Husserl maintains that his **epochē** involves no sceptical doubt about or straightforward denial of the veracity of experiences, but rather a putting out of action of the general positing that characterizes naive experience. Husserl always insisted that the application of the **epochē** and the performance of the **phenomenological-transcendental reductions** were necessary features for the practice of the phenomenological method. Husserl claims to have discovered the phenomenological reduction some time around 1905 in his Seefelder manuscripts; and its discovery marks a sharp break between the **descriptive psychology** of the *Logical Investigations* and the transcendental phenomenology of the mature Husserl. Husserl first introduced the **epochē** in print in his *Ideas* I (1913) §§ 31–2, but he had been lecturing on it from his 1906–1907 *Lectures on Logic and Epistemology* (Hua XXIV) as well as in his *Idea of Phenomenology* lectures of 1907 (posthumously published as Hua II). The term does not appear in his 1910/1911 'Philosophy as a Rigorous Science' essay. In *Ideas* **I**, having introduced the **natural attitude** which humans normally occupy in their worldly everyday life, Husserl proposes to suspend it, exclude it, or alter it radically. To be more precise, Husserl proposes to suspend or alter just one aspect of the **natural attitude**, namely its 'general positing' (*Ideas* I § 30), or its thetic character, i.e. the way in which it presents entities in the world as factually existing actualities. Husserl is explicit that the general positing is not a distinct existential judgement rather:

> It [the general positing] is after all, something that lasts con-
> tinuously throughout the whole duration of the attitude, i.e.,
> throughout natural waking life. (*Ideas* I § 31, p. 57; Hua III/1 53)

The suspension is characterized by Husserl as an **epochē**. Slightly earlier, in *Ideas* I § 18, Husserl refers to 'the philosophical **epochē**' which 'shall consist of our complete abstaining from any judgement regarding the doctrinal content of any previous philosophy'. But this philosophical **epochē** is only a prelude the phenomenological **epochē**, which is also often called by Husserl 'the phenomenological reduction'. In fact, in the text of *Ideas* I, Husserl refers to 'reductions' in the plural and there is much discussion of how many Husserl envisaged and how he same them as related to the initial performance of the **epochē**. The phenomenological **epochē** consists in putting out of action or excluding the general thesis:

> With regard to *any* positing we can quite freely exercise this
> peculiar *epochē, a certain refraining from judgment which is
> compatible with the unshaken conviction of truth, even with
> the unshakable conviction of evident truth.* The positing is 'put
> out of action,' parenthesized, converted into the modification,

'parenthesized positing,' the judgment simpliciter is converted
into the *'parenthesized judgment.'* (*Ideas* I § 31, pp. 59–60;
III/1 55)

The aim is to somehow place the whole 'pregiven world' in a position
where it makes no validity claim on us. The **epoché** plays an extraordinarily
important role in Husserl's conception of phenomenology. The break with
the natural attitude and its 'worldly' commitments is decisive. In his later
writings, and especially in the *Crisis* documents, emphasis is placed on
suspending the natural attitude in order to break through to the transcendental attitude. In his Author's Postface to *Ideas* I (written in 1930), Husserl
says the 'phenomenological reduction' should more properly be called
the 'transcendental phenomenological reduction' (*Ideas* II, p. 412; Hua V
145). The **epoché** is a central feature of the ***Cartesian Meditations*** as
well as in the ***Encyclopedia Britannica*** **article**. In CM § 8, Husserl speaks
of the concept of the 'overthrow' (*Umsturz*) of the sciences in Descartes'
Meditations and on the parallel need to bracket and parenthesize all
positings:

> This universal depriving of acceptance, this 'inhibiting' or
> 'putting out of play' of all positions taken toward the already-
> given objective world … or, as it is so called, this 'phenomeno-
> logical *epoché*'. (CM § 8, p. 20; Hua I 60)

He goes on in the same section to say that:

> The epoché can also be said to be the radical and universal
> method by which I apprehend myself purely: as Ego, and with
> my own pure conscious life, in and by which the entire Objec-
> tive world exists for me and is precisely as it is for me. (CM §
> 8, p. 21; I 60)

According to CM, the **epoché** is a way of moving from psychological
subjectivity to transcendental subjectivity. I uncover myself as 'subject for
the world' and I discover the world as something that gets its 'meaning
and validity' (*Sinn und Geltung*) only from me. The mature Husserl does
generally distinguish between **epoché** and **reduction**. The **epoché** is a

form of disconnecting or putting into parenthesis or putting out of play of the natural attitude and especially its '**general thesis**'. The reduction, by way of contrast, begins with the 'philosophical reduction' but also includes moving from the particular to the *eidos* (through the employment of imaginative variation). This is often referred to as the phenomenological reduction. Then, following the eidetic reduction, there is the move to understand all objectivities as achievements or productions of transcendental subjectivity. Hence the 'transcendental reduction'. In mature works such as *Crisis*, Husserl proposes that the **epochē** be understood as a way of overcoming the naiveté of the natural attitude. In the reduction, there is a radical 'upheaval' (*Umsturz*) of one's commitments to the extent that one even 'ceases to be human', losing all connection to the empirical, natural human ego and its psychological states (*mein natürliches menschliches Ich und mein Seelenleben*). In the *Crisis* in particular, Husserl acknowledges that the 'Cartesian way' of **epochē** and reduction that he had developed in the *Cartesian Meditations* was too abrupt and brought the ego into view in one bound, as it were, but, in so doing, revealed it as 'apparently empty of content' and, hence, passed over the whole apparatus which constituted the 'life-world' (*Crisis* § 43). Husserl had a number of different theoretical reasons for introducing the notion of reduction. First, it allowed him to detach from all forms of conventional opinion, including our commonsense psychology, our accrued scientific consensus on issues, and all philosophical and metaphysical theorizing regarding the nature of the intentional. We must put aside our beliefs about our beliefs, as it were. Second, it allowed him to return to and isolate the central structures of subjectivity. By putting aside psychological, cultural, religious and scientific assumptions, and by getting behind or to one side of the meaning positing or thetic acts normally dominant in conscious acts, new features of those acts come to the fore. Most of all, the reduction is meant to prevent what we have won by insight being transformed or deformed into an experience of another kind, a change from one kind to another, a '*metabasis in allo geno*' (*Ideas* I § 61). There is an almost inevitable tendency to 'psychologize the eidetic'. Husserl thought there would be no need for the reduction were there a smooth transition from the factual to the eidetic, as there is in geometry, when the geometer moves from contemplating a factual shape to its idealization (*Ideas* I § 61, p. 139; Hua III/1 116). In other areas, however, especially in grasping consciousness, the move to the eidetic is difficult to achieve, hence the need for the vigilance of the **epochē**. Husserl characterized the practice of **epochē** in many different ways: 'abstention' (*Enthaltung*), 'dislocation' from, or 'unplugging' or 'exclusion' (*Ausschaltung*) of the positing of, the world and our normal unquestioning faith in the reality of what we experience. He speaks of 'withholding', 'disregarding', 'abandoning', '**bracketing**' (*Einklammerung*), 'putting out of action' (*außer Aktion zu setzen*), and 'putting out of play' (*außer Spiel zu setzen*) all judgements which posit a world in any way as actual (*wirklich*) or as 'there', 'present at hand' (*vorhanden*). But the essential feature is always to effect an 'alteration of attitude' (*Einstellungänderung*), to move away from naturalistic assumptions about the world, assumptions both deeply embedded in our everyday behaviour towards objects, and also at work in our most sophisticated natural science. The change of orientation brings about a 'return' (*Rückgang*) to a transcendental standpoint, to uncover a new transcendental domain of experience. The **epochē** then is part of the reduction. Above all else, the transcendental must not be thought to be simply a dimension of my own mind, reached through psychological reflection. Husserl always regarded his formulation of the reductions as the real discovery of his philosophy and as necessary in order to reveal non-psychologically the essence of intentional consciousness and of subjectivity as such. To experience the reduction is to experience an enrichment of one's subjective life, it opens infinitely before one. Husserl is always insistent that reduction provides the only genuine access to the infinite subjective domain of inner experience, and that he who misunderstands reduction is lost:

> But in the final analysis everything depends on the initial moment of the method, the phenomenological reduction. The reduction is the means of access to this new realm, so when one gets the meaning of the reduction wrong, then everything else also goes wrong. The temptation to misunderstandings here is simply overwhelming. For instance, it seems all too obvious to say to oneself: 'I, this human being, am the one who is practicing the method of a transcendental alteration of attitude whereby one withdraws back into the pure Ego; so can this Ego be anything other than just a mere abstract stratum of this concrete human being, its purely mental being,

abstracted from the body?' But clearly those who talk this way
have fallen back into the naive natural attitude. Their thinking
is grounded in the pregiven world rather than moving within
the sphere of the *epoché*. ('Phenomenology and Anthropology', *Trans. Phen.*, p. 493; Hua XXVII 173)

Essence (*Wesen, Essenz, Eidos*) See also **apodicticity, apriori, eidetic
insight, *eidos*, exact essence, laws of essence, morphological essence
Phenomenology** is a science of essences. Because of confusions around
the German term '*Wesen*', from *Ideas* I onward, Husserl prefers to use
the Greek word **eidos**. Husserl distinguishes between 'matter of fact' and
'essence' in *Ideas* I § 2. Essence does not relate to what factually exists but
defines precisely what is possible. The essence of something characterizes
what belongs to it invariantly, its 'what' (*Was*) or 'whatness' (*Washeit*) or
what it is in terms of its universal and necessary predicates. It is a 'new sort
of object' (*Ideas* I § 3) distinct from the individual contents of empirical
intuition. Husserl sees the great breakthrough of Greek philosophy was
the recognition of the *eidos* or essence by Socrates and Plato. By the same
token, Husserl regards it as one of the great errors of modern **empiricism**
that it has rejected the concept of essences and of directly apprehending
essences in eidetic or **essential intuition**. Husserl distinguishes between
exact essences (e.g. the essence of a circle), which can be completely and
exhaustively defined, and **morphological essences**, which are essentially
inexact and have vague boundaries (see *Ideas* I § 74). Husserl speaks of
phenomenology as a science of essences, an eidetic science, which he
sometimes calls a 'new **eidetics**'. Essences are grasped by a kind of idealizing abstraction from the concrete individual entity using **imaginative
variation**. Essences have an 'unrestricted universality' that is different
from the kind of generality attaching to the laws of nature (see *Ideas* I
§ 6). According to Husserl, there are *eidetic singularities* (the essences
of individual entities) and there are also essences belonging to **species**,
regions, and so on.

Ethics (*Ethik*) See also **axiology, categorical imperative, Kaizo
articles, Scheler, value, will**
Husserl frequently lectured on ethics in Göttingen and Freiburg. He gave
lectures in Göttingen on **axiology** and ethics in 1902, 1908/09, 1911,

and 1914 (see Hua XXVIII) and his Freiburg lecture courses on 'Introduction to Ethics' (repeated between 1920 and 1924) have been published in Hua XXXVII). Ethics is also discussed in his lecture courses 'Introduction to Philosophy' (1919/20 and 1922/23, Hua XXXV), and in the 1922–4 'Essays on Renewal', published in **Kaizo** (see Hua XXVII). Husserl's ethics is largely a response to **Kant**, Fichte and **Brentano**. His earlier lectures stress universalism and objectivism where his later lectures emphasize love and the holistic nature of the **person**. For Husserl, acts of intellection found acts of **feeling** and **willing**. In his earlier lecture courses, under the influence of Brentano, Husserl proposes various ways of overcoming what he sees as the unsatisfactory and 'abstruse formalism' (Hua XXXVII 415) of Kant's categorical imperative. He thinks that ignoring the content of what is willed is absurd. He offers revised imperatives such as 'always do the best that is attainable within one's sphere of practical life'. Husserl regards the categorical imperative as central to ethics and a way of recognizing the objectivity of ethics. In his later work on ethics, he came to regard love as operating on a different level from that of imperatives and also introduces the notion of **teleology** and the desire to live as rational a life as possible.

Europe (*Europa*)   See also **Europocentrism, humanity**
Especially in his ***Vienna Lecture*** and in his ***Crisis***, Husserl speaks of Europe as a spiritual concept rather than a geographical place. 'Europe' broadly speaking means the cultures that have given birth to western philosophy and the sciences that emerged from philosophy. As Husserl had claimed in his 1934 Prague lecture, it is Greek philosophy that created the idea of Europe as a 'spiritual, self-enclosed, unified form of life' (Hua XXIX 207) rather than as a geographically defined place. This theme is repeated in the ***Vienna Lecture*** (1935), in which he states that the name 'Europe' refers to 'the unity of a spiritual life, activity, creation, with all its ends, interests, cares and endeavors, with its products of purposeful activity, institutions, organizations' (*Crisis*, p. 273; VI 319). The origins of European intellectual tradition are in Greece and Husserl includes as 'European' those people who have embraced the theoretical attitude. The spread of European ideas means that North America and Japan can be considered to participate in the European project of universal rationality whereas groups such as the 'gypsies' can be excluded. The scientific transformation of European culture that has taken place since the seventeenth century was occasioned, according to

Husserl, by **Galileo**'s '**mathematization of nature**' (*Mathematisierung der Natur, Crisis* § 9). In one of the drafts for his **Kaizo** articles, Husserl says that European culture has lost its way and strayed from its inborn *telos* (Hua XXVII 118) of freely given autonomous **reason**. Husserl states his overall aim as the 'rebirth (*Wiedergeburt*) of Europe from the spirit of philosophy' (*Vienna Lecture, Crisis*, p. 299; VI 347). Building on this Greek foundation, the West has a 'mission' (*Sendung*) to accomplish nothing less than the development of humanity (*Menschheit*) itself (*Crisis*, p. 299; VI 348). It was Greek philosophy that originally gave humanity a 'revolutionary' change of attitude and a 're-orientation' (*Umstellung*) – or 'transformation (*Verwandlung*) – through the promotion of the ideas of *abstraction* and *infinity*:

> But with the appearance of Greek philosophy and its first formulation, through consistent idealization, of the new sense of infinity, there is accomplished in this respect a thoroughgoing transformation (*Umwandlung*) which finally draws all ideas of finitude and with them all spiritual culture and [its concept of] mankind into its sphere. (*Crisis*, p. 279; Hua VI 325, trans. mod.)

According to Husserl, this emergence of the idea of **infinity** through idealization is revolutionary and cuts off scientific culture from all prescientific culture.

Europocentrism   See also **Europe**, *Vienna Lecture*
Husserl, especially because of his later writings, *Crisis* and *Vienna Lecture*, has been accused of 'Europocentrism' or 'Eurocentrism', i.e., of assuming that all science and philosophy had its origins in Europe and specifically in the 'breakthrough' to the **theoretical attitude** in Greek philosophy. Husserl does not use the term, and regards the European breakthrough as offering a new universal style of self-responsible life which is open to all humanity.

Evidence (*Evidenz*)   See also **apodicticity, givenness, knowledge, truth**
Husserl's concept of *Evidenz* is variously rendered as 'inner evidence', 'self-evidence', or simply 'evidence'. Husserl understands evidence as

'an experiencing of something that is and is thus; it is precisely a mental seeing of something itself' (CM § 5). It is 'nothing other than adequate self-givenness' (IP, Hua II 59). **Knowledge** in the strictest sense requires 'evidence', that is, cognitions given with **insight (*Einsicht*)** and with a certainty to be sharply distinguished from blind belief or a psychological feeling of conviction. All genuine knowledge rests on For Husserl, 'the most perfect 'mark' of correctness is evidence' (LU *Prol.* § 6). To know something is to be able to verify it by tracing it back to some evident experiences that ground it fully. Evidence can be immediate but more usually is a gradual process. As Husserl will clarify in FTL:

> Evidence ... designates that *performance on the part of inten-tionality which consists in the giving of something itself ... The primitive mode of the giving of something itself* is *perception*.
> (FTL § 59)

Husserl insists that there is no apodictic final evidence about empirical entities, due to their perspectival mode of givenness. An act of knowing is evident when it displays or 'gives' itself with all the requirements necessary for knowledge, or when it has self-evidence, in the sense that one is fully warranted in holding the belief. Evidence is not to be understood as a psychological feeling of some kind, or any kind of hunch, but is 'immediate intimation of truth itself' (LU *Prol.* § 6). Indeed, according to Husserl, evidence is achieved only after long and hard endeavours. In the Sixth Logical Investigation, Husserl explains evidence as the insight that occurs when the *meant* (*das Gemeinte*) comes into complete correspondence with the *given* (*das Gegebene*, LU VI § 36). For Husserl, self-evidence is not confined to the mathematical or logical domains. There are many different kinds of evidence, for Husserl, depending on the domain of knowledge. His standard examples of self-justifying evident acts are our normal perceptual acts, e.g. acts of seeing which normally present the object with all the accompanying evidence necessary to warrant a judgement of the form 'I see x'. To get someone else to see requires drawing their attention to it, nothing more. Evidence is an ongoing, everyday '**achievement' (*Leistung*)** in all cognitions where the object is given in a satisfactory form, with 'intuitive fullness' (*anschaüliche Fülle*) or as Husserl prefers to say, in which the object gives itself. Husserl emphasizes that self-evidence involves the transition from empty intentions to fulfilled ones (a *process* in the sense of '**fulfilment'**), that it is the ('absolute') 'self-givenness' of the object (itself), so that it's the *mode* of the givenness of an object, that it's something that belongs to the *form* of our acts. Husserl also discusses *Evidenz* in his *Formal and Transcendental Logic* (§§ 105–107) and *Cartesian Meditations* § 6.

Exact essence (*das exakte Wesen*)   See *eidos*, **essence, morphological essence**
Exact essences are found in the exact sciences and are idealizations (e.g. geometric figures) and function Husserl says like 'ideas in the Kantian sense' (*Ideas* I § 74) in that they provide ideal limits. They are contrasted by Husserl with **morphological essences**.

Expectation (*Erwartung*)   See also **protention, time consciousness**
'Expectation' (*Erwartung*) Husserl's term for the intentional consciousness that looks forward to the future for fulfilment. Expectation is an intentional state based on **protention**. Anticipation is taken to be a different kind of intentional **act**.

Experience (*Erfahrung, Erlebnis*)   See also *cogito*, **empiricism, lived experience, self-experience, transcendental experience**
Husserl regularly employs two terms for experience – the more usual German noun *Erfahrung* (literally: an 'encounter') and also the German term ***Erleben***, which is often translated as ***lived experience***. Husserl usually reserves the verb *erleben* and the noun *Erlebnis* for the personally undergone experience, something lived through. Husserl speaks of evidence as an experience of being thus and so (CM § 5), of 'perceptual experience' and of 'experience of the world' (all using *Erfahrung*) and claims to have discovered with the **reduction** a new domain of 'transcendental experience' (*transzendentale Erfahrung,* CM § 9) understood as 'self-experience'. Husserl criticizes modern **empiricism** for having a too narrow sensualistic conception of experience. He praises Descartes' discovery of the ***cogito*** for uncovering a domain of apodictic evidence and for moving from natural self-experience to transcendental self-experience (CM § 11). The 'experience of the other person' is called *Fremderfahrung* by Husserl (see CM § 42).

Experience and Judgment (Erfahrung und Urteil, 1938)   See also
Landgrebe
Husserl's last published work, *Experience and Judgment* (1938), was written
in collaboration with Husserl's former assistant Ludwig **Landgrebe**. The
book was in press in Prague when Husserl died in 1938. The invasion of
Czechoslovakia by the German army meant the book was suppressed,
apart from a few copies that had already been shipped in Britain and
the United States. Landgrebe presents the book as a companion piece to
Formal and Transcendental Logic (1929). According to Landgrebe, he
drew heavily on Husserl's unpublished lectures especially the *Analyses of
Passive Synthesis* but also acknowledges that he also drew on his memory
of Husserl's verbal utterances and that the work cannot be judged on the
basis of philological exactitude. A draft of the work was already written in
1930 and had been annotated by Husserl but Landgrebe put it aside and
did not return to it until 1935. Husserl authorized Landgrebe to finish the
work for him. *Experience and Judgment* had a strong influence because
of its discussion of **passive synthesis** and of pre-predicative experience.
This work defends the idea that all formal **judgement**s including those of
logic depend on a pre-predicative and pre-linguistic form of experiencing.
Experience and Judgment claims to explore the 'genealogy' of logic and
offer a 'genetic' account of the origin of experience.

Expression (*Ausdruck*)   See also **indication, language, meaning, sign**
Expressions are a particular class of **sign**. As opposed to mere **indications**, which point to objects directly (e.g. flags, signals, signposts, warning
signs), expressions refer to objects through a **sense** (*Sinn*) or **meaning**
(*Bedeutung*). *Expressions*, for Husserl, are primarily *linguistic* acts and he
excludes gestures or facial expressions (which signify only by indicating),
as well as signs such as signals, flags. Linguistic signs which function as
'expressions' (*Ausdrücke*) are more than indicators, their relation to an
object is mediated *through* (*mittels*) a *meaning*: 'it is part of the notion of
an expression to have a meaning' (LU I § 15 I 201; XIX/1 59). Expressive
signs *express* meanings, i.e. they instantiate an ideal sense. A 'meaningless'
(*bedeutungslos, sinnlos*) expression is, strictly speaking, not an expression
at all. A set of sounds (a chain of noises) only becomes a communicable
meaning when endowed or 'animated' (*beseelt*) with a meaning intention by
the speaker (LU I § 7). In that sense, a parrot cannot generate an expressive

act even if he can articulate or mimic spoken sounds. An act of investing the sounds with sense is required for the sound sequence to be an expression. As he will later write: an expression intends a 'meaning' (*Meinung*) and 'in speaking we carry out an internal act of meaning [*Meinen*] that melds with the words, as it were, animating them' (APS 14; Hua XI 360).

Meaning depends on inner acts of intending-to-mean. With regard to expressions, Husserl distinguishes between the act of expressing or intending to mean, the psychological state of the person expressing, the ideal identical meaning expressed and the object referred to. He also discusses the manner in which different instances of the same expression differ in physical nature (e.g., the same word spoken in different accents or at different pitches or tone) and the same expressed sense. While the single instances are multiple, the same identical meaning is expressed, and hence that meaning must be an ideal unity entirely distinct from the physical sound pattern. This leads Husserl to discuss many different situations in which the same sense can be expressed in different expressions or in which different expressions refer to the same object using different senses, e.g., Napoleon can be referred to as 'the victor of Jena' or as 'the vanquished at Waterloo'. Husserl also considers the case of proper names (e.g., 'Socrates') and what he calls 'essentially occasional expressions' (indexicals such as 'here', 'there' 'now, 'this') where the object referred to depends on the occasion in which the expression in used. Expressions, of course, also serve as indications in that they indicate to someone that a meaning is being communicated; that is, they motivate the hearer to believe that the speaker is undergoing a mental process, entertaining a content and seeking to communicate something (LU I § 7). Husserl calls this the 'intimating function' (*die kundgebende Funktion*) of the sign: when someone is speaking, I listen to him as someone thinking, recounting, etc. The questioner signals his question in uttering the sentence. Husserl is here drawing on a fairly traditional account of the function of signs as found in Mill. But these kinds of indication, which are often found 'interwoven' (*verflochten*) with expressive acts, differ sharply in essence from the essence of expression as such (see Hua XXVI § 3). Whereas logic is interested only in the expressed meanings and their formal interconnections (e.g., relations of inference), their essential kinds and differences (LU I § 29), phenomenology focuses on the meaning intending act. Husserl rejects the traditional view of expressions that accounted for them solely in terms of the set of physical sounds or written marks, on the one hand, and a sequence of mental states, on the other hand, joined associatively to the physical sounds. This account ignores the role of the ideal sense. Words spoken with intention incarnate sense or meaning. For Husserl consciousness of sound and of meaning are interwoven into a complex unity that serves as the basis for further modifications. In his 1908 reprise of this discussion, Husserl said that instead of the inadequate physical word/psychical event distinction, he had begun from Brentano's tripartite distinction between the word as communicating some information, as expressing a meaning, and as naming an object (Hua XXVI § 3). Normally, in seeing a word written on a page, we attend to and 'live in' what is signified not the word itself, although this is clearly founded on seeing the word (Hua XXVI § 4). Our object of interest is not the physical or aural trace of the written word but what it refers to (Hua XXVI § 4b). I listen to the content of what is being said, as opposed to, for instance, the person's accent. The awareness of the word has the specific function of conducting us to the consideration of the object. In his 1908 lectures, Husserl is clear that the consciousness of the word has itself the phenomenological feature of both *self-effacement* and of *conducting beyond* itself to its object. Normally we are not conscious of this 'pointing-away-from-itself' feature of our words. We rather live in what is meant (APS 15; Hua XI 361). This holds true even in 'solitary mental life' (*im einsamen Seelenleben*; LU I § 8), in one's private mental thinking to oneself. Here expressions continue to function as they do in public communication, without, Husserl believes, the intimating function being operative as it is now unnecessary. One does not need to intimate to oneself. This becomes an issue for Derrida in his *La Voix et le phénomène* (1967), trans. David Allison, *Speech and Phenomena and other Essays on Husserl's Theory of Signs* (Evanston, IL: Northwestern University Press, 1973). The words (whether a phrase or a sentence) still perform the function of expressing meanings (*Bedeutungen*), but the thinker doesn't have to signal to himself or herself that he or she is having such a thought. Expression of meaning then is an essentially different act from 'communication' or 'intimation' (*Kundgabe*), although, of course, the different functions are usually found together in the one speech act. Moreover, we normally experience an expression as a set of words and meanings that are so unified they cannot be separated. They have fused into a whole.

—F—

Fact (*Faktum, Tatsache*)   See also **essence, facticity, Hume**

Husserl speaks of 'facts' and even invokes **Hume**'s English phrase 'matters of fact' (*Ideas* I, Introduction) in contrast to **essences**, laws, generalities and other **idealities**. Hume contrasts 'matters of fact' with 'relations of ideas'. For Husserl, facts are contingent, actual occurrences that take place in space and time and are opposed to mere possibilities. The existence of the human species is simply a fact (Hua VII 55). Husserl occasionally speaks of the 'irrational fact' of the existence of the **world**. Scientific knowledge is always more than an assembly of facts. **Knowledge** has to provide a theoretical framework within which facts can be understood and interpreted. Phenomenology is an a priori discipline that focuses on **essences** and is not interested in the facts concerning the empirical world.

Facticity (*Faktizität*)   See also **fact, Heidegger**

'Facticity' is a term originally found in German Idealism (Fichte), and taken up by the neo-Kantians and logical positivists to express the status of matter-of-fact, empirical facts as contingent in contrast to **a priori**, ideal necessities, generalities and **values** (*Geltungen*). The term is not common in Husserl but he uses it in the 1920s and 30s largely continuing its broad neo-Kantian meaning (see Hua VII 35, 54, 139). Husserl regularly speaks of the existence of the world, of nature, of history, and of human beings, as sheer irrational **facts**. There is a general facticity or contingency to human life that can never be overcome. In *First Philosophy*, Husserl speaks of the 'facticity of **life**' as belonging not to phenomenology but to **metaphysics** (Hua VII 394). In the *Crisis* § 52, Husserl contrasts individual facticity with the domain of lawful generality (cf. CM § 64). The term 'facticity' is more prominent in **Heidegger**. In his Freiburg lectures in the early 1920s, Heidegger sought to develop what he called 'a hermeneutics of facticity'. Hans-Georg **Gadamer** defines facticity as follows: 'Facticity is obviously that which cannot be clarified, that which resists any attempt to attain transparency of understanding. Thus it becomes clear that in every understanding there remains something unexplained, and that one therefore must ask about what motivates every understanding' (see H.-G. Gadamer, 'Subjectivity and Intersubjectivity, Subject and Person', *Continental Philosophy Review* 33 (2000), p. 281).

Fantasy (*Phantasie*) See also **image consciousness, memory, perception, presentification, representation**

Husserl was interested in all the central mental acts including **perception**, **memory**, and fantasy. He regards an act of fantasizing or imagining (as distinct from seeing pictures as pictures: '**image consciousness**') as a special **modification** of perception. Without perception there could be no fantasy. Fantasy is characterized as a kind of re-presentation or '**presentification**' or '**presentiation**' (*Vergegenwärtigung*) since it does not have the full 'fleshly' (*leibhaftig*) character of perception. Husserl distinguishes between image consciousness (*Bildbewusstsein*) and fantasy (*Phantasie*). Image consciousness is rooted in the perception of a present object that, as image, refers to an other (absent) object (Hua XXIIII 82). The fantasy, by way of contrast, is not based on the perception of a present object but is a quasi-perception of a sensuous object. Fantasy differs from perception in that perception presents the object with the character of existing in the present whereas the existence of the fantasized object is irrelevant in acts of fantasy and imagination. Existence is simply left to one side. What is fantasized is not necessarily past, present, or future, but is presented 'as-if' (DR § 4), and is not an actual perception. This is a structural feature of fantasy itself: it has the character of 'depicting' rather than presenting (XXIII 16). In fantasy, there is no positing the object. Husserl writes in his 1907 ***Thing and Space*** lectures:

> In phantasy, the object does not stand there as in the flesh,
> actual, currently present. It indeed does stand before our eyes,
> but not as something currently given now; it may be possible
> to be thought of as now, or as simultaneous with the cur-
> rent now, but this now is a thought one, and is not that now
> which pertains to presence in the flesh, perceptual presence.
> The phantasized is merely 'represented' (*vorgestellt*), it merely
> places before us (*stellt vor*) or presents (*stellt dar*), but it 'does
> not give itself' as itself, actual and now. (DR § 4, p. 12; Hua
> XVI 15)

Imagination neutralizes or suspends the thetic function. One is indifferent to the existence of the imagined object. Furthermore, the object seen in fantasy does not have the sense of being located in the same space as an object is understood to be in a perception. The fantasy object 'hovers' or floats before us; it not continuous with the objects or the space around it. Second, there is no temporal distance or gap experienced as there is in the case of memory. The fantasized image is apprehended in the present tense although that present is not itself experienced as perceptual present tense. By the same token, the fantasized image can reappear and be recovered in memory, so it has a certain kind of identity transcending the act of fantasy. Third, the imagined object (in earlier works Husserl speaks of a 'representation', *Vorstellung,* XXIII 18) does not have the same identity conditions or 'selfhood' (*Selbstheit*) of the perceptual object. It is characterized by a certain confusion or indistinctness. Husserl also distinguished between clear and unclear fantasies. Unclear *Phantasie* is always sudden, unexpected, abrupt and intermittent. Fantasy presentations (*Phantasievorstellungen*) are mediated through a 'presentation' (*Vorstellung,* XXIII 24) that is lacking in the case of perception. There is a kind of 'non-presence' (XXIII 58–9) associated with the imagined object. Husserl altered his position on fantasy several times in his life. **Sartre** criticized several aspects of Husserl's interpretation on fantasy. Sartre challenged Husserl's account of fantasy as perception modification; for Sartre, fantasy was an original and fundamental form of consciousness. There are several texts in which Husserl treats fantasy as an original kind of act rather than perception modification. In these writings, he considers fantasy as equiprimordial with perception, rather than based on perception.

Feeling (*Gefühl*) See also **emotion**

Husserl has a wide concept of feelings: including pleasure, displeasure, like, dislike, approval, disapproval, valuing, disvaluing, etc. (LU V § 15 (b)). He locates feelings in the passive sphere of that which consciousness undergoes. In **Logical Investigations**, he discusses whether feelings are mere psychological states or whether they are intentional acts directed at intentional objects (esp. LU V § 15(b)). For Husserl, certain feelings – pleasure at hearing music, displeasure at a shrill sound, joy, hatred etc. – are related to specific objects and are intentional. Others, e.g. pain, appear to be non-intentional but, and here Husserl follows Brentano, such feelings seem to overlap with **sensations**. Feelings then can be either intentional acts or mere states of sensation. For Husserl, however, feelings are not merely natural components of our psycho-physical nature but belong to our intentional and motivational lives. Brentano thought that feelings themselves were intentional although they were founded on **judgements** and **presentations**. There are certain objects that we necessarily experience with a specific feeling quality, which, for Husserl, implies that the relation between these objects and our feelings is not contingent. Our feelings motivate but do not completely control our will and reason. We act freely when act not blindly but with insight and reason. Feelings are subordinated to the **will**. In the sphere of ethics, Husserl accuses **Kant** of 'sensualizing' the sphere of feelings. Husserl maintains Kant maintained the naturalist prejudice that our affect consciousness is ruled solely by natural laws.

Fichte Lectures **(1917)**   This was a series of three lectures delivered in Freiburg in the last months of the Great War on *Fichtes Menschheitsideal* (*Fichte's Ideal of Humanity*), lectures that earned him the Iron Cross for his assistance to the military effort. (See Husserl, 'Fichtes Menschheitsideal. Drei Vorlesungen,' *Aufsätze und Vorträge (1911–1921)*, Hua XXV 267–93). The lecture series was delivered on 8–17 November 1917, and repeated on 14–16 January 1918, and 6–9 November 1918, just before the armistice. According to Husserl, German Idealism, 'indigenous to our people' (XXV 268), was once fully understood but now fallen into neglect and misunderstanding. It will return now that 'one-sided naturalistic mode of thinking and feeling is losing its power' (XXV 269). Husserl draws a historical parallel with the situation in Germany after Napoleon's victory at Jena. It was Fichte who was able to find spiritual resources in that defeat. Fichte offers more than theoretical philosophy, as 'the great man of praxis' (Hua XXV 271) he offers the true critique of practical reason, putting Kant's philosophy on the secure footing by genuinely uniting theory and practice and ridding it of obscure 'things in themselves'. Husserl briefly sketches how **Descartes** and **Kant** overturned naive **belief** in the world, by showing that the 'world is posited by us in our thought' (XXV 272), and that **space, time, causality**, are 'the basic forms of a thinking which belong inseparably to our kind of mind' (ibid.), leading to the Kantian view that 'subjectivity is world creative, shaping the world from out of the pregiven materials of sensation in accordance with its firm laws' (XXV 273). For Husserl, 'Kant's results are the points of departure for Fichte' (XXV 274). Kant had, unfortunately, maintained that the transcendent things in themselves affect our sensibility even if we cannot know anything about them. Fichte sweeps away this remnant of dogmatism, and along with it Kant's assumption that sensibility must be passively stimulated from without before it can be active. For Fichte, human subjectivity is itself not fact (*Tatsache*) but action (*Tathandlung*), action that brings the experience of world into being:

The Fichtean I … is the self-positing action out of which in infinite succession ever new actions originate. (Hua XXV 275)

Moreover, these actions are teleological or goal oriented, and thus:

To write the history of the I, of the absolute intelligence, is therefore to write the history of the necessary teleology in which the world as phenomenal comes to progressive crea-tion, comes to creation in this intelligence'. (Hua XXV 276)

This absolute 'I' splits itself into individual humans. Philosophy consists in grasping the world as the product of this self-splitting ego through immersion in the essence of the 'I' and bringing the world to progressive reconstruction (XXV 276). Furthermore, Fichte's particular genius was to have identified the moral dimension of this idealism. The ego has a drive towards reason, towards the ideal of a moral world order (another name for God). Husserl himself, looking to a universal moral community beyond any narrow national self-interest, cites Fichte's hope for a 'total rebirth of humanity' (XXV 279). Finally, for Fichte, human self-understanding is the self-revelation of God. Husserl's description of Fichte's idealism is everywhere positive and endorsing: 'How elevating is this philosophy for the noble self-consciousness of the human being and the dignity of his existence when it proves that the entire world-creation is achieved in the absolute intelligence for his sake' (XXV 279). Like Husserl himself, Fichte is an optimist seeking a reformation of Germany and humanity in dark times.

Fink, Eugen (1905–1975)   Eugen Fink was born in Konstanz, Germany, in 1905. He attended school there and then studied literature for one year at the University of Münster (1924–5), before moving to Freiburg in 1925 to study with Husserl and later (in 1928) also with **Heidegger**. In 1928 he became Husserl's salaried personal assistant (until 1930) and thereafter cooperated with him as his 'co-worker' until Husserl's death in 1938. In

1929 he submitted his doctoral dissertation on 'Presentification and Image', a phenomenological description of the work of the **imagination**. Fink assisted Husserl with the German edition of the *Cartesian Meditations* and even drafted his own *Sixth Cartesian Meditation* (written in 1932 but not published until 1977), which he intended to submit for his *Habilitation* but this became impossible in 1933 because of Fink's association with Husserl who was Jewish. Fink wrote a number of important articles defending Husserl's philosophy including 'The Phenomenological Philosophy of Edmund Husserl and Contemporary Criticism' in *Kant-Studien* in 1933 to which Husserl himself added a Foreword supportive of Fink. Fink was involved in assisting **Leo Herman Van Breda** with the rescue of Husserl's manuscripts when they were smuggled out of Germany to the newly created Husserl Archives in Leuven, Belgium. Fink worked at these Archives from 1939 until 1940 when he was arrested after the German invasion of Belgium. He was conscripted during the war but afterwards returned to Freiburg as a professor. Fink was interested in Hegel and in reconciling Husserl and Heidegger's philosophies. He proposed a 'transcendental theory of method' to justify phenomenology as a critical enterprise, to develop a 'phenomenology of phenomenology'. Fink believed that phenomenology interrogates the very 'pregivenness' of the world in all experience. Behind the world lies the transcendental ego which has, relative to the being of the world, the 'meontic' status of non-being. Fink's aim was to clarify the status of the 'transcendental onlooker' stance which is that operated within the transcendental **epochē** of phenomenology. In his later writings, Fink became interested in Nietzsche. Fink had a strong influence on **Merleau-Ponty** and on Jan **Patočka** and participated in the important conference in Royaumont in 1959 on the occasion of the centenary of the birth of Husserl.

First philosophy (*erste Philosophie*)   Aristotle uses the term 'first philosophy' (Greek: *protē philosophia*, Latin: *philosophia prima*) in his *Metaphysics* to refer to the science of ultimate principles of all things, which includes the study of substance and cause, and whatever is most universal and general. First philosophy is often taken to be equivalent to the term 'metaphysics' or 'ontology', the study of being. The full title of Descartes' *Meditations* includes a reference to 'first philosophy' (*Meditations on First Philosophy*) and Descartes seems to mean a self-justifying science of knowledge, in other words, **epistemology**. Husserl often uses the term 'first philosophy' (*Erste Philosophie*, *philosophia prima*) to refer to the self-grounding, self-justifying presuppositionless science of all science, namely phenomenology. Husserl also entitled one of his Freiburg lecture courses given in 1923–4 *Erste Philosophie* (now published in two volumes as *Husserliana* VII and VIII). The first volume offers Husserl's 'critical history of ideas' including discussions of the emergence of transcendental philosophy in Descartes and the subsequent naturalization of the Cartesian impetus in the work of Locke. **Berkeley**, **Hume** and **Kant** are also discussed in some detail, foreshadowing the discussion in Husserl's **Crisis**. The second volume offers extended meditations on the nature of the **reduction**. Subsequently, **Emmanuel Levinas** has reacted against the primacy given to metaphysics in the western tradition of philosophy and has argued that ethics is the true first philosophy.

Flow of consciousness   See **stream of consciousness**

Formal and Transcendental Logic (Formale und transzendentale Logik 1929)   Husserl published his *Formal and Transcendental Logic* in 1929 in his **Yearbook of Philosophy and Phenomenological Research** (now reprinted in Hua XVII). The work is subtitled *An Attempt at a Critique of Logical Reason*. It is a sustained rethinking of the issues first discussed in the **Logical Investigations**, namely, the objectivity of truth and meaning and the phenomenological structures that constitute it, but it is also a sustained discussion of the possibility of transcendental logic. One of the specific aims of the book is to distinguish between formal logic and mathematics. The book offers a distinction between the study of formal structures of judgement, **apophantics**, and the study of the possible formal objects of **judgement** (formal ontology). *Formal and Transcendental Logic* contains an interesting discussion of the history of transcendental philosophy from Descartes to Kant. He criticizes Kant for having no way of tackling the difficult problem of the constitution of ideal objectivities from conscious achievements. For Husserl, traditional logic was blind to the transcendental problem and hence logic was a positive science. FTL begins with a discussion of the nature of *logos* and examines the elementary structures of judgement. It then discusses formal apophantics, the theory of deductive systems and the theory of manifolds. The second half of the book is a long analysis of the emergence of transcendental logic.

Formal ontology (*formale Ontologie*)   See also **material ontology, object, part, region, regional ontology, whole**
In the Second Edition (1913) of the ***Logical Investigations***, Husserl uses the term formal ontology to include the pure theory of **wholes** and **parts** outlined in the Third Logical Investigation (see Introduction to Third Investigation). In general, Husserl defines formal ontology as the theoretical account of all possible objects of whatever kind (see *Ideas* I, *Experience and Judgment* § 1), the theory of something in general (***Formal and Transcendental Logic*** § 54). Formal ontology develops **Brentano**'s, **Twardowski**'s and **Meinong**'s conception of *Gegenstandstheorie*, theory of objects, the account of what it is to be an object or a property or a relation, unity, plurality, state of affairs, number, and so on. For Husserl, the objects of mathematics simply form one part of formal ontology, but there are other kinds of formal object that have nothing to do with numbers. Husserl maintained that formal ontology can in fact be pursued independently of **logic**. Purely formal categories include object, relation, property, one, number, whole, part, magnitude (listed in Third Logical Investigation). In *Ideas* I § 10, he lists property, quality, state of affairs, relation, identity, similarity, set, collection, number, etc. **Part** and **whole** are formal essences applicable to any material domain. The entities of formal ontology constitute no **region** at all, but have all *material regions* under them.

Formal or pure grammar (*reine Grammatik*)   See also **meaning, mereology, part, whole**
In the Fourth Logical Investigation Husserl outlines a 'pure grammar' (Second Edition 'pure logical grammar') of the formal **a priori** laws governing the combining or binding of **meanings** (*Bedeutungen*) into a unity that makes sense rather than simply yielding a nonsensical string of words, and is, generally speaking, an application of his part–whole theory to the field of semantics. He speaks of the 'pure theory of semantic forms' (*die reine Formenlehre der Bedeutungen*; Fourth Logical Investigation § 14). The aim is to provide a pure morphology of meaning that lays the basis by providing possible forms of logical judgements, whose objective validity is the focus of formal logic proper. Husserl is explicitly reviving the old idea of an a priori grammar against both the psychological interpretations of grammar dominant in his day and the empirical theorists who were imprisoned in a false paradigm (e.g., assuming Latin grammar as the

paradigm, LU IV § 14). Just as simple objects can be combined to produce complex objects, *simple* meanings combine to produce *complex* meanings (LU IV § 2). Moreover, meaning parts need not mirror parts of the object, and vice versa. Meaning has its own **parts** and **wholes**. Husserl maintains that all combinations are governed by laws; his aim is to find the least number of independent elementary laws (LU IV § 13). It must be possible to identify the rules of all such possible valid combinations a priori, combinations that produce well-formed expressions as opposed to nonsense (such as 'this careless is green', LU IV § 10). Husserl famously distinguished (LU I § 15 and LU IV § 12) between *nonsense* (*Unsinn*) and *countersense* or absurdity (*Widersinn*). The concept of 'square circle' is neither senseless nor nonsensical, but constitutes an absurdity, a contradiction in terms, a 'countersense' that cannot be realized. Formal grammar, on Husserl's account, can eliminate only nonsense not absurdity and is therefore not yet formal logic in the sense of specifying what can be objectively valid. In later writings, notably the **Formal and Transcendental Logic** and **Experience and Judgment**, Husserl continued to maintain that formal grammar provided the bedrock rules for meaningfulness that made possible formal logic. The laws of formal logic lay down the principles under which some part of meaning is to be understood as a **nominalization**, for instance.

Formalism (*Formalismus*)   See also **Hilbert**

Formalism in mathematics and logic is the view that statements in these sciences consist of a set of consistent, interconnected but uninterpreted signs or symbols that are organized according to rules. Logic and mathematics are purely formal sets of rules and are not about anything. **David Hilbert** was a formalist who sought to prove that mathematics was both consistent and complete. The formalist project in mathematics was challenged by Kurt Gödel's Incompleteness Theorem.

Formalization (*Formalisierung*)   See also **generalization**

In *Ideas* I § 13, Husserl distinguishes between formalization and **generalization**. Formalization abstracts from the material properties of a given entity and focus on the object as in terms of pure, empty categorial forms. Thus, for example, a physical material object will be formalized as 'an entity'.

Foundation (*Fundierung, Begründung*)   See also **primal establishment**
Husserl uses the term 'founding' or 'foundation' (*Fundierung*) to refer to a
logical, epistemological or ontological relation of dependence (he speaks of
an eidetic law or law of essence) according to which something A depends
on something else B either for its existence or for its essential nature
or sense and without which it would not exist or be what it is. Husserl
discusses the foundation relation in the Third Logical Investigation § 14 to
explain the way in which parts depend on wholes. Husserl's examples of
foundation include the manner in which colour is founded on (depends on)
extension. Nothing can be coloured that is not also extended, although the
notion of colour does not 'contain' the notion of extension. Extension, by
way of contrast, can exist without colour. The founded **moment** cannot
exist apart from the founding moment. Foundation can be one sided or
reciprocal (i.e. mutually dependent), mediate or immediate. Following
Brentano, a judgement is one-sidedly dependent on a presentation (Third
Logical Investigation § 16). Husserl also distinguishes between immediate
and mediate foundation. A fulfilment is likewise founded on a signitive act
whereas a signitive act does not dependent on its fulfilment. According to a
separate sense (see also **foundationalism**), Husserl sees **phenomenology**
as self-founding and hence providing an **absolute foundation** or 'final
foundation' (*Letztbegründung*) for all the sciences.

Foundationalism   See also **empiricism, foundation, rationalism**
Foundationalism in epistemology usually refers to the doctrine that the
framework of **knowledge** rests on certain basic truths that are absolutely
certain and indubitable and which are not themselves the outcome of
further inferences. Foundationalism is usually contrasted with coherentism,
which claims that knowledge is justified by each knowledge claim being
related by coherence with other relevant knowledge claims, where no
belief has absolute priority. According to **empiricism**, these foundational
truths are sensory observations that are self-justifying and with which we
are immediately acquainted, whereas **rationalism** holds that these foundational truths are a priori intuitions such as the **Law of Non-Contradiction**
or the *cogito ergo sum* that have axiomatic status and that all other truths
can be deduced from these basic intuitions. Husserl was a foundationalist
to the extent that he wanted **phenomenology** to be a pure presuppositionless science that provided an ultimate foundation for all other sciences.

However, he was not a foundationalist to the extent that he accepted neither the rationalist nor the empiricist suppositions about absolute foundation. Furthermore, Husserl did not assume in advance that any particular science (e.g. mathematics) offered a model or normative ideal for what science as systematic knowledge should be (see *Cartesian Meditations* § 3). In some respects, Husserl was a coherentist in that he maintained that science itself consisted in a web of interrelated beliefs. Husserl's main claim was that all knowledge worthy of the name had to be justified by **evidence**.

Framework of sense (*Sinnzusammenhang*)   Term used by Husserl to refer to the interconnecting network of constituted meanings that is the result of intentional activity. The term *Zusammenhang* ('interconnection', 'nexus') is frequently used by **Dilthey** to express the seamless interconnectedness of life. Husserl also speaks of the 'interconnectedness of life' (*Lebenszusammenhang*).

Frege, Gottlob (1848–1925)   German mathematician and philosopher responsible for his radical reconceiving logic. Born in Wismar in 1848, Frege entered the University of Jena in 1869, received his doctorate from Göttingen (where one of his teachers at Göttingen was **Hermann Lotze**) in 1873, and his *Habilitation* from Jena in 1874. Frege then taught at the University of Jena until his retirement in 1917. He died in 1925. Frege outlined his new symbolic notion for logic in his *Begriffsschrift* (*Concept Notation*, 1879). His main works include *The Foundations of Arithmetic* (1884), and *The Fundamental Laws of Arithmetic,* published in two volumes (1893/1903). Frege is regarded as the father of mathematical logic and of modern analytic philosophy. Frege was committed to the logicist project of reducing mathematics to logic. His articles 'On Sense and Reference' (1892) and 'Concept and Object' (1892) are seminal contributions to the philosophy of language. Frege had an enormous influence on Husserl, Russell, Wittgenstein, and **Carnap**. Husserl was one of the first philosophers in Germany to recognize Frege's work and the two engaged in correspondence although they never met. In his *Philosophy of Arithmetic* in 1891, Husserl criticized Frege's account of definition and identity, and, in 1894, Frege in turn reviewed Husserl's *Philosophy of Arithmetic* in a penetrating but somewhat intemperate manner. According to Frege, Husserl treated number naively as properties of things or of aggregates rather than as the extensions of concepts. Husserl had seen number as deriving from our intuition of groups or multiplicities and since neither one nor zero is a multiple, strictly speaking they were not positive numbers for Husserl. Frege criticized Husserl's account of zero and one as negative answers to the question 'how many?'. Frege states that the answer to the question 'How many moons has the earth?' is hardly a negative answer, as Husserl would have us believe. Furthermore, Frege believed, Husserl seemed to be confusing the numbers themselves with the *presentations* of number in consciousness, analogous to considering the moon as generated by our act of thinking about it. Crucially for Frege, in identifying the objective numbers with subjective acts of counting, Husserl was guilty of **psychologism**, the error of tracing the laws of logic to empirical psychological laws. If logic is defined as the study of the laws of thought, there is always the dangerous that this can be interpreted to mean the study of how people actually think or ought to think; understanding necessary entailment, for example, as that everyone is so constituted psychologically if he believes P and if he believes that P implies Q then he cannot help believing that Q is true. For Frege, Husserl has collapsed the logical nature of judgement into private psychological acts, collapsing together truth and judging something as true. According to the journal kept by W. R. Boyce-Gibson, who studied with Husserl in Freiburg in 1928, Husserl later acknowledged that Frege's criticisms had 'hit the nail on the head'. Partly in response to Frege's criticisms, and partly through his reading of Bolzano, Husserl became a stern critic of psychologism in the first volume of the *Logical Investigations, Prolegomena to Pure Logic* (1900) where he writes:

> I need hardly say that I no longer approve of my own fun-
> damental criticisms of Frege's antipsychologistic position set
> forth in my *Philosophie der Arithmetik*, I, pp. 129–32. I may
> here take the opportunity, in relation to all of the discussions
> of these *Prolegomena*, to refer to the Preface of Frege's later
> work, *Basic Laws of Arithmetic*. (LU, *Prol.* § 45)

Fulfilment (*Erfüllung*)   See also **coincidence**, **empty intention**, **intuition**, **signitive act**
From the ***Logical Investigations*** onwards, Husserl distinguishes between **empty intentions** and filled intentions. An act can intend an object in

an empty manner, for instance if I am simply thinking about or remembering my garden. The act of actually seeing the garden now is an act of intuitive fulfilment. The experience of fulfilment is actually not just the presence of the perceptual object given in a bodily present manner but the experienced sense of the *identity* between what is intended and what is actually intuited. In other words, fulfilment is the experience of the **coincidence** between the empty intention and its fulfilling object. All perceptual experiences contain an interwoven mixture of empty and filled intentions, e.g. when I actually perceive the front side of the object, the back side is perceptually present in an empty manner (see APS, p. 44: XI 9). Husserl's examples of the progress from intuition to fulfilment are complex and often drawn from logic or mathematics. He talks for example about the manner in which a complex mathematical expression e.g. 5^3 has to be fulfilled through a chain of **signitive** intentions. He also talks about the gradual progress towards fulfilment when a roughly drawn sketch is filled in to be a complete drawing.

Functioning subjectivity (*fungierende Subjektivität*) See also **intentionality, subjectivity**

Functioning subjectivity is a term used in the later Husserl (e.g. *Crisis* § 72 – but first introduced at *Crisis* § 13; see also Hua XXXV 98) to refer to the kind of anonymous, background, pre-reflective, passively experiencing subjectivity that is continuously functioning in **passivity** to produce the unified experience of the **world** as pregiven in experience. The term 'living … functioning intentionality' appears in FTL § 94 and it also appears in The *Internal Time Consciousness* lectures. The term was picked up by **Merleau-Ponty** in the Preface to his *Phenomenology of Perception* (1945), in which he speaks of 'functioning intentionality' (*funktionierende Intentionalität,* PP, p. xviii; xiii) which he translated as 'operative intentionality' (see also PP, p. 418; 478) and which he contrasts with active intentionality. **Fink** speaks of it as 'performance consciousness' (*Vollzugsbewusstsein*) and Merleau-Ponty also cites Fink. Husserl frequently speaks of the 'functioning lived body (*Leib*)' at CM I 172) and of normally functioning organs (*Ideas* II), and generally of 'functioning consciousness' or 'functioning ego' (*Ideas* II, Hua IV 337). Husserl usually sees functioning as a kind of anonymous passive process that precedes and lays the ground for all the intentional activity of the ego.

Fundamental belief, primal belief or proto-doxa (*Urdoxa*, *Urglaube*)   See also **belief, doxa**

In *Ideas* I § 104 and elsewhere, Husserl uses the term 'fundamental' or 'primal belief' (*Urglaube*) as a technical term to name the 'doxic modality' or presumption (which, of course, never is explicitly made thematic by naive consciousness in the **natural attitude**) that my perceptual experiences have unquestioned validity (certainty) for me and the objects of the experiences have the character of existent actuality. There are many different modalities of epistemic or doxastic attitude but the fundamental or most basic one is sheer perceptual belief or acceptance, perceptual certainty (*Ideas* I § 103). This bedrock certain conviction has primacy of place in our conscious doxastic attitudes for Husserl: 'belief certainty is belief simpliciter in the pregnant sense' (*Ideas* I § 104). This mode of certain belief can be 'modalized' or modified into other belief states such as uncertainty, questionability, deeming possible, deeming likely, and so on.

— **G** —

Gadamer, Hans-Georg (1900–2002)   See also **Heidegger, historicity, horizon**

Hans-Georg Gadamer was born in Marburg in 1900 and enrolled in the University of Breslau in 1918 before moving to Marburg University in 1919 to study philosophy and classics. He completed his doctorate on Plato under Paul Natorp and Nicolai Hartmann in 1922. He then travelled to Freiburg to meet Heidegger in 1923, and while there attended Husserl's seminars. He returned to Marburg to study with Heidegger from 1924 to 1928, completing his *Habilitation* in 1928, published as *Plato's Dialectical Ethics* (1931). Gadamer first taught as *Privatdozent* at Marburg, before securing a temporary post in Kiel from 1934–5 in controversial circumstances, as he was replacing a friend, Richard Kroner, a Jewish lecturer who had been dismissed under the new Nazi laws. Gadamer returned to Marburg in 1935, becoming a professor in 1937. In 1938 he moved to Leipzig, where he remained through the war. He was appointed

Rector of the University of Leipzig in 1946–7, but soon left for a position in Frankfurt, where he was active in bringing Adorno and others back from exile in the USA. In 1949 Gadamer was appointed professor in Heidelberg, where he has taught until his retirement in 1968. Although Gadamer had published books and articles (mainly on classical Greek philosophy and Hegel), it was his book, *Wahrheit und Methode* (*Truth and Method*, 1960) that brought him to prominence as a philosopher. In this work, Gadamer has a long engagement with Husserl and especially with his *Crisis of European Sciences*, on the notion of **historicity**. Gadamer makes extensive use of the concept of **horizon**. In his autobiographical *Philosophical Apprenticeships*, he records his memories of Husserl as a lecturer. After his retirement in 1970, Gadamer lectured at universities in Canada and the United States, including Boston College. He was Professor Emeritus in Heidelberg until his death in 2002. Gadamer begins from Heidegger's insight in *Being and Time* (§§ 32–4), that understanding (*Verstehen*) is *the* central mode of human being-in-the-world, a world encountered and inhabited in and through language. Hermeneutics, for Gadamer, signifies this ongoing, never completable process of understanding in the light of human *finitude* and 'linguisticality' (*Sprachlichkeit*). As Gadamer puts it in *Truth and Method*, 'language is the medium of the hermeneutic experience'.

Galileo Galilei (1564–1642)   See also **Descartes, Koyré, mathematization of nature, nature**

Galileo was an Italian mathematician, astronomer, physicist, philosopher, and experimental scientist, best known for popularizing and defending the Copernican heliocentric system, for employing the newly invented telescope to examine the heavens, for inventing the microscope, and for carrying out practical experiments involving dropping stones from towers and masts (to challenge the Aristotelian view that heavy bodies fall faster than lighter ones), examining the regular movements of pendula. Through his use of the telescope, Galileo discovered mountains on the moon, and spots on the surface of the sun, as well as observing Jupiter's moons, and the phases of Venus. Because of a lack of uniform standards of measure, he had to set up his own units and standards of measurement for length and time, and Husserl emphasizes this contribution. Through experiments involving objects moving along inclined planes, he discovered the law of free fall, according to which, in a vacuum, all bodies would fall with the same acceleration, expressed as proportionality to time squared. Galileo has the distinction of being both the first modern experimental scientist and for creating the a priori discipline that became known as mathematical physics and historians have argued over which had prominence in his career. Galileo Galilei was born in Pisa, the son of a musician, and first studied medicine at the University of Pisa before transferring to mathematics. In 1589, at the age of 25, he was appointed to the chair of mathematics in Pisa. Some three years later, in 1592, he moved to Padua where he taught geometry, mechanics, and astronomy until 1610. Galileo discovered that a pendulum takes a uniform time to traverse its arc, no matter how large the arc is (isochromism), a discovery that allowed Galileo, late in his life (1641), to realize that the pendulum could be used in clocks. Husserl talks of Galileo not only in Section 9 of the **Crisis** but in several associated texts including the draft now known as '**The Origin of Geometry**' (this title was actually bestowed on the fragment by Husserl's assistant Eugen **Fink**). Whereas Husserl had a career-long interest in mathematics, his sudden interest in Galileo's specific achievement is puzzling and various authors have suggested theories as to what occasioned it. David Carr in particular has suggested it was visits by **Alexandre Koyré**, then an emerging Galileo scholar, that sparked Husserl's interest and influenced his interpretation. Reinhold Smid, editor of *Husserliana* XXIX, a collection of supplementary texts to the *Crisis*, however, has argued that Koyré's last visit with Husserl was in July 1932, prior to Koyré having published his Galileo study. Furthermore, Koyré himself remarked in 1937 to Husserl's long-term student, Ludwig Landgrebe that he was in agreement with Husserl's Galileo interpretation (see Hua XXIX il) so it is more likely that Koyré was influenced by Husserl rather than the other way round. **Aron Gurwitsch** has suggested that Husserl depended heavily on **Ernst Cassirer**'s treatment of Galileo in his *The Problem of Knowledge in the Philosophy and Science of Modernity* (Vol. 1, 1906), a work Husserl relied heavily on in his lectures (see *First Philosophy*) for its account of modern philosophy. However, Husserl's copy of Cassirer's book does not contain any annotations (and Husserl was in the habit of marking up texts that he read intently). In fact, Husserl had been interested in Galileo's use of geometry from his earliest days (c. 1892) when he was attempting to write the (subsequently abandoned) second volume of the *Philosophy of Arithmetic*. Thereafter, references to Galileo regularly reappear in Husserl's work (see the material in **Experience and Judgment**, § 10, written after the *Crisis*). For example, at the beginning of his 1929 *Formal and*

Transcendental Logic, Galileo and Descartes are mentioned as participating in the 'reshaping' of modern science and philosophy through the establishment of a 'new logic'. It was quite common for German philosophers of the period (including **Cassirer** and **Natorp**) to see Galileo as one of the founders of modern *philosophy* not just modern science, and to emphasize his theoretical accomplishments over his experiments and empirical observations. It is important to recognize at the outset that Husserl is not concerned with Galileo as a historical person but rather as a figure standing for the origins of the modern scientific worldview (see VI 58). Galileo is not a proper name, as **Derrida** puts it in his *Introduction to the 'Origin of Geometry'* and Husserl considers his reflections to be part of a wider set of 'historical reflections' (*geschichtliche Besinnungen*, *Crisis* p. 57; VI 58) necessary for our current philosophical and also cultural situation. Husserl admits that he is using the name Galileo to name a whole set of tendencies relating to the whole 'bestowal of meaning' (*Sinngebung*, VI 58) of what has been constituted as 'natural science'. His general aim is to arrive at a 'reflective form of knowledge' (*reflektive Erkenntnisgestaltung*, p. 59; VI 60) concerning what he will speak of as the 'primal establishment' (*Urstiftung*) of modern science (*Crisis* § 16, p. 73; VI 75). A crucial outcome of Galilean science in its impact on modern philosophy is a certain kind of **dualism**, a 'splitting' (*Zerspaltung*, *Crisis* § 10, p. 60; VI 61) of the world into that which is 'nature' and has '**being in itself**' and another world which is the world of the psychic, which is the world of '**subjective-relative properties**'.

Geiger, Moritz (1880–1937)   See also **realist phenomenology**

Moritz Geiger was born in Frankfurt in 1880 and initially studied law at the university of Munich before being attracted by the philosophy and psychology of Theodor **Lipps**. He then studied for a period with Wilhelm **Wundt** at Leipzig before completing his doctorate with Lipps. He was one of the Munich students who moved to Göttingen to study with Husserl. He was a co-editor of the *Yearbook for Philosophy and Phenomenological Research* and published articles in it himself. He taught at Munich and Göttingen but, as a Jew, was forced to leave Germany in 1933. He emigrated to the USA where he taught at Vassar and later as a visiting professor at Stanford. He wrote on a broad number of issues including phenomenological aesthetics, the nature of feeling, the unconscious, but also on issues connected with relativity theory and geometry. He was a follower of **realist phenomenology** and rejected Husserl's transcendental turn.

General thesis or general positing (*Generalthesis*)   See also **attitude, epochē, fundamental belief, natural attitude**

For Husserl, the **natural attitude** is characterized by a 'general thesis' or act of universal positing (Greek *thesis* means 'positing') that means that all conscious intentional acts involve a presupposed commitment of **belief** in the existence and reality of the objects of the experiences in question (see *Ideas* I § 30). Husserl speaks of this as 'positing' (*Thesis, Position, Setzung*). Not just the perceived objects but the **world** itself is always experienced in every **lived experience** as simply 'there' for the perceiver, 'on hand', having the character of factually given reality or 'actuality' and experienced as having an overall unity. Further, without any doubt or question, I experience myself as belonging to this world. I have no reason to doubt these experiences. Moreover, the general thesis has the character of 'acceptance' or unquestioning basic belief. The **natural attitude** is characterized by its naive acceptance of this general thesis. It is precisely this 'general thesis' or 'general positing' that has to be unplugged or disabled in the 'phenomenological **epochē**' (see CM § 8).

Generalization (*Generalisierung*)   See also **formalization**

Generalization is the process, discussed in *Ideas* I § 13, whereby one moves from the individual to the **species** and the genus. Beginning with an individual physical object (e.g. a stone) one moves to the species 'spatial, material thing'. The traditional logical tree (Porphyry's tree) that sees humans as animals and animals as living beings is an example of generalization. Husserl distinguishes this process from **formalization**. Husserl gives the example of the individual *red shade* (called a **nuance** by Husserl) being included under the species *red* and this again under the genus *colour*, which is under the higher genus *quality*. Pure forms arrived at through formalization, by way of contrast, cut across these species–genus hierarchies and yield pure formal categories, such as unity.

Generativity (*Generativität*)   See also **genetic phenomenology**

Husserl coins the term 'generativity' (*Generativität*) in his later writings (e.g. *Crisis*, p. 188: VI 191 and XV 207–209) to express the constitutive processes through which the cultural, human world is the outcome of successive acts of **constitution** by human beings over generations in history. Husserl uses the term both for general processes of becoming – which he usually refers to as 'genesis' – and for the historical process that occurs whereby language, cultural legacy and tradition are handed down from one generation to another. Human communities are made up of layers of generations. The concept of a 'generation' was already found in Dilthey and the idea of belonging to one's generation is discussed by Heidegger in *Being and Time*. Husserl speaks of generative problems of life and death in CM § 61. Husserl occasionally speaks of a 'generative phenomenology' that can be seen as a part of **genetic phenomenology**.

Genetic phenomenology See also **active and passive genesis, phenomenology, primal establishment**

The term 'genetic phenomenology' is used by Husserl in CM § 34, a form of phenomenology that especially attempts to grasp the constitution of a living **ego** which is a concrete **person** evolving and developing in **time**, with a personal **history** (see APS Hua XI 336). Husserl began to speak about 'genetic' phenomenology around 1917 and saw it as an attempt to uncover the sedimented layers of constitution that underlie our experience of objects, what he called the 'history of objectivation' (Hua XI 345). Genetic phenomenology has to explain how the concept of **world**, for instance, comes about for the **ego**. Genetic phenomenology in this sense contrasts with **static phenomenology** (see CM § 37). Husserl distinguishes phenomenological genesis from psychological genesis. Psychological genesis would concern itself, for example, with how a child in early infancy first learns to relate to objects. Phenomenological genesis, contrariwise, examines the structures involved in such a generating of the concept of object in infancy, not from empirical study but by eidetic variation attempting to grasp the essence of such object constitution, and encounters such things as **primal establishment** (*Urstiftung*, CM § 38). The problems of the constitution of time and of the ego in time belong to **genetic phenomenology** whereas static phenomenology studies the 'finished' products of constitution (APS, p. 634; Hua XI 345).

Genetic psychology (*genetische Psychologie*) See also **Brentano, description, descriptive psychology**

Franz Brentano uses the term 'genetic psychology' in his *Psychology from an Empirical Standpoint* (1874) to mean a kind of causal, physiological study in contrast to **descriptive psychology**. Genetic psychology examines the physiological basis of psychic acts and studies causal relations between the physical and the mental, and is an inductive science. Brentano also calls this 'physiological psychology', which is similar to **Wilhelm Wundt's** term. According to Brentano, descriptive psychology (also called 'psychognosy', or later (around 1889) 'descriptive phenomenology') was an *exact* science, like mathematics, independent of, and *prior* to, 'genetic' or physiological psychology (DP 8), which studies causal relations between the physical and the mental. Brentano acknowledged that the mental depends on the physical (PES 48) but the physical does not explain the mental, which is explicable only on its own terms. Genetic psychology may ultimately discover that intentional phenomena have a physico-chemical substratum, but this is independent of the **description** of mental states. In his *Descriptive Psychology*, Brentano strengthened this claim: that consciousness can be explained by physico-chemical events represents 'a confusion of thought' (DP 4).

Genuine or authentic presentations (*eigentliche Vorstellungen*)   See also **intuition, presentation**
Brentano had distinguished generally between what he termed 'genuine' or 'authentic' (*eigentlich*) presentations, where the object is directly given, and non-genuine, 'inauthentic' or 'symbolic' (*uneigentlich, symbolisch*, XII 193n1). Husserl develops this distinction in his ***Philosophy of Arithmetic***. We can have genuine presentations of small numbers (e.g. 5, 7) but we cannot intuit very high numbers directly but have to symbolize them e.g. 10^6 . Thus, Part One of *Philosophy of Arithmetic* is entitled 'The Genuine Concepts of Unity, Plurality, and Number', referring to those smaller numbers that can be grasped immediately on the basis of a sensory presentation of distinct concrete multiplicities (numbers smaller than a dozen). Indeed, in his dissertation defence in 1887, Husserl lists among the theses he will defend: 'One can hardly count beyond three in the authentic sense' (PA, p. 357; Hua XII 339). Husserl's account of the nature our authentic, genuine experiences of the smaller numbers in the first part of PA was retained essentially unaltered in later writings. It is at the very heart of his conception of intuition as either empty or full. Thus in the *Lectures on Passive Synthesis*, Husserl speaks of the fact that the presented object is the same in both the cases of empty and full presentation (APS Hua XI 245).

Emptiness means a potential towards **fulfilment**. Husserl remarks that this thinking 'in the mode of emptiness' (*im Modus der Leere*, Hua XI 245) is at the centre of linguistic and logical thinking. Higher logical operations are entirely symbolic and thus the challenge is to give an account of their legitimacy and justification.

Givenness (*Gegebenheit*)   See also **absolute givenness, appearance, fulfillment, intuition, phenomenology, principle of principles**
'Givenness' (*Gegebenheit*) is one of the central concepts of Husserl's phenomenology. It is invoked so frequently in phenomenology that **Heidegger** even characterizes it in his 1920 Freiburg lectures as the 'magic word' (*Zauberwort*) of phenomenology. According to Husserl's **principle of principles**, what is given in intuition has to be accepted precisely in the manner in which it is given. This is the basic principle of phenomenology: to return to and attend to givenness in all its forms. 'Givenness' characterizes the fact that all experience is experience of something to someone, according to a particular manner of experiencing. There is something that comes to appearance or is given in the experience. In **perception**, something is perceived; in **imagination**, something is imagined, and so on. Givenness also implies that there is a conscious **subject** who apprehends or undergoes the experience; there is a 'dative' element in the experience, a 'to whom' of experience. There is a third aspect to givenness, namely, that there is a particular manner or mode in which the given comes to light to the experiencer. For instance, **memory** and **fantasy** provide different modes of givenness to **perception**. There are different modes of givenness and there are different degrees of givenness; Husserl speaks of adequate givenness and absolute givenness. The givenness of memory can never be adequate relative to the kind of immediate bodily givenness of the perceived object in perception. Perceptual givenness can never be adequate because all perceptual experiences are given in **profiles**. In the *Idea of Phenomenology* and *Ideas* I, Husserl claims that **lived experiences** (*Erlebnisse*) themselves are given absolutely and adequately, just as they are, but he later moves away from this claim. Ideal entities are also given absolutely according to Husserl. The *cogito* is often given as an example of absolute givenness. In his later work, Husserl sees absolute givenness as an ideal limit rather than something that can actually be achieved. Husserl's concept of 'givenness' was reinterpreted by Heidegger as disclosure or

manifestation; it has been reinterpreted in recent French philosophy, e.g. Jean-Luc Marion, under the concept of 'donation'.

Göttingen Philosophical Circle   During his Göttingen years (1901–16), Husserl attracted many brilliant students, e.g., Johannes Daubert (1877–1947), **Moritz Geiger** (1880–1937), **Adolf Reinach** (1883–1917), **Max Scheler** (1874–1928), **Hedwig Conrad-Martius** (1888–1966), **Roman Ingarden** (1893–1970) and **Edith Stein** (1891–1942), all drawn to Husserl's new way of approaching logical and epistemological problems, which broke with the tradition. Many psychologists with studied under G. E. Müller (1850–1934) also took part in Husserl's seminars and developed many of his phenomenological insights, including Erich R. Jaensch (1883–1940), Wilhelm Schapp (1884–1965), David Katz (1884–1953), Heinrich Hofmann and Jean Héring (1890–1966). In 1907 Theodor Conrad founded the Göttingen Philosophical Society, whose founding members included Katz, Hofmann, Schapp, and others. Edith Stein attended the Friday night meetings of the Society.

Governing, holding sway (*Walten*)   See also **lived body, will**
Husserl speaks of the manner in which the ego has a direct relationship with its **lived body** as a 'governing' or 'holding sway' (*Walten*). I experience my body as a set of capacities or what Husserl calls 'I can's. I can turn my eyes left, I can turn my head, tilt it, reach out my hand and so on. I experience my body primarily as a centre of this governing. That is, I have immediate voluntary control over it. This sense of governing can be inhibited in various forms of disability, disease, or brain dysfunction.

Gurwitsch, Aron (1901–1973)   Aron Gurwitsch had a lifelong interest in phenomenological psychology and particularly in the nature of **perception**. He was particularly close to the Gestalt psychologists and also developed the non-egological account of consciousness later found in Sartre. Born in Lithuania in 1901 into a Jewish family, he moved to Danzig, but spent most of his life as a stateless person. In 1919 he attended the University of Berlin to study with Carl Stumpf among others. In 1921 he went to Freiburg to study with Husserl but could not be enrolled because of his status as a stateless person. He then went to the University of Frankfurt to study Gestalt psychology with Gelb and Goldstein. His dissertation was entitled 'Phenomenology of Thematics and the Pure Ego: Studies of the Relation between Gestalt Theory and Phenomenology'. There was no one to supervise the thesis in Frankfurt and Gurwitsch eventually sent it to **Scheler** (due to arrive in Frankfurt as professor) but Scheler died suddenly in 1928 and the thesis was eventually examined by **Moritz Geiger**. In 1933 Gurwitsch emigrated to Paris where he knew **Lévy-Bruhl** and Koyré and met **Maurice Merleau-Ponty** at the home of Gabriel Marcel. Merleau-Ponty acknowledged having read the *Phenomenology of Thematics and the Pure Ego* and being influenced by it. Gurwitsch made Goldstein's unpublished papers on the Schneider case available to Merleau-Ponty. He met Schutz in Paris in 1937. Gurwitsch developed a non-egological theory of consciousness (later replicated by Sartre). In 1940 with the help of Schutz he emigrated to the USA to a post in Johns Hopkins University. He taught physics at Harvard and later mathematics at Brandeis before eventually getting a post in philosophy in the New School for Social Research in 1959. A major study, *The Field of Consciousness*, was published in 1964 and a collection of essays, *Studies in Phenomenology and Psychology*, in 1966.

—H—

Habit (*Gewohnheit, Habitus, Habitualität*)   See also **ego, sedimentation, style**

Husserl uses the term 'habit' (German: *Gewohnheit*, but he also uses the Latin-derived terms *Habitus* and *Habitualität*) in relation to the manner in which certain beliefs and ways of behaving settle down to become part of the **ego**'s character and contribute to its personal **style**. The concept of habit is to be found in classical philosophy, e.g. Aristotle's *hexis*; in medieval philosophy, e.g. Thomas Aquinas' *habitus*; as well as in modern empiricism, e.g. Hume's 'custom and habit'. Husserl sometimes discusses the concept of habit in criticism of **Hume** whom he accuses of circularity in attempting to understand habit in terms of **causality** while at the same time explaining causality in terms of custom and habit (see Husserl, *Introduction to Logic* *and Theory of Knowledge* (1906–1907), § 51). In ***Ideas*** II, Husserl discusses the notion of habit (*Gewohnheit*) especially in §§ 54–6 where he is discussing motivation as 'the fundamental lawfulness of spiritual life'. In the Fourth Cartesian Meditation, Husserl speaks of *habitus* and 'habituality'. Husserl does not restrict habituality to our pre-predicative perceptual life or to the life of instincts and drives but also discusses the manner in which judgements become sedimented as passive **convictions**. A person can hold the conviction (of voting Labour in elections, for instance). Husserl speaks of being thus-and-so decided. People develop habitual styles of thinking and feeling. Habit is also understood by Husserl as the manner in which an overall '**attitude**' or 'stance' or 'collective mindset' is lived through, as in Husserl's 1910/1911 *Logos* essay 'Philosophy as a Rigorous Science'. There, Husserl's writes of 'habitus' as an overall disposition of, for instance, a natural scientific researcher:

> In keeping with their respective habits of interpretation (*herrschenden Auffassungsgewohnheiten*), the natural scientist is inclined to regard everything as nature, whereas the investigator in the human sciences is inclined to regard everything as spirit, as a historical construct, and thus both thereby misinterpret whatever cannot be so regarded. (PRS, p. 253/294; Hua XXV 8–9)

Similarly he claims:

> It is not easy for us to overcome the primeval habit (*die urwüchsige Gewohnheit*) of living and thinking in the naturalistic attitude and thus of naturalistically falsifying the psychical. (PRS 271/314; Hua XXV 31)

And again:

> *Experience* as personal habitus is the precipitation of acts of natural, experiential position-taking that have occurred in the course of life. This habitus is essentially conditioned by the way in which the personality, as this particular individuality, is motivated by acts of its own experience and no less by the

> way in which it takes in foreign and transmitted experiences
> by approving of or rejecting them. (PRS 284/329; XXV 48)

There is, furthermore, a difference between the habit (*Habitus*) of the natural man in his daily living and that of the phenomenologist. The mature Husserl has a sense of habitus as forming an essential part of the character or attitude of natural life and also of expressing the self-consciously adopted stance of the phenomenologist. Husserl speaks of the 'theoretical habitus' (Hua XXVIII 402) of the scientist and philosopher and even of the 'habitus of the **epochē**' (Hua XIII 208). In a supplement written around 1924 to the *Basic Problems of Phenomenology*, Husserl writes:

> The *habitus* of the phenomenological *epochē* is a thematic
> *habitus*, for the sake of obtaining certain themes, the discover-
> ies of theoretical and practical truths, and to obtain a certain
> purely self-contained system of knowledge. This thematic
> *habitus*, however, excludes to a certain extent the *habitus* of
> positivity. Only in its being closed off to the latter does it lead
> to the self-contained unity of phenomenology as 'first' phi-
> losophy, the science of transcendental pure subjectivity. (GPP,
> p. 123; Hua XIII 208)

Heidegger, Martin (1889–1976)   Martin Heidegger was born in Messkirch in 1889 and educated at the Heinrich-Suso-Gymnasium in Konstanz. After a short period in a Catholic seminary he entered the University of Freiburg initially to study theology but shifted promptly to philosophy. He wrote his doctorate on **psychologism** (*The Doctrine of Judgement in Psychologism*). Husserl met Heidegger soon after his arrival in Freiburg in 1916. Heidegger had recently received his *Habilitation* supervised by **Heinrich Rickert** on The *Theory of Categories and of Meaning in Duns Scotus* and Husserl wrote to him for a copy of his thesis. Husserl was instrumental in getting the thesis published later in 1916, and he is thanked in the dedication to the published version. The two kept in contact when Heidegger was called up for military service. When Heidegger returned from the war to lecture in Freiburg, commencing in January 1919, he initially became Husserl's salaried assistant. He lectured at Freiburg until he moved to the University of Marburg in 1923. Throughout the 1920s Husserl and Heidegger were very close, with Heidegger accompanying Husserl on family holidays. Husserl assisted Heidegger to secure a post at the University of Marburg (writings references to **Natorp**), and, in February 1927, published *Being and Time* as Volume VIII of the *Jahrbuch für Philosophie und phänomenologische Forschung*. Husserl helped Heidegger with the page proofs of the publication. Later published with Max Niemeyer Verlag (Tübingen), *Being and Time* is dedicated to Husserl. After the highly acclaimed publication of *Being and Time*, Husserl promoted Heidegger as his successor for the chair at the University of Freiburg the former would vacate in 1928. Heidegger's philosophy stems from a radicalization of Husserl's transcendental phenomenology into a fundamental ontology whose focus, however, is not on the elaboration of the constitution of the intentional horizon of phenomena but rather on the question pertaining to the meaning of being from the explication of the temporality proper to being itself. In an effort at intellectual cooperation in late 1927, Husserl invited Heidegger to cooperate on the 'Phenomenology' article for the 14th edition of the *Encyclopaedia Britannica*. They worked through several drafts together from September 1927 through to February 1928, but their views diverged radically and, in the submitted version, Husserl had excised much of Heidegger's contribution especially the latter's introductory paragraph locating phenomenology within fundamental ontology. Similarly, Husserl was initially satisfied with the version of his *Lectures on Internal Time Consciousness* published by Heidegger in 1928, but he quickly came to find fault with the truncated form in which the lectures were published, for which he blamed Heidegger. Relations between Husserl and Heidegger became strained in the 1930s, most particularly after 1933 when Heidegger became Rector of the University of Freiburg, soon after the establishment of the Nazi regime in Germany. Although no longer rector at the time (Heidegger's rectorship of the University of Freiburg lasted only 10 months), Heidegger did not attend Husserl's funeral in 1938, saying he was ill at the time. In the 1930s Heidegger's thought moved in a new direction, turning away from phenomenology towards what he called the 'thought of being'. Heidegger's most noteworthy influences in this turn were Nietzsche, Schelling, Hölderlin and implied also a return to pre-Socratic thought.

Heraclitean flux (*Heraklitischer Fluss*)   See also **consciousness, stream of consciousness, time consciousness**

Husserl regularly uses the image of a 'stream', 'current' or 'flow' to express the nature of consciousness (*Bewusstseinsstrom*, Hua XXV 362; *Erlebnisstrom, Lebensstrom*). He speaks of a 'Heraclitean flux' (CM Hua I 18, 191) to refer to the fact that consciousness is a continuously changing temporal stream of experiences that, like Heraclitus' image of the river, never stands still. All conscious experiences are essentially temporal and every **now moment** passes into a **retention**. No two conscious experiences (even of the same object in the same manner) can be identical because they occur at different times. Each ego has its own **stream of consciousness** that cannot be shared with another ego. At best the two streams run in parallel.

Hilbert, David (1862–1943)   See also **Cantor, formalism**

David Hilbert was German mathematician who worked at Göttingen and was instrumental in bringing Husserl there from Halle. Hilbert supported **Cantor**'s theory of infinite sets and transfinite numbers. He was one of the early defenders of **formalism** in mathematics. In 1900 he outlined a number of outstanding problems in mathematics that would dominate twentieth-century mathematics.

Historicity (*Geschichtlichkeit, Historizität*)   See also **generativity, horizon, spirit**

The mature Husserl employs two German terms for 'historicity' – *Geschichtlichkeit* and *Historizität* – that he probably found in the writings of **Dilthey**. In his English translation of the **Crisis of European Sciences**, David Carr renders *Geschichtlichkeit* as 'historicity' and *Historizität* as 'historical development' (e.g. *Crisis*, p. 336; VI 271), but Husserl does not always differentiate between these two terms. The term 'historicity' is used by Husserl in a somewhat different sense to the manner in which it is used by **Heidegger** in *Being and Time*. Heidegger tends to use the term to express the manner in which human existence has the capacity to live its life in a historical way. There is no direct evidence that Husserl was influenced by Heidegger's conception, indeed it is possible that the reverse is true and that Husserl's use of the term influenced Heidegger in their discussions during the 1920s (when both were reading Dilthey). For Husserl, each cultural grouping has its own historical trajectory, i.e. a 'historicity'. Humans live in groups, nations, and other supranational unities (such as 'Europe', 'China', and so on). In his late writings, Husserl speaks of nations having their own 'living historicity' (*lebendige Geschichtlichkeit*, XXVII 187). He also speaks of societies having different *levels* of historicity, i.e. their own levels of collective social, political and spiritual development. Strictly speaking, Husserl writes, there are no 'first' humans (XXIX 37); rather families give rise to families, generations to generations. Nations live in a 'homeland (*Heimat*, XXIX 9) or '**homeworld**' (*Heimwelt*) with a sense of what is familiar and what is strange and foreign (each nation has its opposing nation, XXIX 38–9, 41). Human cultures begin from a natural 'animism' (XXIX 4; 38), whereby nature itself is experienced as a living person. The mythic perception of the world is animistic. Things are not experienced as pure things; the dead, for instance, are considered to continue to inhabit the world (Husserl is echoing similar claims to be found in Lévy-Bruhl). However, a second stage of historicity is arrived at with the breakthrough to science enabled by the **theoretical attitude** (XXIX 41). In this text from November 1934, Husserl speaks of the differences between the French, German and other nations with their specific senses of history and indeed the manner in which they form 'higher order persons' and the Papuan who has strictly speaking no biography, life history (*Lebensgeschichte*) or 'history of the people' (*Volksgeschichte*). Spiritual life depends on tradition (*Crisis*, p. 354; VI 366).

Homeworld (*Heimwelt*)   See also **alien world, historicity, normality, world**

Especially in his later period, during the 1930s, Husserl frequently uses the term 'homeworld' (*Heimwelt*, Hua XV, Hua XXXIX, *Crisis* VI 303) to express the claims that the world is always presented within a familiar context (e.g. the world as 'normal lifeworld' *normale Lebenswelt* Hua XV 210). Husserl also uses the term 'near-world' (*Nahwelt*, VI 303) as equivalent. He means the familiar world. Husserl also speaks of the 'human environment (*Umwelt*)' or the 'generative homeworld' (*generative Heimwelt*, Hua XXXIX 335). The **world** is neither the totality of objects in a physical sense nor the whole of all our subjective activities. Rather, *my* present world (full of meanings, spiritual and cultural values and objects) is inevitably enrooted in traditions and customs (Hua XXXIX, Beilage XLIII). Homeworld is in this manner the peculiar unity between present horizon and meanings. The notion of 'homeworld' highlights the manner in which the world is shared with others and, especially, with those who live in close proximity with us. Homeworld is contrasted with alien world. It is not easy to define the boundaries that separate the homeworld from alien worlds. Husserl regards the distinction between homeworld and alien world as transcendental. Every world is constituted according to the conditions of **normality** and abnormality (Hua XXXIX 58). That is, the world unfolds necessarily within relations of proximity and remoteness. If the world is, as Husserl states, a meaningful horizon that emerge continually in the unity of our history (*Crisis*, Beilage V; Hua IX, Beilage XXVII), it is inevitably lived through different perspectives and distances. In this continuous movement, we can distinguish between familiar and strange elements, customs and people. Furthermore, different worlds can be interwoven. We can share, for example, the same place or town with other people whose habits or approaches to the world are radically different to ours. In this way we would not consider them our 'home comrades'. The unfolding of the world in terms of home and alien world is related to the problem of history (*Crisis*, Vienna Lecture; Hua XXXIX 48): the world is always meaningful within a historical and intersubjective horizon. *Our* world is not only linked to our own experiences and remembers, but it bears in its core the stamp of the others (aliens and home comrades) (Hua XXXIX 17).

Horizon (*Horizont*)   See also **life-world, world**

Husserl uses the term 'horizon' based on an analogy with the meaning of the term in ordinary language. A visual horizon defines the range of one's vision and includes everything that can be seen from a particular standpoint. Horizon, then, is a context of our experience which acts as an apparent unsurpassable limit (the Greek *horos* means 'boundary'). Horizons can be temporal, spatial, historical, cultural and so on. There are both subjective individual horizons and shared horizons (e.g. the horizon of a language or a culture). Husserl speaks of humans living within the horizons of their **historicity** (*Crisis* § 2). The first discussion in print of the concept of horizon occurs in *Ideas* I, in which he talks about the world as the 'collective horizon of possible investigations' (§ 1). For Husserl, objects are not perceived in isolation but against a *background* (*Hintergrund*) and in the midst of a 'surrounding world' (*Umwelt*) of other objects and also of other living bodies which are also other persons, animals, and so on (*Ideas*

II § 51). The 'horizon of all horizons' is the world (*Ideas* I § 27) which has the sense of being infinite and unbounded in every direction. Husserl speaks of a 'world horizon' (*Welthorizont*) and recognizes that all individual intentionalities take place against a backdrop of a world horizon. How the same object is experienced as the same by multiple co-subjects is precisely the problematic of how a 'world' comes into being (*Ideas* II, IV 80). According to Husserl, every lived experience bears with a set of unique essential possibilities that go to make up what he calls the 'horizon' of the experience. These horizons are not just empty possibilities, but rather are 'intentionally predelineated in respect of content' (CM § 19, p. 44; Hua I 82), that is, they are 'predelineated potentialities' (CM I 82). There is a 'horizon of references' built in to the experience itself:

> [E]verything that genuinely appears is an appearing thing only by virtue of being intertwined and permeated with an intentional empty horizon, that is, by virtue of being surrounded by a halo of emptiness with respect to appearance. It is an emptiness that is not a nothingness, but an emptiness to be filled out; it is a determinable indeterminacy. (APS 42; Hua XI 5–6)

Things are given within a 'perceptual field' whereby the entity is experienced with internal and external horizons (*Crisis* § 47). A perceived thing has a context of immediately present things, but also a context of possible things. A word or sentence has meaning against the background context of all the other meanings in the languages. A horizon is a system of references. The side of the object that appears in a series of **adumbrations** always promises more, there are pointers to other sides, an inside. But the horizons do not stop there. There are not just the other sides of the object, but also the possibility that the **perception** itself could have been conducted in a different way (from a different angle, distance, etc.). Thus, for example, I know if I approach the wooden table more closely, certain features of the grain will stand out more clearly. These leads to a certain indeterminacy within the experience of the object and yet also a certain determinateness and a certain set of further determinables. The object is a 'pole of identity' (*ein Identitätspol*, CM § 19) for a set of experiences, 'a constant X, a constant substrate' (APS 42; Hua XI 5). *Inner horizons* consist of the set of anticipations and prefigurations that I have already in mind as I approach the object (APS 43; Hua XI 7; see also CM). Husserl sees the process of perceiving an object as a dynamic procedure involving progressive fillings and emptyings. Certain prefigurations get filled in intuitively while new expectations are opened up. But in APS, Husserl specifies more clearly the role of retention in this process. What becomes invisible is not lost as it is retained when the new side of the object is seen (APS 45; Hua XI 9). Thus every perception invokes a whole series or system of perceptions. There is no final perception that can exhaust the thing completely. Indeed, to be a physical thing is precisely to be essentially inexhaustible. Every **lived experience** has a past that fades into an indeterminate horizon of the past and similarly it has one of the future. Our visual perception has a horizon. The character of a horizon is of a limit that can never be reached and which seems to recede as one approaches it. A horizon is therefore non-objectifiable and non-determinate. In FTL, Husserl says that in LU he still lacked the concept of 'horizon intentionality'. The concept of 'horizon' was subsequently taken up by **Heidegger** and Gadamer, in particular. **Gadamer** thinks of mutual understanding taking place through a certain 'overlapping' of horizons. In *Truth and Method*, Gadamer explains a horizon as 'not a rigid boundary, but something that moves with one and invites one to advance further' (p. 245).

Horizontal intentionality (*Längsintentionalität*) See also **horizon, time consciousness, transverse intentionality**

Especially in his analyses of **time consciousness**, Husserl distinguishes between 'horizontal' and 'transverse' intentionality (*Querintentionalität*). Both are forms of retentional consciousness. Horizontal intentionality is the retentional consciousness of the lapsed phases of time whereas transverse intentionality refers to the continued consciousness of the intended act or object through the temporal phase.

Humanity, humanness (*Menchentum, Menschheit*) See also **Europe**

Husserl uses several terms (*Menchentum, Menschheit*) to express humanity. He often speaks in the plural about 'humanities' (*Menschheiten*), by which he means the different cultural paths in which human societies have developed. Husserl's aim is for philosophy to play a central role in the development of a rational self-responsible humanity. According to the draft programmatic plan for completing the manuscript of the *Crisis*, Part Five (never written) was to cover the 'indispensable task of philosophy: humanity's responsibility for itself.' He regarded 'European humanity' as having developed philosophy and science and have experienced the breakthrough to the '**theoretical attitude**'.

Hume, David (1711–1776)   David Hume was a Scottish philosopher and historian, author of *A Treatise of Human Nature* (1739–40) and *Enquiries concerning Human Understanding* (1748). He is a classic empiricist, although he was widely regarded by his contemporaries as a sceptic. According to **Immanuel Kant**, Hume awoke him from his dogmatic slumbers. Hume criticized the view that causation was an observable real connection in nature rather human observers assume a constant conjunction between certain events based on their occurring contiguously, in direct succession, and so on. In general, Hume attributes to custom and **habit** many of our assumptions that we apply to the external world of nature. Hume similarly denied that there was a real ego behind the stream of conscious experiences. Husserl was influenced by Hume throughout his life. He discusses Hume's distinction between relations of ideas and matters of fact and his account of presentations in the ***Logical Investigations*** but he returns to discuss Hume in his *First Philosophy* lectures and in *Crisis* §§ 23–4. For Husserl, Hume is one of great transcendental philosophers. Hume's achievement was to recognize that causality was not a feature of the objective world but was an achievement of subjectivity. However, Hume's philosophy ends in fictionalism. Husserl also criticizes Hume's appeal to concepts such as 'custom', 'human nature', 'sense organs', which imply transcendence and thereby are in essential contradiction with his own stance (see *Idea of Phenomenology*, p. 17; Hua II 20).

Hyle (*Hyle*)   See also **hyletic data, matter, morphē, sensation**
Hyle is an ancient Greek word originally used by Aristotle to refer to the material principle that is formed by the formal principle to produce the material thing. Husserl uses the transliterated term *hyle* or '**hyletic matter**' or '**stuff**' is refer to the sensuous constituents of our intentional experiences, e.g. acts of perceiving, willing, valuing, and so on. In *Ideas* I § 85, Husserl introduces the Greek term *hyle* to refer to this sensible, temporally flowing, matter of experience in contrast to the intentional *morphé* or form. Sensuous matter is enlivened and ensouled by the **form**. Husserl leaves

open the possibility that there might be 'formless stuffs or 'stuffless forms' (*Ideas* I § 85).

Hyletic data (*hyletische Daten*)   See also **content, *hyle*, intention, matter, perception, sensation, stuff**

In ***Ideas*** I § 85, Husserl uses the term '**hyletic data**' to refer to the sensuous constituents of our intentional experiences, e.g. the raw sensuous content or '**stuff**' (*Stoff*) of acts of seeing, hearing, touching, etc. The term 'hyletic' come from the Greek word for matter (*hyle*) and Husserl speaks also of a 'sensuous *hyle*', which he contrasts with the intentional form (***morphē***) of acts. For Husserl, conscious experiences have a certain sensuous component that belongs to the **matter** of the act, e.g. there is something it feels like to perceive, to be in pain, to be thirsty, to have sexual desire, experiences of pleasure, being tickled, and so on (see *Ideas* I § 85). Husserl thinks that hyletic data should not be considered to be atomic, discrete **sense data**. He does think hyletic data are sensory but include the experiences of **drives**, feelings and emotions as consciously apprehended states. Husserl characterizes these hyletic data as part of the immanent or '*reell*' content of experience – that is, they are genuine component parts of the temporally extended lived experience itself. They arise and disappear with the experience itself (the colour seen, the noise heard). Hyletic data are present as part of the matter of the lived experience but are not the primary intended objects. As such the hyletic data are merely experienced and are not themselves intentional. As Husserl says in the Fifth Logical Investigation, I see the *box*, I do not see my own *sensations*. The same object can be apprehended through different hyletic data (I can *see* John visually or *hear* John on the phone aurally) or again the same hyletic data can be the platform for different intentional objects, depending on how these hyletic data are taken up, apprehended or interpreted. There are different kinds of hyletic datum – not just the data of the senses but also the peculiar felt qualities of imaginative, emotional and other experiences. Husserl also distinguishes between the felt matter of the experience and the objective quality of the object that is conveyed through the experience, e.g. one can distinguish between the peculiar sense in one's fingertips and the *smoothness* or *roughness* of the touched surface. Husserl was never satisfied with his account of hyletic data.

—**I**—

Idea of Phenomenology, The (*Die Idee der Phänomenologie,* **1907**)   See also **absolute givenness, evidence, givenness**
Between 26 April and 2 May 1907 Husserl delivered five lectures at the University of Göttingen, which were posthumously published in 1950 as *Die Idee der Phänomenologie* (*The Idea of Phenomenology*) as *Husserliana* volume II. These lectures were designed to serve as an introduction to his **Thing and Space** lectures given in the summer semester of 1907. *The Idea of Phenomenology* lectures focus on the **reduction** as a way of moving from the psychological to the truly epistemological domain. In this lecture series, Husserl characterizes **phenomenology** as the 'science of pure phenomena' and focuses especially on the phenomenology of **knowledge** and the possibility of justifying the objectivity of knowledge. Husserl discusses sceptical challenges to the possibility of knowledge, especially Cartesian doubt which puts everything in question. Phenomenology is presented in transcendental terms in relation to **Kant**. His problem is the 'how' (*wie*) of knowledge. The essence of knowledge has to be clarified with reference to pure **intuition**. In the Third Lecture, Husserl introduces the **epistemological and phenomenological reductions** in terms of an overcoming of the **natural attitude**, suspending all concerns with existent actuality and focusing solely on the **lived experience** or *cogitatio* and what is given in it. Husserl introduces the *epochē* in these lectures.

Idealism (*Idealismus*)   See also **absolute being, annihilation of the world, consciousness, correlation, transcendental idealism**
The term 'idealism' has many senses and first appears in modern philosophy in the eighteenth century. In Latin, the term appears in 1734 in Christian Wolff's *Psychologia Rationalis* §36, as the doctrine that nothing exists outside God and other spirits, clearly a reference to the Irish philosopher George Berkeley, who did not himself use the term. The term also appears in Diderot's *Encyclopédie* in the 1750s. Plato is counted as an idealist by Leibniz in 1702, as are the followers of **Descartes**. **Berkeley**'s claim, in his *Treatise Concerning the Principles of Human Knowledge* (1710) that *esse est percipi*, that the being of any object (other than a mind) is its being perceived by a mind (either the divine or the human mind), is usually seen as both

inaugurating modern idealism and formulating it in paradigmatic manner. Idealism of this kind arises from the need to address sceptical worries concerning the mind's access to an 'external world' thought of as having an 'absolute existence' of its own. Kant describes Berkeley's idealism as a 'material' or subjective idealism that thinks of reality as mind dependent. In the First Edition of the *Critique of Pure Reason* (1781), the term 'idealist' is introduced precisely in terms of the existence of an external world:

> By an **idealist**, therefore, one must understand not someone who denies the existence of external objects of sense, but rather someone who only does not admit that it is cognized through immediate perception and infers from this that we can never be fully certain of their reality from any possible experience. (A368–9)

In the Refutation of Idealism section of the Second Edition (1787) of the *Critique*, Kant opposes what he calls 'psychological' or 'material idealism':

> Idealism (I mean **material** idealism) is the theory that declares the existence of objects in space outside us to be either merely doubtful and **indemonstrable**, or else false and impossible. (B274)

Responding to the challenge of Berkeley, Immanuel Kant proposed a new form of idealism – **transcendental idealism** – which held that **objectivity** and **subjectivity** stand in an **a priori correlation**. Husserl's *Logical Investigations* defends the ideality of species, universals, essences and states of affairs and this was interpreted by critics as a move towards Platonic idealism. In the Second Edition of the *Logical Investigations* (1913), Husserl acknowledges that his position could be called idealism in a certain sense. He writes:

> To talk of 'idealism' is of course not to talk of a metaphysical doctrine but of a theory of knowledge which recognizes the 'ideal' as a condition for the possibility of objective knowledge in general, and does not interpret it away in psychologistic fashion. (LU II, Intro. **II**, p. 238; XIX/1 112)

After 1907 Husserl explicitly began to describe his philosophy as an 'idealism' and specifically as the final development of **transcendental idealism**. The first published announcement of this idealism (without using the word) came in *Ideas* I (1913) and this idealist turn was widely repudiated by Husserl's Munich and Göttingen followers. Husserl later conceded that this 'scandal' affected the reception of *Ideas* I (see V 150). Husserl makes his commitment to idealism explicit in his *Formal and Transcendental Logic*, *Cartesian Meditations* and in the *Crisis* as well as in his Author's Preface to the English translation of *Ideas* I by Boyce-Gibson. Husserl always rejects any version of subjective idealism that treats the objective material world as illusory or as merely a content of consciousness (Hua XXXV 276). He sees the similarity between his new form of idealism and the forms of **transcendental idealism** developed by German Idealism. However, for Husserl, the true founder of transcendental idealism is **Descartes** (rather than Kant) with his discovery of the apodictic certainty of the *ego cogito*. Husserl's idealism includes his notorious thought experiment concerning the **annihilation of the world**. Even if the stream of experiences becomes chaotic, there is still a consciousness that is experiencing this stream. Consciousness then is absolute. No objectivity is thinkable without reference to conscious subjectivity. Subjectivity is absolute because it is self-constituting and purely for itself (Hua XXXV 278). Husserl believes the world is constituted by the community of subjects, by the **community of monads** acting in consort.

Ideality (*Idealität*)   See **being in itself, Platonism**

In the **Logical Investigations**, Husserl defends the need to recognize 'idealities' (*Idealitäten*), that is, ideal entities that are characterized by identity across time such that they may be said to be supratemporal. Mathematics and **logic** are concerned with idealities such as the *number 4*, or the *Pythagorean theorem*. These ideal entities have a certain **being in itself**. There are many different kinds of ideality or ideal unity, e.g. meanings (the word 'dog'), concepts, universals, essences, the contents of judgements, art objects, and so on. For instance, Husserl believed that an artwork had an ideal, timeless identity that remained the same across all its instantiations. Thus, for example, a piece of music will remain the same ideal unity whether reproduced on vinyl, cassette, CD, analogue or digital format. Husserl was accused of **Platonism** for his defence of idealities. Husserl himself acknowledged the influence of **Hermann Lotze**'s interpretation of Platonic ideas in helping him to understand **Bolzano**'s '**propositions in themselves**' (*Sätze an sich*) as the ideal senses of statements and not as mysterious kinds of thing that existed in some kind of heavenly realm.

***Ideas Pertaining to a Pure Phenomenology and to a Phenomenological Philosophy, First Book (Ideen zu einer reinen Phänomenologie und phänomenologischen Philosophie* 1913)**   See also *Ideas* **II**
In 1913, Husserl published the First Book of his planned three-volume *Ideas Pertaining to a Pure Phenomenology and to a Phenomenological Philosophy* (usually referred to as *Ideas* I) in Volume 1 of the new **Yearbook for Philosophy and Phenomenological Research**. The subtitle was 'General Introduction to Pure Phenomenology' and this volume represents the first of Husserl's many 'introductions' to phenomenology as a 'method'. Like many of his other published books, it was written in a single feverish burst over eight weeks of the summer of 1912. It was originally planned to replace the then out-of-print **Logical Investigations** as a primer of phenomenology, but Husserl instead opted to bring out a second, revised version of the earlier work to accompany the new *Ideas* I. *Ideas* I introduced many new phenomenological themes, including (among many others), the **natural attitude** (*Ideas* I § 27), the phenomenological **epochē** (§ 32), the phenomenological **reduction**, the general positing or **general thesis** (§ 30), the concept of pure or transcendental **consciousness** (§ 33), the **principle of all principles** (*Ideas* I § 24), the **noesis** and **noema** (§§86–96), the notion of **hyle** (§ 85, 97), and the **neutrality modification** (§ 111). In addition, Husserl provides clarifications of the distinction between the factual and the eidetic, and distinguishes between **formalization** and **generalization** (§ 13). *Ideas* I aims to introduce the 'general doctrine of phenomenological reductions' (*Ideas* I, p. xxi; Hua III/1 5) which give access to the domain of pure (also called 'transcendental' consciousness and also to give a general account of the a priori (eidetic) structures of pure consciousness (*Ideas* I § 34). Phenomenology is presented as an entirely new science, an a priori science of essences, a 'new **eidetics**' (*Ideas* I § 33). Husserl says that he will avoid the term '**a priori**' as much as possible and instead employ the Greek term **eidos**. The a priori is to be understood as based on essence. *Ideas* I introduces the notion of the natural attitude and of normal sciences as carried out in this attitude and in its theoretical complement ('the natural theoretical attitude', *Ideas* I § 1). It was in this work that Husserl

emphazises the 'worldly' nature of the sciences of the natural attitude and their dogmatic nature, which must now be confronted by a critical turn, activated by an *epoché* or 'suspension', which puts out of play all worldly positings of consciousness in order to grasp its very essence. This work is extraordinarily ambitious in that it even attempts to lay the groundwork for a phenomenology of reason. In *Ideas* I § 49, Husserl introduces a thought experiment concerning the possible **annihilation** or **dissolution of the world**. He maintains that consciousness cannot be thought away in such an experiment and hence must be understood as having 'absolute being' whereas reality has to be understood as dependent being. Husserl also styles the world of consciousness as 'immanent' being. Lived experiences are understood to be 'immanent' whereas transcendent perception are those where the object is given in **adumbrations**; a lived experience is not given in adumbrations (*Ideas* I § 42), but is as it is perceived. Husserl also gives prominence to the presence of the pure **ego** in consciousness, also known as the **cogito** (*Ideas* I § 37; § 46). Husserl's *Ideas* I was reviewed positively by **Paul Natorp** who saw Husserl as moving towards a reconciliation with **Kant** through his presentation of phenomenology as a form of **transcendental philosophy**. Contrariwise, *Ideas* I caused consternation among Husserl's realist followers who thought he had strayed from the realism of the *Logical Investigations*. Heidegger criticized Husserl's account of **consciousness** as immanent and absolute as a continuation of the presuppositions of Cartesian metaphysics. Husserl did not publish another book for over a decade and for many philosophers *Ideas* I (1913) remained the definitive introduction to Husserl's phenomenology. In 1931 *Ideas* I was translated into English by Boyce-Gibson and Husserl wrote an author's preface to the translation. In 1950 *Ideas* I was translated into French by Paul **Ricoeur**.

Ideas Pertaining to a Pure Phenomenology and to a Phenomenological Philosophy, Second Book (Ideen zu einer reinen Phänomenologie und phänomenologischen Philosophie. Zweites Buch: Phänomenologische Untersuchungen zur Konstitution, Ideen II/Ideas II)   See also **Ideas Pertaining to a Pure Phenomenology and to a Phenomenological Philosophy, First Book**

Ideas Pertaining to a Pure Phenomenology and to a Phenomenological Philosophy, Second Book or *Ideas* II, a set of studies in the phenomenology of **constitution**, is one of Husserl's most original and successful works although it was published posthumously. Husserl made an initial draft in 1912, just after he had written *Ideas* I, and from 1916 to 1918 his assistant **Edith Stein** worked on the manuscript incorporating new material on the nature of **spirit** (as found in Section Three). A later assistant, Ludwig Landgrebe, also worked on the manuscript in consultation with Husserl from 1925 until 1928. It was finally published in 1952 edited by Marly Biemel. *Ideas* II begins with the discussion of the 'idea of **nature**' in general and then goes on to discuss material, animal and human nature, the last being the realm of personhood and spirit. In discussing the nature of the personal 'I', Husserl discusses the manner in which we relate to our living animate bodies and to the surrounding world. Husserl's account of the constitution of the **lived body** has been very influential especially his account of the double sensation and the intertwining of the senses of sight and touch. Husserl also talks about the role of **kinaesthetic sensations**. **Heidegger** acknowledges the importance of the *Ideas* II manuscript in *Being and Time* and Maurice **Merleau-Ponty** read the typescript of *Ideas* II in the Husserl Archives in 1939 and was deeply influenced by it. In *Ideas* II, Husserl introduces the idea of **motivation** as the law of spirit. He also distinguishes the **naturalistic attitude** from the **personalistic attitude.**

Ideation (*Ideation*)   See also **essential insight, intuition**

In general the term 'ideation' is used in **psychology** to refer to the process of forming ideas, e.g. suicidal ideation refers to the process of entertaining thoughts of suicide. Husserl uses the term only occasionally in the *Logical Investigations* and elsewhere (see *Ideas* I § 3, in which he identifies ideation with eidetic seeing; and *Phenomenological Psychology*, Hua IX 83). He describes ideation as a kind of direct non-sensuous seeing that takes place at the level of intellection and is directed at universals or essences. In *Ideas* I, Husserl says that he used the term ideation in LU for an eidetic seeing that grasped the essence in an adequate way, but now he wants to use the term more broadly to include even vague apprehension of the essence. Ideation involves grasping a concept and may proceed either through abstractive **generalization** or through **formalization**. There is a different kind of ideation involved in abstraction than in **eidetic insight** (*Ideas* I § 74).

Image (*Bild*)   See also **image consciousness**

Husserl is critical of the view that lived experiences or conscious episodes should be understood, as the classical empiricists did, as inner images or representations. He was interested in the status of physical images that can be perceived not just as physical objects but as images precisely through a unique form of consciousness which he called **image consciousness (*Bildbewusstsein*)**, a particularly complex mental process whereby we see a picture as a picture. For instance, we can look at a postcard of a bridge and see that is a physical piece of cardboard but also that it is an image or picture of a bridge (what Husserl calls the 'subject' or theme of the picture). Normally the perception of the physical image is suppressed and only the image as represented (the 'image object') is seen. Picture consciousness is a particular kind of 'seeing-in' (Husserl's term) as described in aesthetics according to which a particular material composition (photograph, painting, sculpture) is understood as a figure of a certain kind. This 'image object' is described by Husserl as non-real and as a kind of 'nullity' or 'absence'.

Image consciousness (*Bildbewusstsein*)   See also **fantasy, image, memory perception, presentification**

Along with **memory** and **fantasy**, image consciousness is a form of presentification or 'presentiation'. For Husserl, image consciousness (*Bildbewusstsein*) is a kind of **presentification** but it also involves a **perception**, where what is actually intended is not the same as what is sensuously presented. For instance, in looking at a photograph of a person, we actually see first and foremost that *person* but this 'seeing' is founded on the actual perceptual seeing of the photograph (as a piece of paper with colour on it). In the **Logical Investigations**, Husserl distinguishes between perceiving, imagining, 'picture consciousness' (*Bildbewusstsein*) and sign consciousness or 'signitive consciousness' (LU V § 14). He later elaborated on these mental acts in his lectures in Göttingen (see especially Hua XXIII). Fantasy is a certain way of orientating oneself towards something that is not asserted as existing. Image consciousness (or 'depicting consciousness', *Bildbewusstsein*) is a new kind of representative consciousness but a very complex one. It is a specific modality of consciousness. The error of modern philosophy had to been to misconstrue perception itself as an image consciousness. In fact, perception and image consciousness are entirely different constitutional processes (*Ideas* I, III/1 186). To say that perception involves depiction would lead to an infinite regress. According to Husserl, seeing a photograph or a postcard with the picture of a bridge on it, involves both seeing a physical object and imaging a picture (of a bridge). There is a blend of perceiving and imaging. The photograph is a genuine object that is perceived (XXIII 19). It is a kind of paper, can be felt, tasted, etc. But it is a special kind of physical thing: a 'picture thing' (*Bildding*, XXIII 489). The actual 'image' on the photograph – the bridge – floats somewhat free of the physical object and is an appearance. In his lectures of 1904/1905, Husserl calls the image itself the 'representing object' (*das repräsentierende Objekt*) or the 'image object' (*Bildobjekt*, XXIII 19). It is distinct from the actual object presented (the real bridge which the photograph shows), which Husserl often calls the 'subject' of the picturing (*Bildsujet*, XXIII 489). The picture object is an 'apparent thing' (*Scheinding*, XXIII 19), belonging to the 'world of appearance' (*Scheinwelt*) yet it appears as vividly as a perceptual object. Husserl says it is not a real part of the physical object. The colours and lines are real **parts** of the photograph but the image object is not a real part of it. Husserl sees the image as a kind of 'nullity' (*Nichtigkeit*, see XI 351), as is an image in fantasy. Image consciousness differs from fantasy in that fantasy needs no physical substrate or support (*Bildding*). The fantasy is not based on a physical object and indeed belongs within consciousness itself. Moreover, the image does not survive the end of the act of imagining or fantasizing, whereas a picture based on a physical object does survive. The picturing thing is in a different time and space from the physical object (XXIII 537). It is an ideal object. A picture consciousness is also different from the consciousness of an illusion (XXIII 486). A statue is not an illusion; it is a real object grasped in perception, but also there is picture consciousness operating that sees it as a statue of, say, Napoleon. When we look at a wax figure in a wax museum, knowing what I am experiencing, then I see it as *representing* a woman. But I can even be mistaken and perceive it simply as a woman (cf. LU V; also Hua XI 350–52; XXIII 487). In that case, it is an instance of straight perception, but it is illusory. Only after the assumed object has 'exploded' and we see it as a wax figure on which is superimposed the figure of a woman we have a more complex situation, part perception and part image consciousness.

Imaginative free variation (*Phantasievariation, freie Variation, Variation*)   See also **eidetic insight**, *eidos*, **essence, fantasy**
The concept of 'free variation' (CM Hua I 167), 'imaginative variation'

(*Phantasievariation*; Hua IX 74), or 'free arbitrary variation', 'eidetic variation', or 'free fantasy', is central to Husserl's methodology for moving from the individual instance to the viewing of essence, but it is rarely discussed in detail in his writings. The main treatments of the topic are in **Phenomenological Psychology** (1925, see especially *Phen. Psych.*, § 9 53–65; Hua IX 72–87) and **Experience and Judgment** (1938). Imaginative free variation plays an essential role in allowing the **eidos** or **essence** of the **phenomenon** to manifest itself as the structure of its essential possibilities, what is invariant across all possible variation. Husserl is concerned that the imaginative variation be 'pure' (*rein*), i.e., unconstrained by reference to actual existence and by assumptions concerning the real features of actually existing objects or processes. The particular example chosen at the beginning is supposed to be irrelevant (Hua IX 74). The aim is to free oneself from all constraints from the world and to proceed in the realm of pure possibility. Husserl distinguishes imaginative variation from alteration (which involves changing real parts of the object under consideration, Hua IX 75). In **Phenomenological Psychology**, he gives the example of beginning with a specific shade of red and running though variations until one arrives at the *eidos* red (Hua IX 82). In the **Cartesian Meditations**, Husserl gives the example of seeking the essence of an act of perceiving. Beginning with any current perception, e.g. seeing a table (even one carried out in imagination, i.e. imagining *seeing a table*), one then seeks to alter the constituent parts of the object, while retaining the perceiving element in the act. The essential features are those which cannot be varied in our imagination. Husserl writes:

> Starting from this table perception as an example, we vary the
> perceptual object, table, with a completely free optionalness,
> yet in such a manner that we keep perception fixed as percep-
> tion of something, no matter what. Perhaps we begin by
> fictionally changing the shape or the colour of the object quite
> arbitrarily ... In other words: Abstaining from acceptance of its
> being, we change the fact of this perception into a pure possi-
> bility, one among other quite 'optional' pure possibilities – but
> possibilities that are possible perceptions. We so to speak, shift
> the actual perception into the realm of non-actualities, the
> realm of the as-if. (CM § 34, 60; Hua I 104)

Imaginative free variation takes aspects of our original intuition and substitutes parts in a manner that allows the essence to come into view and anything merely contingent to drop away. The whole point of free variation is to open up new aspects of the experience and especially those invariant aspects – aspects which belong to the essence of the experience. Husserl distinguishes *variation* from **generalization**. Pure universals are arrived at by free variation whereas empirical universals are arrived at by inductive generalization. The concept of *variation* as a way of arriving at what is truly universal and necessary is already mentioned in the **Logical Investigations** (LU III § 5) and it is discussed under the title of imagination or **fantasy** in *Ideas* I. Husserl recognizes that there cannot be an endless entertaining of individual examples. It is enough to see the *identity* of the essence in question and to recognize that the process of examining examples can go on endlessly. There is an 'open infinity' of examples but once one has insight that none of these examples threatens the identity of the essence and that it is pointless to continue (to keep performing 'and so on), then the essence has been arrived at. The variation is supposed to be completely arbitrary (retaining no links with actuality) but there are problems deciding, for instance, what object to start with and how to isolate the properties to be varied. In this regard, the method of eidetic variation has been criticized as circular: one must know what **type** the instance falls under in order to vary it to find the **essence**. In *Phenomenological Psychology*, Husserl gives the example of starting with a tone, but how do I know my original example is a *tone* at all?

Immanence (*Immanenz*)   See also **transcendence**

The term 'immanence' has several senses for Husserl. It is used primarily to refer to the manner in which **consciousness**, its **lived experiences** and intentional objects are to be understood after the **phenomenological reduction**. Husserl contrasts immanence with **transcendence** and speaks of **phenomenology** as proceeding in immanence. After the **reduction**, the entities in **consciousness** and even the **ego** itself has to be understood as a 'transcendence in immanence' or 'immanent transcendence' (*immanente Transzendenz*; CM § 47). Husserl criticizes the misleading and false conception of immanence found in modern philosophy after Descartes. In his **Idea of Phenomenology** (1907), Husserl rejects as absurd the modern philosophical understanding of immanence as meaning that the objects of knowledge are apprehended as representations in **consciousness** and that it is the task of **epistemology** to determine how these representations point beyond themselves to the transcendent objects in the world. Husserl claims phenomenology offers a new conception of immanence and of 'transcendence within immanence' (CM Hua I 169). Husserl often speaks of the Cartesian return to the pure or 'primordial' immanence of the *cogito*. Self-experience is a domain of pure immanence and Husserl speaks of the importance of a new 'inner psychology' (*Innenpsychologie*) to explore this domain.

Inauthentic presentations   See **genuine presentations**

Indication (*Anzeichen*)   See also **expression, sign, signitive intention**
In the First Logical Investigation, Husserl distinguishes between **expression** and **indication**. Indicative signs merely point to their object without the mediation of a meaning. All **signs** (*Zeichen*) signify 'something'. Some signs operate purely as 'indications' or 'indices' (*Anzeichen*), simply pointing or signalling beyond themselves to something else. Such pointing takes the form of establishing some link between two actually existing things: smoke indicating fire, or a fossil as a sign of a mammal, or a flag standing for a nation, a knot in a handkerchief serving as a reminder, where no intrinsic 'meaning' or 'content' links sign and signified and the 'indicative relation' between sign and the signatum is causal or conventional, that is, external (LU I § 2; see also Hua XXVI § 3) Indications as such do not *express* meanings. Signals are an example of indications.

Inexistence (*Inexistenz*)   See also **Brentano, intentionality**
'Intentional inexistence' (*intentionale Inexistenz*) is the expression used by **Franz Brentano** in *Psychology from an Empirical Standpoint* (1874) to characterize the mode of being of the **intentional object** in the act of intending. An intentional act can be directed to an object which may or may not exist. I can hope that I find the Holy Grail, or search for an ideal partner, entertain the concept of a round square, and so on. 'Inexistence' as used by Brentano is his translation of the medieval Scholastic term *inesse* (literally: 'being-in' or 'indwelling') which was used to express the inherence of an accident *in* a substance, e.g. the manner in which 'whiteness' resides in the 'white paper', or knowledge resides in the knower. The concept 'in' here

does not have spatial connotations but rather expresses dependence. Later in the 1911 Edition of *Psychology from an Empirical Standpoint*, Brentano admitted his earlier account was ambiguous (PES, 180 note), saying he had considered replacing the term 'intentional' with that of 'objective' (another Scholastic technical term) but this would have given rise to more misunderstandings by those who did not appreciate the Scholastic meaning of 'objective being' (*esse objectivum*) the manner in which things are 'objectively' in the mind as opposed to their 'formal being' (*esse formale*), how they exist in reality. This Scholastic distinction is found in Descartes' Third Meditation, for instance. The later Brentano repeatedly emphasized that the intentional object is best described not as a special object with 'inexistence' but as the real object *as thought by* the mind. Frequently Brentano himself invokes Descartes' distinction between objective and formal reality in explanation of the status of the intentional object. In the Fifth Logical Investigation, Husserl expresses his unhappiness with the term 'inexistence', which he thinks in misleading in his discussion of Brentano's conception of intentionality.

Infinity (*Unendlichkeit*)   See also **Cantor,** *Vienna Lecture*

The term 'infinity' (*apeiron*, literally: 'without limit') was introduced by Aristotle in his *Physics*. Aristotle denied that an infinity can be realized actually. Every infinite is only potential, for Aristotle. Actual infinity became a property of God in medieval thought. In medieval mysticism, God is described as an infinite sphere whose centre is everywhere and whose circumference is nowhere. Husserl sees the discovery of infinity as one of the great breakthrough concepts of Greek philosophy (*Crisis* § 9). From early in his career as a mathematician Husserl was interested in **Cantor**'s work on transfinite numbers as well as Brentano's exploration of the notion of infinity. For Husserl, science has to be understood as an infinite project with 'infinite tasks'. Experience has to be understood as an infinite horizon of possible experiences (*Crisis* § 42). Space time in science has to be understood as an infinity over and against the experience of the **life-world**.

Ingarden, Roman (1893–1970)   Polish philosopher and phenomenologist

best known for his writings on metaphysics and aesthetics, Roman Ingarden was born in Krakow in 1893 and studied with Husserl at Göttingen and Freiburg. In 1918 he published his doctoral thesis on Henri Bergson. In

1925 he published his *Habilitation* (written in Poland) entitled 'Essential Questions'. He was a close friend of **Edith Stein** and maintained a steady correspondence with Husserl until the latter's death in 1938. He became a lecturer in philosophy in Lvov, Poland and published two important studies *The Literary Work of Art* (1931, in German) and *The Cognition of the Literary Work* (1936, in Polish). After the war he taught at Jagellonian University, Krakow. He died in 1970. His critique of Husserl's idealism was published as *On the Motives which led Edmund Husserl to Transcendental Idealism*, translated by Arnor Hannibalsson (The Hague: Nijhoff, 1976).

Inner perception (*innere Wahrnehmung*)   See also **Brentano**, *cogitatio*, *cogito*, descriptive psychology, outer perception, perception

Inner perception refers to the manner conscious acts themselves are reflexively grasped while the subject is engaged in acts of external perception. In his *Psychology from an Empirical Standpoint* (1874), **Brentano** advocates a **psychology** based on 'inner perception' (*innere Wahrnehmung*) which he contrasts with inner observation (*innere Beobachtung*) or introspection. Brentano explains his distinction between mental and physical phenomena as follows: 'The object of an inner perception is simply a mental phenomenon, and the object of an external perception is simply a physical phenomenon, a sound, odor, or the like' (PES 210). One cannot *observe* one's own mental states while occupying them. But, by careful training, one can *perceive* one's inner mental states as they engage outer phenomena, and this perception grasps them whole. Brentano maintained that inner perception could intuitively apprehend the 'ultimate mental elements' (PES 45; DP 13), i.e., the real parts of psychic acts. Inner perception yields necessary, apodictic truths. For Brentano, it as a feature of psychic acts that they present with certainty, though that certainty can be overlooked and obscured for various reasons. He writes: 'The thinking thing – the thing that has ideas, the thing that judges, the thing that wills – which we innerly perceive is just what we perceive it to be. But so-called outer perception presents us with nothing that appears the way it really is.' For Brentano, inner perception is an accompanying, concomitant or additional consciousness (*Bewußtseinsnebenbei*), whereby the essential features of the primary act are grasped 'incidentally' (*en parergo*; PES 276). There is no perceiving without the possibility of apperception (DP 171; PES 153). We inwardly perceive only what presents in the now, and in immediate memory. According to Brentano, whatever is given in inner perception is given with certain apodictic **evidence** (**Evidenz**). In the Appendix to the Sixth Logical Investigation and elsewhere, Husserl criticizes Brentano's account of inner perception.

Insight (*Einsicht*)   See also **eidetic insight, evidence, intuition**

Husserl speaks of 'insight' and especially of 'essential insight' as a specific cognitive process whereby some object is apprehended with **evidence**. Insight is a bedrock feature of cognition and, for Husserl, must be given its full due in epistemology. Evidence has to be ground in original experience and insight (Hua I 6). There is insight into logical and mathematical axioms and into our immediate conscious living (see *Ideas* I § 78). The model of apodictic insight is **Descartes'** discovery of the apodictic certain truth of the *cogito ergo sum*.

Instinct (*Instinkt*)   See also **drive, stimulus**

Husserl considers that the ego is a centre of actions and affections and is passively affected by instincts, desires and impulses. There is an *instinctive* self (*Instinkt-Ich*) at the very basis of the **ego** where drives, needs and instincts are working out perhaps without conscious presence. Husserl thought that below our conscious, intentional life there is a complex of instincts that affect and awaken the ego's interest and motivate it to respond. In his research manuscripts, he gave a detailed and extensive account of drives and instincts, chiefly in the C manuscripts, (now published as Husserl, *Materialen Band* VIII). There is a deep instinct to make sense of experience, to connect our temporal experiences into a unity, to retain the stability of past experiences into the future, and so on. Instincts and drives have a kind of *directedness* that can already be characterized as intentional; he refers to this directedness of drives and instincts as 'primal' or 'proto-intentionality'. Husserl therefore occasionally speaks about drive intentionality. This proto-intentionality founds the intentional performances of fully conscious activity. Husserl even speaks of 'transcendental instinct' and of 'instinctive reason'. Life, for Husserl, is always a drive or striving for satisfaction. The manner in which the ego responds to instinctual pulls is, however, very complex and many layered. Instincts can be taken up and interpreted at the level of consciousness and can be acculturated. There is also an instinctive proto-intentionality toward an other, which provides a foundation for the higher level constitutive achievements of intersubjectivity. In Husserl's account, the mother–child relationship is the most fundamental one of all relationships. The child is *instinctively* directed toward his or her mother.

Intending (*Meinen, Meinung*) See also *cogito*, intentionality, meaning

Husserl often used the term *Meinung* (present participle) or the verbal noun *Meinen*, meaning 'to intend' or 'to mean' or 'to refer to', to express the **intentionality** of our conscious states. Intending is a meaning something, a 'wanting-to-say' or 'wanting-to-think' something. Paul Ricoeur translates intentionality as *vouloir-dire*. All conscious acts are intending that intend something (CM § 20). For instance, at CM § 4, Husserl says that 'judging is intending' (*Meinen*). He also speaks of 'pre-intendings' or 'expectant meanings' (*Vormeinen*) and 'accompanying intending or meanings' (*Mitmeinen*) at CM § 15 and elsewhere. All perception involves intending more than is actually explicitly presented, and in this instance Husserl speaks of *Mehrmeinen* (CM, Hua I 84). This intending can be 'empty' or it can be 'full', as when the intended object satisfies the intending with its self-presence, that is, with **evidence**.

Intentional content (*der intentionale Inhalt*)   See also **content, intentional essence, noema, object**

In the Fifth Logical Investigation, Husserl seeks to overcome deficiencies in Brentano's account of intentionality by a series of complex distinctions. **Brentano** loosely referred to what the intentional act aimed at as its '**content**' or '**object**'. Husserl was aware that **content** and **object** can be used in a loose sense to pick out the same objective pole of the act, but that careful further discriminations were needed. Intentional content is an ambiguous term for Husserl. In one sense, 'intentional content' can mean the object intended. Husserl, however, wants to distinguish between the object that is intended and the object as it is intended (the Fifth Logical Investigation § 17). The same object may be intended in different ways, e.g. Napoleon can be presented as 'the victor of Jena' or as 'the vanquished at Waterloo'. The intentional content of an act also includes the **act quality** and the **act matter**. In *Ideas* I, Husserl introduces the notion of the **noema** to overcome ambiguities in the conception of content and object.

Intentional essence (*intentionales Wesen*) See also **intentional content**

According to Husserl's Fifth Logical Investigation (§21 and § 37), the intentional essence of an intentional act is the unity (Husserl even says *identity*) made up of the act's **matter** and the **act quality** as they are combined to form the act's descriptive content. Husserl analyses the intentional **act** in a very complex manner in order to overcome deficiencies in what he takes to be **Brentano**'s dyadic act content scheme. By *intentional essence*, Husserl wants to express the nature of the intentional object of the act as modified by the kind of act (act quality) under which the object is being apprehended. So if the intentional act is 'John imagines a white horse', the intentional essence of the act is not just the intentional object 'white horse' but rather the very specific intentional object, 'white horse as imagined'. There are other aspects of an intentional act – e.g., **sensations** – that do not fall under the notion of 'intentional essence'. Husserl says that intentional essence does not exhaust the act phenomenologically (Fifth Logical Investigation § 21). Husserl also distinguishes between the intentional and the **semantic essence** of the act. The semantic essence is the concrete act of meaning that which in the act allows for the **meaning** to be abstracted. The intentional essence is meant to convey that which allows two acts (Husserl's example is Greenland's icy wastes being thought about by two different people) that are actually individually different in their presentations to be essentially the same. It is not that the two acts need share a common part or even be similar to one another; rather their act qualities and act matters combine to yield the same intentional essence.

Intentional object See **intention, intentional content, noema, object**

Intentionality (*Intentionalität*) See also **correlation, descriptive psychology, noema, noesis, phenomenology**

Intentionality can be described as the 'aboutness' or 'directedness' of our conscious states. The phenomenological approach, for Husserl, broadly means the intentional approach. Husserl even claims that '[i]ntentionality is the title which stands for the only actual and genuine way of explaining, making intelligible' (*Crisis* § 49, p. 168; VI 171). Husserl speaks of the need to go back to the 'intentional origins' and attempt to follow the build-up of sense ('sense formations') that we eventually experience in a completely immediate way as the whole intuited life-world, understood as a nexus or 'framework of meaning' (*Sinnzusammenhang*, *Crisis*, 284; VI 331) or 'meaning structure' (*Sinnbildung*, *Crisis*, 378; VI 386). Husserl inherits the concept of intentionality from **Franz Brentano**, who in turn credits the Scholastics. Husserl begins by specifying what he means by '**consciousness**', bracketing discussion of the relation of conscious acts to an **ego**, and focusing exclusively on the intentional character of conscious experiences deriving from Brentano's rediscovery of intentionality. However, Husserl regards Brentano's characterization of intentionality as misleading and inadequate, trapped inside the old **Cartesian dualism** of subject and object and with all the problems inherent in that representationalist account. Under the notion of 'objectifying act' he offers a more precise account of what Brentano called '**presentation**' (*Vorstellung*), and goes on to address what he calls 'cardinal problem of phenomenology', namely, the doctrine of **judgement** (LU Hua XVIII 14). Husserl is especially critical of the many unsorted out ambiguities in Brentano's foundational concept of 'presentation' (*Vorstellung*) and carefully differentiates between the many senses of the term (LI V § 44), stressing, however, that logic must decide which meaning of 'presentation' is most appropriate for its own needs. Logic does not follow linguistic usage as logical definition is a kind of artifice (LI IV § 3). In *Psychology from an Empirical Standpoint* (1874), Brentano had held that all psychic acts are characterized by 'directedness' or 'aboutness':

> Every mental phenomenon is characterized by what the Scho-
> lastics of the Middle Ages called the intentional (or mental)
> inexistence of an object, and what we might call, though
> not wholly unambiguously, reference to a content, direction
> towards an object (which is not to be understood here as
> meaning a thing), or immanent objectivity. (PES, 88)

In a general sense, every psychic act intends an object, although not necessarily something existent. Husserl paraphrases: 'In perception something is perceived, in imagination, something is imagined, in a statement something stated, in love something loved, in hate hated, in desire, desired, etc.' (LU V § 10, **II** 95; Hua XIX/1 380). Brentano himself came to realize that his expression 'intentional **inexistence**', which he claimed he had used to express the concept of inherence or *inesse* of the Scholastics, had been misunderstood as a special kind of subsistence. In his later writings, he claimed he never intended to say that the intentional object is merely some kind of object in our minds, some purely immanent thing. Husserl rejects Brentano's attempt to distinguish between 'psychical' and 'physical' phenomena, but sees his discovery of intentionality as having independent value (LI V § 9). Husserl is likewise cautious about using Brentano's term **'act'** without qualification, but, above all, wants to avoid misleading talk of 'immanent' objectivity. He insists that all objects of thought – including the objects of fantasy and memory – are *mind transcendent*. Even when I am imagining something non-existent, e.g., if I am thinking of the mythical god Jupiter, that god is not *inside* my thought in any sense, it is not a real element or real part of the experience (LI V § 11). Rather, even fictional objects are *transcendent* above our mental experiences, intentional experience always transcends itself towards the object, its character is a 'pointing beyond itself towards' (*über sich hinausweisen*) something. Husserl offers a new global distinction between the **matter** and the **act quality** of intentional acts. Acts of different quality (judgings, wishings, questionings) may have the same matter. Not all our experiences are intentional in the sense of presenting something to our attention. According to Husserl, **sensations** in themselves are not intentional, they are not the object that we intend, rather they accompany the intentional act and fill it out. Sensations belong to the 'matter' (and are grasped as such only in reflection), whereas the act quality provides the form of the act. Husserl also distinguishes between the contents of the **lived experience** and the properties of the mind-transcendent **object**. When I see an object, I only ever see it from one side, in a certain kind of light, from a certain angle and so on. As I walk around the box for example, I see different **'adumbrations'** (*Abschattungen*) or 'aspects' of the box, and yet I know I am getting glimpses of the same object in the different perceptual acts. The same object is presenting itself to me in different modes. Husserl's distinction in the Fifth Investigation (LI V § 17) between the object which is intended and the particular mode under which it is intended forms the basis for his later distinction between **noesis** and **noema** in *Ideas* I. In his *Formal and Transcendental Logic* (1929), Husserl claimed that Brentano had failed to recognize the true meaning of intentionality because he had not seen it as a 'complex of performances' that end up being layered in sediments in such a way as to make up the unity of the intentional object:

> Brentano's discovery of intentionality never led to seeing in it
> a complex of performances (*Zusammenhang von Leistungen*),
> which are included as *sedimented history* in the currently
> constituted intentional unity and its current manners of given-
> ness – a history *that one can always uncover following a strict
> method*. (FTL § 97, 245; Hua XVII 252)

For Husserl, the most significant and unifying feature of conscious acts is that they are intentional, they aim at some object, they are *about* something. It was Brentano who brought Husserl to recognize that all conscious acts, all mental processes or lived experiences (**Erlebnisse**) to use Husserl's term (also found in Dilthey) have sense or intend towards something (*etwas 'im Sinne zu haben'*, *Ideas* I § 90). Husserl expresses this claim in the *Logical Investigations* as the view that all consciousness consists of a set of meaning intentions (not to be identified with expectations, which are a narrower class of intention) and **fulfilments.** The key to consciousness is the way it 'reaches out beyond' (*hinausreichen*) what it actually experiences, in a kind of 'meaning-beyond-itself' (*hinausmeinen*, LU VI § 10). Husserl often used the term '*Meinung*' or the verb '*meinen*', meaning to 'intend' or 'to mean to refer to', to express the intentionality of our conscious states. Mental acts are content bearing, object-directed acts. They carry some kind of relation (*Beziehung*) to something objective (*ein Gegenständliches*; LU V § 13, **II** 101; Hua XIX/1 392). Furthermore, it is a structural feature of any mental act, for Husserl, that it can be reflected upon and hence function as the object, or as Husserl says the 'target' (*Ideas* I § 98), of another mental act. The reflexive nature of conscious acts is a very important structural feature that allows one to reflect on acts themselves, whereas normally we are preoccupied by the objects disclosed through the acts. Husserl does not offer an explanatory account of how it is that our minds are able to hook onto the world. Husserl just assumes that we can make intentional reference. His interest is rather in a taxonomy of myriad kinds of intentional reference and an account of the a priori structural laws governing intentional acts. This is the domain of **descriptive psychology** and later of what Husserl came to call '**phenomenology**'. Husserl's main critique of Brentano is that the latter thought that all modes of intentional presentation were the same whereas he diagnosed myriad different kinds. Later on Husserl speaks on intentionality more generally in terms of an **a**

priori correlation between world and subject. The key to intentionality is that phenomenology is an accomplishment or **achievement** of subjectivity. As Husserl asserts: '[A]ll real, mundane objectivity is constituted accomplishment' (*Crisis* § 58, p. 204; VI 208).

Interpretation (*Interpretation, Deutung, Auffassung*) See also apprehension, hermeneutics, matter, sensation

In the Sixth Logical Investigation (LU VI § 26), Husserl states that, in the different forms of intuiting, there are different complex relations between interpretative grasp and its **matter**. For instance, purely **signitive intention** needs no relation between the sensuous marks and the intended object to make the objective attribution; whereas in other forms of **presentification** some kind of internal relation (based on similarity and resemblance) is necessary. In general, Husserl does not discuss in detail what he means by 'interpretation', other than to suggest that it is an *intuitive* grasp or apprehension that does not involve inference or reasoning.

Intersubjectivity (*Intersubjektivität*) See also solipsism, transcendental intersubjectivity

The term 'intersubjectivity' has its origins in German Idealism, especially Fichte. Husserl employs the term already in his Göttingen lectures of 1910–11 (*Basic Problems of Phenomenology*) and discusses it in depth in his *Cartesian Meditations*. He links the issue to overcoming the problem of 'transcendental **solipsism**'. Husserl's research manuscripts, especially those now published as the volumes on intersubjectivity, contain a rich amount of material on this topic. In the *Crisis*, the phenomenon of cooperating intersubjectivity is read back from the experience of a common world 'for all':

> Constantly functioning in wakeful life, we also function to-
> gether, in the manifold ways of considering, together, valuing,
> planning, acting together. (*Crisis* § 28, 109; VI 111)

This is the domain of what Husserl calls 'we-subjectivity' (*Wir-Subjektivität*, *Crisis*, 109; VI 111) and which he regards as inaccessible to traditional psychological reflection since it is always presumed by the psychological approach (*Crisis* § 59). Husserl had already addressed the problematic of the communicative function of speech in his First Logical Investigation. The experience of the 'other ego' is a problem he encountered already in the work of **Theodor Lipps**.

Intuition (*Anschauung*) See also **categorical intuition, eidetic intuition, givenness, principle of principles**
The German term *Anschauung* is formed for the German word meaning 'to see', 'to watch', 'to look at' (*schauen*) just as the Latin *intuitus* is related to the verb, *intuire*, to see. **Kant** distinguished sharply between two separate faculties – *sensibility* (*Sinnlichkeit*) and *understanding* (*Verstand*). These two faculties provide two distinct 'sources of knowledge' for Kant. Kant introduces the term 'intuition' in place of the more usual '**sensation**' (*Empfindung*) because he wants to be able to say that space and time are apprehended in intuitions and not through sensations. For Kant, intuitions have both matter and form. The matter is 'the raw stuff of sensory impressions' and the form is space and time. According to Kant, the combination of the sensory impressions into a manifold cannot be the work of the sensory impressions themselves but must come from the form of intuition. Kant claims to have shown that human beings have only sensible intuition and he denied that human beings had the capacity for *intellectual intuition*. For Kant, the introduction of the distinction between intuitions and concepts was a way of separating himself from the Leibnizian–Cartesian heritage according to which sensations were considered to be 'confused thoughts'. Descartes included sensation and imagination in his list of mental, thinking activities in the *Second Meditation*. For **Descartes**, sensing (*sentire*) is a 'special mode of thinking'. In the *Logical Investigations*, Husserl offers a complete reworking of Kant's distinction between intuitions and concepts. Husserl begins with the notion of sensuous intuition as an immediate grasping of the object as in direct perception but he expands the notion of intuition to include non-sensuous **categorial intuitions**. According to Husserl, cognitions are to be related back to 'primal sources' (*Urquellen*) in 'giving intuitions' (*Ideas* I § 1; III/1 7). Immediate seeing consists not only of sensuous seeing but is to be understood as original, giving intuition of whatever kind appropriate to the level of cognition involved (*Ideas* I § 19). Husserl speaks of an 'originary giving intuition' as the basis of all **knowledge**.

— J —

Judgement (*Urteil*), judging (*Urteilen*)   See also **apophantic logic, presentation, proposition, state of affairs**

Husserl's account of judgement is shaped by his studies in logic (**Bolzano, Lotze**) as well as his understanding of the theories of judgement found in Aristotle, **Descartes, Kant** and in **Brentano**. Husserl developed his theory of judgements in opposition to Franz Brentano, who had challenged the traditional notion of judgement as a synthesis of subject and predicate, and had interpreted the judgement 'the sky is blue' as an asserting or positing of 'blue sky'. Brentano maintained a judgement consisted of giving or withholding one's assent to a **presentation**. Judging was a kind of 'yes-saying' or 'no-saying' to a presentation. When I think or say 'the sky is blue' I am affirming the blue-sky presentation. In the *Logical Investigations*, Husserl that the fundamental structure of *judgements* in a manner opposed to Husserl denies that judgements can be treated as nominal acts, as simply *naming* complex states of affairs (LU V § 17). We can, of course, turn a judgement into a nominal act, by nominalizing the content of the judgement. This belongs as an a priori essential possibility to judgements (LI V § 36). So, to the judgement 'the cat is black' corresponds the **nominalization** 'the cat's being black' which can then function as the basis for further judgements. But this internal relation between judging and nominalizing does not mean that they are essentially the same kind of act. Husserl, following Bolzano, declares judgements to be essentially different from presentations. Judgements *assert* something to be the case (LI V § 33). A judgement *articulates* and specifies in a 'many-rayed act' the parts of the situation that a nominalizing act presents in a 'single-rayed act', as Husserl puts it. The relation between **presentation** and **judgement** is not as described by Brentano except to say that a judgement is founded on a presentation. The object of a judgement is an 'affairs complex', a **state of affairs** or '**situation**' (*Sachlage*). Husserl developed his most detailed account of judging in his *Formal and Transcendental Logic*. For Husserl, judgement involves a stance or **position taking** on the part of the judger. A judgement then involves (as Descartes thought), an act of **will**. Judgements can become sedimented. I can be someone who **believes in** global warming. My becoming 'thus and so' decided can be life changing.

It can become an abiding **conviction** (Überzeugung). Judgement is crucially important for knowledge and for human beings as rational subjects. Our life is a striving for cognition and that means a striving for judgements. Husserl speaks of our 'judicative life'. Judgement is linked to **truths** and with establishing as valid (APS 97; Hua XI 56). He approaches judgement as a higher order activity that builds on the more basic acts of perceiving, imagining, remembering, etc. He makes many attempts to develop a phenomenology of judgement (e.g. LU VI, APS, FTL and finally in EU). Already in LU, he had been concerned to distinguish **perception** from judgement as acts with essentially different structures. Although perceptions may very well motivate judgements, they are not judgements. They are different forms of **intentionality** (APS, 94; Hua XI 54), although clearly there are, for Husserl as for Kant, perceptual judgements, judgements of perception, as a distinct and important class. Previous philosophers have not made much progress in the theory of judgement precisely because they misconstrue the subjective dimension of judging (FTL § 85). The act of judging has been confused with the judged proposition. While he has much to say about the structure of the judged, the 'proposition', especially in earlier years, in phenomenological terms, he is specifically interested in the judgement as a performance, as an egoic act of position taking, as a categorial activity, an act of *kategorein*, accusation (EU § 47, 198; 233). Judgements are voluntary acts of the will, and when I retain a judgement, I *will* it continuously (EU § 48). He also employs Kantian terms, whereas perception belongs to receptivity, judging is a higher order activity of 'predicative spontaneity' (EU § 49). Judging is essentially involved with conceptualization and **generalization**. When I judge S is red, there is already involved a relation to redness, and an essential generality (EU § 49), although this generality ('redness') is not explicitly thematized. Husserl begins from the simplest cases of judgement, namely the perceptual judgement, which he takes to be a categorial formation of the form S is P, where a certain objective unity S is focused on and enriched by having a predicate P asserted of it. In APS and EU, he discusses how continuous perception where there is a sharpening of focus on a property of the object is the intuitional basis for this kind of perceptual judgement, e.g. looking at a copper bowl, we let our glance run over it and we can tarry over distinctive features and examine them singly but we remain consciousness of the abiding unity of the object itself:

> In all this we are continually oriented toward the entire object;
> we have apprehended it and hold fast to it as a thematic sub-
> strate. (EU § 24, 117, 130)

From such perceptual chains the concept 'subject' emerges, as does the concept 'predicate'. Indeed, Husserl maintains all the conceptual categories involved in judgement have their foundation in 'pre-predicative experience':

> It is true, we can only begin to speak of logical categories in
> the proper sense in the sphere of predicative judgment ... But
> all categories and categorial forms which appear there are
> erected on the prepredicative syntheses and have their origin
> in them. (EU § 24, 115, 127)

This is the basis for his 'genealogy' (his term) of the forms of judgement in FTL and EU. Husserl criticizes Brentano's view of judgement as the approval (*Anerkennung*) of or 'yes-saying' to – or denial of or no-saying' to – a presentation. Judgement cannot be construed as a certain attitude of belief supervening on the presentation of an object. For a start, while judgement has an act-object intentional structure, the object of a judgement is a 'state of affairs' or 'fact that something is the case' and not a simple object or cluster of objects as in a perception (LU V § 28). But in LU, Husserl is mainly concerned to articulate the object of a judgement (a state of affairs) and its content (what is judged, the 'proposition') as something ideal. Against Frege and Brentano, Husserl revives the Aristotelian account of judgement as a relation between subject and predicate. More clearly than Aristotle, he emphasizes that judgement is a *positing* and not just an entertaining of a proposition. It is a thetic act. Judgement is involved in positing or 'constituting' higher order categorical objectivities ('that the cat is on the mat'). In FTL, Husserl speaks of these constituted objects of judgement as irreal: 'in judging, something irreal becomes intentionally constituted' (FTL § 63). In his later discussions, Husserl focuses a great deal on the different levels of conviction that a judgement can articulated with respect to the situation judged. Judgement in the true 'predicative' sense is founded on modalities present in perception and the 'sense certainty' of perception:

What one so hotly debated under the rubric of the theory of
judgment in the newer logical movement since Mill, Brentano
and Sigwart is at its core nothing other than the phenomenological clarification of the essence of the logical function of the
certainty of being and the modalities of being. (APS 66; Hua
XI 28)

Judgement only emerges from perception when there is a 'splitting' of the
perception so that a certain part of its content is offered ambiguously and
calls for a decision. The 'concordant' perception 'harbours' a decision (APS
104; Hua XI 63). But perceptions themselves do not harbour judgements.
The empty intuitive grasp of the non-presented side of an object is not
a matter of inference. Husserl does not accept the view that all seeing is
propositional 'seeing-that', e.g. seeing *that the ball is uniformly spherical
and green*. Seeing is a living experience of being in the presence of the
object. It is not yet the yea-saying affirmation of the object, but it provides
the foundation for such an affirmation:

When it [the ego] simply perceives, when it is merely aware,
apprehending what is there and what, of itself, is presented
in experience by itself, there is no motive for taking a position
provided that nothing else is present. (APS 93; Hua XI 53)

In part, Husserl thinks that the difference between perception and judging
has to do with the role of the ego. Judging is an activity of the ego (FTL
§ 63; EU § 47). It is a specific act of position taking that requires a certain
amount of uncertainty, of opposing motives being in play. Judging can arise
'in the primordial sphere of a motivating perception' but that is only when
a conflict has been apprehended. In ordinary 'smooth' perceptions where
no conflicts present themselves, there is no role for the ego. Judging, by
way of contrast, requires active appropriation on the side of the ego. When
I judge something to be valid, it becomes an abiding part of my convictions; it is accepted by me as settled. Perceptions are not incorporated in
the same way, but have to be continually renewed. There is a different
temporal reference in perception in comparison with judgement (if I break
off a perception, I still have perceived the object; if I break off in the middle
of judging, the judgement is not actualized). Judgings have different levels

of clarity and distinctness. A judgement can be completely vague FTL § 16)
and it can progress or be articulated into clarity.

—K—

Kaizo articles, 1923/1924   See also **renewal**
In 1923/1924 Husserl contributed three articles on the theme of *renewal*
(*Erneuerung*) to a Japanese intellectual journal, *Kaizo* ('Renewal', now
reprinted in Hua XXVII), to which Heinrich **Rickert** and Bertrand Russell
had also contributed. Husserl's theme was the **renewal** of philosophy
and science through the creation of a universal moral order, and through
a surpassing of narrow nationalisms in order to found true community in
shared interests. Here, echoing the mood of many Germans, he bemoaned
the appalling state of affairs in the Weimar Republic where 'psychological
tortures' and economic humiliation had replaced war. Husserl saw the only
hope for overcoming *Realpolitik* and rebuilding the confidence of a people
was through a spiritual retrieval of the human sense of purpose, a renewal
of the ideals of the European Enlightenment (which culture, in his opinion,
Japan had recently joined). Of course, this renewal consisted in philosophy
as a rigorous science, but now a science of the human spirit was needed to
complement and give moral purpose to the exact sciences. Husserl proposes
'the a priori science of the essence of human spirituality' (HSW 329; Hua
XXVII 9). Human beings are in essence rational animals:

> The human being is called *animal rationale* not merely because
> he has the capacity of reason and then only occasionally regu-
> lates and justifies his life according to the insights of reason,
> but because the human being proceeds always and every-
> where in his entire, active life in this way. (XXVII 33)

This rationality emerges in practical striving that has given itself the goal
of reason, which in its ideal limit, is also the idea of God (XXVII 34). 'All

specifically personal life is active life and stands as such under the essential norms of reason' (XXVII 41). Essentially, in these years Husserl was developing his philosophy as a kind of 'higher humanism', a vision he would develop in his last work, **Crisis** (1936).

Kant, Immanuel (1724–1804)   Immanuel Kant was born in Königsberg, Prussia, in 1724 into a strictly religious Pietist family. He lived all his life in Königsberg and studied and taught at the university there. He initially was formed in late Scholastic philosophy and in the work of Leibniz. He claimed to have been awoken around 1771 from his 'dogmatic slumbers' by **Hume**'s scepticism. He went on to write the three critiques for which he is famous, including the first critique – The Critique of Pure Reason (1781; 2nd edition 1787). Kant advocated a critical philosophy that inquired into the conditions for the possibility of objective knowledge. He advocated a **transcendental idealism**, claiming that space and time are the forms of sensible intuition rather than simply existing independently as part of the world. Kant claimed all human knowledge has only two sources – sensibility and understanding – and he dismissed the possibility of a purely intellectual intuition. Husserl's relationship with Kant is complex and evolved over his life. Initially, Husserl followed **Brentano** in being dismissive of Kant. But in his early years in Göttingen, especially after 1905, Husserl began to engage with Kant in his lectures and seminars. Thus, for example, in his 1907 **The Idea of Phenomenology** lectures, he acknowledges the affinity between his own problematic and that discussed by Kant in his Prolegomena to Any Future Metaphysics, namely, how objectivity comes into play in the difference between judgements of perception and judgements of experience. But Husserl distinguishes himself from Kant, who could not free himself from the grip of '**psychologism** and **anthropologism**':

> Kant did not arrive at the ultimate intent of the distinction that must be made here. For us it is not a matter of merely subjectively valid judgements, the validity of which is limited to the empirical subject, and objectively valid judgements in the sense of being valid for every subject in general. For we have excluded the empirical subject: and transcendental apperception, consciousness as such, will soon acquire for us a wholly different sense, one that is not mysterious at all. (IP, pp. 36–7; Hua II 48)

Similarly, in his *Thing and Space* lectures of 1907 he denies that he is posing the problematic of the constitution of objectivity in terms of Kant's question (in his famous *Letter to Markus Herz* of 1772), how subjective representations reach outside themselves to gain knowledge of the object. To pose the question in this way is already to surrender to representationalism. As Husserl says, such questions are 'perversely posed' (DR § 40, p. 117; Hua XVI 140). It is not the existence of the perceived that is in question for Husserl but the *essence* of perception or cognition and the *essence* of the perceived thing or the cognised thing as such. As he will later say in the *Crisis*: 'The point is not to secure objectivity but to understand it' (Hua VI 193).

In this sense, Husserl agrees with Kant that a 'transcendental' inquiry is one which seeks 'conditions of possibility'. Husserl treats Kant extensively in his *First Philosophy* lectures of 1923/1924 as well as in the *Crisis*. Husserl sees Kant as recognizing that naive **objectivism** ignores the role of anonymous functioning subjectivity. Kant was right to seek the subjective conditions of the objectively experienced world (*Crisis* § 29). Husserl criticizes Kant for not taking seriously the need to explore the realm of the transcendental ego uncovered first by Descartes. Kant did recognize the role of 'knowing subjectivity' (*Crisis* § 27) but he remained imprisoned in his own naturalistic preconceptions whereby he understood this subjectivity in a psychological sense. As a result Kant never uncovered the anonymous structures of the **life-world** and never made the appearance of the world problematic. Kant also postulated mythical entities such as faculties and 'things in themselves' that Husserl rejected as absurd. There are many areas where Husserl comes close to Kant especially in his recognition of the role of **synthesis, time consciousness** and the **transcendental ego.**

Kaufman, Felix (1895–1949) Felix Kaufmann was born in Vienna and graduated in jurisprudence and philosophy from the University of Vienna. He an enthusiastic reader of Husserl's phenomenology, attended meetings of the circles around Hans Kelsen (his doctoral supervisor), the economist Von Mises, and the group that eventually became known as the Vienna Circle. Kaufmann had a significant influence on the social phenomenology of the young **Alfred Schütz,** and his book on the *Infinite in Mathematics and its Exclusion* (1930) was highly regarded by Husserl. Kaufmann often discussed Husserl at meetings of the Vienna Circle (supposedly much to the annoyance of Schlick and some others) and also wrote on the relations between phenomenology and logical empiricism. In 1938 Kaufmann emigrated to the United States where, as an academic (teaching law and philosophy) at the New School for Social Research, he wrote several papers on the relation between phenomenology and analysis and, indeed, debated with his fellow émigré **Rudolf Carnap** on the nature of induction and truth in the pages of the **newly founded Philosophy and Phenomenological Research**. It is clear from this exchange that Carnap respected Kaufmann and that Kaufmann was recognized as an influential mediator between phenomenology and the emergent logical positivist tradition. He contributed an important paper, 'Phenomenology and Logical Empiricism', to *Philosophical Essays in Memory of Edmund Husserl*, edited by Marvin Farber in 1940. In particular, Kaufmann defended Husserl's concept of **eidetic insight**, *Wesensshau,* against **Moritz Schlick**'s criticisms (which we discuss later), and argued that Husserl's concept of **evidence** (*Evidenz*) had been misunderstood by those critics who regarded it as a subjective feeling of certainty.

Kinaesthetic sensations (*kinästhetische Empfindungen*) See also **sensation, sensings**
Kinaesthetic sensations or ***Kinaestheses*** are those sensations in which I move myself, i.e. 'sensations' by which I am aware of movements on and in my body (sometimes these are called 'motor sensations'). This term was frequently employed by nineteenth-century German, British and American psychologists (e.g. Müller, Münsterberg, William James), not just Husserl. The term 'kinaesthetic sensations' is somewhat inexact and Husserl himself is not consistent in his terminology. It is not clear, for instance, if kinaesthetic sensations include all proprioceptive experiences, including muscle sensations, experiences of effort, force, balance, and so on, or only those experiences that contribute to perception and movement. He speaks of 'sensations, 'complexes', 'circumstances', 'appearances', 'processes', 'kinaestheses' (*Crisis* § 47), 'kinaesthetics processes', 'systems', and so on. Following German psychology, Husserl, somewhat misleadingly, calls these 'kinaesthetic' sensations, by which he seems to mean that they are sensations of movement (*kinesis*) than can be freely undertaken (although they are not fully modes of will, XV 330). In EU he writes:

> We call these movements, which belong to the essence of
> perception and serve to bring the object of perception to
> givenness from all sides in so far as possible, *kinaestheses*. (EU
> § 19, p. 84; 89)

They are ordered into systems:

> In this way, from the ordered system of sensations in eye
> movement, in head movement freely moved, etc., there unfold
> such and such series in vision … An apprehension of a thing
> as situated at such a distance … is unthinkable, as can be
> seen, without these sorts of relations of motivation. (*Ideas* II §
> 18, p. 63; Hua IV 58)

With regard to the 'kinaesthetic', Husserl is not referring to the physiological movements of the body (the physical range of movements of
which the body is capable) but rather our first-person experiential sense of
the moving of our eyes, tilting and turning the head, looking up or down,
and so on, especially in so far as those movements are *freely* undertaken.
Husserl uses the term to the experiences as of moving one's head etc. he
also refers to seeing, hearing, as well as lifting, carrying, pushing, and so
on (*Crisis* § 28). In this sense, for Husserl, the lived body is a 'freely moved
sense organ' (*Ideas* II 61; IV 56). Of course, when the barber moves my
head, there is still an element of freedom in that I choose to *cooperate*
and not stiffen the neck muscles but his act of turning and tilting my
head is not the same as one I undertake myself. Sometimes he speaks
about these as 'internal' sensations in contrast to the actual movements
performed in the real world. A kinaesthetic sensation, for Husserl, must
have its 'locus' or 'position' (*Stellung*) in a particular part of the body; it
also has the character of 'I can' and it can be controlled through 'practice'
(Übung). Husserl speaks about 'kinaesthetic processes' at *Crisis* § 47 that
have the character 'I do' and 'I move' or even 'I hold still'. There are internal
kinaesthetic processes corresponding to external bodily movements. Husserl
speaks here of a 'two-sided character' (VI 164). Continuing to fix my eyes
on something requires a conscious act of attending or 'concentrating'. In
turning my head, I have an expectation of perceptual continuity of a certain
kind. There is an 'if-then' character to my perceptual experience; a system

of kinaesthetic capacities that are at the back of every perceptual certainty. There is a strict correlation between the series of kinaestheses and the series of appearances of the object. Husserl uses the term 'kinaesthesis' for the ego's own motility (see *Crisis*, 106; VI 108). It covers much of our experience of ruling over or **governing** the living body, 'holding sway' (*walten*, *Crisis* § 28; § 62). My relation to my kinaestheses is one of immediacy and familiarity. I know what moving my eyes and head feel like but I also know to move them to inspect the object from a particular viewpoint. My holding sway is peculiar to each kind of perception (*Crisis* § 62): seeing with the eyes, touching with the fingers. My kinaestheses are not exactly in space like the movements of my body. They are only indirectly 'colocalized' in the movement (§ 62, p. 217; VI 221). My kinaestheses go to make up the experience of objective space so they cannot themselves be objectively spatial in the same way.

Knowing or recognition (*Erkennen*)   See also **achievement, epistemology, fulfilment, knowledge, synthesis of identification**
Husserl emphasizes that **knowledge** does not consist solely of its objective side, namely the set of true propositions or **truths**, but also has the subjective side, namely, the acts of knowing (*das Erkennen*), i.e. the ineliminable cognitive activity or **achievement** understood in a specific non-psychological sense. Objective knowledge, Husserl insists (not just after his transcendental turn) is an achievement or accomplishment of **subjectivity** or, more accurately, of subjects cooperating together in intersubjective agreement. According to Husserl, systematic knowledge (**science**) comprises not just a set of true propositions about a domain of objects but also a set of achievements, accomplishments or performances (*Leistungen*) of knowing subjects, 'a unity of acts of thinking, of thought dispositions' (LU *Prol*. § 62). Every item of knowledge is gained, achieved and preserved in specific acts of judgement. Any theory of knowledge must recognize the fundamental contribution of subjectivity without 'psychologizing' it. Husserl is interested in the **epistemology** and not in the psychology of knowing. In the Sixth Logical Investigation § 8, Husserl speaks of knowing or recognition as the experience of the identity (through a **synthesis of identification**) between what is intended and what is presented in intuition.

Knowledge (*Erkenntnis*)   See also **epistemology, evidence, fulfilment, knowing, science**

In the *Logical Investigations*, Husserl associates **phenomenology** with **epistemology** or the theory of knowledge (*Erkenntnistheorie*), which he sometimes also calls 'the critique of knowledge'. In his earlier writings, phenomenology is seen as having the function of providing a secure foundation for scientific knowledge through **clarification** of the underlying assumptions concerning the relations between **subjectivity** and **objectivity**. Prior to **Descartes**, knowledge was understood naively as a direct contact between the subject and the world. Husserl is sympathetic to the Kantian project of discovering the necessary conditions for the possibility of knowledge. However, he regards his inquiry as more far reaching than **Kant**. For Husserl, the highest kind of knowing is a direct intuition where the intention is fulfilled by the presence of the object intended. Husserl equates knowledge with the **fulfilment** of an **intention** (Hua XIX/2 735), that is, when there is recognition of a **coincidence** between what is intended and what is grasped fully in intuition (see Sixth Logical Investigation). Husserl also speaks of knowledge as equivalent to **evidence** and distinguishes knowledge from opinion or *doxa*. Knowledge is insight (*Einsicht*) into **truth**. In his later writings, especially the *Crisis*, Husserl considers that **objectivity** comes through intersubjective agreement.

Koyré, Alexandre (1892–1964)   See also **Galileo Galilei**

Alexandre Koyré was born in Russia of Jewish parents. He studied in the University of Göttingen with Husserl and **Hilbert** from 1908–11 and was a member of the Göttingen Philosophical Society. However, he left Göttingen to study with Bergson in Paris. In 1914 he joined the French Foreign Legion. After the war, from 1922 he lectured at the *École Pratique des Hautes Études*. Due to the German invasion, Koyré left France for Cairo and subsequently emigrated to the USA where he taught at the New School for Social Research, Johns Hopkins University and eventually settled at Princeton. He was an expert on mathematics and especially the development of mathematics in modernity, writing serious studies of Galileo and Newton and also his *From the Closed World to the Infinite Universe* (1957) that charted the emergence of the concept of an infinite universe in the thought of early modern mystical philosophers such as Nicolas of Cusa and Giordano Bruno. Koyré attended Husserl's lectures in Paris in 1929 and visited Husserl in

Freiburg in the early 1930s. Koyré's last visit with Husserl was in July 1932. Koyré and Husserl agree in presenting Galileo as a revolutionary genius whose real breakthrough was in conceiving of **nature** in term of Platonic mathematical forms (the book of nature is written in numbers) rather than as an empirical scientist. Koyré published his Galileo studies as *Études galiléennes* in Paris in 1939.

—L—

Landgrebe, Ludwig (1902–1991)   Ludwig Landgrebe was born in Vienna in 1902 and entered the University of Vienna in 1921. Influenced by Max **Scheler**, he went to Freiburg to study with Husserl and became his assistant from 1923 until 1930. In 1927 he completed his doctoral thesis under Husserl on *Dilthey's Theory of the Human Sciences*. He then went to Prague to complete his *Habilitation* thesis on Anton Marty's theory of language with **Brentano**'s former student Oskar Kraus. In the late 1920s he began to work with Husserl collecting and organizing his research manuscripts. Landgrebe was partly responsible for editing **Ideas** II. He also selected from Husserl's manuscripts on passive synthesis to produce Husserl's last publication, **Experience and Judgment**, published in Prague in 1938. He went to work at the newly opened Husserl Archives in Leuven in 1939 but was deported by the Nazis when they invaded Belgium and he returned to Germany. After the war his *Habilitation* was eventually submitted to Hamburg University where he began teaching in 1947. His students there included Hans Blumenberg. In 1954 he moved to become director of the newly founded Husserl Archives in Cologne where he worked until his retirement in 1971. He died in 1991. Among his publications are *The Way of Phenomenology* (1963), *Phenomenology and History* (1968) and *Phenomenology and Praxis* (1976).

Language (*Sprache*)   See also **Derrida, expression, grammar, meaning** In general, Husserl did not make language thematic in this work, but he recognizes the necessity of language for the expression of thought. Already in the **Logical Investigations**, Husserl recognizes that systematic knowledge depends on language and that cognitive judgements need to be expressed in language. In the First Logical Investigation, he discusses language primarily from the point of view of the speaker. A speaker intends a **meaning** (*Bedeutung*) and has a desire to communicate. Language, therefore, has an expressive function (articulating a meaning) and also a communicative function (*kundgebende Funktion*), in that the speaker wants to convey something to the hearer (e.g. a command, a question, an agreement, disagreement, and so on). A linguistic **expression** (*Ausdruck*) expresses a meaning (i.e. the embodiment of an ideal meaning) and also seeks to communicate or intimate something to the hearer. Husserl at times seems to have been committed to the idea of a philosophically purified language. In LU *Prolegomena* § 9, he acknowledges that language is imperfect because it is ambiguous. He follows Mill in believing that logic must offer clarification to language (LU Introduction § 1). Husserl claimed that formal logic needed to be grounded on a formal grammar that specified the formal rules for the combination of meanings into significant unities. Husserl's procedure of **reduction** was challenged because it did not make any allowance for the assumptions embedded in everyday language. In his late work on the **life-world** Husserl recognized the **historicity** and contextuality of linguistic meaning. However, Husserl never develops an account of the hermeneutics of language as found in **Heidegger**. In his **Origin of Geometry**, Husserl acknowledges the specific role of written signs in the preservation of the identity of meaning across generations. Husserl's discussion of linguistic signs and writing had an enormous impact on the work of **Derrida**. Husserl believes that new senses that gain currency in the language need a primordial or 'originary foundation' (*Urstiftung*) or institution that brings them into being and constitutes them as having an ongoing identical meaning over time.

Lask, Emil (1875–1915) Emil Lask was an independent philosopher of broadly neo-Kantian outlook and student of Heinrich Rickert at Freiburg. He completed his *Habilitation* under Windelband. He taught at the University of Heidelberg. He was influenced by Husserl's account of **categorial intuition** in the Sixth Logical Investigation and attempted to develop his own theory of the categories in his *The Logic of Philosophy and the Doctrine* *of Categories*. He corresponded with Husserl who had a high opinion of his work but lamented it was too abstract and formal. Lask accepted Husserl's account of **intentionality** and maintained that values have to be given in experience, while believing that everything given in experience has to be subsumed under a category. Lask became a professor in 1914 but his career was cut short and he was killed in action in the Great War in 1915. His publications include *Fichte's Idealism and History* (1902), *Philosophy of Law* (1905), *The Logic of Philosophy and the Theory of the Categories* (1911) and the *Doctrine of Judgement* (1912). Lask had a deep influence on the young Heidegger, who was also a student of **Rickert**.

Laws of essence (*Wesensgesetze*)   See also **analyticity**, **essence**
One of the aims of phenomenology is to identify a priori necessary laws that govern the essences of things, situations, and all entities encountered in experience. In his **descriptive psychology, Brentano** also sought to identify the essential laws governing the domain of the psychic, e.g. every judgement depends on a presentation. Husserl claims to find many a priori laws governing each material and formal region of essences, e.g. no colour without extension: 'There is no colour without extended surface' (LU III, §11). Husserl's writings are full of such laws of essence, e.g. no mind that is not embodied. There are essential laws of **logic**, **consciousness**, **knowledge**, and so on. Husserl's method of **eidetic variation** involves the testing of putative eidetic descriptive laws. **Eidetic free variation**, which operates in pure **fantasy**, has aims at generating possible counterexamples to falsify the presumed law. This characteristic of being falsifiable by counterexamples constructed in pure fantasy marks out eidetic descriptive laws from merely empirical **generalizations**.

Levinas, Emmanuel (1906–1995)   Emmanuel Levinas was born in Lithuania in 1906 and witnessed the Russian Revolution of 1917. He emigrated to France and in 1923 enrolled in the University of Strasbourg, initially to study classics, psychology and sociology. In 1928 he spent two semesters at the University of Freiburg, attending Husserl's and then Heidegger's seminars. He gained his doctorate from Strasbourg in 1929. Levinas was present at Husserl's lectures in Paris and Strasbourg in 1929 (which were given in German) and, with Gabrielle Pfeiffer, translated Husserl's ***Cartesian Meditations*** into French. Levinas' doctoral dissertation, entitled *The Theory of Intuition in Husserl's*

Phenomenology, appeared in 1930 and was hugely important for the French reception of Husserl. With the outbreak of war in 1939 Levinas served in the French army and was interned by the Germans during the Second World War. Because he was an officer he was protected from persecution as a Jew. Almost his entire family, however, perished in the Holocaust. After the war he was appointed Director of the *École Normale Israélite Orientale* and published many studies on the Jewish Talmud. He also continued to write on phenomenology and the history of philosophy, including several essays critical of Husserl and Heidegger as well as developing his own philosophical thought centered on the singularity of the 'Other', which, according to Levinas, could be reduced to neither the Husserlian horizon of intentionality nor to the Heideggerian being-with others. In 1961 he published *Totality and Infinity*, which explicated the ethical 'step beyond' transcendental phenomenology and fundamental ontology. This 'step beyond' was radicalized in the 1974 work, *Otherwise than Being or Beyond Essence*. Levinas was particularly critical of Husserl's approach to **intersubjectivity** in the Fifth Cartesian Meditation. He believed Husserl began from a solipsistic approach that resulted in a reduction of the singularity of the 'Other' to an *alter ego*, another self. Consequently, in both *Totality and Infinity* and *Otherwise than Being or Beyond Essence* Levinas critically rereads the western tradition for prioritizing being and totality, and thus truth and meaning, over the singularity of the Other. For Levinas, ethics as responsibility for the Other – and not the question of being and totality – must carry the name of **first philosophy**. He became Professor of Philosophy at Poitiers (1963), then Paris-Nanterre (1967) and finally at the Sorbonne (1973). His publications include *Existence and Existents* (1947), *Time and the Other* (1947), *Discovering Existence with Husserl and Heidegger* (1949), *Totality and Infinity* (1961), *Otherwise than Being or Beyond Essence* (1974), *Ethics and Infinity* (1982), and *Of God who comes to Mind* (1986).

Lévy-Bruhl, Lucien (1857–1939) Lucien Lévy-Bruhl was a prominent French intellectual, philosopher, sociologist, ethnologist, and theoretical anthropologist, an almost exact contemporary of Husserl's, who had a major influence on philosophers such as **Ernst Cassirer**, psychologists such as Piaget and Jung, as well as anthropologists such as Claude Lévi-Strauss and E. E. Evans-Pritchard. Trained in philosophy, he achieved his *aggrégation* from the École Normale Supérieure in 1879 and, subsequently, taught philosophy at Poitiers (1879–82) and Amiens (1882–3), before moving to Paris where he completed his doctorate at the University of Paris in 1884 with a thesis on 'The Idea of Responsibility'. He taught at the École Normale from 1886 and was appointed to the Sorbonne in 1904 as professor of the history of modern philosophy. He initially published purely philosophical works. He had a strong interest in empiricism (especially Hume) and positivism (Comte). Under the influence of the sociologist Émile Durkheim, however, he began to develop a strong interest in sociology and theoretical anthropology. This interest in other cultures is first marked in print in his *Ethics and Moral Science* (1903), where he argues for the study of morality based on a scientific sociology of different moral systems (including those found in primitive societies), and rejects the possibility of an absolute universal ethics. In this work, he acknowledged the incommensurability of the thought systems in different cultures. From then on he began to embark on a number of studies on the mentality of the primitive (he coined the phrase *la mentalité primitive*) concentrating on the difference between preliterate societies and modern European cultures. The first of these works was *Les Fonctions mentales dans les sociétés inférieures* (Paris, 1910, translated as *How Natives Think*), followed by *La Mentalité primitive* in 1922 (translated as *Primitive Mentality*). In 1925, together with Marcel Mauss and Paul Rivet, he founded the Institute of Ethnology at the Sorbonne, dedicated to the memory of Émile Durkheim, who had died in 1917. He eventually resigned from the Institute and the Sorbonne in 1927 to devote himself to writing and travel. Lévy-Bruhl subsequently lectured at Harvard, Johns Hopkins and the University of California. He died in Paris on 13 March 1939. Lévy-Bruhl was present at Husserl's Paris lectures in 1929. He corresponded with Husserl sending him copies of his books. Husserl's letter to Lévy-Bruhl in 1935 is reprinted in Edmund Husserl, *Briefwechsel*, edited by Karl and Elizabeth Schuhmann. This letter had a major influence on **Merleau-Ponty** and in it, Husserl speaks of the 'lack of history' (*Geschichtlosigkeit*) of primitive peoples who live in the flowing present. In his '**Origin of Geometry**', Husserl will write, doubtless with Lévy-Bruhl in mind: 'Every people has its "logic" and, accordingly, if this logic is explicated in propositions, its "a priori"'.

Life (*Leben*) See also **consciousness**, **life-world**, **lived experience**, **living present**

Husserl regularly characterizes the aim of phenomenology as the description of the life of consciousness. Husserl speaks of life as a continuous temporal stream of **lived experiences**. Husserl takes over Dilthey's view of the unified interconnectedness (*Lebenszusammenhang*) of conscious life. Moreover, life is originally determined by **instinct**. There is a desire to survive, to overcome pain, hunger and discomfort, to achieve satisfaction. According to Husserl, all life is 'striving' (*Streben*). The life of **consciousness** is always ego centred, the concept of an ego-less consciousness is regarded by Husserl as an eidetic impossibility. Moreover, consciousness is always embodied. Husserl also speaks not just of life in the **natural attitude** but of transcendental life which is a striving towards living self-responsibly according to rational goals as a **person** related to other persons in relations of mutual recognition. In this regard, although individual human beings are subject to birth and death, Husserl believes that transcendental life is endless.

Life-world (*Lebenswelt*) See also **Avenarius, Heidegger, natural attitude, nature, Schutz, world**

The concept of **world** as a horizonal backdrop for our experiences is already to be found in Husserl's *Logical Investigations*. The world is the ever present horizon of experiences, the basis for all assumptions, the backdrop for all '**positing**': 'to live is always to live-in-certainty-of-the-world (*Inweltgewissheitleben*, *Crisis* § 37). 'Life-world' or 'world of life' (*Lebenswelt*) is Husserl's term in his mature writings for the concrete world of everyday experience, the 'everyday world' (*Alltagswelt*), the 'intuitive world of experience', the world as experienced in the **natural attitude**. This life-world has both subjective and objective aspects. Husserl did not invent this term *Lebenswelt*, which could already be found in the writings of the poet Hugo von Hoffmannsthal (c. 1908) and also in philosophers such as Georg Simmel and Rudolf Eucken. The term *Lebewelt* (world of living being) was also in use by the palaeontologist biologist to signify the sphere of living beings. Husserl himself uses the term *Lebewelten* in *Ideas* I § 50, which the editor Karl Schuhmann corrected to *Lebewesen* (living things). Husserl acknowledges the influences of Richard **Avenarius** and Ernst Mach in his formation of the concept of life-world. Both men advocated a return to the prescientific world of immediate experience. They wanted to determine the nature of the 'natural concept of the world' (*natürlicher Weltbegriff*) prior to scientific theorizing and indeed prior to the split between physical and psychical. Husserl himself explicitly associated his concept of a 'naturally experienced world' with Richard Avenarius' concept of the 'pregiven' world of experience, especially in his lectures of 1910/1911 *Basic Problems of Phenomenology*. In *Ideas I* § 28, Husserl speaks of 'my natural surrounding world' (*meine natür-liche Umwelt*). This is the world in which I find myself all the time and which supplies the necessary background for all intentional acts, and is the 'ground' (*Boden*; see *Crisis* § 40), the 'meaning fundament', for all other worlds it is possible to inhabit (e.g., the world of science, the world of mathematics, the world of religious belief, and so on). The term 'life-world' (*Lebenswelt*) appears with increasing frequency in the 1920s and 30s to capture the peculiar character of the pregiven environing world. In *Cartesian Meditations* § 58, Husserl refers to the 'natural surrounding world'. Life-world is an all-embracing term that includes the 'surrounding world' (*Umwelt*), both that of nature and of culture, including humans and their societies ('the world of culture'), things, animals, our overall environment. Husserl speaks of our 'world-life' (*Weltleben*, VI 127), our 'natural worldly life' (*Crisis* § 43) and indeed characterizes humans as essentially belonging to the world, as 'children of the world' (*Weltkinder*). Life-world includes, in particular, the realm of that affecting us subjectively, of the fluctuating character of experience, what Husserl calls the realm of ***doxa*** (commonly held opinion) or the '**subjective-relative**', which remains constantly functioning for human beings even when they are absorbed in the practice of science. The life-world is not just *my* world but the world 'for everyone' (*für Jedermann*) or 'for all'. It has an a priori universality that can be construed as objectivity. It is a 'universal field fixed in advance' (*Crisis* § 36). It is 'a realm of original self-evidences' (*Crisis* § 34d). It is also the world of our **interests** and purposeful activities and **habitualities** (*Crisis* § 36). The life-world is variously characterized by Husserl as the world that is 'prescientific' (*vorwissenschaftlich*), 'concretely intuited', 'pregiven' (*vorgegeben*), 'always already there' (*immer schon da*), 'on hand' (*vorhanden*), 'familiar', and 'taken for granted'. Husserl even claims that the 'life-world' is not a partial problem but the universal problem of philosophy (*Crisis* § 34f). This world is always experienced as the 'one, existing world' (*die eine seiende Welt*, *Crisis*, 317; VI 296). Husserl says that 'the plural makes no sense' when applied to world (*Crisis* § 37). In other words, the concept of world is so all inclusive that it makes no sense to speak of life-world in the plural. According to Husserl, the life-world of contemporary western culture is actually shot through with scientific insight and technological determination. Although Husserl often contrasts the life-world with the world of science, he also insists that the scientific world 'belongs' to the life-world (see *Crisis*, § 34e). For Husserl, however, the life-world has a certain overall primacy and fundamentality as that from which all science develops. Galileo however introduced a transformation that effectively cut off the life-world such that it became, as Husserl says, the 'forgotten meaning fundament' of the sciences (*Crisis* § 9h). At this point Husserl writes:

> It is this world [the pregiven world] that we find to be the world of all known and unknown realities. To it, the world of actually experiencing intuition, belongs the shape of space time together with all bodily shapes incorporated in it; it is in the world that we ourselves live, in accord with our body (*leiblich*), personal way of being. But here we find nothing of geometrical idealities, no geometrical space or mathematical time with all their shapes. (*Crisis* § 9h; VI 50)

The life-world provides a set of horizons for all human activity including scientific activity. It is, Husserl says, 'the ground of all *praxis*' (*Crisis* § 37). The life-world 'grounds' the world of science (*Crisis* § 34e), it is the 'grounding soil' (*gründende Boden*, VI 134) of the sciences. It is a world into which we are inserted in an embodied manner. Space and time as we experience it are lived space and time. Husserl's conception of the 'life-world' raises many questions: If modern technological practice is an integral part of the life-world, how can we still maintain the distinction between world of experience and scientific world? Is there a danger of conceiving of the life-world solely in terms of the primitive, prescientific world? Is it not rather, for Husserl, the living context for the pursuit of purposeful social and cultural life? For Husserl, moreover, attention to the life-world meant attention to history, tradition and culture. If the life-world is constantly varying with culture and history, how can Husserl speak of 'invariant' features of the life-world? In *Crisis*, Husserl is interested in tracking the *invariant* features of the life-world. Because we always live within the taken-for-granted life-world we rarely make it explicit. In fact, Husserl claims, the manner in which life-world functions as 'subsoil' (*Untergrund*; *Crisis* 124; VI 127) of our practices has never before been examined. The life-world can be approached from different perspectives from the point of view of phenomenology. On the one hand, it is possible to have a general 'science of the life-world' (*Crisis* § 38), documenting the 'ontology' of the life-world – the kind of human, social entities that belong to the world of our experience (handshakes, kisses, tools, equipment, etc). Husserl speaks of a 'general science' of the *Lebenswelt* that will identify the lawful 'essential typicalities' that correspond to it. This is, for Husserl, a straightforward or 'naive' way of approaching the life-world. On the other hand, this science cannot be objective and logical but must somehow be prior to or higher than all of that (Crisis § 34a). It is, however, not to be understood as psychology in any naturalistic sense. Employing the **epochē**, it is possible to reveal the life-world in the 'how of its givenness' (*Crisis* § 38). Husserl recognizes the paradoxical character of trying to have a science of the life-world. The life-world cannot be objectified without betraying its very sense. The real challenge is to understand the relationship between objective logical thinking and intuition. Both Fink and Husserl stress that human beings are normally completely absorbed in the world so as to be 'captivated' or 'ensnared' by it (equivalent to Heidegger's conception of 'fallenness'). Husserl's conception of the 'life-world' has been widely adopted in philosophy, sociology, and other human sciences. Martin **Heidegger** discusses the concept of *Lebenswelt* as early as 1919–23 in his lecture courses in Freiburg. Like Husserl, Heidegger focuses on the problem of world alienation and self-alienation resulting from objectivism in the formal-logical sciences and their assumption of unquestioned acceptance as the lead authorities in our culture. Unlike Husserl, however, Heidegger locates the problem in the specifically ahistorical character of scientific objectivity, which tends to run counter to the genuine historical nature of the life-world and life-world experiences. Heidegger is critical of the primacy of the theoretical. **Alfred Schutz** wrote on the topic of human natural and social experience in his *The Phenomenology of the Social World* (1932). Schutz claims that the recognition of the other is the basis of the social and of the experience of the world. In his 1932 work, he distinguishes between different dimensions of world including the 'world of predecessors' (*Vorwelt*) and the 'world of one's successors' (*Folgewelt*) as well as the social world of the present. Following Husserl, he emphasizes the importance of temporality in the constitution of social reality. Through Schutz, life-world became an important theme in sociology especially in the United States. **Jan Patočka** published his *Habilitation* thesis in Czech entitled *The Natural World as a Philosophical Problem*.

Lipps, Theodor (1851–1914) See also **descriptive psychology, empathy, realist phenomenology**
German philosopher, aesthetician and psychologist. Born in Wallhalben, he studied theology and natural science at Erlangen, Tübingen, Utrecht, and Bonn. In 1884 he became Professor of Philosophy at Bonn, then Breslau (1890), and finally the took the chair in Munich (1894), replacing Stumpf, where he remained until his death in 1914. Lipps was influential for his approach to psychology, for his investigations of aesthetic experience and, most importantly, for his theory of empathy, which had a strong influence on Scheler, Stein and Husserl. Lipps followed an introspectionist way of doing psychology. **Psychology** is the study of 'inner experiences' and inner experiences can be apprehended by inner perception. Lipps supported the idea of the unconscious and was greatly admired by Freud (who drew on Lipps' book on humour). Lipps thought of **empathy** as a kind of entry into the psychic life of another. This is done through an almost instinctive and motor 'inner imitation'. His publications include *Fundamentals of Psychic Life* (1883), *Aesthetics* (1903/1906), *The Comic and Humour*, *Guidelines to Psychology* (1909), and *Psychological Studies* (1926). In the first decade following the publication of the *Logical Investigations*, many of Lipps' students at Munich became followers of Husserl. Husserl criticized Lipps' theory of empathy. Lipps influenced the Munich School of phenomenologists as well as **Scheler** and **Stein**.

Lived bodiliness (*Leiblichkeit*) See also **body, lived body**
Lived bodiliness is Husserl's term for the first-person human experience of being embodied in a way that one experiences oneself as 'governing' or '"holding" sway in a body with feelings of willful self-movement. See *Crisis* § 62.

Lived body or animate body (*Leib*) See also **body (*Körper*), ego, governing, kinaesthetic sensation, lived bodiliness**
The lived or animate body (*Leib*), i.e. the body as organism, is distinguished by Husserl from the **body** (*Körper*) understood as a piece of physical nature in many of his works, including **Ideas II**, *Ideas* III, **Cartesian Meditations**,

and **Crisis**. In one sense, the human living body can behave exactly like any other body in nature. It enters into causal and gravitational relations with other bodies in the world. In this sense the body is, borrowing Descartes' phrase, *res extensa*; it has volume, mass, weight, physical parts, and so on. The main difference between *Leib* and *Körper*, however, is that the animate body (*Leib*) is always given as *my own* body (*Crisis* § 28) and I experience myself as 'holding sway' over this body. The lived body is not just a centre of experiences but a centre for action and self-directed movement. It consists of a series of 'I can's. My own experience of my own body is unique, given in a unique way. My **apperception** of 'my body' has an absolute primordiality for Husserl. It is given as a unity but I am not given to myself as 'human being', but rather, as Husserl says, as an 'I am' (see **cogito**) with capacities of moving (kinesis), fields of **sensation**, and so on. I can of course genuinely perceive my body externally (my hand, say) as an external transcendent object, but at the same time I have an inner sensuous awareness of it. It belongs to my 'interiority' (*Innerlichkeit,* Hua XIV, 4). This leads Husserl even to speak of the manner in which my own body is given as 'subjective-objective' (Hua XIV 6). It is not a simple 'in itself'. Husserl later emphasizes the sense in which I am always present to myself within my own sphere of experience. I have furthermore a sense of myself as '**governing**' or 'holding sway' (*waltend*) in this region. Husserl speaks of a 'living embodied egoity' (*leibliche Ichlichkeit, Crisis* § 28). Each of us experiences our embodied 'soul' in our individual case in a primordial way (*Crisis* § 62). The living body is never absent from the perceptual field (*Crisis* §28, p. 106; VI 108). Husserl thinks of the lived body as constituted in 'strata' – perceptual, actional, and so on. The living body, however, is also the centre of my experience. It is the means of my perceptual encounter with the world. It is an 'organ of perception'. Husserl uses many cognate expressions to emphasize different aspects of our experience of embodiment, including 'I body' (*Ichleib*), corporeal body (*Leibkörper*), and so on. The body is grasped primarily through touch and **kinaesthetic sensations**. In *Ideas* III (V 118), Husserl explains that the lived body (*Leib*) should not be thought of as a physical body with a consciousness added on (as in **Descartes**) but rather has to be thought of as a sensory field, a field of localization of sensation. Husserl is interested in the problem of how we constitute the living body in our experience. A physical body becomes a body in the lived sense not just be being seen (this would present merely a physical *Körper*) but by having touch, visual, pain, movement sensations localized within it. (*Ideas* II § 37) For Husserl, there is a normal optimal situation for the body – upright, looking forward. The body is only an 'incompletely constituted thing' for Husserl. Husserl lists various characteristics of the lived body. It is a centre of orientation, the 'zero point' of my space. It is also the centre of my '**now**'. It is a unifying locus for all my sensory and kinaesthetic experiences (vision, touch, taste, smell, sense of bodily movement).It is the 'organ of my will' and through my body I experience my capacities for free movement as a kind of immediate 'holding sway' (see *Crisis* § 62).

Lived experience (*Erlebnis*) See also **act, *cogitatio*, *cogito*, consciousness, content, Dilthey, life, Lipps**
Husserl uses the term *Erlebnis* to mean the conscious state as personally lived through and experienced in the first person. It has also been translated as 'lived experience', 'mental process', 'conscious process', 'mental episode'. The more general term for 'experience' in German is *Erfahrung*, but Husserl uses the term *Erlebnis* to refer to individual mental events, states (*Zustände*) or processes that can be identified in the **stream of consciousness.** In *Ideas* I § 78, Husserl says that every lived experience is in itself a 'flux of becoming'. Husserl found the term 'lived experience' (*Erlebnis*) in **Dilthey, Lipps,** among others. In his ***Logical Investigations***, Husserl generally refers to these conscious processes as mental ***acts*** (*Akte*), although he makes clear in the Fifth Logical Investigation that he does not mean to include any sense of wilful activity or action. A lived experience is also called a 'thought' (***cogitatio***, borrowing from **Descartes**)**,** understood in the widest sense to include any identifiable or distinguishable episode in the **stream of consciousness**. Strictly speaking, no mental episode is an independent part of the flow; mental episodes are always embedded in one seamless flow of consciousness. In *Cartesian Meditations* § 20, Husserl says that conscious processes have a priori no ultimate elements as such. Furthermore, conscious life is not a chaos of intentional processes but a highly structured, layered and unified complex – there is a 'unified constitutive synthesis' at work (CM § 21) Under the ***epochē***, consciousness is considered independently of the existing, physical, causal world, in order to be grasped as an appearance in its own right, it is understood as made up of *Erlebnisse*, mental processes, each of which has a *cogito-cogitatio-cogitatum* structure. Every lived experience contains **retentions** and

protentions. Husserl thus speaks of a realm of 'transcendental experience' (*transzendentale Erfahrung*) that is reachable through the **epochē** and transcendental **reduction**.

Living present (*lebendige Gegenwart*) See *cogito*, now moment, protention, retention, time consciousness

The 'living present' is a term common in Husserl's later writings to characterize the manner in which time is experienced by the ego. According to Husserl, the **ego** continually experiences itself in the living present which Husserl characterizes as a 'standing streaming' continuous present. This living present is not the same as the **now moment** (*Jetztmoment*) of conscious **lived experiences** that are always related to a past and a future. The standing, streaming present is the manner in which the ego grasps itself as spread out across time including the **retention** of the past, the now moment, and the anticipatory **protention**. The living present has both the character of gathering into a unity ('standing') and also having the experience of a passing away ('streaming'). For Husserl, the notion of *living* characterizes the very streaming of consciousness (see Hua X 301). The concept of the living present is a rethinking of what is at stake in the *sum* (I am) of the *cogito ergo sum*.

Logic (*Logik*) See also formal grammar, formal ontology, theory of science

Husserl uses the term 'logic' in a wide sense to mean a 'theory of science' in general. The conceptual requirements for the discipline of logic also supply the requirements for science in general. Logic investigates the *form* of science and that includes investigating its own nature (LU, *Prol.* § 42). Pure logic is a set of self-evident truisms or statements that are true in virtue of their own terms (*Selbstverständlichkeiten*). In the **Logical Investigations**, Husserl sketches a threefold division of logic: logic is a theoretical science, a *normative science*, and a practical discipline or 'technology' (*Kunstlehre*). A theoretical science studies pure theoretical truths as such. For example, if one says 'of two contradictory propositions, one is false and the other is true', this states an ideal law with no reference to how one *ought* to think. A *normative* science is concerned to lay down criteria or values to be followed, given that these ideal truths hold. Every pure theoretical law, therefore, has its normative transformation. So, on the basis of the ideal Law of Non-Contradiction, logic, a normative science will prescribe, for

example, that one ought to recognize that of two contradictory propositions, only one can be true. As a normative science, logic holds up an
'idea' of science that all other sciences should emulate (LU *Prol.* § 11).
Logic as a practical discipline is concerned with concrete realization (see
ELE § 9, Hua XXIV 27–32). Schopenhauer, for instance, denied that one
could be educated to be good, since all moral action depended on innate
character. He therefore denied the possibility of morality as a technology,
but maintained a view of morality as a normative discipline (LU *Prol.* § 15;
see also ELE § 9; Hua XXIV 28).

Husserl saw himself as clarifying traditional ideas of logic, sharpening its
concepts of the a priori, of form, of the nature of the analytic, and so on.
He was deeply familiar with logic both in historical and contemporary terms
(Mill, Frege, Schroeder). He was especially inspired by Leibniz, Bolzano and
Lotze. He admired Leibniz's idea of a *mathesis universalis*. Following Bolzano
and Brentano, he criticized Kant's account of analyticity as confused.
However, he also saw himself as amplifying the conception of logic in
several dimensions, including clarifying the concepts of necessity and possibility and showing how these modal forms arise from categorical judgements.
In LU *Prolegomena*, and subsequently, he sided with the Bolzanian tradition,
which characterized logic as *Wissenschaftslehre*, theory of science, and he
never abandoned this conception, although he gave it a unique and original
characterization as including in its highest form a '**theory of manifolds**' or
the 'theory of the forms of theory'. From his earliest days, he had recognized the deep theoretical connection between logic and mathematics and
their common root. From the outset, he saw the essential identity of formal
logic and mathematics: all formal calculation is essentially logical deduction
(ELE § 19, Hua XXIV 84). He was in broad agreement with Frege and with
Russell (somewhat later) who espoused the reduction of mathematics to
formal logic. If anything, Husserl overestimated the possibilities of formal
logic in that he endorsed Hilbert's programme of complete formalization
(with its axiom of the solvability of all mathematical problems) and does not
seem to have anticipated the problems posed by Gödel's Incompleteness
Theorem. Nevertheless, he was not a formalist as such neither was he
committed to symbolic logic. He identified flaws in the then current project
of a purely extensional logic, and was aware of, and possibly even anticipated, Russell's – or Zermelo's – paradoxes regarding set theory. But at the
time of writing LU, Husserl's main gripe was that those who advocated the

reduction of arithmetic to logic had a mistaken conception of logic as a normative or practical discipline and hence were vulnerable to psychologism (ELE § 15, Hua XXIV 56). In LU *Prolegomena*, Husserl reveals a complex and very broad understanding of logic as having a threefold task: First, it was a doctrine of the primitive apophantic and formal ontological categories and the laws combining them. Second, it included the connection of categories in terms of the laws of consequence understood so generally as to include both logic and arithmetic. Third, it included a theory of the possible forms of theory and the corresponding formal ontological theory of manifolds. Logic requires formal grammar (the rules governing meaningfulness as such), *consequence logic* (logic of inference, *Konsequenzlogik*, bound only by the Principle of Non-Contradiction) and what he called 'logic of truth'. In some respects, his account of logic is quite traditional, being centred on the notion of **judgement** or assertion (Greek: *apophansis*) and hence is, following Aristotle, characterized as **'apophantic logic'** (see LU IV § 14 **II** 72; Hua XIX/1 344; see also ELE § 18; Hua XXIV 71), although his detailed account of judgements goes far beyond Aristotle. Husserl always insisted on the judgement or proposition as the highest category in logic and specifically the apophantic form 'S is P', the copulative judgement, as the absolutely fundamental form. Similarly, he took the Law of Non-Contradiction to be one of the absolutely basic ideal laws. One of his innovations is his view that formal logic in the sense of the science of the forms of implication needed to be complemented with a pure formal grammar specifying the rules for meaningfulness in the most general terms, offering an 'anatomy and morphology of propositions' strictly in regard to their sense (ELE § 18; Hua XXIV 71). Formal apophantics, which is concerned with truth and falsity as articulated in judgement, builds on this formal grammar. Before something is true or false, it must meet minimum conditions of coherence and meaningfulness as *a possible truth*, that is, as a possible *piece of knowledge*. Husserl always draws a distinction between the mere elaboration of consistent rules (rules of a game) and the specification of the possible forms of judgements understood as items of genuine knowledge (see FTL § 33; EJ § 3). In FTL and elsewhere, Husserl refers to the unity of formal logic and mathematics as 'objective logic'. The counterpart of formal apophantics is what Husserl calls *formal ontology*, the theoretical account of all possible objects of whatever kind (see EJ § 1), the theory of something in general (FTL § 54). Husserl recognized that formal ontology can in fact be pursued independently of logic. Formal ontology develops Brentano's, Twardowski's and Meinong's conception of *Gegenstandstheorie*, theory of objects, the account of what it is to be an object or a property or a relation, unity, plurality, and so on. For Husserl, the objects of mathematics simply form one part of **formal ontology**, but there are other kinds of formal object that have nothing to do with numbers. Husserl recognized that mathematics itself was moving away from a fascination with objects and engaging in a reflection on its own methods. Thus geometry did not have to remain fixated on geometrical figures but could express its results in terms of axioms and purely formal deductions (ELE Hua XXIV 80). Contrariwise, with his interest in genetic logic, Husserl wants to emphasize the formal ontological concepts such as property, plurality, and the like, actually arise from 'nominalizations' of certain kinds of function that are located in judgements, in formal **apophantics**. In his later years, Husserl became increasingly preoccupied with a genetic account of the emergence of forms of judgement. He was interested in giving an account of the emergence of logical forms from the life-world, from the domain of 'proto-logic'. Husserl begins the *Investigations* with an account of the 'idea of science in general' (LI, *Prol.* § 11), what belongs to science as such, every kind of science, including sciences of the possible, the ideal, and so on. He calls this '**theory of science**' (*Wissenschaftslehre*), following Bolzano (and Fichte), and he further agrees with Bolzano that logic provides the essence of this science. A theory of science is a 'theory of theories', an account of any structured domain whatsoever (a system of things, numbers, meanings, propositions, etc). A theory is a unified set of propositions about any given domain. Husserl holds, moreover, that the set of logical truths, and hence scientific truths, are all interrelated, and thus, he, like Carnap, is committed to the ideal of the unity of science: science is the body of true propositions linked together in a systematic way (LI *Prol.* § 10). All theoretical research, no matter how it is conducted, eventually comes to expression in a body of *statements* (*Aussagen*, LU Intro. § 2) or propositions. Logic, then, studies propositions. What is important for logic and science is the inferential connections between what is stated, between the propositional contents themselves, which has nothing to do with the contingent acts of assertion and judgements which gave rise to them. Logic, as any other theoretical science is 'an ideal fabric of meanings' (*eine ideale Complexion von Bedeutungen*, LU I § 29). Husserl distinguishes between logic as a theory of science and logic as an art or technique of reasoning (*Kunstlehre*). He also distinguishes between logic as a system of ideal truths and logic understood as a normative practice. Husserl's account of logic rejects **psychologism**. Pure logic is an a priori analytic science (see Hua XXVI § 1, 4) consisting of 'truisms' or 'tautologies' (*Selbstverständlichkeiten*). It is concerned with purely formal concepts, as Husserl writes:

> [F]or me the pure laws of logic are all the ideal laws which have their whole foundation in the 'sense', the 'essence' or the 'content' of the concepts of Truth, Proposition, Object, Property, Relation, Combination, Law, Fact, etc. (LU, *Prol.* § 37, I 82; Hua XVIII 129)

Anything that violates these laws is simply absurd:

> A proof whose content quarrels with the principles whose truth lies in the sense of truth as such is self-cancelling. (LU, *Prol.* § 37, I 82; Hua XVIII 129)

Moreover, 'everything that is logical falls under the two correlated categories of meaning and object' (LU I § 29) and 'meanings in the sense of specific unities constitute (*bilden*) the domain of pure logic' (LU II Intro., I 238; Hua XIX/1 112). Pure logic covers the whole domain of the formal a priori (as opposed to the material a priori domain explained in LU III), including mathematics and may be more accurately described as 'formal ontology' (a phrase not used in the First Edition, see ILI 28; 121; XX/1 285).

Logical Investigations (*Logische Untersuchungen*, 1900/1901)

Edmund Husserl published his *Logische Untersuchungen* in two volumes with Max Niemeyer in 1900 and 1901. The first volume, *Prolegomena zur reinen Logik* (*Prolegomena to Pure Logic*) appeared in July 1900. The second volume, subtitled *Untersuchungen zur Phänomenologie und Theorie der Erkenntnis* ('Investigations in Phenomenology and the Theory of Knowledge'), containing six long treatises or 'investigations', appeared in two parts in 1901. Husserl had rushed the work into print and was never satisfied with it. He first planned an extensive revision and then wrote other books (e.g. **Formal and Transcendental Logic** in 1929) with the hope of replacing the *Investigations*. Four editions appeared in Husserl's life: a revised Second Edition of the *Prolegomena* and first five investigations in 1913, a revised Edition of the Sixth Investigation in 1921, and a Third Edition with minor changes in 1922 and a Fourth Edition in 1928. A critical edition, which includes Husserl's written emendations and additions to his own copies (*Handexemplar*), has appeared in the *Husserliana* series in two volumes. This gargantuan work – which Husserl insisted was *not* a 'systematic exposition of logic' (*eine systematische Darstellung der Logik*, LI III, Findlay, p. 435; Hua XIX/1 228), but an effort at epistemological **clarification** and critique of the basic concepts of logical knowledge – consisted of a series of analytical inquiries (*analytische Untersuchungen*) into fundamental issues in epistemology and the philosophy of logic, and also extensive, intricate philosophical discussions of issues in semiotics, semantics, **mereology** (the study of wholes and parts), **formal grammar** (the a priori study of the parts of any language whatsoever in regard to their coherent combination into meaningful unities), and the nature of conscious acts, especially presentations and judgements. In fact, it was these latter detailed descriptive psychological analyses of the essential structures of consciousness, in terms of intentional acts, their contents, objects and truth-grasping character, especially in the last two investigations, which set the agenda for the emerging discipline Husserl fostered under the name **phenomenology**. The origin of Husserl's *Logical Investigations* lay in the studies in mathematics, logic and psychology he had been pursuing, inspired by his teachers Weierstrass, Brentano and **Stumpf**. As he put it, the *Investigations* originally grew out of his desire to achieve 'a philosophical clarification (*eine philosophische Klärung*) of pure mathematics' (Hua XVIII 5). It worried Husserl that mathematicians could produce good results and yet employ diverse and even conflicting theories about the nature of numbers and other mathematical operations. Their intuitive procedures needed philosophical grounding. In search of this grounding for mathematics, Husserl was led to consider formal systems generally and ultimately to a review of the whole nature of meaningful thought, its connection with linguistic assertion and its achievement of truth in genuinely evident cognitions. Husserl suggested that the *Logical Investigations* was originally inspired by Brentano's attempts to reform traditional logic. Husserl never quite finished the text. It is a huge sprawling work – Husserl himself calls it a 'patchwork'. The *Prolegomena* as a free-standing treatise dedicated to securing the true meaning of logic as a pure, a priori, science of ideal meanings and of the formal laws regulating them, entirely distinct from all psychological acts, contents and procedures. The *Prolegomena* offered the strongest possible refutation to the then dominant *psychologistic* interpretation of logic, propounded by John Stuart Mill and others, which Husserl viewed as leading to a sceptical relativism that threatened the very possibility of objective knowledge. Turning instead to an older tradition of logic stemming from Leibniz, **Kant**, **Bolzano** and **Lotze**, Husserl defends a vision of logic as a pure theory of science – in fact, the 'science of science' – in the course of which he carefully elaborates the different senses in which this pure logic can be transformed into a normative science or developed into a practical discipline or 'technology' (*Kunstlehre*). The second volume of the *Investigations* (1901) was published in two parts: Part One contained the first Five Investigations and Part Two the long and dense Sixth Investigation, the writing of which had considerably delayed the appearance of the work as Husserl began to realize the depth of the phenomenological project he had uncovered. Whereas the *Prolegomena* was particularly influential in turning the tide against **psychologism** (**Frege**'s efforts in the same direction being in relative obscurity at the time), it was *Investigations* Volume Two in particular that had a major impact on philosophers interested in concrete analyses of problems of consciousness and meaning, leading to the development of phenomenology. Husserl's *Logical Investigations* had enormous and enduring impact on several generations of philosophers in Europe. It was recognized as a major philo-sophical achievement by leading figures of the time including **Paul Natorp**, **Wilhelm Dilthey**, **Wilhelm Wundt** and **Heinrich Rickert**. Brentano, however, appeared to ignore the work and Heidegger first read it in 1909. The *Logical Investigations* was translated into Russian as early as 1909, and had a major influence on Roman Jacobson's conception of a formal science of language. Through **Roman Ingarden**, who reviewed it in Polish, the *Investigations* played an important role in Polish philosophy, influencing Stanislaw Lesniewski's development of mereology, for instance. It was translated into Spanish in 1929. A French translation of the Second Edition appeared between in three volumes between 1959 and 1963, but, Husserl's influence on French philosophy has begun much earlier through the efforts of his earlier Göttingen students, Jean Héring and later through the writings of **Emmanuel Levinas**, **Jean-Paul Sartre**, **Maurice Merleau-Ponty**, Paul Ricoeur, **Jacques Derrida**, all of whom began their philosophical careers with critical studies of Husserl. In contrast to the situation in continental Europe, the *Logical Investigations* was somewhat slower to gain recognition in the English-speaking world. Bertrand Russell wrote to Husserl on 19 April 1920 saying that he had taken a copy of his *Logical Investigations* with him to jail, with the intent of reviewing it for *Mind*, but the review never appeared. However, in 1924, Russell recognized the *Logical Investigations* as a 'monumental work' listing it alongside his own *Principles of Mathematics* (1903) and works by William James, Frege, G. E. Moore (who, incidentally, also admired Husserl's book), for their efforts in the refutation of German Idealism.

Lotze, Rudolf Hermann (1817–1881)   See also **Bolzano, Frege**
Rudolf Hermann Lotze was an influential German philosopher who taught **Frege** (in Göttingen), Wilhelm Windelband and Carl **Stumpf**. He was an opponent of **psychologism** and defended the ideality of logical entities and meanings. He was born in Bautzen in Saxony in 1817 and studied medicine and philosophy in Leipzig, graduating in both disciplines in 1838. In 1840 he completed his *Habilitation* thesis on infinite series. He published widely in different areas including medicine, psychology, aesthetics, anthropology, metaphysics and logic. His book on anthropology, *Microcosmus: An Essay Concerning Man and His Relation to the World* (1856–64), was had a huge influence on Husserl. The young Husserl credited Lotze's discussion of the Platonic ideas for opening his eyes to the true nature of the ideal **objectivities** that **logic** studied, helping him to understand the **Bolzano**'s **'propositions in themselves'** (*Sätze an sich*) as the **senses** of statements, not as mysterious kinds of thing, thus avoiding Platonic hypostasization. Husserl was unsatisfied with a certain 'psychologizing of the universal' he detected in Lotze's *Logic* (1874), however, especially § 316. Husserl thanks Lotze in his 'Review of M. Palagyi, The Dispute between Psychologists and Formalists in Modern Logic' (EW, p. 201; Hua XXII 156). Husserl offers some criticisms of Lotze in his *Logical Investigations* (see LU II §10 I 322 n.5; Hua XIX/1 138).

—M—

Mach, Ernst (1838–1916)   See also **phenomenalism**

Ernst Mach was an Austrian scientist, physicist and philosopher who was regarded as an early positivist and phenomenalist. He was born in Churlitz, then part of Austria and now part of the Czech Republic. He entered the University of Vienna in 1855 and received his doctorate in physics there in 1860 and his *Habilitation* in 1861. He taught mathematics at the University of Graz and in 1866 was made Professor of Physics there. The following year he moved to a chair in physics at Prague where he remained until 1895 when he moved back to the University of Vienna. In 1901 he retired from the professorship and was made a member of the upper house of the Austrian parliament. Mach was interested in physiology and studied with Fechner and was influenced by his *Elements of Psychophysics* (1860). His scientific research work focused on the recently discovered Doppler Effect and his studies on sound have led to the unit of the speed of sound being named after him. Mach was the author of *The Analysis of Sensations and the Relation Between the Physical and the Psychical* (*Die Analyse der Empfindungen und das Verhältnis des Physischen zum Psychischen*, 1902). His position is regarded as phenomenalist. He claimed that physics ought to describe experience as accurately as possible. Husserl regarded him as one of the forerunners of phenomenology because of his attempt to describe precisely what was given in experience. He was deeply influential on the logical positivism of the Vienna Circle. He also advocated monism and published articles in *The Monist*.

Masaryk, Thomas (1850–1937)   Thomas Masaryk was born to a poor family in Hodonin, Moravia,and, at the age of 12, he left school to work as a blacksmith, but enrolled in the University in Brno and then the University of Vienna in 1872. His first thesis, *Principles of Sociology* (1877) was rejected, largely because sociology was still a suspect discipline, but his second thesis on suicide in 1878 was eventually accepted through the support of **Brentano**. In 1880 he converted from Catholicism to Protestantism. An activist Czech nationalist, he eventually elected President of Czechoslovakia in 1918 and remained in the post until 1935. Thomas Masaryk was a lifelong friend of Husserl. He convinced Husserl to study with Brentano in

1884 and later was active in encouraging Husserl to read the British empiricists. Masaryk was also influential in converting Husserl to Christianity, leading to Husserl's baptism in the Lutheran church in Vienna on 26 April 1886. In 1915 Masaryk became a professor in Slavonic studies in King's College, London. As President of Czechoslovakia he tried to use his position to protect Husserl from political persecution by the National Socialists in Germany.

Material thing in space   See also **adumbration, object, thing**

Husserl considers that the solid material thing in space with rigid boundaries is the exemplary concept of the **thing**. It is grasped directly in **perception** and other kinds of material entity, fluids, water, air, etc., are always grasped relative to material solid things (see *Ideas* II § 16).

Mathematization of nature (*Mathematizierung der Natur*)   See also *Crisis of European Sciences*, **Galileo Galilei**, **primary qualities**, **subjective-relative qualities**

Husserl sees the breakthrough of modern science in the redefinition of physical **nature** as a mathematical manifold. Galileo had stated that mathematics was the key to unlock the secrets of nature. In *Crisis* § 9 he writes:

> [T]hrough Galileo's *mathematicization of nature, nature itself* is idealized under the guidance of the new mathematics; nature itself becomes – to express it in a modern way – a mathematical manifold [*Mannigfaltigkeit*]. (*Crisis*, § 9, 23; VI 20)

Nature so defined is understood in terms of its measurable properties, its so-called '**primary qualities**'. Mathematics covers nature in a 'cloak of ideas'. All **subjective-relative properties** (e.g. colour, taste, rough, smooth, hot, cold) are redefined as merely subjective and are excluded from the domain of objective nature.

Meinong, Alexius (1853–1920)   See also **theory of objects**

Alexius Meinong was born in Lemberg, then part of the Austrian Empire, now Lvov in Poland. He studied at the University of Vienna and received a doctorate in history in 1874. He then studied with Franz **Brentano** and wrote his *Habilitation* thesis on Hume's relationship with nominalism, published in 1878. He then became an unsalaried lecturer (*Privatdozent*) at the University of Vienna and in 1882 moved to Graz, becoming professor in 1889 and teaching there until his death in 1920. Meinong developed the **theory of objects** (*Gegenstandstheorie*) against which Bertrand Russell reacted (see Alexius Meinong, 'The Theory of Objects,' trans. by R. Chisholm in *Realism and the Background of Phenomenology* (Glencoe, IL: Free Press, 1960). Meinong proposed that every object of thought had to have some kind of ontological status in order to be graspable by the mind. He distinguished between entity that actually existed and other kinds of subsistent entity, including non-existent, possible, imaginary, and even impossible objects (such as a 'round square'). An object is understood as a bearer of true predicates. This was criticized by Bertrand Russell. In particular, Meinong felt we had to overcome 'a prejudice in favour of the actual' to allow there to be 'objectives' standing for all our intentional acts. Meinong sought to explain thought's ability to refer to all kinds of things, from actual things to non-existent *possible* things (e.g. gold mountains), ideal things (e.g. numbers, ideal laws) or even *impossible* things (e.g. square circles), by positing these entities as having various special kinds of being distinct from actual existence. Meinong maintained that a 'square circle' had a kind of being, 'being-thus' (*Sosein*), which meant that it truly had the properties of being circular and square even if it could never actually be existent. In correspondence with Meinong, Russell wondered if an 'existent square circle' meant that it also existed. Meinong replied that indeed it did have the property of existence but this was not the same as asserting that it actually existed. Marty, similarly, defended the concept 'the non-being of A' as a genuine object of thought. Meinong's *On Assumptions* (1902), which studied assumptions as a class of mental acts that did not imply the existence of their objects, was seen by Husserl as a kind of plagiarism of his own ideas.

Memory (*Erinnerung*)   See also **imagining, perceiving, presentification, representation, retention, time consciousness**

AHusserl discussed memory in his lectures of 1904-1905, and in research writings throughout his life (see Hua XXIII). According to Husserl, memory is a form of representing or **presentification** (*Vergegenwärtgung*) that is dependent on a prior originary experience, i.e. an experience of **perception**. In general terms, Husserl contrasts the *self-givenness* of perception (e.g. FTL § 86) with that of a very large class of forms of consciousness that are 'representational' (*vergegenwärtig*) or work through a modification of presencing, which Husserl terms *Vergegenwärtigung*, '**presentification**', 'presentiation' or 'calling to mind' (not just in memory, but in **fantasy**, wishing, etc). Perception takes place in the now, in the present, and its object is apprehended as immediately present, 'in the flesh' (*leibhaftig*, as Husserl says), as being there in the same temporal phase as the mental process itself. In memory, however, while the **lived experience (*Erlebnis*)** is in the present, the object remembered is not experienced as being in the present, but precisely as not present and as 'having been'. Memory suffers from an essential *inadequacy* in that things can be represented that were not, in fact, ever perceived (see *Ideas* I § 141), or different memories can be fused into one memory. For Husserl, **retention** (or, in earlier terminology, 'primary memory', Hua II 67) is not yet memory in the strong sense ('secondary memory'), although it forms the basis or ground for both passive and active rememberings. Rememberings present objects as whole entities, whereas a retention is a part of a perceptual awareness, it is a 'just past' that is still there in a reduced or modified sense. It still has a kind of 'impressionality'. Similarly, **protention** is not yet the fully fledged conscious act of anticipation but a structural component of any **lived experience** (*Erlebnis*). Remembering presents something in the 'now' that is apprehended as not belonging to that now. When we remember an object, we do not have precisely the same sense of the immediate, actual, bodily and temporal presence of the object. Indeed, in memory, we are certain that the object is not presently there, but there is still some kind of reference to its being, it is still being posited (as past) in a specific way. Memory posits the real 'having-been' of something. Imagination entails no such positing of the real existence of its object in any temporal mode. Memory, moreover, is not the same as picture consciousness (X 316). It is a *thetic* or positing act, but the object is presented as 'being-past', 'having been' (XIII 164) and as 'having-been-perceived-by-me' (VII 252) and having been originally experienced *in a mode other than memory*. In other words, in an act of remembering, the experience remembered is presented as one originally experienced by me, but now with a *temporal distance* separating it from my current experience. This temporal distantiation is characteristic of memory:

> Recollection is not simply the being-conscious once again of
> the object; rather, just as the perception of a temporal object

carries with it its temporal horizon, so too the recollection
repeats the consciousness of this horizon. (ZB, 113; X 108)

Husserl puts enormous stress on the structural importance of remembering for a number of reasons. It is in remembering that consciousness first comes to meet itself as an object. **Reflection**, therefore, essentially involves memory. There is already a split or chasm between the self that is remembering and the experience of the self that is being remembered. For instance, if I have a memory of myself as a child swinging on that swing, I perceive myself through a different consciousness to that of the child on the swing. There is a **splitting** or **doubling** of consciousness and a peculiar experience of both difference and identity. My empathic grasp of the cognitive life of the other also falls under the general category of '**presentification**' (*Vergegenwärtigung*) for Husserl and he regularly compares **empathy** with acts of remembering. Memory has to be carefully distinguished from fantasy. Brentano had tried to explain the object in memory as a kind of imagined or fantasized object. For Husserl, memory is a modification of perception; it is a reproducing of an earlier act of perceiving.

Mental process (*Erlebnis*)   See **lived experience**

Mereology (*Mereologie*)   See also ***Logical Investigations*, part, piece, whole**
The term 'mereology' comes from the Greek word *meros*, which means a **part**. Mereology is the formal theory of the a priori laws governing the possible relations between wholes and parts. The term *mereology* is never used by Husserl although he inspired the science of mereology as later developed by the Polish mathematician and logician Stanislaw Leśniewski in his *Foundations of a General Theory of Manifolds* (1916), and others. In Third Logical Investigation, especially, Husserl tries to specify a priori laws that govern all possible kinds of inherence of parts in their wholes, the a priori possibilities inherent in part–whole relations in general.

Metaphysics (*Metaphysik*)   See also ***Cartesian Meditations*, first philosophy, formal ontology, intersubjectivity, monadology**
The term 'metaphysics' was developed after Aristotle primarily to refer to his lecture notes that discuss the nature of being and substance (*ousia*).

The science of metaphysics studies the ultimate principles and constituents of reality, not just what is actual, but also what is necessary, possible and impossible. Metaphysics is a term used by Husserl primarily to refer to science of being 'in the absolute and final sense' (IP Hua II 32); the 'ultimate cognitions of being' (CM § 60); the 'universal doctrine of being' (Hua VII 186). In general, Husserl agrees with Kant that metaphysics must be approached from a critical perspective (see IP Lecture One) and that rationalism in particular developed an ungrounded speculative metaphysics, what Husserl calls an 'historically degenerate metaphysics (CM § 60) that was full of 'speculative excess'. Husserl even includes Kant's discussion of things-in-themselves as part of this excessive metaphysical specu- lation. In *First Philosophy*, Husserl says that matters of fact and **facticity**, death and destiny, are matters for metaphysics (VII 182). In ***Cartesian Meditations***, Husserl attempts a new kind of metaphysics that is grounded and overcomes the naiveté of traditional metaphysics (CM § 64). According to this metaphysics, it is impossible to conceive of **monads** that are not in communion with one another. Each monad 'predelineates' a closed universe of possible monads (CM § 60). The absolutely first being is '**transcendental intersubjectivity**'.

Modalization (*Modalizierung*)   See also **belief, neutrality modification**
Husserl speaks of 'modalization' to describe the manner in which a doxic attitude (e.g. **belief**) towards some proposition or judgement can be trans- formed into a different attitude, e.g. certainty can be transformed into doubt, questioning, assuming, actualizing, and so on). There are different **doxic modalities** and Husserl pays particular attention to one such modality, the **neutrality modification** (*Ideas* I § 117).

Mode of givenness (*Gegebenheitsweise*)   See also **givenness**
The mode of givenness is the manner in which an intentional object is presented in an intentional **act**. The mode of givenness is part of what Husserl calls the **act quality** in the ***Logical Investigations***.

Modification (*Modifikation*)   See also **neutrality modification**
Modification is a term originally found in grammar according to which a verb can change from one mood to another, e.g. from the indicative to the interrogative mood. Husserl uses the term 'modification' for a change in the

intentional act that brings about a corresponding change in the intentional object. Thus a **memory** is a modification of a **perception**. The **neutralilty modification** is the most important and far reaching kind of modification, since it modifies the **general thesis** of the natural attitude by nullifying it into a suspension of belief commitment. **Empathy** involves a modification of my own self which is then attributed to the other.

Moment (*Moment*)   See also **mereology, part, whole**

Husserl uses the term 'moment' for a dependent or 'abstract' **part**, that is, a part that depends on another part or a whole for its existence (see Third Logical Investigation § 17). A moment is considered to be some aspect of an object that is identifiable but that cannot exist independently, e.g. the particular red of an apple is a moment or abstract, dependent part of the apple.

Monad (*Monad*)   See also **ego, ego pole, empathy, intersubjectivity, monadology, person, subject**

Especially in his later writings on **empathy** and in the *Cartesian Meditations*, Husserl self-consciously adopts the terms 'monad' and '**monadology**' from Leibniz to express the whole united course of a concrete, ego-centred, personal life understood in the phenomenological sense as a set of flowing experiences centered around the **ego** with its **habitualities**, abilities, personal 'abiding style' embedded in its surrounding world. The term is already appears in Husserl's '**Philosophy as a Rigorous Science**' essay. For Husserl, the ego taken in its full concreteness is a monad (CM § 33); my 'monadic self-ownness' ('*meine monadische Selbsteigenheit*', CM Hua I 125). Husserl speaks in CM § 57 of the 'self-objectivation of the monad'. The idea of the monads is of a human person including its entire life, actions, meanings and so on. A monad is an individual, living, a *concrete* unity (Hua I 157; *eine lebendige Einheit*, XIV 34), established over time (CM § 33), with its own temporal field (*Zeitfeld*, XIV 43), and capacity for self-development (XXV 322) as a life. It is a 'unity of becoming' (*Werdenseinheit*, XIV 34); it includes not just the person at present but how he or she has evolved or become, that is, including the various intentional layers that have sedimented (XIV 35). The monad also includes those parts of a concrete life in which the ego is not awake or appears absent or 'dull', e.g. sleep (XIV 46), as there is no consciousness without hyletic data (XIV 52), a unique

set of hyletic data that belong to it. The monad is a 'substratum of habitualities' (Hua XIV 43) and acquires a personal style or character over time. The
monad is a self that includes his or her history. Monads also seem to contain
within themselves the possibilities of what they may become. Leibniz
believes that monads were the most basic possible substances and as such
contained their whole life experiences within themselves and yet were
simple and without parts. Leibnizian monads were 'windowless' in that they
do not communicate outside themselves and at the same time they exhibit
a pre-established 'harmony'. Husserl, by way of contrast, especially in his
mature writings, insists that his monads *have* windows (Hua XIV 260), the
window being provided by **empathy**. Husserl speaks of an intersubjective,
communicating, open **community of monads** (which is another term for
transcendental intersubjectivity) and also uses the term **monadology**
(see CM §§55–6). Monads are in 'harmony' and the **sense** of a shared,
common world is an **achievement** of the harmony of the community of
monads. Husserl does acknowledge that the introduction of the concept of
monad leads to **metaphysics** (CM § 60) but he not intend his term 'monad'
as a speculative metaphysical postulate but rather as an intuitively arrived
at, descriptive phenomenological term to express the seamless *unity* of an
egoic life. Yet Husserl does think of birth and death as immanent to the
monad, which itself cannot come into being or be destroyed.

Monadology (*Monadologie*) See **intersubjectivity, monad, transcendental intersubjectivity**
The mature Husserl uses the term 'monadology' (see CM § 62), a
term derived from Leibniz, for the phenomenological **transcendental
idealism** that begins from the concrete reality of **intersubjectivity** or
'we-subjectivity' in contrast to the narrow methodological solipsism of the
phenomenology which focuses solely on the **ego**'s self-experience. The
world as such is constituted by the **community of monads** acting in
consort. Husserl argues that it is impossible to conceive of monads dwelling
in worlds that are completely partitioned from one another. Necessarily, all
monads belong to the one world (CM § 60). There can exist only one single
community of monads. Monads are unique, 'absolutely separate' individuals
(I 157), yet nevertheless they are 'communalized' in a community of monads
(EP II Hua VIII 190), a 'harmony of monads' (I 138). There is a transcendental
'universe of monads' (*Allheit der Monaden*, *Monadenall*, XV 609). Part of

Husserl's puzzle is how a monad grasps itself both as an absolute being for itself and also as 'a' monad, one that leaves open the possibility of a plurality of such monads (Hua XV 341). Monads have not only being 'for themselves' but also 'for one another' (*für-einander-Sein*, I 157) in genuine community. The self has not just an 'I sense' but a 'we sense'. These others have reciprocal communal relations with each other leading to the notion of an open community of monads, i.e. '**transcendental intersubjectivity**' (I 158).

Morphē   See also **form**, *hyle*, **matter**, **morphological essence**
The Greek word *morphē* means 'form' and is used by Aristotle in particular to refer to the principle which, when combined with **matter** (*hyle*) gives the things its particular nature. For Aristotle, all material things have a form matter composition, a doctrine often known as *hylomorphism*. Husserl uses the term 'intentive *morphē*' in *Ideas* I § 85 to refer to the act that gives form to the sensational matter (that he sometimes calls *hyle* or **hyletic matter** or simply '**stuff**') in an experience to make an experience of that particular entity. The function of the 'form' is to animate, enliven and shape the experience in a particular way. Husserl speaks of 'formings' as acts of sense bestowal. In *Ideas* I §§ 73–4 Husserl distinguishes between 'exact' essences (such as occur in mathematics) and what he calls '**morphological essences**' that are the essential forms of more vaguely defined entities (e.g. a shoreline as opposed to a geometrical figure such as a circle) such as are studied by the natural sciences. Husserl even describes the descriptive phenomenology of **noesis** and **noema** as 'eidetic morphology' (*Ideas* I § 145).

Morphological essence (*das morphologische Wesen*)   See also **essence**, **exact essence**, **morphē**
In *Ideas* I §§ 73–4, Husserl distinguishes between 'exact' essences (such as occur in mathematics) and what he calls '**morphological essences**', which are the essential forms of more vaguely defined entities such as are studied by the natural sciences. Morphological essences are not faulty or deficient but are absolutely appropriate to the domain of description to which they belong; and they cannot be replaced by corresponding exact essences. The natural and human sciences may be said to study morphological essences. In these cases, there cannot be exact definition. **Exact essences** are ideal and function Husserl says like 'ideas in the Kantian sense' (*Ideas* I § 74); they provide ideal limits.

Motivation (*Motivation*)   See also **causation, position taking, spirit**
Husserl speaks of 'motivation' or 'motivational causation' (*Ideas* II § 55) as
distinct from '**causation**' when attempting to explain human personal and
social behaviour. For Husserl, causation is a real connection between events
in the natural world whereas 'motivation' is a less exact form of causation
that explains events that are produced by human agents acting intentionally
(the **ego** as 'subject of intentionalities'). According to Husserl, causality
belongs to the very essence of the notion of physical thing (*Ideas* II § 60),
whereas motivation articulates 'the lawfulness of the life of **spirit**' (*Ideas* II
§ 56). Husserl thinks we ask about motivations when we ask – what made
me think of that?:

> [*H*]*ow did I hit upon that*, what brought me to it? That ques-
> tions like these can be raised characterizes all motivation in
> general. (*Ideas* II, §56, 234; Hua IV 222; trans. mod.)

No causal explanation can replace the kind of personal understanding one
arrives at through understanding a person's motivations (*Ideas* II § 56(f)).
Motivations are based on assumptions about what a person with free will,
choices, goals, etc., will do in a particular situation. In this sense, motivation
is a basic interpretative tool of history and the human sciences generally.
The phenomenologist Alexander Pfänder distinguished between *drives* and
motivations and the term motivation was also used by **Dilthey** to explain
behaviour in the human as opposed to the natural sciences (Husserl discusses
Dilthey in this context in his *Phenomenological Psychology* lectures). In *Ideas*
II § 54, Husserl speaks of motivation as the 'law of personal life'. According
to motivation, the ego has to become interested in something in order
to turn towards it and carry something out. **Perceptions**, for instance,
motivate **judgements**. Elsewhere, Husserl speaks of **retentions** motivating
protentions (Hua XXXIII 18); a certain kind of content in consciousness
motivates the appearance of another content. Husserl allows for a weak
'passive motivation' based on association but he thinks motivation in the
full sense involves the ego in its active **position taking**. In this sense,
Husserl distinguishes between motivations which operate in the sphere of
passivity (through **association**) and active motivation which involves a
freely willed **position taking** by the ego. For Husserl, motivation is more
basic than causality, in the sense that consciousness as such is involved in

a 'web of motivations'. Motivations can be explicit or implicit. According to **Stein**, motivations flow through the ego, in the sense that is the ego that is really motivated, that, in turn, motivates actions. Reasons can motivate me explicitly or implicitly (in that they don't have to be activated over again). Some motivations can be immediately apprehended, other motivations are below the level of consciousness and can only be uncovered through something like psychoanalysis (*Ideas* II § 56). I can be motivated by real events (e.g. real emotions or passions) or indeed by fantasy emotions (as in the theatre).

Movement sensations (*Bewegungsempfindungen*)   See also **kinaes-thethic sensations**

Husserl speaks of 'sensations of movement' or 'kinetic sensations' (*Bewegungs-empfindungen*) in his research manuscripts and in his *Thing and Space* lecture course (1907). Movement sensations are quite different from those of vision and touch and do not primarily constitute the body in terms of its own characteristics. Experience of walking, sitting and so on are primarily constituted out of touch sensations.

Multiplicity (*Vielheit*)   See also **collective combination,** *Philosophy of Arithmetic*

For Husserl, the concept of a multiplicity or plurality (*Vielheit*) includes the concept of a '**something**' (*ein Etwas*) as well as the concept of some kind of gathering or collection. Husserl maintains that the concept of multiplicity has a certain indefinite extension which he expressed by 'etcetera' or 'and so on' (*und so weiter*). This indeterminacy ('and so on') is included in the very notion of a multiplicity (XII 81). The extension of a general concept, then, e.g. 'animal', has to allow for a certain indeterminacy, for being applied over and over again, and the 'etc.' captures this requirement well. Numbers, then, arise through the 'enumeration of multiplicities' (PA XII 182). I can see different things as part of the same multiplicity by collecting them together and ignoring their properties or 'contents' and concentrating on each one just as an instance of a 'something'. Thus I can see a pen, a table, and a lamp, as a group of objects, ignoring their differences. What makes a mathematical multiplicity exceptional is that it can be a gathering together of *anything* at all – 'physical or psychical, abstract or concrete, whether given through experience or imagination,' e.g., an angel, the moon, Italy (XII 16). Numbers do not designate concepts as such, rather, they are general names for definite multiplicities or sets (Hua XII 182). The number 5, for example, does not refer to the *concept* 5 but any arbitrary set of five items (XII 181). To form a determinate multiplicity, I must *combine* a 'something' with another thing, which gives me the concept of two, and so on. For example, if I want to count an apple, a book, and a colour, I count each one as a 'something', abstracting from the particular characteristics that make it a book, apple, or colour. I simply count *three* individual things.

Mundanization, enworlding (*Mundanisierung, Verweltlichung*)   See also **constitution, transcendental ego, world**

'Mundanization' or 'enworlding' is a term used by Husserl and then by **Fink** to name the constitutive process by which **transcendental subjectivity** constitutes itself as a human embodied subject in the world of nature, time and history. In the **natural attitude**, human beings grasp themselves as entities, human subjects, within the world with others. The subjects within the natural atittude are 'mundane'. The **transcendental ego** is not part of the world but constitutes the world. However, it mundalizes itself as a human subject in the world. The aim of transcendental phenomenology is to uncover the nature of this *mundanization* through unveiling the constitutive activity of the natural attitude itself. Through the **reduction**, the ego can move from its mundane being to grasp its transcendental nature.

—N—

Natorp, Paul (1854–1924)   See also **Platonism**

Paul Natorp was an influential German philosopher and member of the Marburg School of Neo-Kantianism, who wrote on classical Greek philosophy and also on psychology. Born in Düsseldorf, he initially studied classics at the universities of Bonn and Strasbourg before being attracted to philosophy. He wrote his *Habilitation* with Hermann Cohen at Marburg (1881), where he then taught until his death in 1924. His publications include Plato's *Theory of Ideas* (1903) where he advocated the view of Ideas as laws. Natorp was responsible for Martin **Heidegger** being employed (on Husserl's recommendation) in Marburg in 1923. Natorp was also Hans-Georg **Gadamer**'s dissertation director. His other students included Karl Barth and **Ernst Cassirer**. Natorp corresponded with Husserl until his death and reviewed his *Logical Investigations* and later *Ideas* I favourably. In his review of *Prolegomena to Pure Logic*, the first volume of the *Investigations*, in *Kant Studien* in 1901, he portrayed Husserl as broadening the essentially Kantian inquiry into the necessary conditions of the possibility of experience and correctly predicted that Husserl would move closer to neo-Kantianism. In the First Edition of his *Logical Investigations* (1901), Husserl rejected Natorp's conception of a pure **ego** as a necessary non-objectifiable subject of experiences and 'centre of relations'. However, in his 1913 revised Second Edition, Husserl acknowledged that he had since discovered the transcendental ego. Natorp's studies in psychology, including his important essay 'On the Objective and Subjective Grounding of Knowledge' and his *Introduction to Psychology* was carefully read by Husserl. Natorp's concern was the nature of scientific cognition and the nature of philosophy as a science. He argued that all objectification is produced by consciousness which is subjective and cannot be captured by a reflexive intuition. Natorp coins the neologism *Bewusstheit* (**consciousness**) for this kind of non-objectifiable subjectivity (see Husserl's critique in the Fifth Logical Investigation § 8). Natorp, as a neo-Kantian, did not accept Husserl's concept of **essential intuition** and argued that the way to grasp the activity of consciousness is through 'reconstruction' rather than direct intuition.

Natural attitude (*die natürliche Einstellung*) See also **attitude, naturalism, naturalistic attitude, nature, personalistic attitude, phenomenological attitude, philosophical attitude, theoretical attitude**

An **attitude** is a certain stance towards the world, a way the world is made manifest determined by interests. The natural attitude is the most primordial attitude adopted by humans in their engagements with the world. The natural attitude is characterized by a certain 'naturalness', 'straightforwardness' and 'naiveté' (see e.g. *Crisis* § 38): the world of physical things and our own bodies are incessantly there for us (*Ideas* I § 39). The natural attitude is a complex constellation of attitudes that presents the world as 'pregiven' and simply 'there' for me, spread out in space and time, and so on. In *Ideas* II § 11 (and elsewhere), Husserl speaks of the 'natural-scientific attitude'. Husserl can be said to have discovered the 'natural attitude'. He introduced the term 'natural attitude' in print in *Ideas* I §§ 27–31 (but it was discussed earlier, i.e. his 1907 **Idea of Phenomenology**). The natural attitude is the normal, everyday attitude of human beings prior to any sceptical questioning. The 'natural attitude' is the attitude of 'natural worldly life' (*Crisis* § 43). In the natural attitude, attention is turned towards things given in whatever manner they are given, in a mode of acceptance. The natural attitude of naive living in the world is contrasted with a sceptical attitude (which for Husserl characterizes the **philosophical attitude**) that questions the existence of the world. The natural attitude is the 'original' attitude of humans living in the world, Husserl claims in his lecture to the Kant Society in 1924 (now in *Erste Philosophie*):

> The natural attitude is the form in which the total life of
> humanity is realized in running its natural, practical course. It
> was the only form from millennium to millennium, until out of
> science and philosophy there developed unique motivations
> for a revolution. (*Erste Philosophie* I, Hua VII 244)

According to *Ideas* I § 30, the natural attitude is permeated by a particular assumption which Husserl calls 'universal thesis' or 'general positing' (*Generalthesis*), namely the assumption of the existence of the world and the entities within it. This 'general thesis' is a general, unquestioning acceptance of the world and everything in it as objectively there. In the natural attitude, the everyday world is simply taken for granted. In our natural experience, we live 'naively' in this world, 'swimming' with the flow of its givens, that have the character of being 'on hand' (*vorhanden*) and 'actual' (*wirklich*; *Ideas* I § 50). Husserl says that in the natural attitude we simply 'effect all the acts by virtue of which the world is there for us' (*Ideas* I § 50). The natural attitude is prior to the scientific attitude. Thus in *Thing and Space*, Husserl contrasts the nature of platinum as described by the scientist (atomic complex, etc.) with what is grasped experientially, as a heavy lump in the hand (see DR 4; XVI 6). Furthermore, all scientific inquiry, including mathematics and logic, takes place within the natural attitude;

these sciences simply *assume* the world and the extant availability of the objects of their science (e.g. numbers). These sciences are *naive* precisely because they accept the world as 'present' or 'on hand' (*vorhanden*) and 'actual' (*wirklich*). The natural attitude is normally taken for granted to the extent that it is invisible or unknown to itself. Husserl introduces the **epochē** in *Ideas* I to break the spell of the natural attitude. It is only the **transcendental attitude** (an attitude Husserl particularly characterizes in the *Crisis* and in the associated *Vienna Lecture*) that highlights the true nature of the natural attitude. The natural attitude further carries within it the danger that it can deteriorate into what Husserl terms **the naturalistic attitude**, which both *reifies* and *absolutizes* this world. Husserl's assistant, Eugen Fink, compares the natural attitude to the attitude to the shadows taken by the prisoners in Plato's cave. We are 'captivated' by the natural attitude. Due to this captivation by the natural attitude, the manner in which it structures and filters the world is not visible. While Husserl is interested in characterizing the natural attitude and the sciences associated with it, he is also interested in suspending it in a 'bracketing' or 'putting out of action' which he calls **epochē** (Ideas I § 32). We thereby arrive at a new sort of attitude: the phenomenological attitude. This attitude no longer simply lives in the acts it performs but reflects on them (*Ideas* I § 50).

Naturalism (*Naturalismus*) See also **attitude, empiricism, natural attitude, naturalistic, nature, physicalism**
According to Husserl, naturalism recognizes only one domain of possible knowledge, namely **nature**, as it appears in the natural sciences (Hua XXX 18). Naturalism also recognizes only one method for gaining scientific knowledge, empirical observation and induction (Hua XXX 20). The two basic sorts of naturalism are materialism and psychologism (Hua XXX 20; Hua XXV 9). Both versions share a basic understanding of nature as the spatiotemporal physical world unified by mathematically expressible causal laws (Hua XXV 8). A materialist naturalism claims that all psychological phenomena are in reality physical phenomena. Husserl sometimes mentions another version of naturalism, namely, a sense data monism that reduces all physical and psychological being to collections of sensations (Hua XXV 9); such as the monism propounded by Husserl's contemporaries **Ernst Mach** and **Richard Avenarius**. Husserl also ascribes a version of this 'sensualism' to **Hume** (Hua XVII 264). What is shared by all these versions of naturalism

is a commitment to empiricism, i.e. the view that the ultimate justification of all scientific knowledge is to be sought in perceptual experience (Hua XXX 18). Husserl regards this restriction of the possible modes of scientific justification as the fundamental mistake of naturalism (*Ideas* II). According to Husserl, naturalism is blinded by the truly remarkable success of modern natural science. Naturalism is blind to the other great source of scientific knowledge namely eidetic intuition. More specifically, the empiricist prejudice of naturalism results in a misconception of both consciousness and of the absolute norms of rationality (Hua XXV 9). The consequence of this naturalization of logical laws is, according to Husserl, an absurd and self-refuting relativism and scepticism. The attempt to naturalize consciousness as such, Husserl argues, results in similar absurdities. The 'naturalization of consciousness' – a phrase Husserl himself uses – is part of a general attempt to make epistemology into a proper science that, for naturalism, is equivalent with natural science (Hua XXV 15). However, Husserl argues, an understanding of how consciousness can provide valid experiences of objective reality can never itself be provided by a naturalized epistemology that regards consciousness as just another occurrence within the objective psychophysical world. What is required for a proper science of consciousness as such is the shift from the natural attitude to the phenomenological attitude that makes an eidetic investigation of consciousness possible (Hua XXV 15).

Naturalistic attitude (*die natüralistische Einstellung*)   See **attitude, natural attitude, naturalism, nature, theoretical attitude**
The concept of the 'natural attitude' is given its most important characterization in *Ideas* I §§ 27–31, but there is already an important distinction between the natural attitude and the 'naturalistic attitude' introduced in Husserl's 1910–11 essay '**Philosophy as a Rigorous Science**' and also in his 1910/1911 *Basic Problems of Phenomenology* lecture course. The 'naturalistic attitude' is developed in *Ideas* II § 49 where it is contrasted with both the **natural attitude** and the **personalistic attitude**. The naturalistic attitude is subordinate to the personalistic attitude in everyday life (*Ideas* II § 49(e)). Husserl characterizes the 'naturalistic attitude' as a specific evolution and deformation of the natural attitude. It is arrived at by a certain process of abstracting the personal ego from the world and absolutizing the world of physical things (*Ideas* II § 49 (e)). The naturalistic attitude is the attitude

determined by modern science. Indeed in *Ideas* II § 11 (and elsewhere) Husserl speaks of the 'natural-scientific attitude'. The naturalistic attitude is linked with **naturalism**. All activities of consciousness, including all scientific activity, indeed all knowledge, initially take place within the natural attitude (Hua XIII 112). Husserl here also speaks of the 'naturalistic attitude'. The naturalistic attitude is the opposite of the **personalistic attitude**, which is the most concrete and basic way in which humans relate to one another and to the world.

Nature (*Natur*)   See also **life-world, natural attitude, naturalism, naturalistic attitude, spirit**

Husserl understands 'nature' from the phenomenological standpoint as the objective correlate of a very specific **theoretical attitude**, which Husserl calls the **naturalistic attitude**, i.e. as a very special construct ('an artificial product of method' *Phenomenological Psychology*, § 5) studied by modern natural science (see '**Philosophy as a Rigorous Science**' and *Ideas* II §§ 1–2; § 11). Nature, in this sense, is approached scientifically in terms of materiality, space, time, and exact **causality** (sometimes summarized by Husserl under the Cartesian term *res extensa*). 'Nature' understood by natural science as a domain that is regulated by strict laws and divorced from the realm of values (*Ideas* II § 2: 'nature, as mere nature, contains no values') is correlated with the **naturalistic attitude** (*Ideas* II § 49). In science, nature is approached as a 'field of transcendent – specifically spatiotemporal – realities' (*Ideas* II § 1). This is not nature understood as the realm of sensuous experience (and of the 'subjective relative') in particular. In everyday human experience, by way of contrast, the personal and cultural worlds – everything that for Husserl belongs to the pregiven **life-world** – are prior to nature. Nature as experienced by humans in the **natural attitude** is layered over culturally and is experienced in terms of interests and values (e.g. beauty, utility, suitability, etc., see *Ideas* II § 1). Nature, however, as the correlate of modern natural science as inaugurated by **Galileo**, does not include such concepts as 'state, church, right, religion' and so on (*Ideas* II § 11). In this sense, Husserl opposes nature and **spirit**. As part of nature, human beings are understood in terms of physical bodies or as **psychophysical** unities but never as **persons**. Yet, Husserl recognizes that the domains of nature and spirit interpenetrate (see *Phenomenological Psychology*, § 5). Husserl claims that 'physical nature' is the founding substratum for the rest of nature (e.g. living animate things, see *Ideas* II § 49). For this reason he says the term 'physiopsychic' is preferred to 'psychophysical' since it correctly mirrors the order of founding. Everything in nature has some kind of bodily incorporation.

Neutrality modification (*die Neutralitätsmodifikation*) See also **doxic modalities, modalization, neutralization, positing act**
Especially in *Ideas* I § 109, Husserl introduces the original notion of *neutrality modification* as a crucially important capacity or stance that consciousness can adopt towards any of its doxic attitudes. In opposition to the general acceptance that characterizes the natural attitude, one can also adopt an attitude of 'nullness' or non-positing. According to Husserl, the neutrality modification is *universal* in that it can modify not just **beliefs** but all kinds of **position takings**. It is akin to pure entertaining of the content of the judgement without the making of any explicit judgement or taking any stance including a sceptical one. For Husserl, the performance of the phenomenological **epochē** is just one kind of neutrality modification. There is neutrality modification involved in aesthetic suspension of disbelief, in various kinds of scientific attending to phenomena, etc. Moreover, as Husserl sees it, neutralization is not straightforward negation but a very different kind of annulment and abstaining:

> It is included in every abstaining-from-producing something, putting-something-out-of-action, 'parenthesizing-it', 'leaving-something-undecided' and then having-an-'undecided' – something, being 'immersed'-in-the-producing, or 'merely conceiving' the something produced without 'doing anything about it'. (*Ideas* I § 109, p. 258; Hua III/1 222)

Husserl claims this genus of annulment modifications has never before been made the subject of thematic study. Moreover, he wants to consider these independent of all notion of voluntary performing. They are acts in which the 'positing' element has become powerless. It is a *mere-thinking-of*, which has not got to the level of affirming; neither is it a kind of fanta-sizing, although the neutrality modification runs through both **fantasy** and the *epochē*. There is no way of having a reiteration of a neutralization unlike a fantasy (*Ideas* I § 112). The neutrality modification is the opposite of all positing, 'the counterpart of all producing', a 'shadowing' (*Schatten*), pointing to the 'radical separation' in consciousness (*eine radicale Scheidung*, *Ideas* I § 114, p. 269; Hua III/1 232). For Husserl, the neutrality modification is a wholly unique yet universal structural feature of consciousness and one that it is hugely important in that its presence enables the very possibility of philosophical reflection on the life of consciousness. *Epoché*, idle fantasy, etc., are themselves all varieties of neutrality modification. The neutrality modification is a very deep part of consciousness, but, because it makes no claim on truth or validity, it is, according to Husserl, difficult to access.

Nexus (*Zusammenhang*)   See also **consciousness**

Husserl, drawing on **Dilthey** frequently refers to the concrete, flowing and unified life of consciousness as a 'nexus' of internally interwoven psychic states or **lived experiences** (*Erlebnisse*) (see, for instance, *Phenomenological Psychology* § 1). For Husserl, there is a complex intertwining between all psychic experiences and they never occur atomistically in an isolated way.

Noema (*Noema*)   See also **act, intention, intentional content, noesis, noetic act, object**

The 'noema' (from the Greek meaning 'what is thought') is a key technical term introduced by Husserl around 1912 in his research manuscripts. The noema means the **intentional object** *as* perceived, *as* judged, *as* wished; generally speaking: as intended. In *Ideas* I § 96, Husserl claims that mastering the doctrine of the noema is 'of the greatest importance for phenomenology'. Elsewhere, he says that the account of the intentional object as noema provides a 'transcendental clue' to the entire multiplicity of possible experiences or ***cogitationes*** (CM § 21). Husserl's analysis of the noesis and noema is central to his understanding of the practice of phenomenology under the transcendental reduction. The noema is a key element in the eidetic description of consciousness; it is an '***objectivity*** belonging to consciousness and yet specifically peculiar' (*Ideas* I § 128). The noema is always the correlate of a noetic act or '**noesis**'; it is the object *as* it is perceived, thought, imagined, or whatever. There is an **a priori corre-lation** between the noesis and the noema and Husserl criticizes traditional tendencies to separate the study of these elements (as psychology sought to study psychic acts independently of the objects on which the acts were directed, *Ideas* I § 128). The term 'noema' is first used in the pencil draft of

Ideas I in 1912 and Husserl's first published discussion of noema and noesis occurs in ***Ideas*** I. However, the concept of the 'noetic' appears earlier in his 1906–1907 lectures on *Introduction to Logic and the Theory of Knowledge* (Hua XXIV § 27), and the general notion of the noema is discussed (but not under that name) in his summer semester 1908 *Lectures on the Theory of Meaning* (*Vorlesungen über Bedeutungslehre*, Hua XXVI). With the noema, Husserl is positing a single complex entity that will take combinations of what Frege includes under the term 'sense' (*Sinn*), mode of presentation, and the referential function of the act, i.e. the intentional object of the act. Husserl writes: 'the noema in itself has an objective relation and, more particularly, by virtue of its own sense' (*Ideas* I § 128). For this reason, Husserl's noema is not exactly identical with the Fregean concept of 'sense', although it appears to encompass that notion ('sense' is regarded as an abstract form inherent in the noema at *Ideas* I § 132). Husserl is essentially rethinking the relation between the act of giving meaning and the meaning and object intended. The noema is meant to replace what had previously been discussed under the ambiguous notions of '**content**' and '**object**' (*Ideas* I § 129). The noema cannot simply be the object as the object is accessed differently in different kinds of act (perceiving, remembering), neither does it simply provide a route to the object understood as something transcendent to the intentional act. The noema somehow includes both the object intended as something immanent within it and the mode of presentation of that object. The fundamental distinction that underlies the doctrine of noema is already to be found in the Fifth Logical Investigation, where Husserl distinguished between the 'object which is intended' and 'the object *as* it is intended' (LU V § 17), e.g. the Emperor of Germany may be understood as the 'son of Frederick III' or the 'grandson of Queen Victoria'. Husserl later says that the *Logical Investigations* concentrated primarily on the noetic side, i.e., in examining intentional actrs and did not sufficiently address the corresponding noemas (see Ideas I §128 note). In the 1906–1907 *Lectures on Logic and Theory of Knowledge*, Husserl speaks of grasping this intended object immanently, as it is given, without regard to existence (Hua XXIV § 38, 232). Husserl contrasts the real temporal living act of intending with the ideality or non-real nature of the object grasped as it is grasped. The problem is whether the noema as an immanent entity in consciousness is a real part of the occurrent thought, or whether it refers to the object beyond the thought, or whether it is the abstract ideal meaning (*Sinn*) through which the object is given. The exact meaning and precise status of the noema in Husserl's account is controversial. It has given rise to a huge discussion concerning the nature of the phenomenological theory of meaning and the nature of the intentional object. According to one – perhaps the standard – interpretation, originally proposed by **Aron Gurwitsch**, noemata are ideal entities (literally: abstract ideal senses) that allow an intentional act to refer to its intentional object. Husserl himself says that the real tree can be burnt, destroyed, but not the noema 'tree' (*Ideas* I § 89). It is not clear, however, whether as an abstract sense, the noema is meant to be a universal **species** or an individual. Others, e.g. John Drummond and Robert Sokolowski, argue that the noema is simply the **intentional object as intended**. According to this interpretation, the noema is a technical term to refer to the intentional object as explicitly thematized in the phenomenological reduction. On either interpretation, the noema is a complex entity and Husserl speaks of it possessing several different parts or moments. He speaks of the 'full' noema, the noematic 'core' (*Ideas* I § 129), and also of the 'innermost moment' (*Ideas* I § 129) in the noema that performs the task of being a bearer of properties, maintaining unity across different acts of referring, the object as 'determinable X' (see *Ideas* I § 131). The account in *Ideas* I is full of ambiguities. Husserl seems to have become less interested in specifying the technical meaning of the noema in his later writings, and the term is not common in *Cartesian Meditations* or *Crisis* where he speaks usually of the noetic-noematic correlation without further elaboration.

Noesis   See also **act, intention, noema**

The *noesis* is 'the concretely complete intentive mental process' approached in such a way that its noetic components are clearly emphasized (*Ideas* I § 96). The noesis includes what Husserl calls in the **Logical Investigations** the '**quality**' of the act, i.e. what all acts of hoping, or remembering, have in common. But the noesis has a larger function in that it is responsible for bestowing sense, for constituting the meaning of what it grasps. The noesis is always correlated with the **noema**.

Nominal act (*nominaler Akt*)   See also **nominalization, positing act**

A nominal act is an intentional act of **expression** that names or picks out an object through a **meaning**. This may mean an act whereby something is picked out explicitly by a noun or substantive or more generally a nominalization, e.g. the 'being-black of the cat'. Subject-predicate judgements can always be transformed using **nominalization**. Nominal acts are discussed in the **Logical Investigations** and in **Formal and Transcendental Logic.**

Nominalization (*Nominalisierung*) See also **proposition, state of affairs**

In LU V § 38, Husserl refers to the act whereby some complex expression is turned into a name that can then itself function as a subject of predication. The complex statement or **judgement** 'the cat is black' can be turned into the nominalization 'the black cat' or 'the cat's blackness' which then can act as a logical subject in further predicative statements, e.g. 'the black cat is gone'; 'the cat's blackness is striking'. Nominalization is a powerful act that consciousness performs to transform complex acts into single objects.

Non-participating spectator (*unbeteiligter Zuschauer*) See **disinterested spectator**

Normality (*Normalität*) See also **alien world, habit, homeworld, lifeworld, type, world**

The mature Husserl invokes the idea of 'normality' to express the manner in which the world is necessarily given in a horizon of familiarity (see **Experience and Judgment** § 46, § 93). The various objects that we can grasp are revealed in experience through the unity of present, past and future. In this way, the remembered experience outlines an essential order whereby we expect to experience new objects according to the previously given world. Thus, everything presented to the consciousness is characterized as 'normal' (according to an outlined style) or 'abnormal' (in that there is a break or rupture of certain intentions or expectations). The concept of normality is very broad and characterizes not only the way in which subjectivity faces certain objects but also the experience of the intersubjective world (*Ideen* II § 52, § 59). In relation to the **life-world** Husserl unfolds the relationship between normality and abnormality in terms of '**homeworld**' and '**alien world**'. Different meanings of normality and its opposite abnormality can be identified. Normality can be understood as **concordance** regarding the objects of perception (*Experience and Judgment*, § 21), as familiarity with certain experiences and circumstances

(*Ideas* II, § 59), as lack or deficiency of certain faculties and capacities (*Cartesian Meditations*, § 55; also in this paragraph Husserl speaks of the animal life in terms of abnormal life), as the familiar habits and traditions we share in our culture (homeworld), and so on. Moreover, the different senses of normality can be interwoven: a congenital blindness, for example, can be lived as normal (I have always experienced the world in this way) and at the same time as something abnormal (in relation with others I discover that they have an unknown sense for me). Departing from these basic features, we can examine other forms of normality, as '**typicality**'.

Now moment (*Jetztmoment*)   See **absolute consciousness, primary impression, protention, retention, time consciousness**

The 'now moment' is the experience of 'now' that belongs to every currently occurring **lived experience**. It is always related to a retention that retains an echo of the past and a **protention** or anticipation concerning what will happen in future. The 'now moment' is always a part or phase of the full lived experience. Each 'now moment' is replaced by another 'now moment' that marks itself off from the previous 'now moment' by being experienced as currently now, whereas the previous now moment is now characterized as *having-been*. The now moment in the Bernau manuscripts is described as the **fulfilment** of a previous protention and as at the point of intersection between protention and **retention**. The 'now moment' (*Jetztmoment*) gradually recedes and is replaced by another 'now moment' with the consciousness of the identical content. Every now has a just before as its limit (*Ideas* I § 82). Each now has a 'fringe' of moments around it. The original now is modified into a past-now with the same sensuous content except now indexed as 'having run off'. In listening to a transcendent temporal object such as a melody, we hear the present set of notes *as present*, but also hear them *as succeeding* an earlier set of notes, and *as about to be supplanted* by further notes or by silence. This 'now' presence is expansive and shared, it can include several items that are co-temporal. But the matter is complex: the present notes are stamped *as* present by having the character of coming after and coming before. There are '**retentions**' and '**protentions**' involved (X 84). Moreover, the past notes are not just heard in some sense but have the character of being retaine as *remembered* (X 79), the character of *having taken place*, of having once been *now*, they are also have the character of *leading up* to the present tone; they are continually being stamped with new characteristics. Husserl drew 'time diagrams' to illustrate how such a sensuous appearance endures in consciousness (see X § 10; § 43 and X 330–31). Each temporal phase or segment (*Querschnitt* or 'cross-section') seems to involve or is cross-referenced in relation to other temporal phases. This 'retention' is, of course, not an actual recurrence of the original now, but is something *intentionally* held in the current now phase: 'A continuity of elapsed tone phases is intended in the same now' (X 275). These continue to appear but in a modified way. There is a reaching back from the present into the immediate past, and that past, Husserl says, is never empty. As his thought on time developed, Husserl realized that the consciousness of the now cannot itself be 'now' and hence he postulated the idea of an **absolute consciousness** which is not in time.

Nuance (*Nuance*) See also **moment**

Husserl uses the term 'nuance' in the **Logical Investigations** and elsewhere (e.g. *The Idea of Phenomenology*, *Ideas* I) to refer to the individual occurrence of a specific property, e.g. this particular red shade of this billiard ball. He contrasts the individual red shade or nuance (*Rotnuance*) with the **species** *red* (Hua II 57).

Number (*Zahl, Anzahl*) See also *Philosophy of Arithmetic*

In his **Philosophy of Arithmetic**, Husserl, following **Weierstrass**, assumed that mathematics was founded in arithmetic and arithmetic was based on the cardinal numbers. Husserl therefore proposed to clarify the concept of number. He began from the positive whole numbers or cardinal numbers (1, 2, 3, etc.), as the foundation for all other number concepts, including the irrational, imaginary, real numbers, and so on. However, almost as soon as *Philosophy of Arithmetic* was written, Husserl departed from that assumption as it could not deal with more complex aspects of mathematics, especially the so-called *imaginary numbers* (e.g. $\sqrt{-1}$). In a Göttingen lecture of 1901 and in Foreword to **Logical Investigations**, Husserl recognizes that mathematics totally surpassed its original domain of number and quantity. He now sees mathematics as the 'theory of theories', the 'science of theoretical systems in general', and indeed as belonging within his more general **theory of manifolds** (*Mannigfältigkeitslehre*).

— O —

Object (*Objekt, Gegenstand*)   See also **concretum, content, noema, objectivity, thing**

Husserl employs two German terms, *Objekt* and *Gegenstand*, for the term 'object'. Kant also employed these two terms. Husserl defines an 'object' (*Objekt*), in the formal sense as anything that can be the bearer of true predicates (see *Ideas* I § 3). An 'object' in this logical sense is simply something of which something can be said; something to which some kind of property can be applied. In this sense, 'object', understood as any **thing** whatsoever, is a term in **formal ontology**. In *Ideas* I § 15, Husserl distinguishes between the categorial form 'object' which he regards as non-self-sufficient and abstract with respect to material objects, which are regarded as concrete entities (*concreta*). Object is a very broad category that includes real, ideal, concrete, abstract, individual and general objects. Husserl usually reserves the term 'object' (*Gegenstand*) for the object of knowledge, for what 'stands over' (*gegen* = 'against'; *stehen* = 'to stand') and against the subject in an act of knowing, this is often called the **intentional object**. The intentional object as it is apprehended and in the manner in which it is apprehended is also called the **noema**. **Brentano** identified the object and content of the intentional act whereas his students (e.g. **Twardowski**) sought to distinguish them. On Twardowski's reading, the **content** is internal to the act whereas the object (what the act is about) is external to the act. When I see a tree, the object (the tree) is external to my act; nevertheless, my act also has a tree content which makes it a tree seeing act as opposed to some other. Husserl sought to disambiguate different senses of 'content' and 'object' in his review of Twardowski (1894) and also in the Fifth Logical Investigation.

Objectification (*Vergegenständlichung, Objektivierung*)   See also **reification**

'Objectification' or 'objectivation' is at the core of an intentional act (*Ideas* I § 102). Something is presented as an object in some manner. **Natorp** claimed that the **ego** cannot be objectified.

Objectifying act or objectivating act (*objektivierender Akt*)   See also **act, foundation, intentionality, perception, presentation**
In the Fifth Logical Investigation § 37, Husserl distinguishes between objectifying and non-objectifying acts as a way of making clearer what **Brentano** described under the name of **presentation** (*Vorstellung*). Objectifying acts can include nominal acts that simply refer to an object or state of affairs as well as **judgements** that make reference to an object. Husserl believes acts that name an object, **nominal acts**, or acts that perceive an object as well as **judgements** are very different classes of objectifying act. Objectifying acts can be either **positing** or non-positing. Positing acts (*setzende Akte*), such as **perception** or **memory**, affirm the object as existent whereas non-positing acts (e.g. **fantasy**) present the object in a modified form with no commitment to actual existence. Husserl claims every act is either an objectifying act or founded on an objectifying act. Non-objectifying acts include **feelings**, wishes, wants that, for Husserl, do not contribute to the reference to the object (which is supplied by the objectifying act) but instead determine the manner in which the object is presented. Non-objectifying acts stand are founded on objectifying acts (see also **foundation**).

Objectivism (*Objektivismus*)   See also **naturalism, transcendentalism**
Husserl employs the term 'objectivism' mostly in his later writings (*Cartesian Meditations*, *Crisis* – the term does not appear in *Ideas* I) for any theoretical position in philosophy or science that treats the natural world (including consciousness) as entirely objective realm of objective things with objective properties (see *Crisis* § 14) and completely ignores the role of constituting subjectivity. Objectivism assumes there is a world as **being in itself**. Husserl contrasts 'physicalistic objectivism' or 'naive' objectivism with 'transcendental subjectivism' in *Crisis* Part Two, which treats the world as an achievement of subjectivity (see also CM Hua I 5; 46). For Husserl, objectivism was challenged by **Descartes**' discovery of the apodictic truth of the **cogito** but even Descartes did not make the transcendental status of the ego clear and his philosophy collapsed into a form of objectivism (*Crisis* § 18;).

Objectivity (*Gegenständlichkeit*)   See also **object, state of affairs**
The term 'objectivity' is used in the school of **Brentano** to refer anything that has objective status, whether it be an individual entity thing or a

complex counterpart of a **judgement**, usually known as a **state of affairs** (*Sachverhalt*). Husserl often uses it to refer to 'something objective' (*ein Objektives*) that is not necessarily a thing or a concrete individual, but could be a property, a relation, a categorial formation, a state of affairs, an ideal fact, etc. The ego is always in an intentional relation to some objectivity (Hua I 25; see also CM § 30).

Objectivity (*Objektivität*)   See also **objectivity (*Gegenständlichkeit*)**, **objectivism**
Husserl is concerned with the 'objectivity' of knowledge but he is against **objectivism** that ignores the role of subjectivity in the **achievement of knowledge**. In *Cartesian Meditation*, Husserl says that intersubjectively constituted **nature** is the first form of objectivity (CM § 55). Husserl also speaks of the self-objectification of the transcendental ego as an embodied being in the world.

Objectless presentations (*gegenständlose Vorstellungen*)   See also **intentionality, object, presentation**
'Objectless presentations' is a term used in the school of Brentano (e.g. Meinong) to refer to presentations or ideas that represent nothing actually existent, e.g., the thought of 'nothing,' a 'centaur', a 'round square', a 'green virtue' or a 'gold mountain', 'the present king of France'). Objectless presentations can be actually non-existent, or imagined, possible or even impossible entities. They were originally discussed by Bolzano in his *Wissenschaftslehre* Book I §67, and were subsequently taken up by Brentano, Twardowski, Marty, Meinong, Russell, and Husserl. Husserl deals with the issue of objectless presentations in his review of Twardowski and in his 1896 essay on 'Intentional Objects'. The problem is: how is it possible for consciousness to intend something that does not exist.

Occasional expressions (*occasionale Ausdrucken*)   See also **expression**
According to Husserl, there is an entire category of **expressions** that have meaning only in relation to their context or the occasion in which they are used. They are usually referred to as 'indexicals' but Husserl calls them 'essentially subjective and occasional expressions' (see LU I § 26). Husserl uses these expressions to cover those classes of meaning that vary from

person to person and occasion to occasion. For example 'look over there' will have a different meaning depending on when it is said. Examples of essentially occasional expressions include: 'I', 'you', 'here', 'there', 'above' 'below', 'later', 'yesterday', 'now' and so on, but it can also include expressions such as 'the president' when it is not clear to which president the reference is being made (LU I § 26).

On the Concept of Number. Psychological Analyses (*Über den Begriff der Zahl, psychologische Analysen*, 1887) See also *Philosophy of Arithmetic*

On the Concept of Number. Psychological Analyses is the title of Husserl's *Habilitation* thesis, written at Halle under the direction of **Carl Stumpf**, and printed but not publicly distributed in 1887. The mathematician Georg Cantor (1845–1918) was a member of Husserl's examination committee. This thesis was later incorporated – as the first four chapters – into Husserl's first published book ***Philosophy of Arithmetic*** (1891), now reprinted in Hua XII. In his *Habilitation* thesis, Husserl carries out 'psychological analyses' in the sense of **Brentano**'s **descriptive psychology**, namely descriptive analyses of the necessary components of the specific intentional acts that are involved in basic arithmetical operations. In this work, Husserl relies heavily on Brentano's distinction between 'physical' and 'psychical' relations to argue that the way items are identified and collected together in order to be counted requires grasping higher level 'psychical' or 'metaphysical' relations between the items, as opposed to the more usual 'primary' or 'content' relations. The act of **collective combination** that unites objects together in a **multiplicity** whose items can then be colligated or counted requires that the relating together of these objects not be based on any properties of the objects themselves but solely on their being treated as units or somethings.

Ontic meaning (*Seinssinn*) See also **sense**

Husserl frequently uses the term 'being sense' (*Seinssinn*), which David Carr translates as 'ontic sense' (*Crisis* § 33, p. 122; VI 124) or 'ontic meaning' (*Crisis* § 27, p. 100; VI 103), to mean the sense and ontological status that something has for us as a result of intentional **constitution**. According to Husserl in the *Cartesian Meditations* all sense, being and **validity** is an **achievement** of the **transcendental ego** (CM § 41).

Optimality (*das Optimale*)   See also **normality, perception**

Husserl deploys the concept of 'optimality' (usually in its adjective form: 'the *optimal*', *das Optimale*), e.g. 'optimal givenness' *Ideas* II IV 75; IV 131, to identify those possibilities that are offered to consciousness in order to achieve a deeper and better perception and knowledge of which that is perceived, thought, etc. Everything that is subjectively and intersubjectively given to us offers not only a *normal* character (according to the unity of experience) but also different possibilities that point out to new and better approaches to the already apprehended objects or experiences. Awareness of disappointments or deficiencies in our perception, on the one hand, and openness towards a more complete fulfillment, on the other, are the main features of the notion of optimality. Regarding optimality in **perception** (*Ideas* I § 44): certain places or circumstances are more appropriate to an adequate viewing or audition. There is the optimal place in the theatre from which to view the stage and hear the actors. The optimal colour is taken by us to be colour in clear sunlight rather than at twilight. Memories, spatial considerations, empathy and imagination can play a crucial role in determining the optimality of a mode of **givenness** in experience. At a higher level, that of social world and intersubjective products, the notion of optimality is also crucially important. Optimality can be relatively easily identified in sensuous experience, but its ways of realization at the intersubjective level are more difficult to recognize.

Origin of Geometry (*Ursprung der Geometrie*, 1936)   See also ***Crisis of European Sciences*,**

The 'Origin of Geometry' is the title of a draft essay by Husserl written in early 1936 and first published in 1939 in *Revue Internationale de Philosophie* in a special commemorative volume marking Husserl's death. The title of the fragment 'The Origin of Geometry as an Intentional-historical Problem', was actually bestowed by Husserl's assistant **Eugen Fink** who first edited the text. It forms part of the ***Crisis of European Sciences*** collection of manuscripts. This manuscript was later published by Walter Biemel as an appendix to the *Husserliana* edition of the *Crisis* with two paragraphs (omitted by Fink in his edition) referring to the discussion of Galileo. Biemel decided it ought to be grouped with the material on **Galileo** (*Crisis* § 9). 'The Origin of Geometry' was translated into French with a long and influential commentary by the French philosopher Jacques Derrida in

1962. Superficially, the text is a study of the manner in which geometry was transformed from a practical technique of land surveying (among the Egyptians) into an idealized science of pure ideal objects or **idealities**. He aims to make geometry self-evident through a disclosure of its historical genesis (*Crisis*, p. 371; VI 380). Husserl is puzzled how a science can develop into a long chain of insights with one building on the other, without the original foundational insights being re-activated. Instead, these results appear as ready-made insights for science. However, geometry is taken as simply exemplary for all forms of idealization where meaning forms (both those of science and culture) attain an unchanging self-identical status over time (the Pythagorean theorem, the word 'lion' in English). The essay then develops into a 'regressive inquiry' or **'questioning back'** back into the meaning of tradition. It includes a deep meditation on the nature of human historicity and the manner in which empirical forms of history depend on a historical a priori. Written language is identified as playing an essential role in fixing the ideal forms of the geometer and allowing them to preserved as identically the same from one generation to another. Geometry receives a living embodiment in language, a 'linguistic living body' (*Sprachleib*). The essay discusses the way in which meanings become sedimented in tradition and passed along without the original founding insights being actively re-awoken. Husserl maintains that the true nature of history and the development of human culture and tradition cannot be understood until regressive inquiries are conducted into how human **historicity** develops into tradition. This requires an inquiry back into the life-world and its a priori structures which serve as ground of all human activities.

Original sphere (*Originalssphäre*) See also **cogito, ego, sphere of ownness**

The 'original sphere' (CM § 47; *Originalsphäre*; *Crisis* VI 246), 'primordial sphere' (*die Primordialsphäre*; *Crisis* VI 189), or 'sphere of ownness' (*Eigensphäre*; CM § 44 Hua I 125; *die Eigenheitssphäre*; CM § 44; § 49) are terms used by Husserl, particularly in *Cartesian Meditations* §50, to refer to the sphere of immediate first-person experience under the **reduction**. The sphere of ownness refers to the entire sphere of actual and possible experiences that I as an ego can have directly, immediately and in a first-person way with everything foreign excluded through a special application of the **epoché**. At the same time, Husserl recognizes that the experiences of the other in **empathy,** although can never be given in a direct, first-person way, belong to the sphere of original experience. Husserl's discussion of this domain is ambiguous and unsatisfactory. He speaks also of the 'primordinal world' (*meine primordinale Welt*; CM § 49). In the Fifth Cartesian meditation, Husserl explains how the alien original sphere (of someone else) is motivated in one's own original sphere: 'the Other is appresentatively apperceived as the 'Ego' of a primordial world' (Hua I 146; CM 117).

Other (*das Andere, Anderer*)   See **alien world, other experience, self-experience**

Husserl speaks of the 'other' in many different ways. Phenomenology seeks to describe the experience of otherness in all its forms. The other is generally whatever is experienced as not belonging to the domain of **self-experience**. The 'other' can be the object in the external world, the other subject (*Anderer*), living body (*Leib*), person, animal or living thing, or the entire experience of the world as an **alien world**. According to Husserl the first other is the other ego (see CM § 45); sometimes more specifically 'the mother' or 'father' or members of the immediate family (Hua XV 604). The other subject is apprehended in **empathy**.

Other experience (*Fremderfahrung*)   See also **alter ego, empathy, experience, other, self-experience, sphere of ownness**

The mature Husserl uses the term 'other experience' (*Fremderfahrung*, CM § 43) as a general term to include all experiences of the 'other' or the 'foreign' or 'alien', including objects, other subjects (including animals), persons, the cultural word, and the whole world external to one's own self (CM § 44), whatever is characterized as 'not-I' (*nicht-Ich*, CM § 45). For Husserl, it is a phenomenological problem of great depth to explain how the other **person** or **ego** is encountered as a person or ego rather than just as a physical object in the spatial, material world. Husserl believes the other is encountered through **empathy**. Husserl uses the term 'other' primarily to designate the other person, who is over against me, who is 'there' as opposed to my 'here'. The other person is given to me as also possessing an ego, as being another 'I' (literally: an ***alter ego***).

—P—

Pairing (*Paarung*)   See also **analogizing apperception, association, empathy, passivity**

In ***Cartesian Meditations***, Husserl defines pairing as follows: 'Pairing is a *primal form of that passive synthesis* which we designate as "association", in contrast to passive synthesis of "identification"' (CM § 50) and later: '"Pairing" as an associatively constitutive component of my experience of someone else' (CM § 51). Pairing is a kind of **association** that takes place passively on the basis of similarity rather than actively through a collective combination or specific act of active **synthesis**. In CM § 51, Husserl claims that pairing is a universal phenomenon of the transcendental sphere. Two phenomena are passively apprehended as similar before active intentionality does anything to synthesize the appearances. These things (e.g. two colours) simply stand out as being similar in experience. Pairing is a key component of **empathy**. Pairing occurs when we link through an 'apperceptive transfer' one presentation with another, e.g. the gesture of another's body are paired with gestures of my body (see Hua XV 27; XV 249) through an apperceptive transfer or 'carrying over' (*Überträgung*). My **lived body** is sensually prominent for me but the other's body is grasped similarly through a pairing association: '*Ego* and *alter ego* are always and necessarily given *in an original "pairing"*' (CM 112; Hua I 142).

Part (*Teil*)   See also **concretum, mereology, moment, piece, Stumpf, whole**

A 'part' (*Teil*) is anything that can be identified as belonging to an object (Third Logical Investigation § 2), whether or not it can exist independently and separately in a detached way. Inspired by Carl **Stumpf**, Husserl, in his Third Logical Investigation, develops a sketch for a 'pure theory of wholes and parts', now more familiarly known as **mereology** (from the Greek *meros* which means 'part'). In the Second Edition, Husserl includes part-whole theory under '**formal ontology**'. Any independent entity is a **whole**; whereas a part is defined as anything that belongs to a whole, whether or not it can exist independently of the whole. Wholes can themselves be parts of larger wholes (as Ireland is a part of Europe, and parts can have parts (states can have counties). Husserl distinguishes between independent separable parts or **pieces** and dependent or 'abstract' parts that he calls **moments** (*Momente*). If a handle breaks off a cup, the handle is a 'piece' or independent part as it continues to exist independently of the cup. An example of a non-independent part is a colour that can only be presented with extension and has no independent existence apart from extension. Not all parts can be wholes, however. Wholes and parts stand in various relations of **dependency** (*Unselbstständigkeit*) such that one part is *founded* on another. But pieces that are independent cannot be founded on one another as they exist independently of each other. Husserl also speaks of proximate and remote parts. Something P can be an immediate part of some whole W but that W is itself a part of a larger whole Y. In this situation, P is a mediate or remote part of Y (see Third Logical Investigation §§ 18–20).

Passive synthesis (*passive Synthesis*)   See also **passivity, synthesis**
Husserl distinguishes between active and passive syntheses. A synthesis involves an act of combining. A passive synthesis is a uniting or combining that takes place without the active involvement of the ego. Husserl thinks the original unification of the stream of conscious experiences in time is a passive synthesis (*Ideas* I § 118; Hua XV 203) as is the kind of synthesis that presents sensory patterns as already unified in a certain manner through **association**. According to Husserl, every form of active synthesis presupposes a passive synthesis. The sensible world presents itself as already organized through passive synthesis. The 'always already there' character of the world in all experiences is accounted for through passive synthesis. Husserl distinguishes (Hua XV 203) between primary and secondary passivity. Primary passivity refers to the unification of the flow of my own life experiences; secondary passivity refers to the experiences of the intersubjective socially constituted world as already pregiven and formed.

Passivity (*Passivität*)   See also **active and passive genesis, association, receptivity, synthesis**
The later Husserl uses the term 'passivity' to pick out the 'pregiven' stratum of conscious life that precedes all active judging, willing and other active **syntheses** (acts of explicit combining, separating, comparing, distinguishing) and **position taking**. The domain of passivity is highly organized and regulated but not through active syntheses. In this regard, Husserl often

speaks of 'passive synthesis' and of the a priori 'lawfulness' (*Gesetzlichkeit*) that belongs to the passive sphere. The domain of passivity has its own structural organization and regularity. All activity presupposes passivity (*Ideas* II § 54); in *Experience and Judgment* § 23, Husserl states that there is always a passivity in experience (especially sensuous experience) that precedes all activity. The most fundamental form of passivity is the flow of temporal experience whereby **retentions** and **protentions** just occur as part of the experiencing of the present. Moments of **time** and moments of sensuous experience (e.g. apprehending a colour patch as having a uniform colour) are united together by **association**. In the *Origin of Geometryb*, Husserl explains passivity as follows: 'Passivity in general is the realm of things that are bound together and melt into one another associatively, where all meaning that arises is put together passively' (*Crisis*, p. 361; VI 372). The second law of passivity is **association**.

Perception (*Wahrnehmung*)   See also **adumbration, fantasy, image consciousness, memory, presentification**

Husserl wrote a number of studies on perception (both inner and outer), beginning with the Fifth and especially Sixth Logical Investigation, his *Thing and Space* Lectures (1907), right through to the *Passive Synthesis Lectures*, and even spoke of the 'phenomenological theory of perception' (DR Section 1), a term later used by **Merleau-Ponty**. Husserl offers detailed descriptions of the nature of the act of perception, the perceived object and its **adumbrations**, perceptual **sense or meaning**, the nature of perceptual **content**, the role of **time** in perceiving, the nature of the accompanying **horizons**, and so on. Husserl also distinguishes perception for other conscious states including **memory, fantasy, image consciousness** and **signitive intention**. Husserl begins with direct, immediate perceptual experience, which forms the basis of all consciousness. The bedrock mental act is perception. Perception, moreover, offers a paradigm of the kind of consciousness where intention finds **fulfillment**, where the activity of perceiving receives immediate and constant confirmation and collaboration. Hence perception is a paradigm of the **evidence**, the 'primordial form' (*Urmodus*) of intuitiveness, as Husserl puts it (APS 110; Hua XI 68; see also *Crisis* § 28, p. 105; Hua VI 107). The most basic form of perception is the perceiving of material, spatial objects, their properties and relations to other objects. Husserl maintains that we see individual 'things' (*Dinge*), as well as

their 'characteristics' (*Markmale*), 'properties' (*Eigenschaften*), 'determinations' (*Bestimmtheiten*), their independent parts and dependent **moments**
(*Momente*) in Perception can be of static entities (the table) or dynamic
events and processes, the falling of leaves, the bird flying, and so on. For
Husserl, moreover, events and states of affairs (that the pen is resting on
the table) are actually *perceived* although here he is extending the notion
of perception to include categorial intuition. We perceive relations, and we
see things foregrounded against a background. To see a red square is to see
it against a white background. Husserl summarizes his view of perception in
his *Thing and Space* lectures (1907):

> Perception in itself is perception of a perceived; its essence is
> to bring some object to appearance and to posit what appears
> as something believed: as an existing actuality. (Husserl, *Ding
> und Raum* § 40, p. 118; Hua XVI 141)

Similarly in the *Cartesian Meditations* he writes:

> External perception too (though not apodictic) is an experi-
> encing of something itself, the physical thing itself: 'it itself is
> there'. (CM I § 9, p. 23; Hua I 62)

Husserl's account of perception has been seen as a form of direct **realism**.
He stresses that sensuous perception is essentially characterized by the
fact that the object is given as 'itself there' (*selbst da*). Perception has the
character of offering us the thing itself as it actually is, 'it itself' (*es selbst*).
As he puts it in the *Logical Investigations*, it belongs to the very sense of a
perceptual act to be the self-appearance of the object (LU VI § 14 **II** 221;
Hua XIX/2 589). The object is given 'itself' (*selbst*), 'there' (*da*), 'in the flesh',
'bodily' (*leibhaftig*), *in proprie persona*, in the actual temporal present, in its
own being and 'being so' (*Sosein*, EP VII 251):

> [T]he object stands in perception as there in the flesh, it
> stands, to speak still more precisely, as actually present, as self-
> given there in the current now. (DR § 4, p. 12; Hua XVI 14)

Husserl strongly rejects representationalist accounts that substitute an

image, **sign** or picture for the perceptual object itself (see *Ideas* I § 43). In the *Logical Investigations*, for instance, there is a sustained critique of the representationalist accounts of perception found in Locke, **Berkeley**, **Hume**, **Mill**, and others (including, in *Ideas* I, the representationalism of the Gestalt psychologists Koffka, Köhler, and others). Husserl particularly attacks accounts that claim that what one actually perceives is a *sense datum*. Husserl also rejects the claim that every sensory element in perceptual consciousness involves exercise of a concept. The specific essence of perception is distinct from that of judgement. Husserl also rejects **phenomenalism**, whereby the object simply consists of a series of appearances or sense data. His appreciation of the nature of the stream of consciousness led him to reject all 'sensualist' accounts of it as a stream of contents 'without sense in themselves'; rather **consciousness** always involves intending of objects, sense and **constitution**. Husserl also rejects causal accounts of perception. Husserl is clear that perceiving an object does not involve an awareness of a causal connection between the thing and us, rather there is just the conscious sense of the unmediated presence of the object. To hear the doorbell ringing is not to hear the button being pressed even given that the button's being pressed initiates the causal chain that results in hearing the doorbell. For Husserl, we don't hear the *button* at all; we only know that the button is being pressed because we assume a certain scientific and causal view already. We read causation into the perceptual scene rather than finding it there. For Husserl, following **Brentano**, the act of perceiving involves unquestioned acceptance. Husserl often comments on the fact that *Wahrnehmung* in German means literally 'taking-for-true'. Husserl's analyses of perception explore both the noematic (object) side and also the noetic (mental side). On the noetic side, the perceiving is straightforward and has the character of certainty; on the noematic side, the object perceived has the character of existing actuality (CM II § 15). Perception involves 'perceptual belief' and 'perceptual certainty', Husserl says in *Ideas* I (1913) § 103. In his *Passive Synthesis* lectures, he writes that:

- One speaks of a believing inherent in perceiving (APS 66; Hua XI 28).
- Every normal perception is a consciousness of validity (APS 71; Hua XI 33).
- The primordial mode is certainty but in the form of the most straightforward certainty (APS 76; Hua XI 37).

Perception, for Husserl, is normally accompanied by a *'primal belief* or *protodoxa'* (*Ideas* I § 104, p. 252; Hua III/1 216) that is 'unmodalized' (*Ideas* I § 104). This unmodalized certainty can be modified into uncertainty, deeming likely, or maybe into something questionable (*Ideas* I § 103), but the 'unmodified' or 'unmodalized' form of certainty always has a privileged role. Furthermore, perception is essentially simple' or 'straightforward' (*schlicht*, LU VI § 46) for Husserl, this means there is no reasoning or inference involved in perception qua perception. As Husserl writes in the Sixth Logical Investigation:

> What this means is this: that the object is also an *immediately given object* in the sense that, as *this object perceived with this definite objective content*, it is not *constituted* in relational, connective, or otherwise articulated acts, acts founded on other acts which bring other acts to perception. (LU VI § 46 **II**, p. 282)

We receive the object 'in one blow' (*in einem Schlage*) as he puts it. The fact that perception is straightforward means that it delivers the object at once, in the modes of actuality and certainty. But, of course, it does not mean that we see only a single object. We can have simple straightforward perception of complex objects (a pile of books, a book on the table, etc). Husserl is well known for claiming that, in perception, the object is given as it is in itself, while at the same time it is given in *profiles* or **'adumbrations'** (*Abschattungen*). The object as a whole is never given; it always presents from one side or perspective. Nevertheless, although the object is seen from one side, the *whole* object is given in the perceiving. External perception has the 'sense' (*Sinn*) whole object, even if only one side is 'properly' seen. As Husserl makes clear, even if it is the case that the perception is only of one side under one aspect, nevertheless, it is clear that *the whole object* is intended and 'meant' in the act of perceiving. Husserl claims that the other unseen sides of the object are 'co-intended' in an empty way. Imagination can fill in these empty intendings, e.g. when I visualise that the brown colour of this top of the table continues as the colour of the underneath part of the table. Husserl's account of perception and especially the role of the body in perceiving was hugely influential on **Aron Gurwitsch**, Merleau-Ponty, and others.

Person (*Person*) See also **ego, monad, personalistic attitude, Scheler**
Husserl uses the term 'person', following **Kant** and others, to mean the
human **subject** in its full concreteness, especially in its social relations
with other subjects, and in terms of agency, willing, judging, valuing,
and generally exercising rational **self-responsibility** (*Ideas* II § 60). The
discussion of 'persons' is introduced in '**Philosophy as a Rigorous Science**'
and treated especially in *Ideas* II (§ 49–51), *Cartesian Meditations* § 32 and
in his writings on intersubjectivity. Persons are members of social groupings
(e.g. families) and communities, and are correlated with an environment
or surrounding world (*Umwelt, Ideas* II § 50). Persons approach the world
primarily through the '**personalistic attitude**' (*Ideas* II § 34) that considers
human beings in terms of their inner, subjective, mental life and motivations. Persons stand in relation to **values** and in mutual understanding
(through **empathy**) and communication with one another (in what Husserl
calls 'the community of monads). **Scheler** developed a phenomenology
of personhood in his *Formalism in Ethics* (1913) where he distinguishes
between a person and an ego in that for Scheler a person need not be
opposed to another (hence, for Scheler, God is a person). Husserl sees the
ego as the constituting source and the person as the fully concrete agent
in a social world. The subject as person is not visible to someone in the
naturalistic attitude that sees all physical entities as objects of nature (*Ideas* II
§ 51). The person is the focus of moral regard and the bearer of rights. The
person develops a particular **style** of life and acts with typicality and habituality in certain circumstances (*Ideas* II § 60). Husserl allows the concept of
'person' in a broad sense to be applied also to animals that have personal
egos (see CM § 32).

Personalistic attitude (*die personalistische Einstellung*) See **attitude,
natural attitude, naturalistic attitude, person**
The 'personalistic attitude' is Husserl's term for the normal attitude taken
by humans towards themselves and others *as* **persons** (in which they treat
each other as 'I', 'you and 'we'), and the manner humans interrelate in
social groupings, their attitude towards animals, and so on (see *Ideas* II §
49). In specifically personal interactions, in talking to one another, shaking
hands, etc., humans adopt the personalistic attitude. The personalistic
attitude is generally speaking not a theoretical attitude ('personal life is
generally non-theoretic', *Crisis*, p. 318; VI 297); it is primarily practical and

direct. The natural sciences deliberate exclude the person and the person-alistic attitude. Indeed, this self-forgetfulness of the personal ego (*Ideas* II Hua IV, 184) is 'a consistent, but unconsciously applied blinder' (Hua XXV, 25) of modern natural science, which is also blind to value. In *Ideas* II, Husserl sees the **natural attitude** as founded on and subordinated to the personalistic attitude which is the basic stance for human persons to each other. First and foremost, the person is a genuinely objective thing, consti-tuted in objective time and belonging to the spatiotemporal world (IX 418). BY way of contrast, its essence is quite distinct from that of 'real things' (*Ding-Realitäten*, VIII 493). The specifically personalistic attitude is:

> [T]he attitude we are always in when we live with one another, talk to one another, shake hands with another in greeting, or are related to another in love and aversion, in disposition and action, in discourse and discussion. (*Ideas* II § 49, p.192; Hua IV 183)

It is a 'pre-theoretical' attitude. In *Ideas* I, the 'natural attitude' includes our normal relations to others as persons and in their social roles. In *Ideas* II § 62, he speaks of the 'interlocking' (*ineinandergreifen*) between natural and personalistic attitudes, but he explicitly differentiates the personalistic attitude from the natural, and indeed maintains that the natural attitude is in fact 'subordinated' to the personalistic attitude (*Ideas* II § 49). The natural attitude is actually reached through a self-forgetting or abstraction of the self or ego of the personalistic attitude, through an abstraction from the personal which presents the world in some kind of absolutized way, as the world of nature (IX 419).

Personality of a higher order (*Personalität höherer Ordnung*)   See also **person**

The term 'personality of a higher order' is based on the concept of 'objects of a higher order' found in the school of **Brentano**, especially in **Meinong**. The term 'personality of a higher order', for Husserl (the term appears mainly in his *Intersubjectivity* volumes and in the *Kaizo* articles, but see *Crisis* § 55; Hua XV 421), refers to the nature of social entities such as institutions or social groups, which can be treated as if they were subjects. Personalities of a higher order are groups, communities, nations, the church, the state, and so on (see CM

§ 37; *Crisis* § 55). Institutions, corporations, nations can be treated as having certain forms of identity, consciousness and self-consciousness analogous to that of an individual subject. Personalities of a higher order are founded on individual subjectivities but have their own higher order identity, see CM § 58. In genuine communities, the individual is not submerged in the group but expresses himself or herself through the group and in unity with it. Authentic communities are collectivities which emerge from below and do not suppress the individuals who themselves constitute the group. Personalities of a higher order are bound together by norms (XV 421).

Phänder, Alexander (1870–1941)   Phänder was a German philosopher, born in Iserlorn in 1870. He initially studied to be an engineer but moved to study **descriptive psychology** with **Theodor Lipps** at Munich. His first book *The Phenomenology of Willing* (1900) anticipated by one year Husserl's use of the term '**phenomenology**' in the Second Volume of the *Logical Investigations* (1901). He went on to publish studies in **psychology** and phenomenology on such topics as the **will, feeling, motivation**, and **ethics**. He was a member of the Munich Phenomenological Circle. He applied for the position of professor in Freiburg as successor to Husserl but he was unsuccessful, the post going to **Heidegger** with Husserl's support.

Phantasy (*Phantasie*)   See **fantasy**

Phantom (*Phantom*)   See also **perception, thing**
The term 'phantom' is used by Husserl (see *Thing and Space* § 23; *Ideas* II § 10) to denote an experience of a spatial material thing in so far as it is understood purely in terms of its fluctuating perceptual characteristics (its sensuous schema, *das sinnliche Schema*, Hua XVI 343) and not considered as part of the causal nexus. For Husserl, 'the mere phantom is not yet a thing' (Hua XVI 345) and indeed as a phantom is in permanent flux, since, for example, the colour surface of an object is dependent on the changing light whereas in referring to the sensed thing one tends to assume the colour is fixed and unvarying. The thing as purely visually apprehended (*Sehding*) is the 'visual phantom' and likewise there can be 'tactile phantoms' or purely heard aural phantoms (without reference to wider context, background, spatiality, temporality, causality, etc). Husserl also thought there were concretely occurring individual phantoms in the world, e.g. rainbows.

Phenomenalism (*Phänomenalismus*)   See also **Mach, phenomenology**
Phenomenalism is the doctrine that the physical world is entirely explainable
in terms of the experiences of subjects, especially their sensory experiences. The philosopher G. F. Stout explains phenomenalism as holding
that 'all propositions concerning the existence, persistence, qualities and
behaviour of material objects can be translated into equivalent propositions
about sensations actual and possible in their relation to each other' (see
his 'Phenomenalism', *Proceedings of the Aristotelian Society*, 1938–9, pp.
2–18). **Mach** held a version of phenomenalism according to which physical
objects are to be understood as logical constructs out of **sensations**.
Phenomenalism is to be distinguishes from **phenomenology**, which does
not limit **appearances** to sensory appearances or **sensations**.

Phenomenological reduction   See **reduction**

Phenomenology (*Phänomenologie*)   See also **genetic phenomenology, intentionality, phenomenon, static phenomenology**
The word *phenomenology* literally means 'the logic or science of phenomena'
and the term first appeared in philosophy texts in the eighteenth century, in
Lambert, Herder, **Kant**, Fichte, and Hegel. Johann Heinrich Lambert, a
follower of Wolff, employed the term in the title of the fourth section in his
Novus Organon to signify a *doctrine of appearance* (*Schein*). Lambert
inspired Immanuel Kant (1724–1804), who infrequently used the term
'phenomenology' in several early letters. For instance, in a letter to Lambert
of 2 September 1770, Kant says that 'metaphysics must be preceded by a
quite distinct, but merely negative science (*Phaenomenologica generalis*)'.
Similarly, in his letter to Marcus Herz of 21 February 1772, Kant spoke of
'phenomenology in general' (*die Phänomenologie überhaupt*), which
eventually developed into the transcendental aesthetic section of the
Critique of Pure Reason. Kant continues to employ the term in his mature
treatises also. *Phenomenology*, for Kant, is that branch of science that deals
with things in their manner of appearing to us, for example, relative motion,
or colour, properties which are dependent on the human observer. Kant
uses the term in his pre-critical *Dissertation* of 1770, where he understands
'phenomenology' as the preliminary philosophical attitude capable of delim-
iting the content of sensibility thereby preserving rationality pure of
contingency. At this time, Kant still belongs to the 'pre-critical' metaphysical

tradition, which distinguishes between the subjective sensible appearance, on one hand, and the intelligible objective reality, on the other, maintaining thus the divide where rational understanding must remain pure of **sensibility** and, by consequence, where the former is primary in the very construction of empirical knowledge. The critical revolution inaugurated by the *Critique of Pure Reason* (1781) and prepared by the *Letter to Marcus Herz* (1772) throws this pre-critical distinction into doubt and thereby focuses no longer on the confusion brought about by sensible phenomena for the rationality of objective knowledge, but rather on the elaboration of the *conditions of possibility* for objective knowledge. This '**transcendental**' shift implies the substitution of *phenomenology*, as a preliminary philosophical attitude whose task consists in circumscribing the contingency of sensibility and thereby safeguarding the objectivity of rational knowledge, by *aesthetic*, understood as the transcendental explication of the **a priori** conditions for all or any possible intuition. Kant's enquiry into the conditions for the possibility of **objectivity** – as seen from the subjective side – was criticized by G. W. F. Hegel (1770–1831) for failing to develop a conception of mind other than as consciousness. For this reason, Hegel said that Kantian philosophy remained 'only a *phenomenology* (not a *philosophy*) of mind'. After Kant, the word *phenomenology* undergoes, in the development of German Idealism, a profound and radical redefinition. Hegel revives the word phenomenology but nonetheless entirely transforms its definition. Phenomenology, for Hegel, is defined speculatively as the manifestation of spirit in history. In this manner, the *Phenomenology of Spirit* (1807), as first part of Hegel's Absolute system of philosophical knowledge, traces the movement in which consciousness comprehends itself as the self-recognition of spirit, and thus, as the effective and signified reconciliation of 'substance' and 'subject'. Given that one cannot begin, according to Hegel, with the absolute itself, phenomenology is the necessary and first moment in the itinerary or the odyssey of consciousness engaged in the process of its self-recognition as absolute. Phenomenology is seen thus as the movement by which consciousness evolves from the manifest to its self-recognition as speculative. Constituting part of the system of philosophical knowledge, phenomenology in Hegel's thought literally means *from* phenomena *to* logos. In this sense, philosophical knowledge is comprehended as the movement of historical 'becoming': it is first seen as 'immediacy', sensible certainty, and progressively evolves, in and through the necessary deployment of its own figures of manifestation, by and through the essential process of its mediation, to its identification and recognition as spirit. The concept of phenomenology is used to depict this movement of 'becoming' and mediation, in that it describes the different manifestations of philosophical knowledge progressively evolving into their own self-identification and realization as spirit. The phenomenon is thus entirely and always thought in the essential process of spirit's 'becoming' and furthermore the modern opposition between 'representing subject' and 'represented object' is dialectically surpassed within the development of spirit's historical meaning. The phenomenological task of consciousness is precisely to experience this development and thus phenomenology is the name of this progressive experience in which all oppositions or contradictions are surpassed and converted into their mutual and reciprocal comprehension. Such a task implies that philosophical knowledge is conceived in and as being, or furthermore, that knowledge inhabits being and is never to be seen as a simple exterior point of view on being. Johann Gottlieb Fichte (1762–1814) also made use of the term 'phenomenology' in his *Wissenschaftslehre* of 1804 to refer to the manner of deriving the world of appearance, which illusorily appears to be independent of consciousness, from consciousness itself. Husserl encountered the term not in Hegel or Kant but in **Brentano**. In his lectures on *Descriptive Psychology* (1889), Brentano employed the phrase '**descriptive psychology** or descriptive phenomenology' to differentiate this science from genetic or physiological psychology. In the period between 1891 and 1901, Husserl primarily understood phenomenology as the fundamental '**clarification**' (*Klärung*) and 'epistemic critique' (*Erkenntniskritik*) of what he termed the 'idea of knowledge', setting out the a priori structures of the concepts and acts involved essentially in **cognition** and **knowledge** per se. In particular, Husserl is seeking a specific kind of analysis that involves the identification of certain subjective conditions necessary for objective cognition, and trying to distinguish these 'phenomenological' conditions from the empirical, factual or 'psychological' conditions also involved in human cognition. After 1907, he came to recognize the affinity between his approach and that of Kant, and reformulated phenomenology as a new and radical kind of ***transcendental philosophy***. The concept of *phenomenology*, provisionally introduced by Husserl in the Introduction to the *Investigations*, but uncovered gradually only during the course emerging fully blown in the Fifth and Sixth, is not presented primarily as a *method* in the First Edition, but certainly is so considered by Husserl by the time of *Idea of Phenomenology* (1907, Hua II 23). In the First Edition of the *Investigations*, phenomenology is introduced as a presuppositionless mode of approaching epistemological concepts in order to exhibit them their conceptual contents and connections with other concepts with 'clarity and distinctness' (*Klarheit und Deutlichkeit*; LU, Hua XIX/1 10). This clarification of concepts is achieved, not by linguistic discussions, but by tracing back these concepts to their 'origin' (*Ursprung*) in intuition. In his 1902/3 lectures on epistemology, Husserl was already clarifying the distinction between **descriptive psychology** and phenomenology, which he characterizes as a pure theory of essences' (*reine Wesenslehre*, Hua XIX/1 xxx–xxxi). In 1903, in his 'Report on German Writings on Logic for the years 1895–1899' (*Bericht über deutsche Schriften zur Logik in den Jahren 1895–1899*), he explicitly repudiated his initial characterization of the work as a set of investigations in 'descriptive psychology'. Repeating the language of the Introduction to the *Logical Investigations*, he calls for an 'illumination' (*Aufklärung*) of knowledge independent of metaphysics and of all relation to natural, real being, suggesting he is already moving towards the reduction:

> This illumination requires a phenomenology of knowledge; for the lived experiences of knowing, wherein the origin of the logical Ideas lies, have to be fixed upon and analysed in the illumination, but in removal from all interpretation that goes beyond the real (*reellen*) content of those lived experiences. (*Early Writings*, p. 251; Hua XXII 206)

Husserl continues:

> Phenomenology therefore must not be designated as 'descriptive psychology' without some further qualification. In the rigorous and true sense it is not descriptive psychology at all. Its descriptions do not concern lived experiences, or classes thereof, of empirical persons; for of persons – of myself and of others, of lived experiences which are 'mine' and 'thine' – it knows nothing, assumes nothing. Concerning such matters it poses no questions, attempts no definitions, makes no

hypotheses. In phenomenological description one views that
which, in the strongest of senses, is given, just as it is in itself.
(EW, p. 251; Hua XXII 206–7)

Husserl goes on to say that phenomenology aims to arrive at a clear
distinct understanding of the *essences* of the concepts and laws of logic
through 'adequate abstraction based on intuition', a conception of ideating
abstraction which will be sharpened over the years (in *Ideas* I, for instance).
In the Second Edition of the *Investigations*, Husserl added the following
new paragraph:

> Assertions of phenomenological fact can never be epistemo-
> logically grounded in *psychological experience (Erfahrung)*, or
> in *internal perception* in the ordinary sense of the word, but
> only in *ideational, phenomenological inspection of essence*.
> The latter has its illustrative start in inner intuition, but such
> inner intuition need not be actual internal perception or other
> inner experience, e.g. recollection: its purposes are as well
> or better served by any free fictions of inner imagination (*in
> freiester Fiktion gestaltende Phantasie*) provided they have
> enough intuitive clarity. (LU V § 27, **II** p. 136; Hua XIX/1 456)

Between 1901 and 1913 Husserl refined his understanding of phenomenology as an eidetic science, and by the time of the Second Edition of the
Investigations (1913), he had expunged most of the references to phenomenology as descriptive psychology and, throughout the work, had inserted
phrases that emphasized the pure, a priori, essential nature of phenomenology, accessed through pure, immanent, essential intuition, without
reference to reality or actuality. A typical example of these insertions is
found in the Appendix to the Sixth Investigation:

> Phenomenology is accordingly the theory of experiences
> in general, inclusive of all matters, whether real (*reellen*) or
> intentional, given in experiences, and evidently discoverable
> in them. Pure phenomenology is accordingly the theory of the
> essences (*die Wesenslehre*) of 'pure phenomena', the phe-
> nomena of a 'pure consciousness' or of a 'pure ego': it does

not build on the ground, given by transcendent apperception,
of physical and animal, and so of psycho-physical nature, it
makes no empirical assertions, it propounds no judgements
which relate to objects transcending consciousness: it establishes no truths concerning natural realities. (LU VI, App. **II** p.
343; Hua XIX/2 765)

In the same Appendix, Husserl emphasizes that to doubt what is immanent
in consciousness and given exactly as it is would be irrational (*unvernünftig*,
Hua XIX/2 768). In other words, phenomenological method involves tracing
concepts back to their sources in **intuition**, although, in the Second Edition,
Husserl insists that this is not to be understood as a kind of empirical-genetic
investigation of how concepts arise in natural reality. Husserl continued to
develop and expand on his conception of phenomenology. Thus, in the first
draft of his **Encyclopaedia Brittanica** article (1927), he wrote:

The term *phenomenology* is generally understood to designate
a philosophical movement, arising at the turn of this century,
that has proposed a radical new grounding of a scientific
philosophy and thereby of all sciences (*Trans. Phen.*, 83; Hua
IX 237)

From around 1907 Husserl interprets phenomenology as essentially transcendental. As Husserl writes in the first draft of his *Encyclopedia Britannica*
article on 'Phenomenology':

The transcendental reduction opens up, in fact, a completely
new kind of experience that can be systematically pursued:
transcendental experience. Through the transcendental reduction, *absolute* subjectivity, which functions everywhere in
hiddenness, is brought to light along with its whole transcendental life. (*Trans. Phen.*, 98; Hua IX 250)

Around 1917 Husserl began to distinguish static or **constitutive phenomenology** from **genetic phenomenology**. For Husserl, phenomenology
requires this proximity to being and thus refuses the simple epistemological
exterior point of view of a representing subject and a represented object.

It is in this sense that the commandment of Husserlian phenomenology calls for the 'return to the things themselves'. For Husserl, phenomenology does not and indeed cannot establish an absolute comprehension in which knowledge and being would speculatively signify one another as immanently signified dialectical moments of spirit. Husserlian phenomenology consists in explicating the **horizon** from which phenomena are constituted, that is, the plane from which things appear. In this sense, phenomenology for Husserl means to return to the sources of evidence in which things are given. Phenomenology is thus, for Husserl (and contrarily to Hegel), an infinite project which cannot, by definition, constitute itself in an absolute knowledge as spirit. Phenomenology explicates the meaning that the objective world of realities possesses for us in experience. This meaning can in this manner be rendered, revealed but never as such modified. For phenomenology firstly responds to the necessity of describing and comprehending the lived experience of truth without ever falling into psychologism and the relativism psychologism implies. The first form phenomenology harbours is thus of a pure explication of the lived states of thought and knowledge. 'Pure' is meant here as only attributable to the lived states apprehended in intuition and not to the lived states that arise empirically. In this sense, the pure description phenomenology practices reveals the modality by which objects are aimed at and uncovers the intuitions by which these objects are presented. As such, phenomenology generalizes its descriptive operation to all conscious activity, whether spiritual or perceptual, it can be said to operate a general explication of all lived states for consciousness. Phenomenology is an eidetic science whose task is purely descriptive of the immanent configurations of consciousness. The phenomenological description levels hence a critique towards both the classical idealist and realist schemas in that it radically questions the subject–object distinction. For the meaning of the transcendence of the object cannot, in phenomenology, be considered as a mental production or a simple exterior given. However, in order for this critique to harbour any meaning phenomenology must develop a renewed understanding of the transcendental to which Husserl will give the signification of a 'universal ontology' and consequently edict as 'first philosophy'. In this sense, phenomenology studies the modality by which and in which consciousness originally constitutes the objective meaning of all beings. It is in this original constitution that is to be understood the phenomenological concept of reduction (**epochē**). The reduction, also understood as the methodological necessity of a suspension or a bracketing of determined and constituted knowledge, is to be grasped as that modality by which is attained the *a priori* correlation between the transcendental subject and the world in general. The 'natural consciousness' – which also defines, according to Husserl, the scientific activity and attitude – adheres immediately to the certainty of the existence of the world, that is it remains naive by not yet comprehending its own participation in the donation of the world. The importance of the phenomenological reduction is that it reveals consciousness to itself in that it deploys the activity of consciousness in the constitution of the givenness of the world. In this sense, the phenomenological reduction reappropriates consciousness itself by revealing its operative modality in the constitution of the world as given. To pose consciousness as the origin of all position of transcendence is not however, for Husserl, to elaborate an empirical genesis or a link of causality. Why? For the modality of constitution marks solely and uniquely the intentional correlations between **noesis** and **noema**, that is, between the intentional lived states of consciousness and their correlates. Certainly, the **transcendence** which belongs to the meaning of the being of the world is immanent to subjectivity but not in the sense of an inclusion since, for Husserl, the world is never understood as a component of the self. Husserl speaks rather of a '"transcendence", which consists in not-really being included' (*irreellen Beschlossenseins*, CM 26; Hua I 65) meaning thus that he intends on explicating a new transcendental idealism opposed and critical of all psychological idealism. Hence, in phenomenology one must grasp that 'phenomena' are not simple observable things; similarly, they are not the manifestation of an unknown or unknowable being. They are rather, as Husserl states it in the *Cartesian Meditations*, 'my pure life, together with the ensemble of its pure lived states and of its intentional objects' (p. 18); which means phenomena constitute the originary appearing of the things themselves.

Phenomenon (*Phänomenon, phainomenon,* φαινόμενον) See also **appearance, givenness, phenomenology**

Husserl takes over the term 'phenomenon' from **Kant**. It is a transliteration of the Greek word *phainomenon* (φαινόμενον), which means 'appearance'. According to Husserl, phenomenology treats everything that is given or appears as a phenomenon. Phenomenology does not seek for a 'thing-in-iself' or 'noumenon' behind the phenomenon but attends to the phenomenon itself in its manner of **givenness**. The concept of phenomenon includes the idea of something that manifests itself and also the experiencing of that manifestation. In his *Idea of Phenomenology*, Husserl says: 'The meaning of the word "phenomenon" is twofold because of the essential correlation between appearing and what appears. "*Phainomenon*" properly means "that which appears", and yet it is predominantly used for the appearing itself, the subjective phenomenon' (Hua II 14). **Heidegger** later interpreted the Greek word *phainomenon* as meaning 'that which shows itself from itself', the 'self-showing'. In *Being and Time* (*Sein und Zeit*) §7, Heidegger writes: '[W]hat shows itself (the phenomenon in the genuine primordial sense) is at the same time an "appearance" as an emanation of something which *hides* itself in that appearance – an emanation which announces.' This statement dissociates phenomenon from a mere **appearance** and consequently understanding it as a shown given *also* retracting itself from its **givenness**. This radicality, however, could only have been possible by the ground-breaking role played by Husserl in his redefinition of the term phenomenon. What Husserl revealed in the term 'phenomenon' – opening thus the very field of **transcendental phenomenology** – is nothing less than an intentional configuration in which the 'things themselves' manifest themselves to us in relation to the very manner in which *we* are present to them. It is in this sense that the famous call of transcendental phenomenology – the 'return to the things themselves' (*zu den Sachen selbst*) – must be understood. The paradox of transcendental phenomenology is thus that the things themselves *are* phenomena that, and because they do not appear as such to the natural attitude of consciousness (the attitude by which consciousness is simply aware of that which it is confronted or exposed to and not yet to the manner or modality, the condition or possibility by which the things themselves are present to consciousness as phenomena), require, in order to present themselves as they are, the work of transcendental phenomenology. However, and it is important to notice this decisive fact, since phenomena only appear as such through a phenomenological investigation – that is, by the very application of a precise modality of *logos apophantikos* and thus by the actualization of a phenomenological reduction and suspension (**epochē**) of the natural attitude of consciousness – the very structure and essence of phenomena is at the outset *problematic*. It is precisely this problematical character of phenomena that Husserl will stress in the abstract of the 1907 Göttingen Lectures entitled *The Idea of Phenomenology*. In this explicative and introductory text, Husserl notes that the phenomenological study of the modes of knowledge must always be understood as the study of the **essence** from which is brought forth their inherent intentionality, that is, the possibility and the condition of the object of knowledge as well as of the knowledge of the object. Furthermore, this definition means that the phenomenology of **knowledge** is the science of the phenomena of knowledge in this double sense: on the one hand, science of knowledge as explication of appearances, figurations, presentations given to consciousness in which such *givens* configures themselves and become – either actively or passively – object *of* a consciousness *and*, on the other hand, analysis of this objectivity itself, that is of the act, the aim, the constituting mode of consciousness itself in the structuring of the **horizon** from which they are rendered possible. The word *phenomenon* is thus double for Husserl. It signifies both and at the same time, by bringing together and allying, that which appears (*das Erscheinende*) to consciousness and the appearing itself (*das Erscheinen selbst*) of consciousness. This internal difference in and within the concept of phenomenon opens the very possibility of the Husserlian phenomeno-logical project: to *return* from that which appears to consciousness towards the appearing itself of consciousness, which, as such, does not appear. The phenomenon is, in this sense, for Husserl that which appears in that appearance is always and already configured by the appearing itself of that which appears and which as such does not appear. This double nature of the term phenomenon orchestrates and commands the 'reversing' movement and infinite modality of the phenomenological reduction. In this sense, the phenomenological **reduction** (*Re-duktion*, *Zurückführung*) only suspends the validity of the world proper to the natural attitude of consciousness in order to provoke and engage the 'pure spectacle of the world' in its transparency and intentional structures. Hence, the movement of the phenomenological reduction only accomplishes itself when, returning from mere description to the acts conferring signification and to the meaning inherent to the noetic activity which they presuppose, are revealed the intentional phenomena of the 'transcendental life of consciousness', that is, when is deployed in consciousness the internal life of its 'lived present' (*lebendige Gegenwart*). It is in and within this 'lived present of consciousness' that the infinite dynamic of phenomena, the interminable immanence of their proliferation, is properly revealed. When, in the § 7 of *Being and Time*, Heidegger exposes the expectations of the phenomeno-logical method for fundamental ontology not only does he recuperate the entirety of Husserlian phenomenology in order to bring it to its extreme possibility, but also demonstrates in which manner the very potentiality of the phenomenological project was already at work in Greek thought through a proper examination of the words of *phainomenon* and of *logos*. In this manner, for Heidegger following Husserl's initial breakthrough, the meaning of phenomenology coincides with that of philosophy in that both explicate the same singular task: *apophainestai tà phainomena* – bring the appearing of that which appears to apparition.

Philosophical attitude (*die philosophische Einstellung*) See also **attitude, naturalistic attitude, personalistic attitude, phenomeno-logical attitude, theoretical attitude**

Husserl contrasts the **natural attitude** with the philosophical attitude in *The Idea of Phenomenology* (1907). In the natural attitude, the world – and our knowledge of it – is taken for granted. The philosophical attitude, inaugurated by the Greek sophists (e.g. Gorgias) and sceptics, and radicalized by **Descartes** with his universal doubt, puts the world in question and also puts in question the achievement of knowledge. However, tradi-tional philosophy, including the philosophy of **Kant**, did not recognize the novel manner of its own point of view. Phenomenology is required to clarify the meaning and radicality of the philosophical attitude (see PRS). Until this happens, philosophy is incapable of becoming a rigorous science.

'Philosophy as a Rigorous Science' (*Philosophie als strenge Wissenschaft, Logos* 1910/1911) See also **historicism, naturalism, monad**

This is the title of an influential essay, Husserl's only publication between the **Logical Investigations** (1900/1901) and *Ideas* **I** (1913). Husserl was invited by the **Heinrich Rickert** to contribute an essay, *Philosophie als strenge Wissenschaft*, (*Philosophy as a Rigorous Science*, now Hua XXV 3–62), to the first issue of Rickert's new journal *Logos* published in 1910–11. This programmatic essay offered a sustained critique of **naturalism** and **historicism** as leading to **relativism** and **scepticism**. In this essay Husserl refers back explicitly to the critique of psychologism in the first volume of

LU, *Prolegomena to Pure Logic* (1900), esp. §§ 25–9 where he discusses the Principle of Non-Contradiction. Husserl's diagnoses naturalism as containing within it a 'countersense' or 'countersensical circle', which is similar to his earlier claim that psychologism contains an 'absurdity' or countersense. In the essays, Husserl's earlier critique of **psychologism** is extended to all varieties of *naturalism* including the naturalistic psychology of **Wilhelm Wundt**. But he also found a new target in the increasingly influential historical **hermeneutics** of **Wilhelm Dilthey**, which he viewed as a historicism leading to relativism and hence to the collapse of the mission for science. In particular, Husserl singled out Dilthey's 'philosophy of **world-views**' (*Weltanschauungsphilosophie*) for its denial of the objective validity of cultural formations. The elderly Dilthey was upset by Husserl's attack and wrote to him denying the charge of relativism. It was not until years later that Husserl made amends, acknowledging Dilthey's contribution to **descriptive psychology** (*Phen. Psych.*, Hua IX).

Philosophy of Arithmetic: Logical and Psychological Analyses (Philosophie der Arithmetik, 1891) See ALSO *On the Concept of Number. Psychological Analyses*

Husserl published his *Philosophie der Arithmetik. Logische und psychologische Untersuchingen* (now Hua XII) in 1891, translated as *Philosophy of Arithmetic. Psychological and Logical Investigations*. It was his first book. Its aim was to clarify the nature of number 'independent of any theory of arithmetic' (Hua XII 12). In it, Husserl proposed the 'clarification' of the 'essence and origination' (XII 15) of concepts by examining their 'psychological constitution'. His strategy was to apply **Brentano's** method of descriptive psychology to vindicate **Weierstrass's** concept of number. His basic principle, echoing Brentano, is that 'no concept can be thought without a **foundation** (*Fundierung*) in a concrete intuition' (Hua XII 79). He wants to find the 'origin' (*Ursprung*, PA XII 17; 64), 'genesis' (*Entstehung*, PA XII 17), or 'source' (*Quelle*, PA XII 179) of our basic mathematical *concepts* (*Begriffe*), such as 'multiplicity' (*Vielheit*), 'unity' (*Einheit*), '**collective combination**' (*kollektive Verbindung*), 'more' and 'less', and so on (PA, Hua XII 64), basic concepts employed in the constitution of specifically mathematical concepts. Husserl planned a second volume of this work to deal with algebra and geometry, but he was to abandon this project.

Picture consciousness (*Bildbewusstsein*)   See **image consciousness**

Piece (*Stück*)   See also **mereology, moment, part, whole**
In the Third Logical Investigation, Husserl calls an independent **part** a 'piece', e.g. the head of a horse can exist independently from the horse (see especially Third Logical Investigation § 17). A piece can be separated from the whole – the handle can be removed from the cup – and continue to survive. A non-independent part, by the same token, cannot survive apart from the whole (colour cannot survive independently of the coloured surface).

Platonism (*Platonismus*)   See also **eidos, ideality, Natorp**
Husserl was accused by Paul **Natorp** of offering a Platonist account of ideal entities in his ***Logical Investigations***. Platonism in this context means that ideal entities or idealities (such as numbers, or concepts such as unity, identity, equality) are thought to have an independent, timeless, immaterial existence quite distinct from the spatiotemporal material world. Husserl himself acknowledges being a Platonist in this sense. According to Husserl, it was Herman **Lotze's** account of the independent validity of Platonic ideas in his *Logik* that helped him to understand what Bolzano was getting at in talking of 'propositions in themselves'(review of Melchior Palágyi, EW, p. 201; Hua XXII 156. He repeats it in his letter of 17/21 June 1933 to E. Paul Welch, *Briefwechsel* VI, p. 460). In his *Logic* Book Three Chapter Two (§§ 313–21), Lotze attempts a clarification of the meaning of the Platonic 'world of ideas' by arguing they are the predicates of things in this world considered as general concepts bound together in a whole in such a way as to 'constituted an unchangeable system of thought' (§ 314) and which determine the limits of all possible experience (§ 315). According to Lotze, Plato recognizes that in the Heraclitean world of change, black things become white, etc., but *blackness* itself does not change, even if a thing only has a momentary participation in it. Even when a momentarily appearing sound or colour is immediately replaced by another different sound or colour, it still is the case that these two items stand in definite relations of contrast with one another. These relations and indeed the intelligible contents of real things and events may be said to have **validity** (*Geltung*, § 316). Lotze denied that Plato held an absurd doctrine of the independent *existence* of ideas along side the existence of changing material things. He blamed this misunderstanding on

the fact that the Greek language did not have the capacity to express this validity but referred to them only as 'being' (*ousia*). In fact, the forms are ideal unities (*henades, monades*). Plato's ideas have been misunderstood as having 'existence' (*Dasein*) separate from things whereas, according to Lotze, in fact Plato intended only to ascribe 'validity' (*Geltung*) to them. Plato is not trying to hypostasize the ideas by saying they are not in space, rather he simply wants to say they are not anywhere at all (§ 318). Husserl's account of the **being-in-itself** of ideal entities was accused at the time as being a kind of Platonism. Husserl rejects this accusation of Platonism in the Second Edition of the *Logical Investigations*. Husserl credits Bolzano's 'truths in themselves' for the original inspiration, and Lotze's 'brilliant interpretation of Plato's doctrine of ideas' for making it intelligible to him (ILI 36; 128–9; XX/1 297). It amounts to a 'soft' Platonic approach to ideal objects as stable unities having identity conditions but without existence in space or time. It is 'soft' because Husserl does not naively posit these ideal objects as existing in another realm. Husserl dismisses Platonic realism regarding universals as a naive ontology that has already been refuted (LU II § 7). Ideal entities do not dwell in a 'heavenly place' (*topos ouranios*, LU I § 31), neither are they 'mythical entities suspended between being and non-being'. Science requires that there be such stable unities – the number 3 must be identical in all sentences or formulae in which it occurs. Similarly, whole sentences form ideal unities, in terms of their ideal meanings and their corresponding ideal states of affairs. Even a false proposition has a supratemporal ideality, Husserl emphasizes (ELE, Hua XXIV 37). It has an ideal identical meaning character and a truth value. Moreover, two judgements may be considered to be the same if the exact same statements and no others can be made about or drawn from these judgements, and, in that sense, they have the same 'truth value' (*Wahrheitswert*, LU V § 21).

Positing act (*setzender Akt*)   See also **objectifying act**

According to Husserl in his Fifth Logical Investigation §38, positing acts are a species of **objectifying act** that intends the object as actually existent whereas non-positing acts present the object in a modified form with no commitment to actual existence and are 'merely presented'. Both **nominal acts** and **judgements** can be positing or non-positing. Acts of **perception** or **memory** are positing acts whereas acts of **fantasy** are non-positing.

Position taking (*Stellungnehmen, Stellungnahme*)   See also **attitude,**
conviction, judgement
Husserl frequently uses the term 'position taking' (as a verb *stellungnehmen*
or gerund, *Stellungnahme*), or 'stance taking', for the manner in which the
ego takes a stand or position towards his or her beliefs, thoughts, judgements, emotions, and so on. In *accepting* a proposition as true, for instance,
one is taking a stance towards that belief, embracing it as one of one's own
beliefs, affirming it as a **conviction**, and so on. There are many different
stances consciousness can adopt. For Husserl, all life involves position taking.
Husserl speaks of position taking as an active, free decision of the **ego**.
Positions can also be altered and the ability to take different stances towards
a belief is part of the nature of human consciousness. In the **natural**
attitude, there is a general stance of acceptance towards the existence of
the entities which are the objects of **perceptions, judgements**, and so on.

Possibility (*Möglichkeit*)   See also **essence, horizon, imaginative free**
variation
Possibility means what can be and is contrasted with actuality (what is)
and necessity (what must be). Husserl's phenomenology claimed not just
to study consciousness in terms of its apprehension of actualities, but it
also sought to understand how **consciousness** was able to relate itself to
possibilities. Consciousness has various modal forms. Indeed, Husserl often
saw phenomenology as an a priori science of **essences** as the precisely the
science of possibilities, with the actual existence (*Wirklichkeit*) of entities
and conscious states regarded as irrelevant and excluded by the phenomenological **reduction**. Later in *Being and Time*, **Heidegger** would claim that
possibility stands higher than actuality and that phenomenology is primarily
a science of possibilities. Husserl was interested in the manner in which the
essential properties of something by an **eidetic free variation** than ran
through various possibilities altering the object under investigation to see
what remained invariant. Possibilities belong to the **horizon** of an object as
it is experienced. Thus when I see the front side of an object, the possibility
of its rear side being seen is co-intended at the same time.

Prepredicative experience (*die vorprädikative Erfahrung*)   See also
experience, passivity
'Prepredicative experience' is a late Husserlian term (especially in *Experience*

and Judgment) for the region of experience that occurs before it has been explicitly formulated or 'thematized' in **judgements** and expressed in outward linguistic form, i.e. before it becomes packaged for explicit **consciousness**. As Husserl put it, all predicative cognitive activity presupposes a prepredicative domain that is passively pregiven. Furthermore, predicative experience is an articulation of what is experienced at the prepredicative level. In *Experience and Judgment*, Husserl devotes the first part of the work to the prepredicative (receptive) experience. Simple apprehension and explication (§§ 22–32) – on the one hand – and the apprehension of relation (§§ 33–46) – on the other hand – make up the main structure of the prepredicative experience. Sensibility, affection, modalizations of certainty, the unity of time, **association** and **passive synthesis** are some of the topics that Husserl describes as part of the passive constitution of the pregiven world.

Presentation (*Vorstellung*) See also **intuition, objectifying act, presenting, representation**

Vorstelling is the regular used to translate into German an 'idea' in the Lockean sense. It is usually translated as 'presentation' or 'representation'. The German term *Vorstellung* is frequent in eighteenth-century German philosophy (e.g. **Kant**) and in nineteenth-century German psychology (e.g. Franz **Brentano, Meinong,** and his school) to refer to whatever is immediately before the mind in all mental acts including acts of **perceiving, imagining, remembering** or conceptualizing. Brentano distinguished between presentations (which included images, thoughts, impressions, concepts, etc.) and **judgements**, which, for him, were acts of affirming or denying of presentations. As early as 1893, Husserl was carefully distinguishing the kind of 'presentation' (*Vorstellung*) of an object experienced in an act of visual perception from the kind of 'representation' (*Repräsentation*) of the object in acts of fantasy or symbolization, or, for example, in **empty intending** of the kind we perform when we co-intuit the sides of a cube not given directly in perception. In the ***Philosophy of Arithmetic***, Husserl distinguished between lower numbers that are presented immediately or 'authentically' in **intuition**, whereas thinking of higher numbers involved an 'inauthentic' grasp of them through symbols. This led Husserl to distinguish between the empty presentation and the various forms of 'filling' or **fulfillment** (*Erfüllung*) it can undergo. In the Fifth Logical Investigation, Husserl offered a critique of Brentano's conception of 'presentation' and replaces it with the phenomenologically clarified notion of an **objectifying act**. Husserl recognized the importance of being able to have empty significations or **signitive intentions**, the possibility of symbolic thought founds the very possibility of science as such. Contrariwise, seeing something before me right now in its bodily presence is the paradigm of the kind of bodily filling of our experience. A different form of presenting or presencing of the object occurs in acts of recalling that entity in its absence, whether in **memory** or **imagination** or expectation.

Presentation or presencing (*Gegenwärtigung*) See also **apperception, presentation, presentification, representation**
Husserl uses the term 'presenting' or 'presencing' (*Gegenwärtigung*), derived from the German word for 'present', *Gegenwart*, to refer to those **lived experiences** in which the intentional objects are given in intuitive experience, immediately, directly, and with *in propria persona*, 'in-the-flesh' (*leibhaftig*), here-and-now, full presence, e.g. the manner in which the object is presented in acts of perception. Husserl contrasts this kind of presencing (which carries the temporal notion of being now, in the present) with what he calls 'representation' or 'presentiation' or '**presentification**' (*Vergegenwärtigung*) whereby things are given in a less fully present way, as for instance, in acts of memory, imagination, symbolic representation, and so on. In the presenting of a physical object in perception, the presencing always takes place in **adumbrations** and there are also aspects of the object that are represented or presentiated, that is, emptily intended. Every act of presencing of an object is a mixture of elements that are given fully in the present and elements that are co-intended in an empty way. Most forms of **intuition** involve an interweaving of **presentations** and presentifications.

Presentiation See **presentification**

Presentification (*Vergegenwärtigung*) See also **apperception, perception, presentation**
Husserl distinguishes generally between perceptions that present the intended object directly – which he calls '**presentations**' (*Vorstellungen*) and with 'in the flesh' here-and-now presence and representations or 'presentifications' or, according to some translation, 'presentiations' – there is no exact corresponding term in English (*Vergegenwärtigungen*) –whose

objects do not have this in-the-flesh **givenness**. **Memory** and **fantasy** are types of presentification, although they differ in their **positing** character (memory presents the object as having really existed whereas fantasy is not positing in this way). In regular perception, the object is presented through an **adumbration**, but the absent sides which are co-intended are given through an empty presentification.

Presupppositionlessness   (*Voraussetzunglosigkeit*) See also **phenomenology**
Husserl speaks of 'presupppositionlessness' (*Voraussetzunglosigkeit*) as a central presupposition of the phenomenological approach. The term is first introduced in the Introduction to the *Logical Investigations* § 7, where Husserl speaks of 'freedom from presuppositions' as a principle on epistemological investigations. It is meant to overcome the shortcomings of 'naive' science that starts from assumptions the science itself cannot question. In his mature writings, Husserl presents **phenomenology** as a presuppositionless science by which he means a science whose central concepts are phenomenologically clarified. No use can be made of assumptions drawn from the sciences, religion or other sources. For instance, in his 1930 Author's Preface to the English Translation of *Ideas* I, Husserl speaks of philosophy in general as a radical questioning which demands a 'reduction to absolute presuppositionlessness' (Hua V 160). It is linked with Husserl quest for **absolute grounding** or final grounding (*Letztbegründüng*) of his science. The aim of the assumption of presuppositionlessness is to arrive at fully justified knowledge and to be in a position to take complete epistemic responsibility what Husserl calls 'autonomous **self-responsibility**' (Hua V 162).

Primal consciousness (*Urbewusstsein*) See also **time consciousness**
'Primal or originary consciousness' (*Urbewusstsein*) is, for Husserl, especially in his Bernau time manuscripts from around 1917, the absolute bedrock of consciousness and is the source of time (see Hua XXXIII 146, 161, 163, 264, 267). Husserl speaks of a 'flow of orginary consciousness which can only be grasped in reflection' (Hua XXXIII 285).

Primal establishment, primal instituting (*Urstiftung*) See also **constitution, genetic phenomenology**
The mature Husserl frequently uses the term 'primal establishment' or

'originary foundation' (*Urstiftung*, see CM § 51; *Crisis* § 15) to describe the process whereby a particularly sense formation becomes constituted as such for the first time. The term does not appear in *Ideas* I, for instance. In his '**Origin of Geometry**' essay, Husserl claims that geometry has its primal establishment when the earliest geometers had an intuition about space understood as a self-contained entity governed by a priori rules. For Husserl, there are primal establishments for all cultural acquisitions, e.g. seeing a pair of scissors for the first time (CM § 50). Husserl claims that 'each everyday experience involves an analogizing transfer of an originally instituted objective sense to a new case, with its anticipative apprehension of the object as having a similar sense'. Once we grasp its nature, we can perceive similar pairs of scissors even though they have different sizes, shapes, colours, etc. There is an analogical transfer by which I see the new and unfamiliar in the light of the familiar. It is part of the business of phenomenology to seek to reconstruct imaginatively these primal establishments. There are primordial institutions of modern philosophy (by **Descartes**, *Crisis* § 16), of modern mathematical science (by **Galileo**, *Crisis* § 16) and so on (see *Crisis* § 5). In *Crisis* § 15, Husserl speaks not just of 'primal establishment' but also of 're-establishments' (*Nachstiftungen*) and indeed of a 'final establishment' (*Endstiftung*), which represents some kind of final form, e.g. phenomenology is the final form of transcendental philosophy. Merleau-Ponty translates *Urstiftung* as 'institution' and devoted a lecture course to it. All forms of human instituting involve a re-instituting of what is already encountered as instituted. There is no radical absolute beginning.

Primal impression, primordial impression (*Urimpression*) See also **living present, now moment, protention, retention, time consciousness**

For Husserl, every temporal experience has a moment that he calls the 'primal or primordial impression' (*Urimpression*). In early works, he sometimes refers to it as 'primordial sensation' (*Urempfindung*, Hua X 324). Husserl describes this primal impression as the moment of creation (Hua X, 105); it is the very core of the **living present**. However, it is a necessary eidetic law that this primal impression must be modified into a **retention**. The primal impression can be said to found the retention, yet the primal impression as such can appear only in the retention. There is no absolute experience of the primal impression as such.

Primary properties   See also **life-world, subjective-relative properties**
The term 'primary properties' was originally used by **Galileo** to refer to
those properties in nature that could be given an *objective* characterization according to exact measurement. Locke contrasts primary properties
(understood to be observer independent) with 'secondary' properties,
those properties apprehended by the human subject, e.g. colour, taste,
etc. According to **Descartes**, whereas a material object really is extended,
has shape, position, etc., it is not really coloured, but only appears so to
the apprehending human subject. Berkeley argued that *all* properties were
subjective relative, hence mind dependent. The notion of the real world
(being in itself) with its real, exact, objective properties, is, for Husserl, the
result of an idealizing abstraction from the **life-world**. Husserl contrasts
the objective or primary properties sought by the natural sciences with the
'subjective-relative properties' (see *Crisis* § 16 and § 34) experienced by
subjects in the life-world.

Primordial reduction (*die primordiale Reduktion*)   See also **intersubjectivity, primordiality, reduction**
Husserl sometimes distinguishes between the 'primordial reduction' and
the 'egological' or 'phenomenological' reduction. In the Fifth Cartesian
Meditation, he speaks of a second more radical reduction. The egological
reduction uncovers the problem of **intersubjectivity** but does not directly
address it. Husserl thinks that a second reduction is necessary in order to
explain, from a transcendental perspective, the apprehension of **others**
and their role in the apprehension of the common shared world. Thus, as
Husserl explains at the beginning of the Fifth Meditation, the ego recognizes
the presence of other subjectivities and apprehends the world as revealed
intersubjectively. In the *Cartesian Meditations*, Husserl labels the primordial
reduction the 'reduction to ownness' (*Eigenheitsphäre*) (CM, § 44, p. 92:
*Reduction of transcendental experience to the **sphere of ownness***): 'For
the present we exclude from the thematic field everything now in question:
we disregard all constitutional effects of intentionality relating immediately
or mediately to other subjectivity and delimit first of all the total nexus of
that actual and potential intentionality in which the ego constitutes within
himself a peculiar owness' (CM, § 44, p. 93). In this way, for example, he
says: 'If I reduce other men to what is included in my ownness, I get bodies
included therein' (CM, § 44, p. 97). The mature Husserl often stresses

the primacy of **intersubjectivity**: 'Transcendental intersubjectivity is the absolute ground of being (*Seinsboden*) from which the meaning and validity of everything objectively existing originate' (Hua IX 344). According to the Fifth Cartesian Meditation, within the transcendental sphere of ownness, the other is constituted not just as a body but as an *alter ego*: 'Within and by means of this ownness the transcendental ego constitutes, however, the "objective" world, as a universe of being that is other than himself and constitutes, at the first level, the other in the mode: alter ego' (CM, § 46, p. 100). This tension between intersubjectivity and the sphere of ownness remains extremely problematic in Husserl's phenomenology.

Principle of principles (*Das Prinzip aller Prinzipien*)   See also **evidence, givenness, intuition, phenomenology**

In *Ideas* I § 24, Husserl announces the 'principle of all principles' that governs the practice of **phenomenology**. According to this principle 'every originary presentive intuition is a legitimizing source of cognition, that everything originarily (so to speak in its 'personal' actuality) offered to us in 'intuition' is to be accepted simply as what it is presented as being, but also only within the limits in which it is presented there'. The principle of principles requires that phenomenology be attentive strictly to what is **given** in **intuition** and the manner in which the matter is intuited. Husserl's slogan 'back to the things themselves' is to be interpreted as expressing this principle.

Proposition (*Satz*)   See also **judgement, propositions in themselves, state of affairs**

Husserl uses the term 'proposition' or 'sentence' (*Satz*) for the content of the act of **judgement**. The proposition is what is asserted or posited by the judgement. The proposition represents or expresses a **state of affairs** that is the objective correlate of the propositional content.

Propositions in themselves (*Sätze an sich*)   See also **Bolzano, ideality, Lotze, proposition, state of affairs**

'Propositions or statements in themselves' (*Sätze an sich*) and 'truths in themselves' (*Wahrheiten an sich*) are concepts introduced in Bernard **Bolzano**'s *Theory of Science* which were taken up and adapted by Husserl. In *Theory of Science* Book One § 19, Bolzano defined a *proposition in itself* as 'any assertion that something is or is not the case, regardless whether somebody has put it into words, and regardless even whether it has been thought'. A 'truth in itself' is a true proposition (*Theory of Science*, Bk 1 § 25); it asserts what is the case irrespective of any reference to a thinker thinking or affirming that proposition. Examples of a proposition in itself include: 'there are no thinking beings' or 'there are truths which no one knows'. Bolzano sharply distinguished the subjective presentations in the mind which were parts of subjective propositions from the objective meaning content of the proposition it itself:

> 'Idea' in this sense is a general name for any phenomenon
> in our mind ... Thus, what I see if someone holds a rose
> before me is an idea, namely, the idea of a red colour ... In
> this sense, every idea requires a living being as a subject in
> which it occurs. For this reason I call them subjective or mental
> ideas. Hence subjective ideas are something real. They have
> real existence at the time when they are present in a subject,
> just as they have certain effects. The same does not hold
> for the objective idea or idea in itself that is associated with
> every subjective idea. By objective idea I mean the certain
> something which constitutes the immediate matter [*Stoff*] of
> a subjective idea, and which is not found in the realm of the
> real. An objective idea does not require a subject but subsists
> [*bestehen*], not indeed as something existing, but as a certain
> something even though no thinking being may have it; also
> it is not multiplied when it is thought by one, two, three, or
> more beings, unlike the corresponding subjective idea, which
> is present many times. Hence the name 'objective'. (*Theory of
> Science* Book Two, Part One, § 48)

Bolzano strongly influenced Husserl's recognition that the objects of logic, i.e. propositions and their parts and relations to one another, were ideal, timeless objective entities which do not have actual existence (in the sense of a location in space or time), what he called **idealities**.

Protention (*Protention*) See also **now moment, retention, time consciousness**

The now moment, retention and protention are three mutually related, non-independent parts of each conscious **lived experience** according to Husserl's analyses of **time consciousness**. According to *Ideas* I § 77, a protention is the 'precise counterpart' of a **retention**. Just as retention is not yet memory, so protention is not yet anticipation in the full sense which is a form of **presentification**. The protention modifies the already elapsed retention. Husserl speaks in this regard of a backward streaming or backward mirroring (*Rückstrahlung*) of the protention in the retention. Retentions motivate protentions and protentions are founded on retentions. Protentions and retentions belong to passive experience.

Psychologism (*Psychologismus*)   See also **Frege, idealities, logic, psychology, relativism**
Psychologism is the doctrine that the laws of mathematics and logic can be reduced to or depend on the laws governing thinking. The term 'psychologism' (*Psychologismus*) was first introduced in 1866 by the Hegelian Johann Eduard Erdmann to characterize a position that he criticized according to which all philosophical knowledge must be grounded in psychology. For Husserl, psychologism presents a genuine intellectual challenge. His *Prolegomena to Pure Logic* (1900), the first volume of **Logical Investigations**, is dedicated to a critical assessment of the so-called *Psychologismus-Streit* (the 'psychologism feud'). Husserl's *Prolegomena* is perhaps the most influential anti-psychologistic text within German-speaking philosophy. In this text, Husserl argues that although there is a kernel of truth in the anti-psychologistic arguments put forward by authors such as Herbart, Natorp and Lotze, they fail to articulate the real problems of logical psychologism as it had been propounded by Mill and Lipps among others. Husserl's main argument against logical psychologism is that logical laws are exact, can be known a apriori, and do not imply any claims about psychological matters of fact. In contrast, Husserl argues, psychology has until now only produced empirical generalizations about matters of fact. The basic mistake of psychologism is, according to Husserl, a confusion of the temporal act of cognition and the ideal, timeless subject matter of the cognitive act that subsequently leads to a reduction of logical laws to pscyhological laws. What is known are truths and truths are in contrast to the cognitive acts in which they are know atemporal; they have no beginning and no end and must therefore be distinguished from matters of fact. Husserl further argues that by failing to recognize the ideal

or non-factual character of logical laws psychologism is bound to end up in a self-refuting **relativism**, since truth becomes relative to the specific psychology of the human species. **Frege** was another critic of psychologism and Husserl was one of the first philosophers in Germany to recognize Frege's work, and, although Husserl had criticized Frege's account of the nature of identity in the *Philosophy of Arithmetic* in 1891, relations between the two were collegial and mutually respectful. But, in 1894, Frege published an acerbic review of Husserl's *Philosophy of Arithmetic*, in which he accused Husserl of making a number of fundamental errors. According to Frege, Husserl treated number naively as properties of things or of aggregates rather than as the extensions of concepts (The *extension* of a concept is the set of objects the concept picks out). Husserl had seen number as deriving from our intuition of groups or multiplicities and since neither one nor zero is a multiple, strictly speaking they were not positive numbers for Husserl. Frege criticized Husserl's account of zero and one as negative answers to the question: 'how many?' Frege states that the answer to the question, 'How many moons has the earth?' is hardly a negative answer, as Husserl would have us believe. Furthermore, Frege believed, Husserl seemed to be confusing the numbers themselves with the *presentations* of number in consciousness, analogous to considering the moon as generated by our act of thinking about it. Crucially for Frege, in identifying the objective numbers with subjective acts of counting, Husserl was guilty of *psychologism*, the error of tracing the laws of logic to empirical psychological laws. If logic is defined as the study of the laws of thought, there is always the dangerous that this can be interpreted to mean the study of how people actually think or ought to think; understanding necessary entailment, for example, as that everyone is so constituted psychologically if he believes P and if he believes that P implies Q then he cannot help believing that Q is true. For Frege, Husserl has collapsed the logical nature of judgement into private psychological acts, collapsing together truth and judging something as true. According to the journal kept by W. R. Boyce-Gibson, who studied with Husserl in Freiburg in 1928, Husserl later acknowledged that Frege's criticisms had 'hit the nail on the head'. However, there is evidence that Husserl was already moving away from his own earlier psychologism when Frege's review was published, especially in his critique of Schröder's *Algebra of Logic*. Husserl was already embracing **Bolzano**'s *Wissenschaftslehre* with its doctrine of 'states of affairs' and 'truths in themselves', whose precise nature he then came to understand through his reading of Hermann **Lotze**'s account of the Platonic Ideas. Frege is mentioned in the *Prolegomena* to the Logical Investigations in a footnote (*Prol.* §45, I 318; Hua XVIII 172 note) where Husserl writes: 'I need hardly say that I no longer approve of my own fundamental criticisms of Frege's anti-psychologistic position set forth in my *Philosophy of Arithmetic*.' Husserl had abandoned the approach of the *Philosophy of Arithmetic* almost as soon as it was published in 1891. He realized that the cardinal numbers were not the basis of all numbers, and in particular that the psychological approach could not handle the more complex numbers (e.g., the imaginary numbers). In the *Prolegomena*, Husserl explicitly denies that numbers themselves are to be understood in terms of acts of counting although they can only be accessed through acts of counting:

> The number Five is not my own or anyone else's counting of
> five, it is also not my presentation or anyone else's presenta-
> tion of five. (LU, *Prol.* § 46, I 109; Hua XVIII 173–4)

While it is only by counting that we encounter numbers, numbers are not simply products of the mind. This would deny objective status to mathematics. The psychological origin of arithmetic concepts does not mitigate against the independent ideal existence of these concepts as species quite distinct from 'the contingency, temporality and transience of our mental acts' (LU, *Prol.* § 46, I 110; Hua XVIII 175). Two apples can be eaten but not the number two, Husserl says in his 1906/7 lectures. For Husserl, logical concepts contain nothing of the process by which they are arrived at, any more than number has a connection with the psychological act of counting. Numbers and propositions, such as the Pythagorean theorem, are ideal '**objectivities**' (*Gegenständlichkeiten*), which are the substrates of judgements just as much as any real object is. In contrast to 'real' entities that bear some relation to time, if not to space, the pure identities of logic are 'irreal' or 'ideal'. Husserl charac-terized them as '**species**' in the Aristotelian sense, alongside other 'unities of meaning', for example the meaning of the word 'lion', a word that appears only once in the language despite its multiple instantiations in acts of speaking and writing. Whereas Husserl had begun in 1887 with the assumption that psychology would ground all cognitive acts, he ends the Foreword to his *Investigations* by quoting Goethe to the effect that one is against nothing so much as errors one has recently abandoned, in order to explain his 'frank criticism' (*die freimütige Kritik*) of psychologism (LU, I 3; Hua XVIII 7).

Psychology (*Psychologie*)   See also **Brentano, descriptive psychology, empirical psychology, Wundt**

Husserl always characterizes psychology as an empirical 'science of facts', of the psychic states of human beings as animals embedded in physical nature (see LU *Prol*. § 50). Husserl originally begins from Brentano's distinction between **descriptive** and genetic or physiological psychology (see LU Intro to Second Volume § 6 note 3, where in the First Edition, Husserl defines phenomenology as 'descriptive psychology'). He was familiar with the descriptive psychologies of Brentano, Stumpf and others, as well as with the experimental psychology of Wundt. However, he quickly came to the view that all empirical psychology involves the assumption of **naturalism** (beginning from Locke, see *Crisis* § 22). Psychology studies the mental states of actual embodied creatures in the world and is therefore the opposite of an a priori science of pure consciousness. Psychology proceeds by **generalization** from actual instances. For Husserl, in order to clarify psychology, one has to appeal to **phenomenology** now understood as a transcendental science (see *Ideas* I § 78). Empirical psychology is full of conceptual confusions because it failed to make phenomenological clarifications of the essences of the essential notions involved, e.g. the very idea of perception, memory, imagination, willing, and so on. In his mature works, Husserl believed it was possible to enter into phenomenology by a consideration of psychology. There is a 'way' into transcendental phenomenology through psychology because every statement in empirical psychology has a parallel in the domain of transcendental phenomenology (see *Crisis* §§ 56–60). In the *Crisis*, Husserl characterizes psychology as hopelessly beset by confusion because of the manner in which it emerged to address defects in the mathematical natural sciences of the primary properties of natural things. Naive objectivism in natural science and the concentration on quantifiable so-called 'primary' qualities meant that subjectivity has been misconceived by modern philosophy and scientific psychology. Psychology, as it emerged in the naturalistic context of nineteenth century, is set up to explore a domain that can never be more than 'epiphenomenal' since reality has already been characterized in terms of naive objectivism. At the end of *Crisis* Part III B § 72, Husserl writes:

> The surprising result of our investigation can also, it seems, be expressed as follows: a pure psychology as positive science, a psychology which would investigate universally the human beings living in the world as real facts (*als reale Tatsachen*) in the world, similar to other positive sciences (both sciences of nature and humanistic disciplines) does not exist. There is only transcendental psychology, which is identical with transcendental philosophy. (*Crisis* § 72, p. 257; VI 261)

— Q —

Questioning back (*Rückfragen*)   In his late works, Husserl occasionally (quite rarely) uses the term 'questioning back' or 'regressive inquiry' (*Rückfragen*) – he also speaks of 'backwards reflection' (*Rückbesinnung*, see *Crisis* § 15) – to refer to the kind of 'unbuilding' or dismantling that phenomenology undertakes to uncover the 'primal foundation' (*Urstiftung*) of central concepts, e.g. the meaning of **Galileo**'s **mathematization of nature**. (See especially *Crisis* § 15 and also *Crisis* VI § 53.) In *Crisis* § 28, Husserl speaks of the way into transcendental phenomenology though the questioning back from the **life-world**.

— R —

Rationalism (*Rationalismus*)   See also **empiricism, reason**
In philosophy, rationalism is usually regarded as a claim about knowledge, namely that knowledge primarily comes from reason rather than from sense

experience (as empiricism claims). Husserl sees **Descartes** as the founder of modern 'objectivist' rationalism (*Crisis* § 21) and he sees Kant as a critic of classical rationalism (*Crisis* § 28). Husserl believed that the classic rationalism of the Enlightenment was too narrow and naive (*Crisis* § 6) and committed itself to **naturalism**, but he believes to abandon the ideal of rationalism would be to end in irrationalism He therefore proposes **phenomenology** as a new form of rationalism (see *Crisis* § 56). According to the **Vienna Lectur**e, the crisis in the European sciences and culture has its roots in a misguided rationalism.

Rationality (*Rationalität*)   See also **rationalism, reason, *Vienna Lecture***
Husserl often uses the term 'rationality' to refer to the narrower area of *ratio*, i.e. the sphere of logical inference, calculation and procedural rule following such as comes to the fore in modern mathematical science. Husserl follows Kant is seeing human nature as teleologically oriented towards reason. In *Ideas* I, Husserl speaks of the possibility of a phenomenology of reason. He believes modernity introduced a 'one-sided' (*Crisis* VI 338) notion of rationality that sought to explicate the rationality of the world in the manner of geometry (see *Crisis* § 10). The old 'rationality' of the Enlightenment was too narrow and led to a narrow and absurd **rationalism** (see *Crisis* § 6) that was exposed by Hume's **scepticism**. A broader conception of rationality has to be developed; philosophy is on the way to a 'higher rationality … a true and full rationality' (*Crisis* § 73). This new rationality has to be more than scientific rationality and be grounded in the life-world (see ***Vienna Lecture***; Hua VI 343). The great danger is irrationalism brought on by a failure to adequately ground reason and to retreat to **scepticism** or mysticism.

Realism (*Realismus*)   See also **idealism, realist phenomenology**
Husserl uses the term 'realism' in a number of different senses. The account of perception in the **Logical Investigations** may be said to be realist (direct realism) because Husserl thinks that the perceiver perceives the perceived object directly and without mediation. The object is given 'in one blow' although it is also given in **adumbrations**. Husserl is also a realist in considering all physical objects and mental acts to be in **time**. Husserl was also considered to be a realist in the Platonic sense because he affirmed the reality of ideal entities (**idealities**) and **states of affairs**.

In this sense, he is a realist about numbers, logical entities and **values**. After 1907, however, Husserl moved more and more in the direction of **transcendental idealism**, claiming that all **sense** (*Sinn*) and being (*Sein*) is a result of the constituting action of the **transcendental ego**. In general, Husserl remains a direct, naive realist about the world of perception. After his transcendental turn, he takes this direct realism to be a consequence of the **natural attitude** and its '**general** thesis' which involves a commitment to the existence of the objects of experience.

Realist phenomenology   See also **Conrad-Martius, Geiger, realism, Reinach, Stein**

Husserl's *Logical Investigations* inspired small groups of researchers at Göttingen (e.g. Adolf Reinach) and Munich (e.g. Conrad-Martius, Moritz Geiger) to apply his phenomenology to philosophical problems. Theodor **Lipps** and some of his students in Munich saw themselves as developing Husserl's phenomenology as eidetic description (without the turn to the transcendental announced in *Ideas* I). Roman Ingarden (1893–1970), Hedwig Conrad-Martius (1888–1966), and others were attracted by the realism of the *Logical Investigations*. These students did not follow Husserl in his **reduction** (except in so far as they accepted the reduction from fact to eidos) or his **transcendental idealism**. Husserl later characterized realist phenomenology as 'empirical phenomenology' as opposed to his own transcendental phenomenology. **Edith Stein** saw Husserl as re-invigorating the realism to be found in Thomas Aquinas and other medieval neo-Aristotelian philosophers.

Reason   (*Vernunft, ratio*)   See   also   **rationalism,   rationality, self-responsibility**

Reason (*Vernunft*) – sometimes the Latin *ratio* – for Husserl is divided into three different species: theoretical, practical, and axiological or evaluating (*wertende*) reason which address different ontological **regions**. Pure reason can be studied formally in the theoretical domain (by **logic**) but also in the area of value (**axiology**), and in the theory of practice (*Ideas* I § 147). Husserl believes reason has been misunderstood in both the rationalist and empiricist tradition, and he was seeking a new 'concrete theory of reason' (*Ideas* I § 152). Reason is never just procedural, logical calculation but has an evaluative and critical dimension. Reason is essentially teleological, that is, it is motivated by goals and values. Husserl speaks of a 'phenomenology of reason' (also called 'noetics') in *Ideas* I §§ 136–45, which coincides with the whole of **phenomenology**. In his *Crisis* especially, Husserl speaks of the overall crisis in European scientific civilization as a crisis of reason, a crisis concerning the nature, limits, and possibilities of reason itself (VI, 7, 10, 13, 273, 319, 347). Husserl speaks of a narrow kind of scientific or technological reason (Latin: *ratio*) as having replaced a broader normative conception of reason in early modernity. In *Ideas* I, Husserl closely connects the notions of rationality and **truth** and actuality or being (sometimes called 'what is'). In *Ideas* I, Husserl portrays reason in terms of the rightness of an **intention** that is assured through insight with **evidence**. There is reason not just in cognition but in valuing and acting. One can be said to act or to value truly. To act and value rationally is to act and value rightly. Reason is the norm for action. Husserl sees reason as having the character of universality (*Ideas* I § 146) and as a domain of infinite tasks and goals (Hua VI 348). The life of reason is a life of **self-responsibility**.

Recognition (*Anerkennung, das Erkennen*)   See **cognition, fulfilment**
Husserl speaks of 'recognition' in the Sixth Logical Investigation as the experience of the coincidence or identity between an **intention** and its **fulfilment**. In this sense, it is the experience of **truth**.

Reduction (*Reduktion*)   See also **Descartes, epochē, transcendental ego**
'Reduction' means literally a 'leading back' or a 'return', from the Latin verb *reducere*. Husserl uses 'reduction' as a technical term to refer to the procedure of uncovering the noetic-noematic structure of lived experiences once the **natural attitude** has been suspended through the *epochē* and various prejudices have been neutralized. . For Husserl, the application of the reduction aims at overcoming the naiveté of life in the natural attitude and allowing the phenomenologist to grasp the domain of **transcendental experience**. The various 'reductions' that Husserl proposes are positive steps that are to be taken after the negative moment of the *epochē* has taken place. The concept of the 'phenomenological reduction' was first developed by Husserl in his research writings around 1905 but does not appears in his published writings until 1913 in *Ideas* I §§ 31–3. He distinguishes at various times between different kinds of reduction, indeed in *Ideas* I, he speaks

of phenomenological *reductions* in the plural (*Ideas* I §33; § 56), but also emphasizes their collective unity (§ 33). He already speaks of this reduction as involving a 'transcendental **epochē**' (§ 33). The *epochē*, then, may be seen as the first primarily negative or exclusionary step in the procedure of reduction. There are various kinds of reduction and Husserl never finished meditating on what the reduction introduced. These reductions include: the 'philosophical', the 'phenomenological', the 'transcendental', the 'transcendental phenomenological' (e.g. CM § 14), and the 'eidetic' reduction. In his earliest public discussion of reduction, the 1907 lectures series delivered in Göttingen, **The Idea of Phenomenology**, he speaks of a 'philosophical reduction' and a 'phenomenological reduction' (IP 4; II 5) to exclude everything posited as transcendently existing, but he goes on to speaks of an 'epistemological reduction' (*erkenntnis-theoretische Reduktion*) as necessary in order to focus on the pure phenomena of conscious acts as **cogitationes**, and to avoid misleading assumptions about the nature and existence of the *sum cogitans* (IP 33; II 43). Husserl has in mind the specific **bracketing** of a psychological interpretation of what is given in the acts of knowing. Husserl occasionally refers to a 'psychological reduction' as well as *phenomenological, eidetic* and *transcendental* reductions and other specific reductions, such as the 'reduction to the **sphere of ownness**' (CM § 44). In his **Encyclopedia Britannica article**, Husserl distinguishes between what he there terms the 'phenomenological-psychological' and the 'transcendental-phenomenological' reduction. The aim of the reduction is to transcend the **natural attitude** in order to understand it. Belonging to the natural attitude is a passive belief (rather than an active position taking) that the world is there, on hand. This is the **general thesis** of the natural attitude. The reduction aims to lead away from this thesis. The idea is that the reduction leaves a residuum – in *Ideas* I, it is pure **consciousness**. Husserl does not clearly distinguish the different stages and grades of reduction. Husserl often speaks indifferently of *phenomenological* and *transcendental* reductions or indeed of the 'transcendental-phenomenological reduction' (CM § 8, p. 21; Hua I 61; Crisis VI 239). In the *Crisis*, many different forms of reduction are mentioned including: the positivistic reduction (Hua VI 3), the phenomenological psychological (VI 239), the universal (VI 248) reduction. Husserl also discusses several different models for performing the reduction – various ways into the reduction. The following ways are discussed by Husserl: the Cartesian way, the way through psychology (see *Crisis* §§

565–72), the way through critique of the natural sciences, and through ontology (i.e. through questioning the grounds of pure **logic** as in the *Formal and Transcendental Logic*), and through the **life-world** (explicitly introduced in Part Three of the *Crisis*, §§ 28–55). Husserl even talks about the need for a 'systematic theory of phenomenological reductions' (*Ideas* I, § 61, 139; Hua III/1 115); in practice, he was quite lax about distinguishing between the different ways of approaching the one domain. The Cartesian way begins from a universal suspension of belief in the existence of the world and the veracity of its forms of **evidence**. The Cartesian way brings the transcendental ego immediately into view 'in one blow' as Husserl says. But the danger is that it presents the transcendental ego as a worldless subject. The way into transcendental phenomenology which begins from the life-world corrects this approach by recognizing the embeddedness of subjectivity in the world. The way through psychology recognizes that the psychological description of intentional experience parallels the **achievements** of transcendental subjectivity and that through a certain conversion of attitude psychological insights can be converted into transcendental insights concerning the **constitution** of the world.

Reell (*reell*) and Real (*real*)   See also **realism**

In the *Logical Investigations*, and in subsequent works, Husserl operates with a distinction between two senses of the word 'real' using two different German adjectives *reell* and *real*. Husserl uses the term 'real' (German: *real*) to characterize what exists either spatially or temporally (in this sense the *real* contrasts with the 'ideal' or 'irreal' which is timeless). He uses the term *reell* to refer to the any **parts** which can be identified in an experience, regardless of whether those parts actually exist, e.g. the **act quality** and the **matter**. In the *Logical Investigations* First Edition, Husserl wants to explore the phenomenological structure of **lived experiences** and distinguishes between what he calls '*reelle* or phenomenological' contents and 'intentional' contents (Fifth Logical Investigation § 16). The 'phenomenological' contents of the act are all the parts, both concrete and abstract, that can really be identified in it, specifically, its quality and its sensational contents. Thus, to use his own example of a sound pattern, the *reelle* parts are the component sound elements not the 'real' or actual sound waves, bones in the ear, or, indeed, the ideal meaning linked to the sound. Intentional experiences, too, have identifiable 'parts'. These *reelle* parts do not include the object intended, which always *transcends* the act irrespective of whether the object intended belongs to the real world or is an ideal objectivity (LU V § 20). It is important to note that a *reell* part does not necessarily mean actually existent in the usual sense. A fantasy object has *reellen* parts whereas it has no real parts. A *reelles* moment refers to an identifiable element in the immanent temporality of the **lived experience**, in contrast to the *irreellen* moments such as the ideal **sense** or **meaning** (*Sinn*) of the experience (see Hua XXXV 89). The Second Edition offers a clearer picture (invoking the bracketing of everything empirical) of the difference between the immanent **parts** of an act and its transcendent intentional **object**. The later Husserl does not foreground this distinction between the two senses of 'real' and it is not clear that he continues to observe it.

Reference (*Meinung*)   See also **intention, meaning, sense**

Intentionality involves reference to an object. Both Husserl and Brentano speak of meanings as referring to objects. Husserl is familiar with but does not use **Frege**'s distinction between *Sinn* (usually translated as 'sense' or 'connotation') and *Bedeutung* (usually translated as 'reference' or 'denotation'). For Husserl, as for Frege, acts with different **senses** can still intend the same referent, e.g. when Napoleon is meant or referred to both as 'Victor of Jena' or as 'Vanquished at Waterloo'. Husserl regards intentional conscious experiences (and not just linguistically expressive acts) as directed to objects and hence achieving reference. In the *Logical Investigations*, he sees reference as a function of the **matter** of an act. The referent of an intentional act need not exist, e.g. I can dream of a golden mountain or search for the elixir of life. The referent of essentially **occasional expressions** varies with the context.

Reflection (*Reflexion, Besinnung*)   See also **disinterested spectator, questioning back**

In general terms, reflection occurs when any conscious act turns back on itself and becomes conscious of itself, e.g., when I become aware that I am looking closely at something. For Husserl, it is an **eidetic law** that every lived experience can come to self-consciousness through reflection (see *Ideas* II § 6). Reflection is itself a **modification** of **consciousness** that any conscious act can undergo (*Ideas* I § 78). According to Husserl, even God can gain access to his conscious acts only through reflection (*Ideas* I § 78). Husserl distinguishes between '*psychological*' or 'natural' and 'phenomenological' or 'transcendental' reflection (see CM § 15). Natural reflection involves a return from the object of the experience to a consciousness of the experiencing itself and to the ego that is experiencing. But natural reflection takes place in the **natural attitude** and continues to assume the **givenness** of the world, whereas transcendental reflection operates under the *epochē* and takes a stance of **disinterested spectator** towards the world. Husserl speaks of reflection as essential to the phenomenological method since it is through reflection that the correlations of **noesis** and **noema** are uncovered. He distinguishes between reflection and **self-observation** (*Selbstbeobachtung*) or **introspection** as used in early empirical psychology. Phenomenology is not interested in making empirical observations per se. In phenomenological reflection, there is an effort to gain insight into the **essence** and hence this reflection is uninterested in factual existence. Reflection on an imagined perception can be as valuable as reflection on an actual perception. There is a performative self-contradiction involved in denying the epistemic value of reflection, when reflection itself is required to formulate this judgement (see *Ideas* I § 78). Furthermore, Husserl believes that reflection can gain access in an unmodified manner to the essence of what is reflected on. Husserl uses the term 'reflection' (*Besinnung*) especially in his later writings (e.g. *Crisis* § 52), especially to mean a 'teleological' and 'historical' reflection, and philosophy is to be understood as 'self-reflection' (*Selbstbesinnung*, *Crisis* § 73).

Region (*Region*)   See also **formal ontology, regional ontology**
At *Ideas* I § 16, Husserl defines a region as the 'total highest generic unity belonging to a **concretum**'. According to Husserl, especially in *Ideas* I § 9, the highest material genus of **essences** is called a 'region'. The regions Husserl specifically recognizes are: **material, physical being** or **nature**, **consciousness** (also called '**psyche**', *Ideas* I § 17), and cultural reality (also called **spirit**) (see *Ideas* II). Husserl speaks of 'regional ontologies' that explore these regions as opposed to formal ontology which discusses the properties of anything whatsoever. Each region has a determinate set of priori truths that belong to it which determine the content of that region's **material ontology**.

Regional ontology (*regionale Ontologie*)   See also **formal ontology, region**
'Regional ontologies' (*regionale Ontologien*, *Ideas* I § 149) are material

ontologies to be contrasted with **formal ontology** which studies the nature of anything whatsoever. There are distinct domains of being that are distinguished by their 'matter' or content. Thus geometry is the science of spatial entities, number is the science of quantities, biology studies living organisms, and so on. In this context Husserl speaks of 'regional ontologies' as the very broadest possible categories of beings. These regions are for Husserl 'self-contained'. The various regions are material being (which studies physical things), **consciousness**, and cultural reality (also called **spirit**).

Reinach, Adolf (1883–1917)   See also **Lipps, realist phenomenology**
Adolf Reinach was born in Mainz, Germany, in 1883, and enrolled in the University of Munich in 1901, initially to study political economy and law. Inspired by **Theodor Lipps**' lectures, he soon became interested in **psychology** and philosophy. He was particularly drawn to the new way of doing philosophy offered by Husserl's *Logical Investigations* and participated in the Munich philosophical circle, which included Moritz Geiger, Johannes Daubert, and others (including **Max Scheler** after 1906). He completed his doctorate in 1904 under Lipps on the concept of cause in law. He then went to Göttingen to study with Husserl, but soon after returned to Munich, and completed his law training in Tübingen. In 1909 he returned to Göttingen to complete his *Habilitation* with Husserl, eventually becoming his assistant. At Göttingen, Reinach was known as a brilliant teacher. In 1914 he was conscripted into the German army and he was killed in 1917 in Flanders. Husserl regarded Reinach as the most gifted of his students, and was deeply affected by his death, writing an obituary for Reinach in *Kant Studien* in 1919. Reinach's former students put together a collection of his papers, with a foreword by Hedwig **Conrad-Martius**, in 1921. Reinach sought to develop Husserl's earlier **realist phenomenology**, aimed at the identification and description of the **essences** and the overall pursuit of a priori synthetic knowledge of various material regions. Reinach saw phenomenology is a way of doing philosophy and not a particular doctrine. It is aimed at seeing essences, making essential distinctions and repudiating existing distinctions where they are not validly drawn. In this respect, phenomenology aims at conceptual clarification or meaning analysis (*Bedeutungsanalyse*). However, Reinach insists that the clarification of meaning is not the aim of phenomenology but rather only one means.

The real aim of phenomenology is the **intuition** of **essences** and the essential laws governing them. Here Reinach shows how such essential seeing can have extraordinary impact on the understanding of other areas of knowledge. He argues that phenomenology is concerned with essences in a manner in which other sciences (e.g., mathematics) are not. Reinach was widely read in philosophy, especially, Hume, Kant, and William James, and **Frege**. He was especially known as a brilliant philosopher of law, with insights into the social context of utterances. His treatise, *Die apriorischen Grundlagen des bürgerlichen Rechtes* (*The A Priori Foundations of Civil Law*), appeared in the first volume of Husserl's **Yearbook for Philosophy and Phenomenological Research** in 1913. Reinach offers a first attempt at a systematic theory of the phenomena of promising, questioning, commanding, threatening, accusing, enacting, requesting, and other such acts, which he terms 'social acts', thereby anticipating the speech act theory more recently developed by John Austin and systematized by John Searle.

Relativism (*Relativismus*) See also **anthropologism, scepticism, subjectivism**
Husserl speaks generally of 'relativism' as a form of **subjectivism** – that reality can only be apprehended as it appears to the individual knower. In this regard, he refers to the ancient Greek Protagoras who proclaimed 'man is the measure of all things'. In his Logical Investigations, Husserl sees **psychologism** as leading to relativism and also suggest **anthropologism** – the view that truth is relative to the human species rather than relative to individuals – is also a form of relativism. In '**Philosophy as a Rigorous Science**', he presents **naturalism** and historicism (the view that a truth is relative to a specific historical context or period) as tending towards relativism. Philosophy as an ultimately grounded rigorous science is the enemy of all relativism.

Renewal (*Erneuerung*) See also **Kaizo articles**
In the opening paragraph of his first published Kaizo article (1923) Husserl wrote that 'Renewal is the universal call in our present, sorrowful age, and throughout the entire domain of European culture'. The immediate meaning of 'renewal' was the need to renew Europe's values to overcome the pessimism and despair produced by the effects of the First World War (Hua XXVII 3). But Husserl believes more generally that modern people

have lost their faith in culture and there is danger of a 'decline of the west' (*Untergang des Abendlandes*, Hua XXVII 4, Husserl here is invoking Spengler, without naming him). The answer lies in a renewal of the very 'idea of humanity', to shape our lives freely according to a life of **reason**. Only 'rigorous science' (*strenge Wissenschaft*, XXVII 6) can help us, Husserl says, but the problem is to find such a science, one which will be a true science of **humanity**, 'a science that would establish a rationality in social and political activity and a national, political technique'. An a priori science of humanity (akin to the a priori science of mathematical physics that prescribes and regulates how natural science is to be conducted) is needed, a science of the '**spirit**' (*Geist*), 'the *mathesis* of spirit and of humanity'. This new a priori science of human spirit, Husserl continues, will have to come to grips with the 'inwardness' of each individual consciousness; each human being is an 'ego subject' in a relation of empathy with other humans establishing a community together through their intersubjective, social acts. None of this can be understood if consciousness and subjectivity are approached naturalistically as in current experimental psychology as activities belonging to animal organisms causally interacting in a natural world. Husserl believes that we criticize our culture from the standpoint of ideal norms based on our ideal concept of a true and genuine humanity. In one of the drafts for his Kaizo articles, Husserl says that European culture has lost its way and strayed from its inborn *telos* (Hua XXVII 118) of freely given autonomous **reason**.

Retention (*Retention*) See also **living present, memory, now moment, protention, time consciousness**

According to Husserl's analyses of time consciousness, each temporal experience in the present consists of three phases or moments – the **now phase**, the retention and the **protention**. The retention is the echo or 'trace' of what has just gone before, the experience immediately prior to the present and out of which the present is experienced as coming. Paradoxically, the retention is experienced in the present but it presents the retained experience as modified in the form of 'having-been'. For Husserl, retention (or, in earlier terminology, 'primary memory' or 'fresh memory', the 'consciousness of just having been', Hua X 165) is not yet **memory** in the strong sense ('secondary memory'), although it forms the basis or ground for both passive and active rememberings. Rememberings present objects as whole entities, whereas a retention is a non-separable part of a perceptual awareness, it is a 'just past' that is still there in a reduced or modified sense. The just-past retention still has a kind of 'impressionality'. Husserl criticizes Brentano's view that these retentions and **protentions** are actually 'represented' or 'imagined' experiences, and not actually genuine parts of the perceptual process (X 13). They belong to the class of what have been called **'presentifications'** or 'presentiations' (*Vergegenwärtigungen*) rather than genuine perceptions (we shall return to this topic). In his early writings, Husserl treated the retention as part of the now-moment, but in his mature works he recognized that the retention cannot be in the same 'now' as the now moment (Hua X 333).

Rickert, Heinrich (1863–1936) Heinrich Rickert was a German philosopher who, with Windelband, founded the Baden Southwestern School of Neo-Kantianism. Heinrich Rickert was born in Danzig and graduated from the University of Strasbourg in 1888. In 1891 he began lecturing at Freiburg, becoming professor there in 1894. In 1916 he went to Heidelberg as successor to Wilhelm Windelband. Husserl replaced him in Freiburg in 1916. Rickert supervised Heidegger's *Habilitation* thesis. Rickert was interested in the epistemological and logical foundations of the sciences, both natural and human, but disagreed with **Dilthey**'s approach. Dilthey was critical of the phenomenological approach. He regarded the phenomenological reliance on intuition as deceptive since all understanding required conceptualization. As a neo-Kantian Rickert defended the critical role of philosophy to establish 'the validity of values'. Following his mentor Windelband he regarded natural sciences as interested in **generalization** whereas the historical sciences are interested in the individual. Windelband had distinguished between sciences governed by law ('nomothetic') and those whose interest was in the individual ('ideographic'). Furthermore, for Windelband, value can only attach to what is individual. For Rickert, the aim of scientific generalizing thought is to escape relations of value; whereas culture generally aims to establish values. Rickert emphasized the importance of practical reason. He wrote an influential critique of life philosophy. For Rickert, reality itself is an endless, continuous stream that in itself is 'unsurveyable'. The role of scientific concepts is to reform this complex reality so it can be made intelligible. Abstraction from perceptible reality is required for scientific concepts. Natural science conceptualises reality in general terms, whereas the human sciences are more focused on value. As Rickert puts it, in terms borrowed from Georg Simmel, natural science is a 'conceptual science' whereas history is a 'science of actuality'. His works include *The Object of Knowledge* (1892), *The Limits of Concept Formation in Natural Science* (1896–1902),*Cultural Science and Natural Science* (1899), translated by George Reisman as *Science and History: A Critique of Positivist Epistemology* (1962), and *The Philosophy of Life* (1920). Rickert had a strong influence on his students **Emil Lask** and **Martin Heidegger** and on Max Weber, who was his colleague in Freiburg for a time. Husserl corresponded with Dilthey and admired both **idealism** and the critique of **naturalism** of the Neo-Kantians. Husserl discussed Rickert critically in his *Nature and Spirit* lectures.

—S—

Sartre, Jean-Paul (1905–1980)   The French philosopher and writer was born in Thiviers, France, in 1905. His father died when he was an infant and he was educated by his maternal grandfather and then in the *lycées* Henri IV and Louis-le-Grand. He entered the École Normale Supérieure in 1924 where he met Simone de Beauvoir and Maurice **Merleau-Ponty**. Through Raymond Aron he came to learn about **phenomenology**, and in 1933 travelled to Berlin to study, spending time reading Husserl. In 1936 he published *The Transcendence of the Ego*, a critique of Husserl's egological conception of consciousness and several studies on the nature of imagination (see *The Psychology of Imagination* (1940). Sartre initially became a teacher but after the success of his novel *Nausea* (1938) he became a professional writer. In 1941 while in a detention camp he read Heidegger's *Being and Time* and in 1943 published his own major work *Being and Nothingness*. His 1945 lecture 'Existentialism is a Humanism' is a defence of existentialism. He later incorporated existentialism within Marxism, especially in *Critique of Dialectical Reason* (1960). In 1944 he founded the journal *Les Temps Modernes*, with de Beauvoir and Merleau-Ponty and other French intellectuals. He died in 1980. Sartre's books include *The Transcendence of the Ego* (1936), *The Psychology of Imagination* (1940), *Being and Nothingness* (1943). Sartre was inspired by phenomenology because he believed its doctrine of **intentionality** overcame the subject–object divide of traditional epistemology and restored the world in its full concreteness. He accepts intentionality as expressing this bond between self and world. Sartre was critical of Husserl's invocation of the **transcendental ego** and argued for a distinction to be made between pre-reflective egoless consciousness and reflective consciousness. For Sartre, the ego is not a constituent of consciousness but rather is something that becomes apprehended as an object only in reflective consciousness. Sartre characterizes consciousness as 'lack' or 'negation' or 'nothingness' (*néant*) that is always seeking to fill itself with being, an impossible task.

Scepticism (*Skepticismus*) See also **Descartes,** *epistēmē*, **epochē, Hume, knowledge, relativism**

Husserl acknowledges the importance of ancient Greek scepticism for introducing the distinction between how things seem and how things are, between **appearance** and reality, and between belief (***doxa***) and genuine knowledge (***epistēmē***). Husserl presents Socrates and Plato as attempting to overcome the sceptic challenge that denied the possibility of knowledge (see Husserl's 1906–7 Lectures on *Logic and the Theory of Knowledge* and also *First Philosophy*). Husserl sees scepticism as a perennial possibility in philosophy and he refers to its 'immortality' (see *First Philosophy* I, Hua VII 57) and 'Hydra-headed' nature. Scepticism challenges our naive faith in the pregivenness of the world (Hua VII 59). Scepticism takes many forms and Husserl discusses both the ancient Greek sceptics (specifically Gorgias) and also modern scepticism in the form of **Descartes** and **Hume**. Husserl also connects scepticism with **relativism** (in the ancient philosophy with Protagoras), saying that the 'essence of all scepticism is subjectivism' (Hua VII 58). Husserl borrows the notion of ***epochē*** from the sceptics. Husserl distinguishes his use of the *epochē* from the ancient sceptics in that he does not conclude dogmatically to the unknowability of the world, but simply retains the idea of making no belief commitment concerning the existence of the world. Descartes' scepticism had the function of introducing the ***cogito*** and with it the domain of **transcendental subjectivity**. Scepticism plays a role, then, in the discovery of **transcendental philosophy**.

Scheler, Max (1874–1928)   Max Scheler was a German philosopher and phenomenologist, charismatic lecturer and popular author. Born in Munich in 1874, he initially studied medicine in Munich and Berlin. While in Berlin he also studied philosophy and sociology with **Dilthey** and Georg Simmel. He graduated from the University of Jena in 1897 and completed his *Habilitation* thesis there in 1899 with Rudolf Eucken. He then taught at Jena University (1900–1906) and Munich (1907–10), where he joined the Munich Phenomenological Circle that included **Pfänder**, Daubert, **Lipps**, and others. Scheler met Husserl in 1902 and later asked him to arrange for Scheler to lecture at Göttingen after he was dismissed from his post in Munich following a scandal in his personal life. In 1919 he became Professor of Philosophy and Sociology at the University of Cologne where he taught until his death in 1928 (he was due to move to a professorship in Frankfurt). Scheler's parents were Protestant and Jewish but he converted to Catholicism, although later moved away from the Church. He wrote patriotic pamphlets during the First World War. In 1913 Scheler published his important study, *Formalism in Ethics and Non-Formal Ethics of Values. A New Attempt toward A Foundation of An Ethical Personalism* in the first volume of Husserl's **Yearbook**. This work focused on the nature of the **person** as a source of **value** and emphasized the role of **feelings** and of love. For Scheler, feelings relate to values and values are apprehended a priori in people's feelings. There is a hierarchy of values. Max Scheler published his *Zur Phänomenologie und Theorie der Sympathiegefühle und vom Liebe und Hass* [*On the Phenomenology and Theory of the Feeling of Sympathy and of Love and Hate*] in 1913, planned as the first part of a series of studies entitled *Die Sinngesetze des emotionalen Lebens* [*The Laws of Meaning of Emotional Life*], which would include studies of shame, fear, resentment, and the sense of honour. It was later reprinted as *The Nature and Forms of Sympathy*. Scheler also published *Ressentiment,* and *On the Eternal in Man* (1920–22), *Sociology of Knowledge* (1924) and *The Human Place in the Cosmos* (1928). Scheler had a strong influence on **Heidegger, Edith Stein** and on Ortega y Gasset.

Schlick, Moritz (1882–1936)   See also **a priori, essential intuition**
Mortiz Schlick was a German philosopher, advocate of logical positivism and one of the founders of the Vienna Circle. He was born in Berlin in 1882 and studied physics in Heidelberg, Lausanne and Berlin (with Max

Planck). In 1904 he completed his doctorate and, in 1910, his *Habilitation* on 'The Nature of Truth in Modern Logic'. He taught at the universities of Rostok and Kiel before moving to Vienna in 1922. In Vienna, Schlick founded a circle with other philosophers and intellectuals **Rudolf Carnap**, Kurt Gödel, Herbert Feigl, and Otto Neurath. **Felix Kaufmann** was another member who had studied phenomenology with Husserl. Kaufmann defended Husserl's concept of **eidetic insight (*Wesensshau*)** against Moritz Schlick's criticisms, and argued that Husserl's concept of **evidence (*Evidenz*)** had been misunderstood by those critics who regarded it as a subjective feeling of certainty. In 1936 Schlick was shot dead by a student. Schlick criticized Husserl's phenomenology in the first edition (1918) of his *Allgemeine Erkenntnislehere* (*General Theory of Knowedge*). Husserl responded to Schlick's criticisms in the Foreword to his Second Edition of the Sixth Investigation (published as a free-standing volume in 1921). There Husserl asserts that many criticisms drawn from outside phenomenology fail to understand the effect that bracketing has on one's opinions and convictions. He dismisses as absurd the view that Schlick attributes to him according to which 'my *Ideas* asserts the existence of a particular intuition, that is *not a real psychic act*, and that if someone fails to find *such an "experience," which does not fall within the domain of psychology'*. Husserl was annoyed that a doctrine of special or indeed mystical intuition was being attributed to his phenomenology. Husserl believes the meaning of the **epochē** has been completely misunderstood by Schlick. Phenomenology is not a Platonic gazing at essences given in a kind of intellectual **intuition**; it is based on hard work, akin to mathematics. In fact, Schlick had been targeting Husserl's account of **essential intuition** in the **Logical Investigations** from as early as 1910 in his Habilitation thesis, 'The Nature of Truth in Modern Logic'. In general, Schlick was opposed to the idea that *knowledge* (which he conceived of as essentially propositional) could be any kind of intuition. As he puts it in his 1932 paper 'Form and Content: an Introduction to Philosophical Thinking': 'Intuition is enjoyment, enjoyment is life, not knowledge'. For him, the pure content of intuitive experience was inexpressible. He writes: 'The difference between structure and material, between form and content is, roughly speaking, the difference between that which can be expressed and that which cannot be expressed.' And he goes on to say: 'Since content is essentially incommunicable by language, it cannot be conveyed to a seeing man any more or any better than to a blind one.' For Schlick, one can *see* a green leaf and *say* that one sees the green leaf, but one's saying it does not communicate the intuitive *content* 'green'. This is his position *against* phenomenology. Schlick maintained that all knowing involved seeing-as and hence conceptualizing and judging. Pure intuiting, for Schlick, could not have the status of knowing. Ironically, Schlick does not challenge Husserl on the basis of any kind of verificationism. Both Husserl and Schlick were advocates of kinds of empiricism whereby knowledge is founded on perceptual experience, but Husserl always rejected positivism on the grounds that it overly narrowly restricted the content of experience (to sense data) and did not grasp the nature of what Husserl termed **'categorial intuition'**. Schlick again attacked Husserl in 1930, this time attacking Husserl's defense of synthetic **a priori** propositions (Husserl's 'material a priori'), which Schlick regarded as empty tautologies, rather than significant eidetic insights. For Schlick, as for logical positivism in general, there is no synthetic a priori. Schlick followed Wittgenstein's *Tractatus* in holding that a priori statements were simply tautologies and as such did not 'say' anything. For Husserl, by way of contrast, there are certain truths that are a priori but which depend on the nature of the *matter* in question. Thus, something being blue and at the same time yellow is not, for him, a purely formal truth based solely on the Law of Non-Contradiction, but rather an a priori synthetic truth grounded in the essential nature of color as essentially dependent on surface. Husserl may have been particularly irked by Schlick precisely because the latter was repeating a criticism of phenomenology's reliance on intuition that was to be found in orthodox neo-Kantianism. For neo-Kantianism, it was a matter of orthodoxy that intuitions without concepts were blind. Prominent German neo-Kantians of the day, including **Rickert** and **Natorp**, as well as other prominent philosophers such as Hans Cornelius (one of Adorno's teachers), had also criticized phenomenology's assumptions concerning pure unmediated givenness. The logical positivists and the neo-Kantians both saw phenomenology as a new form of irrational or non-conceptual intuitionism, and as such, would be doomed to failure.

Schutz, Alfred (1899–1959)   Schutz was born in Vienna on 13 April 1899. His father, Alfred, died shortly before his birth and two years later, his mother Johanna married his father's brother, Otto, a banker. Alfred studied at the Staatsgymnasium VI. In 1916 he enlisted in the army in the artillery division and fought in the Great War on the Italian front, earning silver and bronze medals for bravery. After the war, he studied in the Faculty of Law and Social Sciences at the University of Vienna and received his Doctorate in Laws there in 1921. His teachers included the political theorist Hans Kelsen and the economist Ludwig von Mises. Schutz attend von Mises' intellectual discussion circle, which included intellectuals such as Friedrich von Hayek, Eric Voegelin and Felix Kaufman. Mises remained a friend of Schutz's throughout his life. Shortly before submitting his doctorate Schutz was began working as a banker. Schutz was deeply influenced by Max Weber (who had lectured in Vienna in 1918 and was a friend of Mises). He was particularly interested in Weber's 'interpretative sociology' (*verstehende Sociologie*), and the latter's insistence that the social sciences had to abstain from value judgements. In the 1920s, especially from 1925 to1927, Schutz became particularly interested in Henri Bergson, especially his unified approach to consciousness and temporal experience in a series of manuscripts subsequently published as *Life Forms and Meaning Structure*. Influenced by the phenomenologist Felix Kaufmann, he began to read Husserl, especially his just published phenomenology of the consciousness of inner time (1928). For Schutz 'the problem of meaning is a problem of time'. In 1932 Schutz produced his major work, *The Phenomenology of the Social World (Der sinnhafte Aufbau der sozialen Welt)*. He sent a copy of this book to Husserl who invited him to become his assistant. Husserl called him 'an earnest and profound phenomenologist'. Schutz first visited Husserl in June 1932 and subsequently they met frequently and corresponded but he could not afford to leave his banking job. Husserl described him as a banker by day and a phenomenologist at night. Schutz attended Husserl's Prague lectures in November 1935, which deeply impressed him. His last visit to Husserl was at Christmas 1937 when Husserl was already quite ill. After the takeover of Austria by the National Socialists, Schutz emigrated to the USA. Together with Marvin Farber, he helped to found the *International Phenomenological Society* and the journal *Philosophy and Phenomenological Research* in 1940. In 1943 he began teaching sociology and philosophy courses at the graduate faculty of the New School for Social Research and was chair of the philosophy department there from 1952–6. He attracted many graduate students including Maurice Natanson and Lester Embree. He died in 1959.

Science (*Wissenschaft*)   See also **evidence, knowledge, logic, theory of science**

For Husserl, the goal of science is **truth**. Science, for Husserl, is understood in a broad sense to include every form of systematic knowing, including both the natural and the human sciences. Science as a theoretical enterprise divorced from purely practical interests is concerned with the possession of truth, with *knowing* (*Erkennen*) or *cognition* (*Erkenntnis*) in a systematic, coherent sense, which means having grounds for one's knowing, possessing truths with evidential insight or **evidence** (LU, *Prol.* § 6). Science has an ideal of **objectivity** and seeks to be a set of truths that are connected inferentially and built on each potentially to form a coherent system that can produce higher meaning formations and so on to infinity (see *Crisis*, p. 380; VI 460 and 355; VI 367). **Logic** as **theory of science** provides the formal framework for the organization of science. In common with the neo-Kantian tradition, Husserl distinguishes between the exact sciences which investigate **nature** and the human sciences which investigate the realm of **spirit**. In his mature works, Husserl sees natural science as the outcome of a particular form of **theoretical attitude**, an idealizing accomplishment that is directed to the infinite ideal of grasping being in itself, reality as it is in itself. For Husserl, science belongs to the **life-world** but at the same time idealizes **nature** as a closed domain of exact causal laws. In natural science, individual objects are treated as exemplars (this piece of gold stands for gold in general) and there is an assumption of an essential iterability and repeatability. The human sciences, contrariwise, operate on the basis of the **personalistic attitude** and interpretation through **motivation**.

Sedimentation (*Niederschläge, Sedimentierung*)   See also **doxa, habit, tradition, type**

Sedimentation is a term found in Husserl's later work, e.g. *Phenomenological Psychology*, **Formal and Transcendental Logic** (Appendix Two § 50), in **Crisis** (§ 9 h, p. 52; VI 52); **The Origin of Geometry** (*Crisis*, p. 361; VI 371); and **Experience and Judgment** § 67. It appears also in his **Lectures on Passive Synthesis**. The term is not found in his earlier work, e.g. the **Logical Investigations** or indeed in his **Cartesian Meditations**. Husserl uses both the noun ('sedimentation') and the verb ('to sediment') primarily to express how new experiences settle down and become habitual convictions that inform a person's cognitive outlook. Thus in *Experience and Judgment* Husserl explains sedimentation as: 'the continuous transformation of what has been originally acquired and has become a habitual possession and thus something non-original' (EU § 67, p. 275). In this context, sedimentation expresses how experiences become embodied in one's actions, become habitual, and forms one's character and individual **style**. What is sedimented belongs in the background of one's beliefs. Husserl speaks of it as belonging to the 'underground' of the **ego** (Hua IX 481). It is what is 'suppressed'. Sedimentation complements spontaneity and the activity of the ego. When something new is learned there is a kind of Eureka moment or 'aha experience' but with familiarity, this new insight becomes bedded down and eventually it simply forms part of one's background beliefs. It may even be forgotten entirely yet continue to operate, e.g. driving a particular route to work becomes routine so that one does not have to think about it. Neither can one necessarily remember the first time one took the route. Sedimentation has a number of stages. There is the primary activation of a **judgement** and then its retention or even abandonment. In the *Crisis*, Husserl says that the implications of a particular theory may perhaps not be seen because they have become obscured through 'sedimentation or traditionalization' (*Crisis* § 9h, p. 52; VI 52). There is a cumulative tradition involving what Husserl calls *sedimentation* (*Sedimentierung*, *Crisis* 362; VI 372) whereby certain earlier experiences become passively enfolded in our ongoing experience, just as language retains earlier meanings in its etymologies. As Husserl puts it in the **'Origin of Geometry'**, 'cultural structures, appear on the scene in the form of tradition; they claim, so to speak, to be sedimentations (*Sedimentierungen*) of a truth meaning that can be made originally self-evident' (*Crisis*, p. 367; VI 377). Knowing how to speak a language is a case of the reactivation of sedimented knowledge. Husserl also speaks of sedimented judgements being 're-activated' when they are consciously endorsed and deliberately embraced. New judgements can be formed on the basis of earlier judgements which give particular shape and direction to experience (FTL, p. 325). Sedimentation complements spontaneity. However, it is not completely passive but has its own peculiar form of activity. Sedimentation is part of what Husserl calls **passive synthesis**. In *The Origin of Geometry* (*Crisis*, p. 361; VI 371) Husserl speaks of an awakening to sense which is experienced passively. Writing down geometrical insights in words brings about their 'sedimentation'. Husserl speaks of sedimentation in this context as a kind of secondary **passivity**. Thus he writes in *Experience and Judgment*:

> It then sinks ever further into the background and at the same time becomes ever more indistinct; the degree of its prominence gradually lessens until it finally disappears from the field of immediate consciousness, is 'forgotten.' It is henceforth incorporated into the passive background, into the 'unconscious,' which is not a dead nothingness but a limiting mode of consciousness and accordingly can affect us anew like another passivity in the form of whims, free-floating ideas, and so on. In this modification, however, the judgment is not an original but a *secondary passivity*, which essentially refers to its origin in an actual spontaneous production. (EU § 67b, p. 279)

Husserl even speaks of this process as governed by the 'law of sedimentation' (EU § 68, p. 282). Sedimentation is brought about by association of like with like so that experience is organized in types. Someone who knows how to play guitar has sedimented or an intuitive knowledge of the appropriate finger movements and pressures to be applied. Sedimentation characterizes the manner in which a learned skill is possessed without being actively present in consciousness. Husserl speaks of 'originally sedimented judgments'. For any act of judging to take place, certain other judgements must already be present in consciousness (EU 23, 46, 48). Sedimentations belong to the realm of **doxa**. They provide the context and material for further judgements and hence are critically important for knowledge. Sedimentations belong to the very experience of being in the world (p. 48). Sedimentations are revealed by a kind of 'regressive inquiry' or **'questioning back'**. Husserl writes:

> We then understand ourselves, *not as subjectivity which finds itself in a world ready-made as in simple psychological reflection but as a subjectivity bearing within itself, and achieving, all of the possible operations to which this world owes its becoming.* In other words, we understand ourselves in this revelation of intentional implications, in the interrogation of the

origin of the sedimentation of sense from intentional operations, *as transcendental*. (EU § 12, p. 49)

Self-experience (*Selbsterfahrung*)   See also **ego, egology, experience, sphere of ownness, transcendental experience**

Husserl distinguishes between 'self-experience' **Selbsterfahrung** (CM § 9), that is, the immediate experience one has of one's self and one's own conscious states and '**other experience**' (*Fremderfahrung*), the experience of everything that is transcendent to the self, including the objective **world** as well as other **subjects**. The domain of self-experience is apodictic in that its **evidence** cannot be contraverted. The **epochē** opens up a new domain of transcendental self-experience freed from the naive presuppositions that dominate the **natural attitude**.

Self-observation (*Selbstbeobachtung*)   See also **essential intuition, inner perception, psychology**

Self-observation is a term commonly used by nineteenth-century psychologists (including Wundt, **Brentano**, **Lipps**, and others) to mean one's self-awareness of one's mental states and episodes. Self-observation is often called *introspection*. Brentano sharply distinguishes between self-observation (understood as introspection) and **inner perception**. Self-observation is considered to be contemporaneous with the psychic episode it is observing and hence to be fallible as a psychological method. We cannot *observe* our own mental states while occupying them. Brentano writes in *Psychology from an Empirical Standpoint*: 'It is a universally valid psychological law that we can never focus our attention upon the object of inner perception', PES 30) But, by careful training, we can *perceive* our inner mental states as they engage outer phenomena, and this perception grasps them whole. Brentano believes inner perception can intuitively apprehend and compile a complete list of the 'ultimate mental elements' (PES 45; DP 13), i.e. the real parts of our psychic act. Inner perception is supposedly infallible for Brentano. 'It is a universally valid psychological law that we can never focus our attention upon the object of inner perception' (PES 30). Husserl discusses the relations between self-observation and phenomenological **reflection** in *Ideas* I § 79. For Husserl, phenomenology was not interested in existence and hence was not interested in the actual experience of the **ego**.

Self-reflection (*Selbstbesinnung*) See also **questioning back, reflection, self-experience**

Husserl speaks of the task of the philosopher as involving self-reflection – an inquiry back into the kind of beings that we are (*Crisis* § 15). Husserl distinguishes between a broader and a narrower sense of 'self-reflection' (*Selbstbesinnung*): pure 'ego reflection' (*Ich-Reflexion*), which is reflection on the whole life of the ego as ego; and reflection (*Besinnung*) in the pregnant sense of '**questioning back**' into the sense or teleological essence of the ego (*Crisis*, p. 392n; 510–11 n1). Self-reflection in the broad sense involves a **person** seeking to reflect on the ultimate sense of his or her existence.

Self-responsibility (*Selbstbeantwartigung*) See also **life, rationality, Vienna Lecture**

Husserl regularly invokes 'self-responsibility' as central to the practice of autonomous philosophy (*Crisis* § 56). The idea of 'responsibility' and 'answerability to oneself as a rational person is a development of Kant's idea of the moral person as the **person** who gives the law to himself. Husserl believes that phenomenology and radical inquiry prepares the person for the life of self-responsibility. Husserl locates the demand for self-responsibility in Descartes' project of radical intellectual honesty (CM § 2). The philosopher has the duty to take responsibility for safeguarding the rationality of all cultural life. In his **Vienna Lecture**, Husserl speaks of a 'new humanity made capable of an absolute self-responsibility on the basis of absolute theoretical insights' (*Crisis*, p. 283; Hua VI 329). Self-responsibility has the highest form of a will resolved to live a life of autonomous self-responsibility guided by reason (*Crisis* p. 338; VI 272).

Self-thinker (*Selbstdenker*) See also **presuppositionlessness, reflection, self-responsibility**

Husserl uses the term 'self-thinker' for the autonomous, self-critical philosopher who had inquired radically into all his or her beliefs in the spirit of **Descartes**' meditator (*Crisis* § 17), has attempted to achieve presuppositionlessness (*Crisis* § 15) and freedom from prejudice, and who seeks **absolute grounding** for knowledge and is seeking to live a life of rational **self-responsibility** (see also *Crisis*, p. 394; VI 512).

Semantic essence (*bedeutungsmässiges Wesen*)   See also **intentional essence, meaning**
The semantic essence of an intentional act is the concrete act of meaning that which in the act allows for the **meaning** to be abstracted (see Fifth Logical Investigation § 21).

Sensation (*Empfindung*)   See also **hyle, hyletic data, kinaesthetic sensations, movement sensations, sense data, sensings, stuff**
Husserl's account of what is primarily given in experience is a broadening and correction of traditional **empiricism**. In the ***Logical Investigations*** Husserl rejects the classical empiricist and positivist doctrine of atomic, isolated 'sense data' (*Sinnesdaten*) or 'data of sensation' (*Empfindungsdaten*). He regards these as a false theoretical construct produced by the 'psychological attitude' (XXXV 82). Husserl also rejects the representationalist view that what we primarily experience are our own sensations. He writes: 'I see the box, not my own sensations' (LU V § 14). For Husserl, sensations and 'sensation complexes' are not in themselves intentional (LU V § 10; *Ideas* I § 36), they belong to the **matter** of experience, i.e. they are merely 'material' features of our intentional experience. Sensations are part of the experienced content of the mental act; they are 'lived through' rather than perceived. Sensations on their own, understood as raw givens, cannot by themselves play the role of constituting objectivities. Husserl rejects the view that there is an 'act' of sensation; sensations do not involve positing. They are simply 'given' as parts of the **lived experience**, but do not become perceptual objects in themselves:

> Any piece of a sensed visual field, full as it is of visual contents,
> is an experience containing many part-contents, which are
> neither referred to, nor intentionally objective, in the whole.
> (LU V § 10)

When I undergo an *Erlebnis*, it simply presents itself as having a certain sensational colouring, its sensory 'filling' (*Fülle*). Although sensations are not the objects of sense, they do play a vital role in perception. As Husserl says in *Ideas* II § 10, 'all objectification of spatial things ultimately leads back to sensation'. Sensations provide '**matter**', or the 'stuff' of experience, but that matter has to be *formed* by a certain kind of interpretative 'grasp' or '**interpretation**' (*Auffassung*, LU VI § 26; *Deutung*, *Interpretation*) to yield an object with a particular sense or meaning. But they are somehow 'bearers of interpretation'. This suggests that there are only acts that *take up* and *interpret* sensational complexes (LU VI, Appendix, **II** 358n. 6; XIX/2 774n). It is an 'animating apprehension' (DR § 46, p. 136; Hua XVI 160), enlivening 'dead matter' (DR § 15, p. 39; Hua XVI 46). In other words, meaning is not given by the sensations themselves but by the *interpretative* act grasping them. In his *Passive Synthesis* lectures, he warns that the 'interpretation' (*Deutung*) of sensory matter is not like reading a *meaning* off signs, but there is some kind of point beyond experienced (XI 17). This is the reason that the same sensational cluster can underlie and ground different intentional experiences: I see a woman; I see a mannequin, based on the same sensations. Similarly, different acts on the basis of different sensations can perceive the same object, e.g. the tone of a violin heard nearer or further away (LU V § 14). Furthermore, there is always a *gap* between the sensed content and the fuller overflowing perception of the thing. This 'excess' (*Überschuss*) or *plus ultra* of perception is provided by the **apprehension**. In so far as these contents are apprehended so as to present the object, Husserl calls them 'presentational contents' (*darstellende Inhalte*, DR § 15, see also *Ideas* I § 36). Thus, in seeing a white paper, the presentational sensation of white is a 'bearer' of intentionality, of an interpretation, but not in itself consciousness of an object. Husserl recognizes a difference between *presenting* and *presented* sensations. The former sensations motivate our attribution of certain sensory features to a body. When I touch a smooth and cold surface, I have certain sensations in my fingers, but I intend through these sensations to the property of smoothness and coolness of the surface. It takes a reflective turn of regard to notice the sensations in my fingers. The sensations seem to be double sided, as it were. They present themselves as belonging to the fingers, but also as 'presenting' (*darstellen*) properties of the object. Certain sensations are routinely attributed to external things while others are located in us in a certain way. I may become aware that the *room* feels cold or I may be aware that *I* feel cold in the room. There are feelings (like my sense of where parts of my body are) that seem to be constituted *internally* so to speak, while others definitely come marked with transcendence. A person suffering from tinnitus may hear the irritating ringing noise as 'inside her head' and can separate it from persistent ringing noises that appear to be transcendent. In

Ideas I § 85, Husserl introduces the Greek term **hyle** to refer to this sensible, temporally flowing, matter of experience in contrast to the intentional *morphé* or form. This concept of a sensory base or 'stuff' of experience is retained in Husserl's later writings. He characterizes it as a sensuous 'residuum'. The same sensory contents can be the basis for motivating different acts of apprehension; and similarly the same act of perceiving (I see John) can be based on different sensory clusters (I see his face; I see the back of his head). There is an even more complex relation involved in cases like memory where my current perceptual *hyle* may not at all be implicated in the remembered presentation. Husserl developed a very complex account of the sensational component in perceptual experience, but his main theme is that sensation is not perception. His later works stresses the highly ordered and regulated nature of the streams of sensations, there is a continuous harmony, a constancy of experience (XI 108; 263). In fact, Husserl always has a certain problem about the nature of the given, in the sense of the 'primordial matter' (*Urhyle*), the 'primordially given (*das Urgebene*), the ultimate residuum in experience. His researches into time consciousness seem to have convinced him that his matter/apprehension account of sensations could not be correct, or else he would have to posit some kind of time sensations for our sensory experience of entities in temporal situations. But in late works the *Urhyle* stands for whatever is given to the ego such that the ego itself awakes to itself in the midst of this givenness. Husserl makes an important distinction between the *sensations* (*Empfindungen*) that are properly speaking *of* sensory properties of the physical object perceived (colour, shape, texture, smoothness), and those *sensings* (*Empfindnisse*) that motivate us to see the object as spatial but which are primarily experienced as modifications of my sensory organs (IV 146). I can touch the table and feel its coldness and smoothness, or I can advert to the sensings in the tips of my fingers (these sensings often linger after the fingers have withdrawn from the object). I can perceive an object an apperceive the kinaesthetic system that accompanies the perception (I realise I am tilting my head to one side to follow the movement of the object, etc).

Sense (*Sinn*)   See also **Frege, ideality, meaning, noema, reference**
The notion of 'sense' (*Sinn*) is central to phenomenology. The term 'sense' carries wider connotations, in that non-linguistic activities, such as perceiving, remembering, and so on, also involve 'sense'. All experiences

have meaning and the kind of meaning an experience conveys has its own particular mode of 'givenness'. To grasp something as an artwork is to grasp it in a mode of meaningfulness distinct from a relic approached through religious veneration or a tool used for a practical purpose. Sense, as understood within phenomenology, is essentially 'two sided', including both subjective and objective dimensions. Husserl speaks of 'sense constitution'; sense is not simply something outside us that we apprehend, it is something that is 'constituted' or put together by us due to our particular attitudes, presuppositions, background beliefs and so on. In short, phenomenology is a reflection on the manner in which things comes to gain the kind of *sense* they have for us. The central focus of phenomenology, it can even be said, is the problem of *sense*, of *meaning* (*Phen. Psych.*, p. 18; Hua IX 25). Husserl in his *Cartesian Meditations* § 43 had already clearly articulated the basic insight of phenomenology as maintaining 'that every sense that any existent whatever has or can have for me – in respect of its 'what' and its 'it exists and actually is' – is a sense *in* and arising *from* my intentional life.' Husserl sometimes distinguishes 'sense' (*Sinn*) from '**meaning**' (*Bedeutung*), although he regularly uses the terms interchangeably. Meanings are related explicitly to linguistic meaning, whereas there can be perceptual 'senses'. Sense is a term also used by **Frege**. Both philosophers separately were developing sophisticated accounts of the difference between the 'sense' (*Sinn*) of an expression and its objective reference. The sense is the ideal intentional content of an experience. In the ***Logical Investigations***, and indeed since 1891, Husserl was fully aware of Frege's distinction between *Sinn* ('sense') and *Bedeutung* ('reference' or 'meaning'), but he does not observe it since it is at variance with ordinary Germany usage. In his **Logical Investigations**, Husserl tends to use the terms *Sinn*, *Bedeutung* and also *Meinung* more or less as equivalent notions, although later, in *Ideas* I § 124, he will restrict '*Bedeutung*' to linguistic meaning only and use '*Sinn*' more broadly to include all meanings, including non-conceptual contents (e.g. perceptual sense). Both Frege and Husserl agree that the *sense* of a statement is an ideal unity not affected by the psychic act grasping it, or by the psychic stuff (mental imagery, feelings, and so on) that accompanies the psychological episode. In themselves, senses are pure **idealities**, remaining unchanged irrespective of their being counted, judged, or otherwise apprehended in psychic acts. As Husserl says in the *Prolegomena*, truths are what they are irrespective of whether humans grasp them at all (Hua XVIII 240).

Despite the fact that the objects of logic are ideal and transtemporal, never-theless, they must also be accessible and graspable by the human mind, as Husserl later explains: '[I]t is unthinkable that such ideal objects could not be apprehended in appropriate subjective psychic acts and experiences' (*Phen. Psych.*, p. 18; Hua IX 25). We can imagine any such ideal meaning or *Sinn* being entertained or judged or considered in some way by a mind. It is simply a fact that these ideal meanings (*Sinne*) present themselves to us as something that is subjectively grasped: '[I]deal objects confront us as subjectively produced formations in the lived experiencing and doing of the forming' (*Phen. Psych.*, p. 18: Hua IX 25). This is their 'being-for'. They are always truths *for* some possible mind, subjective acts are 'consti-tuting acts' for these ideal objectivities. The question then becomes: how are these hidden psychic experiences *correlated* to the 'idealities'? Frege had answered in a naive manner: our minds simply *grasp* ideal thoughts. But Husserl wants to give an account that does justice to the essential two-sidedness of our cognitive achievements by analysing the structure of this expression and grasping of meaning. Some commentators identify the 'sense' with the 'noema', but, strictly speaking, the 'sense' is the 'core' of the **noema**. Husserl even speaks of 'noematic sense'. The same object can be referred to with different senses (Morning Star, Evening Star).

Sense and validity (*Sinn und Geltung*)   See also **meaning, sense**
Husserl often couples together the concepts of 'sense' and 'validity' (*Sinn und Geltung*) that things, people, situations, social actions, and so on, have for us as experiencing subjects in the world. A thing's ontological status cannot be distinguished from its sense or meaning, and hence also Husserl speaks of 'being-sense' (*Seinssinn*), which David Carr translates as 'ontic sense' (*Crisis* § 33, p. 122; VI 124) or '**ontic meaning**' (*Crisis* § 27, p. 100; VI 103). He also regularly speaks of something's 'validity of being' or 'ontic validity' (*Seinsgeltung*, *Crisis*, § 17, p. 77; VI 79). Things not only have meaning but their whole manner of *being* is an **achievement** of subjective and intersubjective **constitution**.

Sense bestowal (*Sinngebung*)   See also **constitution, sense**
'Sense bestowal', 'bestowal of meaning' or 'sense giving' (*Sinngebung*) is a term frequently used by Husserl to speak of the acts whereby an experience or an object is constituted in a certain way through our intentional acts

(see *Crisis* VI 58 where he speaks about how modern science attains its 'bestowal of meaning'). At CM § 48, Husserl speaks of different levels of sense giving in the constitution of transcendence and, at *Crisis* § 70, of the whole of life as a series of sense bestowals and sense havings.

Sense data (*Sinnesdaten, Empfindungsdaten*)   See also **hyletic data, matter, sensation**

'Sense data' (*Sinnesdaten*) or 'data of sensation' (*Empfindungsdaten*) is Husserl's name for the lowest stratum of what is given objectively in perceptual experience (see *Ideas* II § 54), is experienced passively and is not actively constituted by the **ego**. This sensory field of data or givens make up a non-intentional layer of what is merely felt or undergone. Husserl speaks of this layer as belonging to the **matter** of the intentional act. Husserl is an opponent of positivist accounts of sense data which he regards as metaphysical entities. The term 'sense data' was used philosophers such as Bertrand Russell and G. E. Moore for the immediate givens of sensory experience (felt sensations, seen patches of colour, tones, and so on). Husserl criticizes atomistic approaches to sense-data. For him, sense data are constituted in the flow of **time consciousness**.

Sense investigation (*Besinnung*)   See also **reflection, sense**

The term 'sense investigation' is Dorion Cairns' English translation for 'reflection' (*Besinnung*) used by Husserl for the phenomenological investigation or 'explication' of the sense or meaning of a constituted entity, e.g. the sense of modern science, the sense of logic as a theory of science, etc. See *Formal and Transcendental Logic*, Introduction. A sense investigation is a 'sense explication' (*Sinnauslegung*) that involves **clarification** of senses moving from the vague to the clearly defined (see FTL, p. 9; Hua XVII 13).

Sensibility (*Sinnlichkeit*)   See also **empiricism, Kant, sense data**

Kant claims there are two sources of knowledge – sensibility and understanding. He sees sensibility as the source of sensory intuitions. Space and time are the a priori forms of sensibility whereas sensations are the matter that sensibility receives and processes. Sensibility is characterized by receptivity. According to Husserl, Kant follows the empiricists in thinking that what was received was simply **sense data** from the outside:

> As for sensibility ... it had generally been assumed that it gives
> rise to the merely sensible data, precisely as a result of affec-
> tion from the outside. And yet one acted as if the experiential
> world of prescientific man – the world not yet logicized by
> mathematics – was the world pregiven by mere sensibility.
> (*Crisis* § 25, p. 93: VI 96)

For Husserl, the domain of sensibility is much more complex since it includes
everything that is experienced as 'pregiven', the whole domain of **passivity**,
including the experience of the world as 'always already there'.

Sensings (*Empfindnisse*)   See also **perception, sensation, sense data**
In *Ideas* II (especially § 36 and § 40), Husserl introduces the neologism
Empfindnisse, which has been translated as 'sensings'. Husserl rarely
invented new terms so this shows he was struggling to express something
not captured in ordinary language. The term appears to bring together two
other terms: **sensation** (*Empfindung*) and **lived experience** (*Erlebnis*).
Husserl is specifically referring to bodily sensations that are immediately felt
and lived through in a particular part of the body (Husserl also calls them
'localized sensations') but which also communicate further some other
object. There is a distinction for instance between the specific sensings felt
in the finger tips and the smooth surface of the touched object.

Sign (*Zeichen*)   See also **expression, indication, signitive act**
As a mathematician, Husserl was interested in how certain marks or
physical entities can be understood as signs pointing beyond themselves.
In **Philosophy of Arithmetic**, he was conscious that human beings can
only intuit a small number in concrete terms and need to use signs to
signify numbers that cannot be immediately intuited. In general, scientific
knowledge proceeds through signs. Signs are divided by Husserl in his First
Logical Investigation into **indications**, which point directly to their object,
and **expressions**, which refer to their object through a sense or meaning.

Signitive act   See also **fulfilment**
Already in the **Logical Investigations**, especially the Sixth Logical
Investigation, Husserl speaks of 'signitive acts' or 'signitive intentions' as
empty acts of intending that use a sign to aim at some kind of objective

fulfilment. Signitive acts have a certain content which is construed as a *sign* of the **object** or a **state of affairs**. Signitive acts are contrasted with acts of intuition where the object is immediately given. Signitive acts can intend either simple objects or more complex categorical objects or states of affairs. 'A signitive intention merely points to its object, an intuitive intention gives it 'presence' in the pregnant sense of the word' (LU VI § 21). Sometimes Husserl distinguishes between *signitive* and *significative* acts but he is not always consistent. Significative acts are those **acts** that contribute to the *meanings* of expressions. Significative intentions contribute to words having their **meanings** (LU VI § 63) and allow for intentions to be expressible in **language**. The signitive intention is what operates when signs are used to express the meanings. Signitive acts involve signs but not necessarily linguistic signs (Husserl talks about a rough sketch being gradually filled in to a more complete drawing). The sign becomes 'significant' through a signitive intention. An expression has a meaning through a significative intention. Husserl believes his account of intuitive and signitive acts is a better way of presenting what Kant has tried to express with his contrast of intuition and understanding. Husserl speaks about the manner in which signitive intentions may be fulfilled. If one thinks of 'England' one might call to mind a sketch outline *map* of England. The 'map' must not be understood as an image but as a *sign* of England.

Situation (*Sachlage*)   See also **state of affairs**

Husserl uses the term 'situation' or 'situation of affairs' (*Sachlage*) in connection with his discussion of '**state of affairs**'. A 'situation' is the objective correlate of the proposition expressed by a **judgement**. Two different states of affairs can be based on the one situation, e.g. the state of affairs 'The glass is half full' is different from the state of affairs 'the glass is half empty', although both are based on the same situation. States of affairs are founded on situations.

Social act (*sozialer Akt*)   See also **sociality**

Husserl speaks about specifically 'social acts' (*soziale Akte*, Hua XV 478) that involve persons appealing to other persons (Ich-Du Akte, XV 479), making agreements or promises, and so on. The social world is constituted through social acts. Social acts include shared acts where there is a common intentionality – acts where we say 'we' (*Wir-Akte*, XV 479), e.g. '*we* decide to buy a house', as opposed to two persons separately deciding to buy houses. Each person is a participant in a larger social grouping (a social being, *Mitglieder*, *socius*, XV 510), and performs social acts in unity with that group.

Sociality (*Sozialität*)   See also **social act, supernation**
In his late writings Husserl frequently talks about 'socialities' (*sozialitäten*; see Hua VI 327, 432), which are broadly speaking social groups of various kinds, including tribes, clans, communities, clubs, societies, peoples, states and so on.

Something (*ein Etwas*)   See also **collective combination, multiplicity, Philosophy of Arithmetic**
According to Husserl in his **Philosophy of Arithmetic**, the concept of **number** involves the concept of a determinate **multiplicity** and multiplicity requires the concept of a 'something' that is then understood as a 'unit' to be counted. In any intentional act, something is presented. Reflecting on the nature of the object presented in an 'act of presenting' (*Akt des Vorstellens*, Hua XII 80), the concept of a 'something' emerges. This 'something' (*etwas*) is, as it were, the content of a presentation in general formally considered merely as an 'object':

> Obviously the concept *something* owes its origination (*Entste-hung*) to reflexion upon the psychical act of representing (*Akt des Vorstellens*), for which precisely any determinate object may be given as the content. Hence, the 'something' belongs to the content of any concrete object only in that external and non-literal fashion common to any sort of relative or nega-tive attribute. In fact, it itself must be designated as a relative determination. Of course, the concept *something* can never be thought unless some sort of content is present, on the basis of which the reflexion mentioned is carried out. Yet for this pur-pose any content is as well suited as another: even the mere name 'something'. (PA, p. 84; XII 80)

Reflection on the structure of the intentional act provides our concept of 'something' and reflection on this concept generates the concept of a 'unity' or 'unit', itself a necessary part or meaning component of the concept of 'multiplicity' (*Vielheit*). The concept of a multiplicity, or, to use specifically mathematical language, the concept of a *set* (*Menge*), then, requires or involves the more basic concept of a 'unit' or a 'something in general' (*Etwas überhaupt*). Any item can count as an element in a set. In order to be able to entertain a concept of a determinate multiplicity, one needs the more basic concept of a 'something' (*ein Etwas*, XII 80) – a 'unit' – that abstracts from every attribute of the entity to be considered, except that it is a 'something or other'. Moreover, Husserl is emphatic that the notion of a 'something' should not be understood as meaning something in nature, a *res* or a 'thing'. In his 1910/1911 FPP lectures (Hua XIII), he emphasizes the 'existential neutrality' (*Daseinsfreiheit*) of arithmetic, against those who would give an empirical sense to arithmetical propositions:

> The one (*die Eins*) of arithmetic is something in general and
> what falls under it is not only the thingly, the spatiotemporal,
> but precisely something in general, which may also be an idea,
> or even, for example a number. (Hua XIII 128, my translation)

Soul (*die Seele, das Psychische, das Seelische*)   See also **psychology**

In the nineteenth century the new empirical science of **psychology** sought to develop 'psychology without the soul', rejecting the concept of the soul as a metaphysical invention. However, the mature Husserl continues to use the term 'soul' (*die Seele*), or the gerund forms 'the psychic' (*das Psychische, das Seelische*) to refer to the spiritual side of human and animal nature, especially its conscious life. As in Aristotle, the soul is the principle of life, nutrition, self-motion, and so on. However, Husserl also uses the term 'soul' to refer to the transcendental I or absolute consciousness, Soul or psyche also has been referred to in the first-person as a conscious centre and source of agency. At CM § 54, Husserl speaks of the individual 'life of the soul' (*Seelenleben*, see also CM § 56). The soul is intimately interwoven with a **lived body** (*Leib*), and Husserl often speaks of a *psychophysical* unity.

Space (*der Raum*)   See also **kinaestheses**

Husserl was interested in the **constitution** of space both in lived experiences in the **life-world** and as treated in the formal sciences such as **geometry** and physics. Geometry represents an idealized, self-enclosed yet infinite space (see *Crisis* § 8). Husserl's starting point is **Kant**'s account of space as the form of outer intuition as well as the discussions of space in Helmholtz, **Lotze** and **Stumpf**. Husserl's initial interest was in the 'presentation of space' (*Raumvorstellung*) in experiences. Husserl also thinks that there is an **a priori** side to the experience of space. Reality as experienced is temporal and spatial. The primary objects of perception are material objects in space (*res extensa*). Space is co-apprehended along with the apprehension of spatial things. For him, as for the empiricists, the experience of space is constituted primarily out of a combination of sight and touch sensations. There are 'pre-empirical' levels of experience at the sensory level that found the full experience of space. In his **Thing and Space** lectures (1907) Husserl explores the manner in which the three-dimensional spatial field as perceived is build up from two-dimensional visual experiences combined with the experience of embodied touch and movement. Husserl's view is that there is an 'extensional moment' (*das extensionale Moment*) in both vision and touch but that these 'pre-empirical' experiences of spatiality are not yet sufficient to give the experience of objective spatiality. The sensation of *movement* is also necessary for the constitution of space. Husserl influenced **Rudolf Carnap's** dissertation entitled *Space* (published in *Kant Studien* in 1922).

Species (*Spezies, Gattung*)   See also **abstraction**

Husserl uses the term 'species' in the **Logical Investigations** to refer to the general category under which an individual falls, e.g. the species *red* has to be opposed to the individual occurrence of red (which Husserl calls a **nuance**). Husserl begins with the existing individual occurrence, e.g. the particular *red moment* which he says *founds* the *colour* known as 'red', the species *red*, and indeed *colour* itself, the species *colour*. These *species* are *instantiated* in the particular red moment of the object. These *species* are, using the language of the **Brentano** school, 'objects of a higher order'. They differ from individual, temporal particulars in that they do not change over time, have strict identity conditions, and can be multiply instantiated. Husserl writes:

> Redness is an ideal unity (*eine ideale Einheit*), in regard to
> which it is absurd to speak of coming into being or passing
> away. The part (moment) red is not Redness, but an instance

of Redness (*ein Einzelfall von Röte*). And, as universal objects differ from singular ones, so, too, do our acts of apprehending them. We do something wholly different if, looking at an intuited concretum, we refer to its sensed redness, the individual feature it has here and now, and if, on the other hand, we refer to the Species Redness, as when we say that Redness is a Colour. (LU *Prol.* § 39 I 86; Hua XVIII 135)

Species are ideal, supra-temporal unities and are grasped as Husserl put it at that time in an 'act of ideation based on intuition' (LU *Prol.* § 39), but they do not exist in a 'heavenly place' (*topos ouranios*) as Platonists hold, neither do they possess purely psychological or mental existence as the empiricists hold.

Sphere of ownness (*Eigenheitssphäre*)   See also **ego, egology**
'Sphere of ownness' (*Eigenheitssphäre*) or '**original sphere**' (***Originärssphäre***) are expressions used by Husserl to refer to the range of conscious experiences in which one experiences oneself in one's own particular domain of immanent, egoic, conscious experiences, after the transcendental **reduction** has taken place (see especially CM § 44). According to Husserl, the **ego** can perform a series of abstractions from social and cultural life until it is left in the pure zone of self-experience. For Husserl, there is more than simply imagining oneself on one's own (as in the case of Robinson Crusoe), for such a self is still caught up in the intersubjective world of culture, language and so on. The pure sphere of ownness and selfhood is more difficult to access. Husserl believes it is possible through the performance of a very specific **epochē** to abstract from everything constituting one as a human being and to remove everything foreign (including everything associated with the sphere of nature) until one is left in the pure sphere of ownness. This will be a unified, flowing sphere of egological consciousness in which I experience my own temporality and openness towards an indefinite future (CM § 46). There is the immediate experience of my own self-constitution as a flowing, temporal, self-identical living ego.

Spirit (*Geist*)   See also **human sciences, motivation, nature, naturalistic attitude, person, personalistic attitude, *Vienna Lecture*, worldview**
Especially in ***Ideas*** **II** (§ 48FF), Husserl employs the term 'spirit' (*Geist*)

and the 'spiritual world' (*die geistige Welt*) in the usual German sense to mean broadly the domain of 'mind', 'soul', but especially intersubjective 'culture', in contrast to the realm of **nature**. Spirit encompasses human cultural achievements, understood as the products of collective human conscious or mental activity (including the regions of art, religion, politics, culture, and everything encompassed within the **human sciences** (*Geisteswissenschaften*). The late Husserl also uses the term 'spirit' to signify the general mood or spirit of a culture or discipline, e.g. 'the spirit of philosophy', 'the spiritual battles' of western culture (*Crisis* § 3), as well as to mean the specific culture of human beings. He is most usually concerned with the distinction between the natural and the cultural or human sciences as discussed by the neo-Kantians (e.g. Rickert) and Dilthey rather than with Hegel's more developmental notion of the evolution of spirit in his *Phenomenology of Spirit* (1807). In the **Vienna Lecture**, he speaks of the 'spirituality' (*Geistigkeit*) of animals as well as humans, meaning thereby something like the cultural world and behaviour of animals thought as a complex unified whole (see *Crisis*, p. 271; VI 316). In *Crisis* § 2, Husserl speaks of human beings 'in their spiritual existence' and of the 'shapes of the spiritual world'. Different cultures have their own **worldviews** and their own historical trajectories or **historicities**. The correlate of 'spirit' is 'nature', the world understood through the approach of modern natural science. The world of spirit is a world of **persons** interacting with one another as persons and not merely as objects of nature. In *Ideas* II, Husserl gives an account of the constitution of spirit which see **motivation** as the essential law of the domain of spirit.

Splitting of the ego (*Ich-Spaltung, Ichspaltung*) See also **ego, non-participating spectator, reflection**

In his mature works of the 1920s and early 30s Husserl occasionally speaks of the 'splitting of the ego' as occurring when the **ego** reflects on itself (e.g. CM § 15; 'Kant and the Idea of Transcendental Philosophy', Hua VII ; *First Philosophy* II, Hua VIII 96). The ego has this essential character that in its activity it can bend back on itself (Hua VII 262). In pre-reflective life the ego lives in complete anonymity. But it becomes visible in **reflection** whereby a new anonymous, experiencing ego is created. For instance, if I have a **memory** of myself performing an action many years ago there is a sense of identity between my self now and my self then but there is also a sense in which I am an observer of myself and some kind of splitting of the ego has taken place. As Husserl puts it, the self-remembering does not uncover the present ego but the past ego (VII 263). Husserl also speaks of the splitting of the ego when the stance of the non-participating spectator (CM Hua I 16) breaks free from the 'world-captivated ego' (in **Fink**'s phrase) of the **natural attitude** and which can at the same time contemplate its own life in the natural attitude (see Hua XXXIV 11). The contemplating ego while abstaining from all prejudgements is itself a life and must be understood as such, so the concept of the splitting of the ego must recognize that natural mundane life runs on even in the stance of the non-participating spectator (see Hua VIII 93 where Husserl gives the example of the sceptic who can put the existence of the world in doubt and at the same time has to live through an acceptance of the world in his or her practical activities).The natural ego and the transcendental ego coincide in the same person; there has to be both consciousness of identity and at the same time consciousness of difference.

State of affairs (*Sachverhalt*)   See also **objectivity, proposition, situation (*Sachlage*)**

States of affairs belong to the class of '**objectivities**'; they are the objective correlates of complex synthetic intentional acts such as **judgements**. The judgement 'the cat is on the mat' is directed towards a complex, structured object, which itself contains other objects, and whose nature may be expressed linguistically in several different ways, e.g. 'the cat being on the mat'. The concept of 'states of affairs' was discussed in the Brentano school by **Meinong**, Marty, and **Reinach** and later by Husserl and Wittgenstein. According to Husserl, states of affairs are complex, non-linguistic ideal unities, the ontological counterparts of propositional contents or meanings. States of affairs can combine objects with other objects (the cat, the mat) or objects with predicates (properties, relations, etc). Indeed it is a structural feature of states of affairs that any kind of thing, including real, existing spatiotemporal objects, can be a part of them, e.g. 'the state of affairs of this spider on Mars'. States of affairs are what they are whether we assert their validity or not (LU I § 11); in other words the spider being on Mars is a conceivable state of affairs even if it is not actually true at present. According to the convention developed by Husserl, Wittgenstein and others, states of affairs are said to 'hold' (*bestehen*) or not to hold rather than to exist. When they hold, the proposition expressing this state of affairs is said to be true. Husserl speaks of a state of affairs being a 'unity of validity' (*Geltungseinheit*). When I believe that it is raining, then I am intending the state of affairs *that it is raining*. States of affairs should not be confused with the meaning contents of judgements or sentences. States of affairs are ontological entities. They function to make the sentences expressing them true (Sixth Logical Investigation § 39). It is part of the nature of states of affairs that they can be expressed as nominalizations, e.g., the *rose's redness*, the *being red of the rose* and be the subject of further predications. (See Husserl, Fifth Logical Investigation § 36.)

Static phenomenology (*statische Phänomenologie*)   See also **genetic phenomenology, phenomenology**
Static phenomenology studies the objects of conscious intentional acts as they are experienced as complete unities, almost as if they were simply there in nature like the objects studied by the natural sciences or 'natural history' (CM § 37 Hua I 111). On this account, the objects encountered are arranged in **types**. In static phenomenology, for instance, the **ego** is understood as already relating to a **world**. Another name for static phenomenology is **constitutive phenomenology**.

Stein, Edith (1892–1942)   Edith Stein was born into a bourgeois Jewish family in Breslau, Prussia (now Wroclaw, Poland). She attended the Victoria Gymnasium in Breslau and then entered the University of Breslau in 1911 to study psychology. One of her professors was the psychologist William Stern and she took philosophy classes with Richard Hönigswald (1875–1947), a Kantian philosopher. In 1913 she transferred to the University of Göttingen to study phenomenology with Adolf Reinach and Husserl. Shortly before the semester began, Husserl's *Ideas* I was published which caused consternation because of its idealist turn. Stein also attended the lectures **Max Scheler** gave to the Göttingen Philosophical Society. In 1914 and 1915 she served as a nurse during the Great War. She completed her doctoral dissertation with Husserl in 1916, published as *Zum Problem der Einfühlung* (*On the Problem of Empathy*) in Halle in 1917. From 1916 to 1918, she became Husserl's private assistant, working on the manuscript of *Ideas* II he had originally drafted in 1912. She also laboured on Husserl's *Lectures on the Consciousness on Internal Time* (1905–17), although these were eventually brought to press by Heidegger in 1928. Stein made several attempts to be allowed register for a *Habilitation* but her application was ignored and eventually rejected. Undeterred, she actually wrote a *Habilitation* thesis on 'Contributions towards the Philosophical Foundation of Psychology and Science ('*Psychische Kausalität*' or *Beiträge zur philosophischen Begründung der Psychologie und der Wissenschaft*) which eventually was published in Husserl's **Yearbook** Volume Five in 1922. While visiting Hedwig **Conrad-Martius** at Bergzabern in the summer of 1921, she had a religious experience reading St. Theresa of Avila's autobiography and converted to Catholicism, being baptized on 1 January 1922 with Hedwig Conrad-Martius as her godmother. She taught at a Dominican school in Speyer from 1921 until 1932, when she moved to teach at the German Institute for Scientific Pedagogy in Münster. She continued to correspond with Husserl, Ingarden and others, and contributed an article to Husserl's 70th birthday *Festschrift* (1929) on 'An Attempt to Contrast Husserl's Phenomenology and the Philosophy of St. Thomas Aquinas'. She translated Thomas' *De Veritate* (*Disputed Questions on Truth*) and her later writings (e.g. *Potency and Act*) attempted to reconcile phenomenology with Thomistic metaphysics. Following the rise to power of the National Socialists in Germany in 1933, she was not permitted to give further lectures at Münster. In October 1933 she entered the Carmelite convent at Cologne, and in April 1934 entered the novitiate, taking the religious name Teresa Benedicta of the Cross, after the mystic who had inspired her conversion. In 1938 she was transferred to the Carmelite convent at Echt in the Netherlands. With her sister Rosa, also a Catholic convert, Teresa Benedicta was arrested by the Gestapo in August 1942 at the convent in Echt and shipped to the concentration camp at Auschwitz where she died with her sister on 9 August 1942. In 1998 she was declared a saint. Her most famous work is a study of **empathy**.

Stimulus (*Reiz*)   See **allure**

Stream of consciousness (*Bewusstseinsstrom*)   See also **consciousness, life, time**
Husserl regularly invokes the metaphor of the temporal 'flow' of **consciousness** as a 'stream' (*Strom*) or 'flux' (*Fluss*). He often calls it a 'Heraclitean flux' where nothing remains the same. The sense that consciousness is constantly flowing and streaming while somehow

remaining unified into a single personal, egoic consciousness is at the heart of Husserl's conception. This account of the holistic stream of consciousness can be compared with similar conceptions in William James and Henri Bergson. For Husserl the psychic stream is immensely complex with many nodes, even as it progresses seamlessly from moment to moment. **Lived experiences** (*Erlebnisse* or *cogitations*) are never distinct from one another; Husserl speaks of them as 'waves' in the stream. He also speaks of 'canals' where two consciousness run in parallel streams without intersecting. At times individual experiences can stand out from the flow, e.g. as when an explicit idea comes into my head. Of course, there are also gaps in consciousness, e.g. during sleep, and here the mystery is how the newly re-awakened consciousness regains its mode of givenness, so that the I can again recover itself as bearer of these habitualities, memories, and so on. **Time consciousness** and the sense of the **living present** are at the heart of consciousness.

Stuff (*Stoff*)   See also **content, *hyle*, matter**

Husserl often uses the term 'stuff' (*Stoff*) for the sensuous content of experiences as thought of prior to the act of intention which 'ensouls' or 'enlivens' these contents into the appearance of a constituted objectivity (see *Ideas* I § 85). He is referring to an idealized conception of a raw matter of sensory stimuli prior to their being organized and structured in a formal manner.

Stumpf, Carl (1848–1936)   See also **Brentano, descriptive psychology, Gurwitsch, Lotze, part, whole**

The German philosopher, psychologist and ethnomusicologist Carl Stumpf was born in Wiesentheid in Franconia into a Catholic family in 1848. He was always interested in music and entered Würzburg University to study music, but became interested in philosophy and was especially captivated by Franz **Brentano** who was teaching there at the time. On Brentano's advice, he went to Göttingen to study with **Lotze** who supervised his doctoral dissertation on Plato (1868). After graduating he returned to Würzburg to study theology, but became disillusioned and returned to Göttingen and Lotze for his *Habilitation* on mathematics (1870). Stumpf then taught at Göttingen until 1873 when he moved to Würzburg. In 1879 he moved to Prague, where he worked with Anton Marty; he then moved to Halle in 1884, in 1889 to Munich, and finally Berlin where he became friendly with **Dilthey** and founded an institute of experimental psychology. He became Rector of Berlin University in 1907–08. He died in Berlin in 1936. Stumpf was interested in both experimental psychology and philosophy. At Göttingen, he met Fechner and Weber, two advocates of psychophysics. His *On the Psychological Origin of the Presentation of Space* (*Über den psychologischen Ursprung der Raumvorstellung* 1873) influenced Husserl's early discussion of the apprehension of **space**. Stumpf's two-volume *Psychology of Tones* (*Tonpsychologie*, 1883 and 1890) is an important study of the apprehension of music and auditory phenomena generally. It was reviewed by Paul **Natorp**. Against **Hume**, Stumpf argued for the direct experience of causality. Husserl studied with Stumpf in Halle on the recommendation of **Brentano** and completed his *Habilitation*, *On the Concept of Number*, there in 1887. Stumpf and Husserl became lifelong friends. Stumpf was a personal friend of the psychologist William James and introduced Husserl to James' work. Stumpf's theory of **parts** and **wholes** strongly influenced Husserl's Third Logical Investigation. Husserl's *Logical Investigations* is dedicated to Stumpf. In *Ideas* I § 86, Husserl distinguishes his own transcendental phenomenology from that of Stumpf, which is more accurately a study of appearances or a study of the sensuous contents of experiences. Stumpf influenced Gestalt psychologists such as his students Wolfgang Köhler, Max Wertheimer and Kurt Koffka. He had a particularly strong influence in Aron **Gurwitsch** who studied with him in Berlin.

Style (*Stil*)   See also **habit, type**

Husserl often uses the term 'style' (*Stil*) to put into relief how different acts or objects reveal us not only particular properties but outline at the same time something more general bound with an essential or typical way of being, one that establishes a certain continuity across time. For example, when I reflect on my actual perceptual acts, I am focusing at acts that are unique and unrepeatable (I accomplish them in this concrete situation, within this context, etc.) but we can say that those acts show us a general style and a connection with other experiences whereby we recognize the way in which those acts and objects are given (see as example CM, § 54, p. 118, 120). In the same way, Husserl speaks of individual human subjects or egos developing their own personal 'enduring style' which is unique to them and expresses their character (CM § 32) – bodily expressions, ways of moving, intonations of voice, and all forms of behaving which mark out one's individual particularity. We do not need all a person's properties to recognize them; a few properties identify their 'style'. By means of present sensuous data, we anticipate and pre-delineate the sense of a whole sequence of actions in general. Therefore, the style cannot be reduced to a definition or a definitive set of properties. Humans have a specific 'style of life' (Lebensstil, CM Hua I 149) with its own typicalities. Even though the concept of 'style' is deliberately vague, it is essential for characterizing and for first outlining the sense of an object, person or set of acts. Husserl speaks about the 'causal style' of the life-world (see *Crisis* pp. 344–5; VI 358). Husserl's concept of 'style' is later taken up by **Merleau-Ponty**, especially in his discussion of painting.

Subjective-relative properties   See also **dualism, primary properties**
According to Husserl, the prescientifical world is experienced in natural living in a 'subjective-relative' way (*Crisis* § 9). Early modern philosophy (e.g. Descartes, Locke), following Galileo, divided the world into those **primary properties** which were objective and measurable by mathematics, and those subjective-relative properties (e.g. colour, taste, warmth, tone) that depended on the human subject who apprehends them. At *Crisis* § 9 (i) Husserl speaks of Galileo's doctrine of the 'merely subjective character of the specific sense qualities', which was later formulated by Hobbes as the subjective nature of the sensibly intuited world in general.

Subjectivism (*Subjektivismus*) See also **objectivism, relativism, scepticism**
Husserl believes that the essence of scepticism lies in subjectivism, the belief that one cannot have objective knowledge of the world and that all that one can know is one's own subjective approach to the world: all that I can know is my own experience (Hua VII 59). Husserl opposes subjectivism to **objectivism**, which involves a naive belief in the givenness of the world. Descartes' discovery of the **cogito** overcomes sceptical arguments and introduces a new dimension to philosophy through its discovery of transcendental subjectivism.

Subjectivity (*Subjektivität*) See also **consciousness, intentionality, intersubjectivity, objectivity**
One of the key insights of Husserl's phenomenology is that the modern

sciences have taken an objectivist turn and have completely misunderstood the functioning and achievements of subjectivity. Subjectivity stands for the first-person point of view that is ineliminable from the very concept of knowledge. In his later works, Husserl speaks of 'functioning subjectivity' as an anonymous pre-egoic form of subjectivity which is responsible for the givenness of the world and its 'always already there' character.

Supernationality (*Übernationalität*)   See also **homeworld**
In his later works (e.g. *Vienna Lecture*; Hua VI 320; see also Hua XV 171, 179), Husserl speaks of the notions of an 'over-nation' or 'supernation' (Übernation), and of a 'supernationality' (*Übernationalität*), for example, in his March 1935 letter to **Lévy-Bruhl**, where he speaks of each national and supranational grouping having its own representation of the **world**. He also invokes the idea of a 'supernation' in his discussion of the evolution of modern states. Husserl sees human beings as living in larger horizons including one's family, nation and also 'supernation', e.g. 'Europe' or socially agreed formations such as the League of Nations.

Surrounding world (*Umwelt*)   See **world**

Synthesis (*Synthesis*)   See also **constitution, passive synthesis, passivity**
'Synthesis' (from the Greek meaning 'to place together'), as the act of drawing together or combining parts into a unity or a whole, is a key concept for Husserl, which essentially articulates the manner in which consciousness functions. The concept of synthesis has a long history in philosophy from Aristotle to **Kant**. For Aristotle, combination (*synthesis*) and separation (*diairesis*) are fundamental to **judgement**. Husserl is particularly influenced by Kant's use of the term (Husserl even calls it 'the obscure Kantian term', Hua XXXV 86). In *Ideas* II § 9, Husserl says that the only kind of synthesis Kant had in mind was the 'aesthetic synthesis', understood as uniting different sensory manifolds in the constitution of the perceived thing. Following Kant, Husserl maintains that synthesis is 'a mode of combination exclusively peculiar to consciousness' (CM § 17, p. 39; Hua I 77) and furthermore that it is essential to the operation of consciousness (CM § 18). In *Cartesian Meditations* § 18, Husserl states that identification is the fundamental form of synthesis. He also speaks

of synthesis as being essentially a 'positing' (*Thesis*, *Ideas* I § 120). It is through synthesis that conscious experiences connect together into a *unity*, and than an identical object is grasped in the manifold of appearances. Husserl has been exploring the notion of synthesis since **Philosophy of Arithmetic**, where he already recognizes the importance of the mental act of synthesis, which he calls '**collective combination**', which plays an important role in many different kinds of mental process, including our emotional experiences (PA, Hua XII 75) and is crucial to the understanding of relation in general. Synthesis is discussed in detail in **Ideas I**, where Husserl speaks of the 'continuous synthesis of harmony' (§ 151) in the flow of perceptual experience, as well as 'syntheses of conflict' which can give rise to the experiences of illusion, disappointment, and so on. The most basic form of the synthesis of identification occurs in our internal consciousness of **time**:

> The *fundamental form* of this universal synthesis, the form
> that makes all other syntheses of consciousness possible, is the
> all-embracing *consciousness of internal time*. (CM § 18, p. 32;
> Hua I 81)

There is an ongoing synthesis involved in the unity of mental processes into the one stream of conscious life and there are also the syntheses involved in the constitution of the unities of objects apprehended in experience. There are also what Husserl calls 'many-membered syntheses' (*Ideas* I § 118) whereby conscious acts combine into complex unities e.g. 'ruefully remembering thinking Mary was beautiful'. Husserl distinguishes between **active** and **passive synthesis**. He also distinguishes broadly, following Kant, between aesthetic synthesis and categorial synthesis (*Ideas* II § 9). It is through synthesis that an **ego** is formed as a unity in the stream of experiences, and through synthesis that an object remains the same in the sequence of its appearances. Husserl calls this 'synthesis of identification' (*Ideas* I § 41), but there are other kinds of synthesis: synthesis of unity, of harmony, of discordance, of determination otherwise, of contradiction (*Ideas* I § 138), explicative synthesis, synthesis of 'overlapping' (*Überschiebung*, EU § 24), and so on. For Husserl the greatest synthesis of all is the constitution of the *world* as a unified context of entities. This is also for Husserl the 'greatest enigma' (*Crisis* VI 184).

—T—

Teleology (*Teleologie*) The term 'teleology' (from the Greek *telos*, τέλο□, meaning 'purpose' or 'goal') means goal directedness, being directed to goals or ends. According to Aristotle both living and non-living things have particular ends (states) towards which they are directed, .e.g. it belong to the nature of water and earth to seek a lower place. Living beings especially consciously strive towards their ends, e.g. humans strive towards happiness (for Aristotle). Modern science, since **Galileo** and **Descartes**, is opposed to teleological explanations of natural events (in terms of 'final causes' or the ultimate purposes that things are supposedly for). Husserl uses the term 'teleology', especially in his later works, to refer to the specific networks of ends that motivate human life and culture. **Intentionality** as directedness has an inbuilt teleological character, for Husserl, e.g. **empty intentions** aim at **fulfilment**. Husserl specifically talks about the 'teleology' of western culture in the *Crisis* and associated texts (e.g. **Vienna Lecture**). Western culture since the Greeks manifests a certain inbuilt striving towards **rationality** and living the life of reflective **self-responsibility** (*Crisis* § 15). Indeed, for Husserl – and this has proved controversial –only **Europe** has a *teleology* in the strict sense, that is, a driving force aiming at a higher goal. The history of philosophy also displays a particular teleology (see *Crisis* § 15) as does human history in general, for Husserl (he speaks of the 'inborn teleology of history' at *Crisis* §16). Modern philosophy has a teleological direction towards becoming **transcendental philosophy** for Husserl. Phenomenology is the 'final form' of transcendental philosophy.

Temporalization (*Zeitigung*) See also **now moment, protention, retention, time consciousness**
Husserl speaks of 'temporalization' in terms of the manner in which the **ego** constitutes itself in **time** with its experience of time. Husserl discusses the concept of temporalization in relation to **Kant** (*Crisis* § 30) and in relation to the identity of the **ego** across past, present and future experiences (*Crisis* § 50). The ego *becomes* itself across time through its own peculiar form of temporalization. Husserl also speaks (in the manner of Heidegger) about temporality temporalizing itself. At times Husserl speaks of this

temporalizing as the activity of the **transcendental ego**. The term is later taken up and developed by **Heidegger**.

Theoretical attitude (*die theoretische Einstellung*) See also **attitude, disengaged spectator, natural attitude, transcendental attitude**
For Husserl, the 'theoretical attitude' is an alteration of the **natural attitude** to produce an attitude of self-conscious detached inspection. The theoretical attitude is a very general possibility that accompanies all acts but through a specific focusing of this attitude it becomes the foundation of scientific knowledge. Husserl speaks about the theoretical attitude in *Ideas* II § 3 and later in the *Vienna Lecture*. In *Ideas* II § 6, he distinguishes between the general capacity for **reflection** that accompanies all straightforward conscious acts (perceiving, remembering, judging, and so on) and the specific theoretical stance that involves a more explicit objectification of the intentional object of the act and a bracketing of practical interests (aside from the pure interest in **knowledge**). The reflective attitude is a more straightforward coming to self-awareness that does not exclude interests and values (such as aesthetic pleasure, admiration, and so on). For Husserl, in the *Vienna Lecture*, the theoretical attitude is a somewhat late arrival on the scene of human accomplishments. It was specifically inaugurated by Greek philosophy and has been the basis of the outlook of western **science**. Although the Indian and Chinese civilizations do have a universal interest in the sense they have produced mythopoeic cosmologies, they have done so from the standpoint of practical interests. Husserl writes:

> But only in the Greeks do we have a universal ('cosmological')
> life-interest in the essentially new form of a purely 'theoretical'
> attitude, and this as a communal form in which this interest
> works itself out for internal reasons, being the correspond-
> ing, essentially new [community] of philosophers, of scientists
> (mathematicians, astronomers, etc.). (*Crisis*, p. 280; VI 326)

Husserl maintains that the Greeks broke through to a new form of life – the form of life of *theoria*, dominated by what Husserl calls 'the theoretical attitude'. This theoretical attitude operates at a remove from the concerns of practical life as experienced in the natural attitude. The theoretical attitude is the attitude of **theoria**, of detached contemplation, of the **disinterested** or non-participating **spectator**. The theoretical attitude is characterized by wonder or amazement at the world. The theoretical attitude does not merely live through epistemic states of believing, judging, but rather involves self-conscious attentiveness to these acts as they are being carried out. The theoretical attitude necessarily involves a shift of attention or focus away from practical engagements. It involves applying an **epochē** to all practical interests and focusing purely on the demand for truth, and in this way, Husserl believes it prepares human subjects for the life of 'self-responsibility' (*Crisis*, p. 283; VI 329). The theoretical attitude opens up a world of infinite tasks and unites humans together on the quest for rational **self-respon-sibility** (*Vienna Lecture*). The theoretical attitude is not the same as the attitude of the phenemenologist but it is a precursor to it.

Theoria (Theoria, θεωρία)   See also **theoretical attitude, Vienna Lecture**

Theoria (θεωρία) is a Greek term meaning 'looking', 'contemplation, 'consideration'. Husserl speaks of the Greek discovery of *theoria* as the **theoretical attitude**. *Theoria* is usually contrasted with *praxis*, the active life (Hua VI 329). Husserl discusses the breakthrough to *theoria* in the **Vienna Lecture** (Hua VI 326, 328, 332). It is *theoria* or disinterested contemplation that makes possible the idea of **science**.

Theory of manifolds (Mannigfältigkeitslehre)   See also **logic**

In his **Logical Investigations**, Husserl proposes the theory of manifolds or the 'theory of the forms of theory' as the highest kind of **science** (see LU *Prol.* §§ 69–70). He returns to the concept in *Introduction to Logic and the Theory of Knowledge* §§ 18–19, *Ideas I* §§ 71–2; *Formal and Transcendental Logic* §§ 51–4, and *Crisis* § 9, among many other places. The concept of manifolds is originally drawn from mathematics and is found in **Cantor** (who wrote a work entitled *Foundations of a General Theory of Manifolds*, 1878) and Riemann. In Cantor the term originally meant something like 'set theory'. The term is used in geometry (topology) to describe complexes (e.g. a collection of points) in terms that belong to simpler spaces (e.g. a line). Husserl does not offer a detailed account of what he meant by theory of manifolds but he regards it as one of the highest parts of **logic**. He begins from the idea of a 'manifold' as an aggregate, assembly or class of entities. One can construct a manifold quite arbitrarily and then specify rules for how that manifold is to be organized. A purely formal theory of the nature of manifolds as such would be a theory of theories. It is not merely an abstract set of rules (like a game of chess) but includes a reference to objects, and hence is related to **formal ontology**.

Theory of objects (*Gegenstandstheorie*) See also **Meinong, object, objectivity, thing**

The 'theory of objects' is a term used in the school of Brentano and specifically by Alexius **Meinong** for an overall ontology of objects that tries to categorize all forms of objecthood, including not just actually existent entities but fictional entities, abstract entities, possible entities and even impossible entities (e.g. round squares). Meinong believed it was important to suspend our prejudice in favour of actuality in order to be able to catalogue the true range of objects. For Meinong, as Bertrand Russell objected, a triangle is an object but so also is the triangularity of the object, and so on. Quine referred to this as an ontological jungle. Husserl's account of objecthood in the *Logical Investigations* is close to Meinong and indeed Husserl often complained that Meinong was copying his work.

Thesis (*Thesis*) *Thesis* is a Greek word used by Husserl to mean 'positing' (*Setzung*). The natural attitude is characterized by its **general thesis**, which treats its intentional objects as actual and existent.

Thing (*Ding*) See also **formal ontology, object**

Husserl understands the concept of 'thing' in many different senses. First and foremost, **perception** encounters things and the 'world of things' (*Dingwelt*), i.e., material, solid things that are occur in space and time, and that are apprehended in **adumbrations** or profiles. A thing is formally understood as a unity that can be bearer of properties. Husserl terms this 'object'. This concept of thing as pure '**object**' in general belongs to **formal ontology**. In **logic**, Husserl speaks of the notion of the 'something in general'. In epistemology, the thing is always encountered as an **object** in relation to a **subject**.

Thing and Space (*Ding und Raum*, 1907) See also **kinaesthesis, phantom, sensation, space**

Husserl gave a series of lectures on the constitution of the material thing in space in Göttingen in 1907, now published as *Husserliana* volume XVI (Husserl also called this text his *Dingvorlesung*, thing lecture). These lectures offer Husserl's most detailed and intense analyses of the constitution of the intended object in acts of **perception** and **kinaestheses** as well as the constitution of the presentation of **space** itself. Husserl begins from the simplest cases of perception – seeing a static object with one eye (monocular vision) and then discusses the constitution of the visual field first two dimensionally and then in three dimensions. In these lectures, Husserl first introduces the notion of the 'double sensation' according to which the living body (*Leib*) is able to touch itself. His aim is a description of the constitution of the physical thing in perception, an 'understanding of the givenness of the thing' (DR § 40), primarily focusing on spatiality but abstracting from the consideration of **causality** that fleshes out and concretises our conception of material thinghood beyond what Husserl calls the 'sense schema' or '**phantom**'. In *Thing and Space* Section § 47, as part of a general discussion of the phenomenon called '**kinaesthesis**' (the sensations of self-moving of our body and its parts), Husserl discusses what '**sensations**' (*Empfindungen*) contribute to the experience of spatiality. In each unilateral or 'unifold' perception, Husserl distinguishes between 'presentational contents' (*darstellende Inhalten*) and 'moment of apprehension' (*Auffassungscharakter*; DR Hua XVI 142). We see the same thing under changing conditions: the same colour under different colour profiles or shadings. The presentational **contents** are not first there and then apprehended, rather the **apprehension** itself 'animates' (*beseelt*) them in a unified way.

Thing as idea in the Kantian sense (*Das Ding als Idee im Kantischen Sinne*)   See also **adumbration, Kant, perception, thing**

Husserl understands a material thing as having more 'sides' or **adumbrations** than are given to any current viewing or consideration. A thing always exceeds our cognitive encounter with it and at best we can form only an inadequate intuition of a thing. This leads him to say that the thing is really best understood as an 'idea in the Kantian sense' (*Ideas* I § 143; see also § 83). A Kantian 'idea' is really an ideal, a regulative notion. Husserl says in *Ideas* I § 143 and elsewhere (see FTL § 16c), that every transcendent thing is really a Kantian idea, e.g. 'An idea that lies at infinity belongs to every external perception' (APS 58; Hua 21) and that the thing is a 'rule of possible appearances' (*Ideas* II § 18g, p. 91; Hua IV 86). No finite consciousness can run through all the courses of possible experience belonging to any transcendent object, any physical thing in nature. However, this does not rule out that what we see is actual sensible, material thing. The sensible present appearance is a component in the larger non-sensory aspect of **perception**:

> We always have the external object in the flesh (we see, grasp,
> seize it), and yet it is always at an infinite distance mentally.
> What we grasp of it pretends to be its essence, and it is it too,
> but it remains so only in the incomplete approximation, an
> approximation that grasps something of it, but in doing so, it
> constantly grasps an emptiness that cries out for fulfillment.
> (APS 58–9; Hua XI 21)

As each trajectory of experience is explored, a series of ordered and harmonious results are achieved. The thing is determined ever more closely with this particular attribute, and so on. In this sense, Husserl believes we are experiencing the object more deeply; it is not that we do not experience the object at all and grasp only its partial determinations.

Three basic classes of psychic act (*drei Grundklasse psychischer Akte*)   See also **Brentano, judgement, presentation**

In his *Psychology from an Empirical Standpoint* (1874), Brentano postulates three 'basic classes' of psychical acts, namely, *presentations, judgements,* and what he called '*phenomena of love and hate*' (attraction and repulsion, which included both willings and feelings). Brentano acknowledged this his division echoed Descartes' trifold distinction between ideas, judgements and willings. Brentano distinguished these acts in terms of the ways they related to their content. Presentations simply present an idea, an image, an impression, a thought. Judgements, contrariwise, affirm or deny, accept or reject a presented **content**. Every judgement presupposes a presentation. Feelings of love or hate, however, relate to the judgement. Brentano related feelings and will as aspects of the same phenomenon. For him, to feel a pain is to want it to end. Brentano maintained that every mental act really contains a combination of all three basic classes. Husserl discusses critically these three basic classes of acts in his Fifth Logical Investigation. He rejects the simple threefold classification, claiming that there are myriad different kinds of intentional act. In the Fifth Investigation, Husserl provides an exhaustive analysis of the different senses of the term 'presentation', and distinguishes various classes of acts including positing and non-positing acts and more generally his notion of '**objectifying acts**' (LU V § 37) as a correct way of expressing what is true in Brentano's loose conception of a 'presentation'. Husserl also proposes a more general distinction between **act quality** and **matter** to take care of features more crudely gathered under the name 'content'. Husserl's maintained that Brentano's true discovery was that **intentionality** had the specific character of 'relating beyond itself' and that there are different forms of relatedness that must be analysed.

Time (*Zeit*)   See also **now moment, protention, retention, temporalization, time consciousness**

Husserl furnishes his clearest and most succinct phenomenological analysis of the question of temporality in his 1904–05 winter semester seminar, entitled the *Phenomenology of the Inner Consciousness of Time* (Hua X). It is not surprising that the analysis of temporality – contrarily to the majority of the Husserlian concepts, which were subjected to profound and constant revisions, precisions, and clarifications – is explicated right in the very early stages of Husserl's philosophical enterprise. For temporality, as **Heidegger** also recognized, is the foundational element of Husserl's entire phenomenological project. Not only because time is essentially and structurally allied to the movement and the method of the phenomenological **reduction**, but also, and more importantly, because temporality is, for Husserl, the very modality in which the unity of **consciousness** is structured. Husserl returns to the centrality of temporality and elaborates in great detail the *a priori* correlation of temporality and intentionality – most specifically in *Ideas* I (1913) § 77 and §§ 82–3, in the *Cartesian Meditations* (1931) §§ 37–9, and also in the *Crisis* (1936) § 49 and § 59. But it is quite remarkable that, after the 1905 explication of temporality, he never questions or doubts the centrality of time as providing the unity of the phenomenological consciousness in general. In this sense, time constitutes for Husserl the underlying and presupposed element of all thinking. Furthermore, the fundamental essence of temporality signifies, strictly speaking, that **intentionality** is wholly grounded in temporality. This question however, which aims at situating the centrality of time in the explication of a unified intentionality of the phenomenological consciousness, is in fact presupposed by a more precise formulation elaborated in the Introduction to the *Phenomenology of the Inner Consciousness of Time*, namely, how can consciousness relate 'objective time' and the 'subjective consciousness of time'? The emphasis is placed here on the relation between time as a measurable entity of objective phenomena and the modality in which the subject appropriates phenomenality itself in and within a consciousness of temporality. Here thus the distinction between objective time and subjective time is slowly transmuted for Husserl into the difference between constituted time and constituting time. In this sense, Husserl will concentrate the entire phenomenological investigation of time on that which forms the *consciousness of time* itself, bracketing and reducing the objective, measurable and determinable temporality in which phenomena are simply given to the subject. For Husserl, thus the primordial hypothesis – reaching far beyond the Brentanian theory, which stipulates that the seat of time lies in the passage from **perception** to **imagination** – can be formulated as such: in and within the subject a 'temporal extension' underlies all actual **lived-experiences** of consciousness, 'temporal extension' which pre-determines the consciousness to the articulated field in which phenomena are constituted and consequently appear. The phenomenological investigation commands thus a *return* to the 'immanent duration' of temporality in and within consciousness, and remains focused strictly and uniquely on the lived experiences of consciousness in which will be revealed the 'phenomenological *datum*' of a unified consciousness grasping in one 'originary intuition of time itself' the three appearances of temporality: past, present and future. Hence, the phenomenological reduction is here called upon to bracket the constituted/objective time in order to reveal the temporality of time itself in its structure and modality as **retention** and **protention** and thus reveal its originary 'flux' as that self-constituting element in and within subjectivity. Husserl's phenomenological investigation of time focuses explicitly on the very *being* of consciousness as temporal and furthermore, by explicating the modes of constitution of temporal appearances in their intentionality, aims at displaying the self-constitution of temporality itself.

Time consciousness (*Zeitbewusstsein*) See also **Heraclitean flux, horizontal intentionality, living present, now moment, protention, retention, transverse intentionality**

Time is 'the most difficult of all phenomenological problems' according to

Husserl (Hua X 276). For Husserl, time is at the very basis of consciousness and his analyses of the a priori structures of time-consciousness are among his deepest, most difficult and also most influential writings. His *Lectures on Internal Time Consciousness*, originally given in 1904–1905, and repeated in subsequent years, were edited by **Stein** and **Heidegger** and published in Husserl's **Yearbook** in 1928. More recently, more manuscripts on time, especially those written at Seefeld and Bernau (mostly composed in 1917) and the C manuscripts (1929–34, *Husserliana* Materialen Band VIII), have appeared in the *Husserliana* series. Husserl discusses temporality in a briefer way in his published works in *Ideas* I §§77, 82; *Cartesian Meditations* § 37; and *Crisis* § 49, § 59. Husserl took great interest in the temporal character of conscious acts and the manner of temporality of the intentional objects of conscious acts. Husserl's meditations on time were influenced by Augustine and also by **Brentano**, **Stumpf**, William James, Bergson and the neo-Kantian tradition. From **Kant**, he took the idea that time is a kind of **synthesis** of experiences. All conscious experiences are temporal through and through. Husserl also agreed with Kant that the experience of a sequence of nows is not at all the same as an experience of temporal *succession*. Temporal succession requires an ordering of now moments and their differentiation. In his **Philosophy of Arithmetic**, Husserl already discusses the question whether the arithmetic series derives from the experience of succession, as some neo-Kantians maintained. Husserl's time lectures of 1904–1905, however, are primarily in response to Brentano's analysis of time. To speak of time-consciousness as such is somewhat ambiguous. It is not as if one has consciousness of *time* itself as an object. Strictly speaking, for the early Husserl at least, time only appears in conjunction with an appearing intentional act and intentional object. Similarly, for Husserl, the idea of empty 'now' or empty time is a nonsense; the flow of time is always 'filled' (Hua XXIV 271). In his lectures on internal time consciousness, Husserl distinguishes three layers of tempo-rality: objective time (the time of nature); pre-empirical time, and absolute time. 'Objective time' is the time experienced in the world (also called 'clock time', or the 'time of nature'). When the **phenomenological reduction** is applied then objective time – the time of **nature** – is bracketed (see Hua XXXV 88; X 339). 'Pre-empirical time' refers to the immanent flow of appearing experiences with their linked inner temporal structures (remem-bering, anticipating, experiencing as present). These are constituted with their 'now phases and retentions' (X 90). We have to distinguish temporal objects and their parts from the inner temporal structure of the *Erlebnisse* that present these objects (the phases of the musical tone have to be distinguished from the temporal phases of the hearing experience although there is clearly a parallel between them). Further, these experiences flow from an ego which itself constitutes time and so must be characterized as 'absolute' (Hua X 77). This notion of absolute time consciousness is absent from the earliest analyses of time, but it became apparent to Husserl that the ego must in a sense transcend time: 'subjective time becomes constituted in the absolute timeless consciousness, which is not an object' (X 112). This 'primal consciousness' (*Urbewusstsein*, X 292) is the source of time, which in turn is 'the form of all individual objectivity' (X 296). There is a great deal of debate about the status of this absolute time-consciousness. Some commentators (e.g. Dan Zahavi) think of it as the pre-reflective consciousness of the flow of time. Others (e.g. John Brough) understand absolute time consciousness as a sense of the flow indifferent to what it intends, and, considered in itself, is sheer impressional time consciousness, which does not begin, endure, or change in its duration, but simply flows, always in the same way, neither faster nor slower. For Husserl, time is a universal and invariant form: a colour and a sound can differ with regard to their content but not with regard to their temporal form (Hua XI, 127). Conscious **lived experiences** are temporal entities in a dual sense. Precisely as occurrences (distinct from their 'contents') they belong to the natural world (as real as physical objects) and are temporally extended. In other words, they are temporal objects with distinct phases of beginning, duration, an end: 'it belongs to the essence of the perception of a temporal object that it is a temporal object itself' (X 232). They also have *internal temporal relations*: 'Every *Erlebnis* has its internal temporality' (*Erlebniszeitlichkeit*; CM § 18), its 'immanent' temporal structure (IX 310). Every temporal phenomenon is bound by an eidetic law, namely, that it starts from a primal impression that undergoes the modification of its movement into the past. The mental flow is not simple succession in the sense of one thing being replaced by another, there is a certain layering in experience:

> Perception is a process of streaming from phase to phase; in its own way each of the phases is a perception, but these phases are continuously harmonized in the unity of a synthesis, in the

> unity of a consciousness of one and the same perceptual ob-
> ject that is constituted here originally. In each phase we have
> primordial impression, retention and protention ... it is a unity
> of continual concordance. (APS 107; Hua XI 66)

If experience were purely a set of distinct and separate nows, it could never manifest the temporal phases of the intended object as parts of a unified succession. The apprehension of duration requires duration of the apprehension (X 192). Consciousness has to 'reach out' beyond its now and actually apprehend the now as part of a *flow*. It is not easy to articulate the sense of temporality belonging to the conscious experience as opposed to the temporal dimension of the intentional object of the experience. None the less, they are as different as the sensation of red is from the red property of a seen object. Similarly, in turning the faces of a die, one can distinguish the temporality of the object phases (the different sides appearing) from the inner temporal duration and phases of the experience itself. As Husserl characterizes it, the object is experienced as a *unity* in the duration, whereas the experience itself is 'filled duration' (X 273). Husserl's analyses of time typically begin from the perception of an immanent temporal object, such as a musical note. The appearing temporal object (to take the simples case: a musical tone or sequence of tones) is understood as a cluster of sensuous contents apprehended in a certain way, what he calls *Urimpressionen*, primary impressions. Husserl often returns to the deliberately simple example of listening to a single note, e.g. middle C, played on a piano or violin, held at the same intensity over a period of objective time: 'the tone endures, it is now and now again and again' (Hua X 275). Clearly, he acknowledges even this is an oversimplification and a fiction; such a note in reality would have fluctuations (X 86). But the tone can also be considered as an *immanent* object with everything transcendent excluded, as a 'unity in the flow of its time phases' (X 272, 275). These now phases are, as it were, **adumbrations** of the immanent object. By concentrating on the manner of the tone's appearance rather than the qualities of the tone, the 'wonder of time consciousness discloses itself' (Hua X 280). Husserl wants to see how the grasped sensations (sensuous contents) of the tone are regimented into a temporal experience with different phases. The '**now moment**' (*Jetztmoment*) gradually recedes and is replaced by another 'now moment' with the consciousness of the identical content. The original now is modified into a past-now with the same sensuous content except now indexed as 'having run off'. Famously, Husserl drew a number of 'time diagrams' (which he frequently revised) to illustrate how such a sensuous appearance endures in consciousness (see X § 10; § 43 and X 330-331). In listening to a transcendent temporal object such as a melody, we hear the present set of notes *as present*, but also hear them *as coming after* an earlier set of notes, and *as about to be supplanted* by further notes, or by silence if the tune is over. This 'now' presence is expansive and shared, it can include several items that are co-temporal. But the matter is complex: the present notes are stamped *as* present by having the character of coming after and coming before. There are 'retentions' and 'protentions' involved (X 84). Moreover, the past notes are not just heard in some sense but have the character of being *remembered* (X 79), the character of *having taken place*, of having once been *now*, they are also have the character of *leading up* to the present tone; they are continually being stamped with new characteristics. Each temporal phase or segment (*Querschnitt* or 'cross-section') seems to involve or is cross-referenced in relation to other temporal phases. This 'retention' is of course not an actual recurrence of the original now, but is something *intentionally* held in the current now phase: 'A continuity of elapsed tone phases is intended in the same now' (X 275). These continue to appear but in a modified way. There is a reaching back from the present into the immediate past. Each temporal experience consists of a **retention**, a **protention** and a **now moment**. It is an eidetic law that every now-moment has to submit to being modified into a retention. Similarly, protention is not yet the fully fledged conscious act of anticipation but a structural component of any *Erlebnis*. The present 'now' is not a knife edge but has a certain thickness. Husserl criticizes Brentano's view that these retentions and protentions are actually imagined experiences or presentiations (*Vergegenwärtigungen*). For Husserl protentions and retentions are genuine non-independent parts of the perceptual process (X 13). But what precisely in the sensory apprehension of a musical tone provides the element of 'now consciousness' such that it is then retained? I hear a whistling sound and then I can become conscious of the now of the experience itself (X 113). Do the object sensations (whistling sounds) somehow also carry or add up to a *sensation* of time itself? These sensations or impressions cannot be simply elements appearing the now or else they would simply have now consciousness, rather than temporal becoming (X 322). Initially, Husserl thought of the sensations or **hyletic data** as strictly speaking non-temporal and attributed the temporal element to the apprehension (*Auffassung*) grasping these sensations. In regard, to temporal consciousness, the schema of **apprehension**/content (*Auffassung/Auffassungsinhalt*) became problematic, and in later, more speculative, discussions Husserl talks of an 'primary matter' (*Urhyle*) as if itself were the source from which temporality flowed. In his mature works, Husserl became more interested in characterizing the temporal 'streaming' of **the ego** itself. Time is the form of all egological genesis (CM § 37). The ego constitutes itself by unifying its past, present and protentional moments into the unity of a history. In this regard Husserl speaks of the 'self-temporalizing' of the **ego**. The deepest truth of consciousness is that its origins lie in an upsurge of temporality itself and this raises the question as to whether the source of this temporality has to be something non-temporal. Husserl describes it paradoxically as something 'absolute' and 'standing' in a kind of permanent present (Latin *nunc stans* or 'stationary now') and also as something flowing.

Transcendence (*Transzendenz*)   See also **immanence, transcendental idealism**

'Transcendence' means literally 'to climb beyond', 'to ascend beyond', 'to step over', 'to step across', to 'surmount', 'to exceed'. The term 'transcendence' and its counterpart 'immanence' is taken over by Husserl from modern philosophy and specifically Kant. Husserl introduces term in *Idea of Phenomenology* (1907) and discussion of the various forms of transcendence plays a central role in *Ideas* I (1907). It is also discussed in *Cartesian Meditations*. Husserl speaks of 'transcendence' in several senses. There is the **natural attitude** assumption that the objects of knowledge *transcend* the subject. Indeed, Husserl says that '"transcendence" is part of the intrinsic sense of anything worldly' (CM § 11). Any object given in profiles transcends the immanent flow of consciousness. Husserl speaks of one sense of transcendence as the assumption that the object of knowledge transcends the act of knowing and is not really contained in the act. Husserl criticizes the traditional epistemological problem of how the mind transcends itself to gain knowledge of external objects (a problem expressed by Kant in his *Letter to Markus Herz* of 1772) as nonsensical. Husserl offers a new phenomenological account of transcendence – 'transcendence in immanence' (CM § 47). According to Husserl, especially in *Ideas* I, there are several entities that are said to 'transcend', e.g. the physical thing, the ego, the consciousness of the other, even God. Thus, the 'physical thing is said to be, in itself, unqualifiedly transcendent' (*Ideas* I § 42, p. 90; Hua III/1: 77), i.e. it does not form an immanent part of the flow of the consciousness that apprehends that object. Similarly **the ego** as subject pole is not an immanent part of the object. Universals and essences are also ideal unities that transcend consciousness (*Ideas* I § 59). God as a 'transcendence' is explicitly excluded by the phenomenological reduction (*Ideas* I § 58). The ego is said to be a 'transcendence in immanence'. According to Husserl's transcendental idealism, 'transcendence' in every form is an *immanent* characteristic, constituted within the ego. Every imaginable sense, every imaginable being, whether the latter is called immanent or transcendent, falls within the domain of transcendental subjectivity, as the subjectivity that constitutes sense and being' (CM § 41, p. 81).

Transcendental (*transzendental*) See **Kant, transcendental philosophy**

Although the term 'transcendental' is evidently connected with Kant, it is given an original meaning by Husserl. Husserl reproaches Kant on two main points. First, Husserl challenges the very elaboration of what Kant labelled the **a priori** conditions of possible experience. For Husserl, this conditionality is the result of a primordial confusion between the **natural attitude** and the phenomenological attitude of consciousness. For Husserl, there *is* no 'in itself' unknowable to the transcendental subject beyond phenomena. Rather phenomena are the *in itself* of subjectivity. Second, Husserl criticizes Kant's conception of the a-temporality of the transcendental subject. Husserl, in this sense, challenges the Kantian idea of a subjectivity whose intentional relation to the empirical remains dictated by the *a priori* elaboration of abstract and categorical laws of experience. For Husserl, **intentionality** is the mark of the transcendental ego in that intentionality constitutes the fundamental trait of all its conscious **lived experiences**. The concept of 'transcendental', for Husserl, implies the development of an eidetic science that establishes its ground only in and from the intuition of a given, or what Husserl also calls 'essential intuition' (*Wesensschau*). Hence, transcendental means, for Husserl, the modality by which the subject engages in the project of an eidetic reduction, or **epochē**, which by means of an 'imaginative variation' or referentiality, discovers the fundamental predicates of the given without which this given could not be thought. In this sense, for Husserl, the subject cannot think a thing without also thinking the space in which the thing is given. The essence of colour contains necessarily within its givenness the predicate of its extension. And furthermore, against **psychologism**, the transcendental subject is required to constitute the ideality of ideal objects (logical and/or arithmetical) even though these cannot be sensibly apprehended. Certainly one can here recognize the primary Kantian question: according to which law can there be universal and necessary truths? The Husserlian difference with Kantianism, however, is marked by the fact that phenomenology begins and is solely marked by its recourse to phenomenal description and consequently by the effective bracketing or suspension of all methodology that would consist in elaborating a priori what is possibly experienced for a categorizing subject. The phenomenological investigation will thus be, first, centred on the phenomenal description of the given that, by means of the bracketing of all *a priori* abstraction, *in turn* will be uniquely concerned with the modality by which the subject's relation to the given is explicated. With this turn, **phenomenology** will be labelled by Husserl as 'transcendental'. The world is thus for Husserl not simply existent, but more precisely a *phenomenon of existence*, that is an intentional given. It is existent only in that its being is that of an intentionality for a 'consciousness-in-the-world'. In this sense, transcendental phenomenology signifies the study of the transcendent intentionality of the world as a phenomenal given for a consciousness. As such, thus, transcendental consciousness will never, according to Husserl, be explicable logically. It is an 'actual consciousness' riveted to intentionality. In this sense, transcendental consciousness is not the logical or **a priori** structuring element of the world. It is rather the consciousness that elucidates, as self-consciousness, the pre-rational intentionality, as origin or foundation, of the given world. It is by the recourse to the notion of intentionality that the reversal of the classical empirical position is accomplished. Transcendental consciousness is, as seen, an abstract forming entity of content, but neither is it, for Husserl, a simple passive and receptive sphere of sensible impressions. Transcendental consciousness, rather, is discovered as that element that constitutes the intentionality of all given phenomenon. Which entails that intentionality is that which is constituted by consciousness. And furthermore, that intentionality is deciphered as the very modality by which consciousness is in the world and thus constitutes the transcendence of the world. The phenomenological reduction is here explicated. It is the discovery that intentionality is the transcendental modality by which is constituted the transcendent world of phenomena. For intentionality is always an aim constituted by consciousness' actuality in the world – that is, the manner in which and for which the world appears to and for consciousness. In this sense, the transcendental consciousness is not separable from the empirical consciousness. Which ought not to mean they are simply and elementarily the same. Rather transcendental consciousness is the modality by which intentionality is given to the empirical consciousness. Does this alliance mean that the word is a result of a solipsistic creation? Is the apparent objectivity of the world simply a subjective illusion according to Husserl? How can transcendental phenomenology escape the trap of solipsism? How does Husserl found the objectivity of experience and affirm the reality of essences? One must, according to Husserl, pose *other* transcendental subjects engaged and exposed to the same experience. Which means: the other must be given as a superior transcendence than the world. What the transcendental subject intentionalizes when it aims the other is an absolute **existence**. In this encounter between subject and other, **being** and **intentionality** coincide. This coincidence between being and intentionality as the relation between the transcendental subject and the other is precisely that which keeps phenomenology from falling into the trap of solipsism for which, contrarily, being is only a reflection or an effect of intentionality. Hence, is posed as transcendental the elaboration of a community of absolute existences.

Transcendental experience (*transzendentale Erfahrung*) See also **self-experience, transcendental ego**
Husserl claims that the **epochē** opens up a new dimension of experience – transcendental experience – and the functioning of **transcendental subject** that is normally hidden is brought to light (see *Trans. Phen.*, p. 98; Hua IX 250). Husserl speaks of this domain as a domain of experience. He claims **Descartes** discovered transcendental subjectivity with his recognition of the apodictic **givenness** of the *cogito ergo sum* but that Descartes did not understand this domain as a domain of possible experience that can be explored in its own terms. It is a domain of syntheses, achievements and horizons of 'self-experience' (*Selbsterfarhrung*).

Transcendental idealism (*transzendentaler Idealismus*) See also correlation, Descartes, *Fichte Lectures*, idealism, Kant, transcendental philosophy

From around 1908 until the end of his life Husserl described his position as 'transcendental idealism'. Strictly speaking, he did not use the term 'idealism' in *Ideas* I (1913) and the phrase 'transcendental idealism' (*transzendentaler Idealismus,* see *Crisis* VI 103; VI 427) only begins to appear around 1915. It features in his **Fichte Lectures** of 1917/1918 (Hua XXVII), for instance (see also Hua XXXVI) and is expressed in print for the first time in his *Formal and Transcendental Logic*, **Encyclopedia Britannica** article (1928) and in *Cartesian Meditations* (1931, see especially §§ 11, 34, 40, 41). Husserl sometimes refers to it as 'transcendental-phenomenological idealism' and he believes it is an **idealism** in a completely new sense. For Husserl, transcendental phenomenology is a 'radical and genuine' and indeed the 'final form' (*Endform*) of **transcendental philosophy** as inaugurated by **Descartes** (*Crisis* § 14). Husserl even offers a history of transcendental philosophy in his **Formal and Transcendental Logic** (especially §§ 94–100) and **Crisis**. The essence of transcendental idealism for Husserl was the **a priori correlation** between objectivity and subjectivity. He also asserted the absolute being of **consciousness** over and against the relative being of all other entities. It was Descartes who inaugurated the transcendental turn by seeking the 'ultimate foundations in the subjective' (*Crisis* § 19, p. 81; VI 83) of all being. Transcendental phenomenology, as he explains in his 1931 Foreword to Boyce-Gibson's translation of *Ideas* I, was to be an ultimate science that encompasses 'the universal horizon of the problems of philosophy' (*Ideas* II, p. 408; Hua V 141). **Transcendentalism** emerges to overcome objectivism in knowledge. According to Husserl, transcendentalism maintains that:

> [T]he ontic meaning (*der Seinssinn*) of the pregiven life-world is a subjective structure (*subjektives Gebilde*), it is the achievement (*Leistung*) of experiencing, prescientific life. (*Crisis* § 14, p. 69; VI 70)

In his *Cartesian Meditations*, Husserl claims that everything in the world gets its 'being and sense' (*Sein und Sinn*) from transcendental subjectivity. Husserl regarded his transcendental idealism as an advancement over and clarification of **Kant** who first used the term. In his *Critique of Pure Reason* (1781) Kant defines transcendental idealism as:

> I understand by the **transcendental idealism** of all appearances the doctrine that they are all together to be regarded as mere representations and not as things in themselves, and accordingly that space and time are only sensible forms of our intuition, but not determinations given for themselves or conditions of objects as things in themselves. (*Critique of Pure Reason* A369)

Later Kant proposed the term 'critical idealism' as less misleading, but central to this doctrine is the distinction between objects as appearances (to subjects) and as 'things in themselves'. After Kant, German Idealism, specifically Fichte, Schelling and Hegel, sought to overcome the residual dualism in Kant and especially the dualism between appearances and the unknowable thing-in-itself. Eventually it evolved into the absolute idealism of Hegel where the infinite realization of the identity of subjectivity and objectivity is seen as the self-realization of absolute spirit. Schelling especially regarded transcendental philosophy, the attempt to explain how knowledge is possible, as a way of identifying and seeking the grounds for the 'prejudice' *that there are things outside us*. Indeed, he regards as one of the great achievements of modern philosophy that it has succeeded in uncoupling the conviction that objects exist outside us from the conviction *that I exist*. According to Schelling, idealism results from thinking of the self as the fundamental principle of all knowledge, whereas realism consists of thinking of the object without the self. His claim is that it is necessary to think the two together, leading to what he calls 'ideal realism' or 'transcendental idealism' (*System of Transcendental Idealism*, 1800). Both Schelling and Hegel, reacting to Kant's continuing dualism of subject and thing in itself, understood idealism as involving the resolution of all things into an infinite consciousness which is at the same time **self-consciousness**.

Transcendental intersubjectivity (*transzendentale Intersubjektivität*)
See also **monad, monadology, subjectivity, intersubjectivity**
In order for there to be an experience of a common shared world of publicly available objects as well as the realm of culture and language, there must be

a transcendental structure of intercommunicating subjects that Husserl calls 'transcendental intersubjectivity'. In this sense, Husserl speaks of the world as the **achievement** of transcendental intersubjectivity (CM § 49), which Husserl also characterizes as a **community of monads** acting harmoniously. In his 1928 *Amsterdam Lectures*, he proclaims:

> Transcendental intersubjectivity is the absolute and only self-sufficient foundation (*Seinsboden*). Out of it are created draws the meaning and validity of everything objective, the totality of objectively real existent entities, but also every ideal world as well. An objectively existent thing is from first to last an existent thing only in a peculiar, relative and incomplete sense. It is an existent thing, so to speak, only on the basis of a cover-up of its transcendental constitution that goes unnoticed in the natural attitude. (*Trans. Phen.*, p. 249; Hua IX 344)

The great challenge of phenomenology is to grasp the deepest meaning of the transcendental subject *as* interwoven with transcendental intersubjectivity (see *Crisis* § 73) or what Husserl calls 'transcendental all subjectivity' (*transzendentale Allsubjektivität*, Hua VIII 482). He speaks of transcendental egos that are not only 'for themselves' constituting the **world**, but also 'for each other' (*füreinander*, VIII 505). I experience others not just as in the world but as subjects *for* the world (CM V § 43). Most often in his later works, Husserl articulates this intersubjectivity in terms of **monads** and a **monadology**.

Transcendental philosophy (*transzendentale Philosophie*)   See also **Descartes, phenomenology, transcendental idealism**
Husserl regards phenomenology as the 'final form' (*Endform*, *Crisis* § 14) of transcendental philosophy. Transcendental philosophy has its '**primal establishment**' (*Urstiftung*) in **Descartes**' discovery of the **cogito**. The danger to transcendental philosophy was the misunderstanding of knowledge as an attempt to prove the existence of the external world and to regard knowledge as an inner representation of that world. Modern philosophy after Descartes interpreted the immediate objects of cognition as mental representations. This led to a *subjective* **idealism** by making impossible direct access to the genuine object of knowledge. This is the 'chief error' of modern philosophy, Husserl says in *Ideas* I:

> The holders of this view are misled by thinking that the tran-
> scendence belonging to the spatial physical thing is the tran-
> scendence belonging to *something depicted* or *represented by*
> *a sign*, (*Ideas* I § 43, p. 92; Hua III/1 78)

According to Husserl in *First Philosophy*, there can be only one method
for transcendental philosophy: '[O]ne must study cognizing life itself in
its own essence achievements' (*das erkennende Leben selbst in seinen*
eigenen Wesenleistungen, EP I Hua VII 248). Transcendental philosophy
sets a task for the whole of **humanity** (Hua VII 236), the task of
becoming universal, self-conscious, rational beings in a community and
world that is recognized as its own accomplishment. Husserl considers the
breakthrough into transcendental philosophy and to the 'transcendental
attitude' as producing a permanent reorientation of human culture towards
higher, more rational and more self-aware goals, even to the extent of
producing a new universal humanity. Consciousness assumes **self-respon-**
sibility (*Selbstverantwortung,* Hua V 162) 'through a 'self-explication'
(*Selbstauslegung*) of its own accomplishment of 'mundane objectivity'
(*Crisis* § 58). This self-explication, for Husserl is permanently ongoing, just as
he speaks of 'endless transcendental life' (VIII 126). Whereas transcendental
philosophy offers a critique of naive life, Husserl goes further in seeking a
critique of transcendental life itself (CM V § 63).

Transcendental reduction   See **reduction**

Transcendentalism (*Transzendentalismus*) See also **Descartes,**
transcendental idealism, transcendental philosophy
Transcendentalism is a general movement of philosophy that inquires behind
the manifest given of experience to inquire into the 'how' of its givenness.
Especially in his *Crisis*, Husserl employs the term 'transcendentalism' for any
philosophy that opposes naive **objectivism** and instead recognizes that all
objectivity is an **achievement** of **transcendental subjectivity** (see *Crisis* §
14). According to Husserl, mature transcendentalism also resists subjective
or psychological **idealism** (such as is found in **Berkeley**). **Kant** defines the
concept of 'transcendental' in the *Critique of Pure Reason*:

> I call all cognition transcendental that is occupied not so much

with objects but rather with our a priori concepts of objects in general. (*Critique of Pure Reason* A11–12)

Similarly, in the *Crisis* Husserl says that he employs the term 'transcendental' in the widest sense to mean:

> [T]he motif of inquiring back into the ultimate source of all the formations of knowledge, the motif of the knower's reflecting on himself and his knowing life in which all the scientific structures that are valid for him occur purposefully, are stored up as acquisitions … This source bears the title *I-myself*. (*Crisis* § 26, pp. 97–8; VI 100–101)

Husserl regards **Descartes** rather than Kant as the discoverer of transcendental philosophy with his discovery of the ***ego cogito*** as an absolute source of **truth**.

Transference (*Übertragung*)   See also **empathy**

'Transference' or 'carrying over' (Übertragung) is the term Husserl uses to refer to the manner in which a **sense** experienced in one context is applied in a different context through a transferring **apperception**. For instance, in **empathy**, I carry over or transfer experiences that I have in the first person to the other person (see CM § 50). Or, to use Husserl's own example, the child who sees a scissors for the first time is subsequently able to utilize different shaped scissors not through explicit 'reproducing, comparing, inferring' (CM § 50), but rather through a 'transfer' of sense.

Transverse intentionality (*Querintentionalität*)   See also **horizontal intentionality (*Längsintentionalität*), time consciousness**

Term used by Husserl in his time consciousness manuscripts in contrast with **horizontal intentionality**. Husserl speaks of an **intertwining** of the two intentionalities; they are regarded as two sides of the same process (Hua X 381).

Truth (*Wahrheit*)   See **evidence, givenness, state of affairs**

In his ***Logical Investigations***, Husserl offers a reconceptualization of the traditional correspondence view of truth. According to the traditional definition, truth is a correspondence (*adequatio*) of the mind to things. According to Husserl's reformulation, truth is '*the complete correspondence of the meant and given as such*' (Sixth Logical Investigation § 39). Husserl also speaks of 'being in the sense of truth' (Sixth Logical Investigation § 38). Truth is experienced as an identity or coincidence between the intentional act and that which is grasped as fulfilling the intention. For Husserl, truth is primarily located in **judgements**. In *Ideas* I § 139, Husserl speaks of truth as being given in an evidential consciousness. Every form of evidential judging (including practical and value judgements) has a relationship to truth. Thus perception is described as a kind of truth apprehension (from the German for perception, *Wahrnehmung*, 'truth grasping'). In one sense, Husserl accepts traditional correspondence accounts of truth (*adequatio rei et intellectus*; LU Hua XIX/2 647). However, considered from the phenomenological point of view, truth is actually an experience, a specific (albeit not necessarily specifically thematized) *recognition* of the coincidence between what is meant and what is given. It is not a question of comparing some representation (in the mind) with some state of affairs outside the mind (which cannot be apprehended independently of the representation) rather truth is an *experience* of coincidence. Truth is best described in Husserl's phenomenology as *recognition of identity* or *disclosure*. Husserl in **Logical Investigations** is a realist about truth in that he considers truths to hold whether or not they are ever thought (see *Prol.* § 65), e.g. the Pythagorean theorem stands as an independent valid truth whether anyone actually thinks it or not. He similarly stated that Newton's laws held prior to their being discovered by Newton. In his late works, however, especially in the *Crisis of European Sciences*, Husserl moves more towards a view of truth as what is intersubjectively agreed; he does not abandon his view that ideal truths are timeless. Ideal truths, for Husserl, are always truths *for* some possible mind, but there does not have to be an actual mind contemplating them. Nevertheless, subjective acts are constituting acts for these ideal objectivities. In later writings, e.g. Crisis, Husserl contrasts the objective truths of sciences with the prescientific non-objectifiable truths of the **life-world**. Husserl's conception of truth as recognition or disclosure was strongly influential on **Heidegger**'s discussion of truth as disclosedness and unhiddenness in *Being and Time*.

Truths in themselves (*Wahrheiten an sich*)   See **propositions in themselves**

Twardowski, Kasimir (1866–1938)   Kasimir (or Kasiemierz) Twardowski was a student of Brentano and author of *On the Content and Object of Presentations. A Psychological Investigation* (Vienna, 1894). He was born in Vienna where he attended gymnasium and the studied philosophy at the University of Vienna from 1885 to 1889, completing his doctoral degree in 1891 with a dissertation on *Idea and Perception. An Epistemological Study of Descartes.* He then studied in Munich, taking courses with **Carl Stumpf,** and in Leipzig. In 1894 he completed his Habilitation published as *On the Content and Object of Presentations. A Psychological Investigation* (Vienna, 1894). In that work, Twardowski sought to clarify ambiguities in Brentano's account of intentionality. Brentano tended to identify the object and the content of the mental act whereas Twardowski carefully distinguished them. Twardowski distinguished the immanent content (or mental picture) from the transcendent, intentional object: 'What is presented *in* a presentation is its content; what is presented through a presentation is its object.' The content, according to Twardowski, is purely a route to the intentional object. The intended object had also to be distinguished from the existing object. Husserl wrote an unpublished review of Twardowski's book in 1896. Twardowski was appointed professor in Lvov, Poland (but then part of Austria) in 1895, and set up a philosophical society there. He taught in Lvov until his death in 1938. Among his students were **Roman Ingarden**, the mathematician and logician Stanisław Leśniewski, and the logician Jan Łukasiewicz.

Type (*Typ*)   See also **association, normality, typicality**
Perceptual experience is primarily directed at individuals but it also identifies groups of individuals according to certain loose generalizations or 'types' constituted on the basis of similarity. In a 1925 letter to Landgrebe, Husserl says he is interested in the idea of 'type' as found in Dilthey and that of ideal type in Weber (*Briefwechsel* IV 247). In *Ideas* II § 60, Husserl claims personal life manifests a **typicality**. There is what is typical for human beings as such, but also what is typical for this individual. In *Experience and Judgment* (§§80–85), Husserl explains how empirical generalities (universals linked to individual objects) are based

on types preconstituted in **passivity**: 'The factual world of experience is experienced as a typified world' (EU § 83). Types function between the mere apprehension of individual objects and the conceptual activity. On the basis of perceptions of different objects, a primal outlining is established according to shared similarities (*Experience and Judgment*, § 83). Thus, through **memory** and **imagination**, new perceived objects are grasped as new examples of the same type, e.g. this animal is very similar to that one, 'familiar and yet new' (EU § 83). According to Husserl, attention and **eidetic variation** lead us into the realm of empirical and pure generalities. Husserl distinguishes *types* from *essences*. In fact, the distinction between extra-essential types and scientific or essential types (*Experience and Judgment,* § 83) helps us understand the vague and passive character of perceptual types. Types do not emerge through active conceptual consideration, but rather through the meaningful connection of experiences. Unlike the Kantian schematism (which seeks to apply the pure concepts to the raw material of sensibility), types are not images, either in the form of mere examples or as simpler figures. There can be types of individual, e.g. my 'type' (stereotype) of how I think about John, or types of humanness or **humanity** (e.g. Indian, Chinese, and so on). Husserl thinks that European humanity through its discovery of infinity overcame its status as a mere type of humanity and became a universal model of rational humanity as such. Husserl's conception of 'type' was subsquently taken up by **Scheler** and **Schutz** (especially in his phenomenological sociology).

—U—

Understanding (*Verstehen*)

Husserl uses this term in the same manner as **Dilthey** to contrast the way of making human intentional experiences intelligible in terms of their **motivations** with the explanatory causal approach of the natural sciences, which the neo-Kantians usually described as 'explanation' (*Erklärung*). **Heidegger** made understanding (*Verstehen*) central to his account of human existence (Dasein) in *Being and Time*.

Universal   See **species**

—V—

Value (*Wert*)   See also **axiology, ethics, valuing**
According to Husserl, values are objective and ideal and are apprehended in a quasi-perceptual way. Values simply attach to things in the world. Apprehending value (*Wertnehmen*) is akin to perception (*Wahrnehmen*). In Ideas I § 27, Husserl speaks about the world of the **natural attitude** as including not just physical things but also things of value. We simply hold certain things, actions, emotions, etc., as intrinsically valuable, in that we are drawn towards them or want to affirm them or reject them in some way. Even perceiving involves applying the value 'true' to what is perceived or experiencing what is perceived as really there. At the same time, values are values independent of their being judged or apprehended by someone. Evaluative acts or evaluating acts (*wertende Akte*) are founded both on **feelings a**nd **presentations.** These evaluations have their origin in a certain kind of value feeling (*Wertfühlen*).

Value apprehension (*Wertnehmen*)   See also **value, valuing**
Husserl gave lectures on value theory along with his lectures on ethics at Göttingen from 1908 to 1914 (see Hua XXVIII). Husserl's lectures were influenced by **Brentano**'s *The Origin of our Knowledge of Right and Wrong*. Husserl uses the gerund *Wertnehmen* (Hua XXVIII 370), apprehending value, to describe the act of recognizing values which he sees as similar to perceiving (*Wahrnehmen*, Hua XXXVII 71–75). Valuable things and their valuable properties are perceived (*Ideas* I § 50) but **values** themselves, which are ideal entities, can also be apprehended through a founded act. For Husserl some values are just passively apprehended while others are

actively constituted by our intendings in acts of rational willing or love. Human beings can constitute the value 'love your neighbour as yourself'. Values are originally felt in an 'act of value feeling' (*wertfühlender Akt*).

Valuing or valuation (*Werten, wertende Akte*)   See also **value, value apprehension**

Husserl distinguishes between **values** and acts of *valuing.* The most elementary level of value experience or valuation based on feeling consciousness. Even at the most basic level of sensuous feeling, objects appear as charged with value and are either attractive or to be avoided. One has to feel attracted to a value before that value can be appreciated as valuable.

Van Breda, Herman Leo (1911–1974)   Herman Leo Van Breda was born in Belgium and studied at the Catholic University of Leuven where he finished his master's thesis in 1938. He became a Franciscan priest in 1934. After his master's degree, he decided to visit to Freiburg to meet Edmund Husserl. However, by the time he arrived, Husserl had died and Van Breda instead met with Husserl's widow, Malvine, and with Husserl's assistant **Eugen Fink**. Van Breda learned of the threat posed by the Nazis to the Husserl's manuscripts and arranged for these manuscripts and other memorabilia to be smuggled out of Germany to Belgium where the University of Leuven was willing to provide a home for them. In 1939 the Husserl Archives opened in Leuven with Eugen Fink and Ludwig Langrebe acting as curators, but soon afterwards Belgium fell to the Germans and the Archives had to be hidden. In 1941 Van Breda completed his doctorate on Husserl. After the war, Van Breda became the first director of the Husserl Archives and a professor at the Catholic University of Leuven. Merleau-Ponty was the first visitor to the Archives in 1939 and spent a week there reading the typescript of *Ideas* II and the then unpublished portions of the *Crisis*. During the war, Van Breda assisted Jean Cavaillès and Merleau-Ponty in gaining copies of Husserl's manuscripts, eventually leading to the opening of a Husserl Archives in Paris.

Vienna Lecture (1935)   See also *Crisis of European Sciences,* **Europe, humanity**

On 7 and 10 May 1935 Husserl delivered his famous lecture, 'Philosophy in the Crisis of European Humanity' (*Die Philosophie in der Krisis der europaïshen Menschheit*), in Vienna (generally referred to as the *Vienna Lecture* and later planned as an introduction to the German edition of the **Cartesian Meditations**).The original typescript for the *Vienna Lecture* is not gathered with the *Crisis* collection of manuscripts. There are two typescripts made by Fink (signatures: M III 5 II a and M III 5 b respectively) and there is as well the shorthand version that is contained in a longer manuscript (K III 1 (Bl. 1–26)). The typescript is somewhat expanded over the shorthand version. In this lecture, Husserl addresses larger topics including the shift from mythic thought to **rationality** brought about by philosophy, the meaning of human **historicity** and cultural intercultural understanding, the inbuilt **teleology** of western civilization towards universal rationality, the threats facing it, and so on. Husserl's overall aim is nothing less than the 'rebirth (*Wiedergeburt*) of **Europe** from the spirit of philosophy' According to Husserl, a 'burning need' for an 'understanding of the spirit' has arisen (*Crisis*, p. 296; VI 344). In this lecture, Husserl attempts to characterize the spiritual character of Europe. For him, the name 'Europe' refers to 'the unity of a spiritual life, activity, creation, with all its ends, interests, cares and endeavors, with its products of purposeful activity, institutions, organizations' (*Crisis*, p. 273; VI 319). This lecture became controversial because of its claim that 'Europe' stands as the name for the idea of universal humanity, and for its allegedly ethnocentric remarks about non-European cultures and about 'gypsies' (*Zigeuner*) whom he excludes from the scientific spirit of Europe. Other 'types' of **humanity**, such as the age-old civilizations in China and India, also lack this 'absolute idea' of European universality and remain 'empirical anthropological types' (*Crisis*, p. 16; VI 14). Husserl predicts global Europeanization of the world but is concerned about its narrow technicized nature due to the distortions inherent in European rationalistic scientific culture as it has developed.

—W—

Weierstrass, Karl (1815–1897) Weierstrass was a German mathematician. He was born in Ostenfelde, Westphalia, in 1815, and studied mathematics at the University of Bonn, but left without completing his examinations. He then studied at Münster with Gudermann and developed his theory of elliptical functions. He worked as a school teacher until one of his papers attracted attention and he received an honorary doctorate from the University of Königsberg. He was eventually offered a post at the University of Berlin. He attracted many able students in Berlin including **Cantor** and Husserl. Husserl wrote his doctoral thesis on the calculus of variations supervised by Weierstrass. Husserl later claimed that he received the ethos for scientific striving from Weierstrass.

Will (*der Wille*) See also **attitude, motivation, Pfänder, position taking**

Husserl rarely makes the will (*Wille*) and willing (*Wollen*) thematic in his phenomenology of consciousness. Indeed, **Alexander Pfänder** offered the first phenomenology of willing. Husserl, in general, divides intentional acts into three main classes: intellective acts such as knowing, acts of feeling that apprehend something's value, and acts of willing. In the ***Logical Investigations*** he includes willing as a **non-objectifying act** that therefore has to be doubly founded on both intellective acts and feelings. In order to will something, I must first have a **presentation** of it and apprehend through **feeling** its **value** as positively desirable. All willing is directed at something that I consider valuable and desirable. This valuation is a necessary condition of willing and the **foundation** for every act of will. All psychic acts are based in the will for Husserl. Willing is the basis of action. But some willings can simply anticipate or intend actions whereas others immediately incorporate actions. With regard to the latter he speaks of the 'acting will' (*Handlungswille*). Husserl believes that the ***epochē*** can be effected by an act of willing. He speaks of human existence as 'willing life'. In his **genetic phenomenology**, Husserl sees acts of willing as motivated by an 'underground' of **drives**, **instincts** and tendencies that the **ego** passively experience. It simply feels drawn towards certain things as attractive, valuable etc. But the will can take a stand with regard to their unconscious tendencies. I can resist the desire to smoke. I can say 'no'; Husserl even speaks of my 'eternal no' (*mein ewiges Nein*; Hua XXXVII 339). Husserl distinguishes a willing from a mere wishing. Only what can possibly be brought about can genuinely be willed, whereas wishing can seek what is impossible. Husserl believes he can identify formal laws of rational willing, e.g. he who wills the end also wills the means. Human experience is organized around an **ego** that has a sense of governing its **body**. It experiences its bodily movements as a series of 'I can's. I can also experience the will as a kind of making something happen. Husserl speaks of this using the Latin term *fiat*: 'let it be done'. We experience our bodily movements in the form 'let it be done' – I raise my hand, I turn my eyes. The **living body** is, for Husserl, 'an organ of the will' (Hua IV 151), a 'willing body' (*Willensleib*). Husserl's distinguishes between a will that is blind and a will that acts with insight. Following Kant, Husserl believes that a rational will is a good will. According to Husserl, Kant underestimated the need for a motivational foundation for the will. Because of this, Kant could not recognize that the will always needs motivation from a concrete material content. In Ideas I, Husserl includes willing under position taking. **Position taking** is a free act of the **ego**.

World (*Welt*) See also **alien world, annihilation of the world, homeworld, horizon, life-world, nature, world presentation, worldview**

By *world* (*die Welt*), in his mature writings, Husserl means the 'collective horizon for all investigations', or alternatively the 'horizon of horizons' (*Ideas* I § 1). 'World' means the widest conceivable context for all human intending, not just the limits of the physical universe or 'totality' (*Weltall*), but also the limits of what is meaningful, the limits of temporality, possibility, and so on. Husserl recognizes many forms of world – natural world (*natürliche Welt*), the world of things (*Dingwelt*), the spiritual world (*die geistige Welt*), the world of values and interests, the environing world (*Umwelt*), the familiar, **homeworld** (*Heimwelt*) or 'near-world' (*Nahwelt*), **alien world** (*Fremdwelt*), universal world (*Allwelt*), and so on. In his later years he also discusses the **life-world** (*Lebenswelt*). Besides these layers of the existing world, there is, as for Heidegger, the world of numbers, of mathematics, of idealities, and so on. The spiritual world is the world of **persons** in an intersubjective community (*Ideas* II § 53). The world is experienced through a very specific kind of 'world intuition' (*Weltanschauung*) or 'world apperception' (*Weltapperzeption*, CM § 41). Discussion of the concept of world is prominent in Husserl's mature writings but is already discussed in his **Logical Investigations**, where it is described as 'the unified objective totality corresponding to, and inseparable from, the ideal system of all factual truth' (LU *Prol.* § 36). From the phenomenological point of view, the world is considered by Husserl as a harmonious, unlimited flow of experiences. In **Cartesian Meditations**, he says that being given in harmonious straightforward experience is constitutive of the sense 'world' (see CM § 44). The world has a 'fixed order of being' (*Ideas* I § 27) and always outruns whatever it is we experience. The world has a two-sided 'infinite' (or indefinite) horizon stretching into the indeterminate past and the indeterminate future. The world of the **natural attitude** is experienced as a world endlessly spread out in space, endlessly becoming and having endlessly become in time' (*Ideas* I § 27). The world includes not just physical things (which science investigates under a particular abstractive sense as 'nature'), but also other **persons**, animals, living things, cultural products, etc. It is a 'world of objects with values, a world of goods, a practical world' (*Ideas* I § 27). All sciences that are carried out in the natural attitude are sciences of the world and all particular sciences are included in the life-world although they do not make the life-world thematic (see *Crisis* § 33). For Husserl, the world is not primarily a collectivity of things, practices, etc., but rather is experienced as a **horizon**. He speaks of 'world horizon' (*Welthorizont*). First and foremost attention is concentrated on the things at hand, but the world is always presumed in the background of all intentional activity. The positing of the world is produced by these horizons which are the correlates of experience. It is an always assumed context for experiencing. In Husserl's mature transcendental philosophy, the 'natural world' is considered to be a constituted product or the correlate of the **natural attitude** (see *Ideas* I § 47); 'nature is there for the theoretical subject; it belongs to his correlative sphere'; *Ideas* II § 2). In the natural attitude, the world is accepted as given and is constantly available, 'on hand' (*vorhanden*), and experienced as **pregiven** (*vorgegeben*) in all waking states. All our experience is in the usual sense **mundane** or worldly. The world (just like all entities contained within the world) is a combination of what is determinate and indeterminate. In all our experiences, the world remains one and the same. We have our own familiar worlds and also we experience the worlds of others as alien to us (*Fremdwelt*). Nevertheless, Husserl is insistent that in fact there is only *one* overall world; world is not something that can be plural. The concept of 'world' appears in *Thing and Space* (1907) § 61, in which Husserl raises the issue of how we constitute the sense of a potentially infinite unified world as the backdrop for perceptual experiences of physical bodies. The concept of a '**worldview**' is also discussed in 'Philosophy as a Rigorous Science' (1910/1911) where Husserl is critical of the 'philosophy of worldviews' (*Weltanschaungs-philosophie*), which he understands as a specific form of relativism born from scepticism. The layers of constitution of natural and spiritual world are discussed in some detail in *Ideas* II. With the emergence of mathematical science in the modern period, Husserl claims that the very concept of 'world' undergoes a complete 'transformation of meaning' (*Sinn-verwandlung*, p. 60; VI 61), since it is now split into 'world of nature' and 'psychic world' (*seelische Welt*, VI 61). The naturalistically given world as explored by science is, for Husserl, not *the* world, but rather is founded on the experience of the pregiven, everyday world (*Ideas* II § 53). How humans relate to world is determined by their interests. Husserl even speaks of a 'world of interests' (*Interessenwelt*). Practical goals have limited or finite horizons but the world of science has a potentially infinite horizon. Husserl sees humans as essentially caught up on a world. Human beings are 'enworlded' – the equivalent to Heidegger's notion of being-in-the-world. There is a kind of '**mundanization'** (*Verweltlichung*) whereby the transcendental ego is not only 'for-the-world' but is necessarily embodied in the spatiotemporal, historical world. I am a human being within the constituted world. In *Ideas* I § 49, Husserl also experiments with the idea of the '**annihilation of the world**' (*Weltvernichtung*). This is a thought experiment. We can imagine the flow of the worldly experience being disrupted to the point where all is chaos. But, according to Husserl, we cannot imagine consciousness being disrupted in the same way. Husserl's **reduction** aims to disrupt or suspend this belief in the world, 'world belief' (*Weltglaube*). This makes visible world as world. In the *Cartesian Meditations*, Husserl criticizes those who interpret the ego subject as merely a 'residuum' left over in the world, the 'tag end of the world' (*Endchen der Welt*).

World constitution (*Weltkonstitution*)   See also **constitution, world**
For Husserl, the world is the product of constitution by the **transcendental ego**, or more precisely by an indefinite number of transcendental egos

working harmoniously as the **community of monads** or **transcendental intersubjectivity**. For the late Husserl, the constitution of the world is a great mystery that has not been addressed by previous science or philosophy that proceeded in the **natural attitude** and took the givenness of the world for granted.

World presentation or world representation (*Weltvorstellung*)   See also **life-world, world, worldview**
Especially in his late writings, e.g. **Vienna Lecture**, and in his writings on the life-world, Husserl speaks of the 'world presentation' (*Weltvorstellung*, Hua VI 317) of particular peoples (see *Crisis* § 53; § 58). Husserl believes cultures accept their particular outlook on the world as actually disclosing the world itself until something happens that makes them realise their own view is just one perspective. In ancient Greek thought, the breakthrough to philosophy occurred when people recognize a difference emerges between their 'world representation' and what they conceive of as the 'world in itself' (Hua XXVII 189). Husserl often uses the term *Weltvorstellung* as interchangeable with *Weltanschauung* but sometimes he uses *Weltanschauung* to have the connotation of a more individualistic life outlook.

Worldview (*Weltanschauung*)   See also **historicism, 'Philosophy as a Rigorous Science', relativism, world, world presentation**
The term 'worldview' or 'world intuition' (*Weltanschauung*) is traceable to **Kant** and was employed by nineteenth- and twentieth-century German philosophers, such as Wilhelm **Dilthey** and Karl Jaspers, to refer to an overall outlook on the world, a mindset or perspective that is a comprehensive and systematic way of presenting the world as a whole. During the 1930s National Socialist ideologues (including some philosophers and anthropologists aligned to the Nazi cause) employed the term in an ideological sense, especially to celebrate the worldview of the Germanic peoples and denigrate other worldviews as inferior. The term 'worldview' can suggest an individual's way of responding to the world in existential terms. Husserl uses the term in a number of different senses. In his '**Philosophy as a Rigorous Science**' (1910/1911), Husserl criticized a philosophy based on worldviews in so far as it simply affirmed the plurality of worldviews and their incommensurability. He regards a 'worldview' as primarily an individual outlook – a way of life incorporating a kind of wisdom. As he puts it: 'Worldview

philosophy teaches just as wisdom teaches: personality addresses personality.' Husserl believes an affirmation of plural worldviews (and of outlooks
that can only be understood from within) leads to a particular kind of
relativism that he calls **historicism**. According to this position, one might
regard the beliefs of the Hindus as 'true for them' but not 'true for us
(non-Hindus)'. Husserl regarded this claim as collapsing into absurdity.
In the *Crisis* (§ 56, p. 196; VI 199 and p. 390; VI 509), Husserl criticizes
a certain kind of existential approach to philosophy as a 'philosophy of
worldviews' (e.g. Jaspers) that claims there can be no scientific knowledge
of the absolute nature of things and that humans must be content with a
'worldview' understood primarily as an individual accomplishment, a kind of
'personal religious faith' which as a result is necessarily limited. Husserl often
uses the term 'worldview' interchangeably with '**world presentation**'
(*Weltvorstellung*). Husserl sees the adoption of a personal worldview as
a way of escaping the demand for a rigorous science of the world. For
Husserl, worldviews do not claim unconditional truth and universality (see
Crisis, p. 390; VI 509) but are 'essentially an individual accomplishment,
a sort of personal religious faith'. In this sense, science is not claiming to
be a worldview but aims at absolute truth concerning the nature of being
in itself. In his later writings on the life-world, Husserl acknowledges that,
for instance, primitive peoples have a worldview, as do different cultures
at different periods in history. He praises the anthropologist **Lucien
Lévy-Bruhl** for his account of the worldviews of primitive peoples outside
of the sphere of European science and **rationality**.

Wundt, Wilhelm (1832–1920)   Wilhelm Wundt is regarded as one of the
founders of empirical **psychology**. He was a medical doctor, philosopher
and psychologist who had enormous influence in Germany. He was born
in Neckerau, Mannheim, in 1832 and studied in Tübingen, Heidelberg and
then Berlin. His *Principles of Physiological Psychology* (1874) is regarded as
one of the foundational texts of empirical psychology. He founded one of
the world's first psychological laboratories in Leipzig. Among his important
publications are his *Contributions to the Theory of Sense Perception* (1862)
and *Lectures on the Human and Animal Soul*. Wundt distinguished **inner
observation** from **inner perception**, although his terminology is more
or less the exact opposite of **Brentano**'s. For Wundt inner observation
is the true method of psychology. Husserl attended Wundt's lectures

on philosophy while studying in Berlin. Later Wundt reviewed Husserl's *Prolegomena* (1900) favourably. Husserl was subsequently quite critical of Wundt.

—Y—

Yearbook for Philosophy and Phenomenological Research (*Jahrbuch für Philosophie und phänomenologische Forschung*)

In 1913 Husserl published the first volume of his newly founded *Yearbook for Philosophy and Phenomenological Research* (*Jahrbuch für Philosophie und phänomenologische Forschung*), jointly edited by Husserl along with Alexander **Pfänder**, Adolf **Reinach**, Moritz **Geiger** and Max **Scheler**. Husserl had been planning a journal since 1907 (see his letter to Daubert 26 August 1907, Hua XXV xv), but the plan was revived when a *Festschrift* was written for **Theodor Lipps** in 1911 containing many phenomenological contributions. Husserl seemed worried that Lipps rather than he would be seen as phenomenology's originator. In his Preface to Volume One, Husserl wrote: 'This journal is intended … to unite in shared work those who hope for a fundamental reform of philosophy by means of the pure and rigorous execution of phenomenological method.' The *Jahrbuch* quickly became a repository of brilliant phenomenological studies. The first volume contained Husserl's *Ideas* I, as well as the first book of Scheler's work *Formalism in Ethics*. The Fifth Volume (1922) contained works by **Edith Stein** and **Roman Ingarden**, whereas Volume VIII (1927) contained **Martin Heidegger's** *Being and Time* together with a work by another Freiburg phenomenologist, Oskar Becker, on the nature of mathematical objects. Volume X was Husserl's own ***Formal and Transcendental Logic*** and Volume XI his Postface to *Ideas* I. The *Jahrbuch* eventually ceased publication in 1930.

—Z—

Zero point (*Nullpunkt*)   See also **lived body, space**

The 'zero' or 'null' point is a metaphor taken from the zero point on a scale (e.g. 0° Celsius) or invokes the point of intersection of the x and y axis on a graph. Husserl uses the term to mean that all sense of space, time, orientation, movement, and so on, takes its reference point from the **lived body** of the perceiver. The concept of a 'zero point' expresses the idea of a limit case (Husserl does use the term 'limit case', *Nullfall* at Hua IV 112), i.e., Husserl speaks of the individual **person** as the 'null case' of social **subjectivity** (Hua IV 197). Husserl speaks about perception as beginning with a 'zero point' that is nothing other than one's own body in **space**. All concepts of 'here', 'there', 'above', 'below', 'now' and so on, take their orientation from the position the perceiver is in at the time, which is understood as an 'absolute' here (*Ideas* II § 32, IV 127). This position is the null or zero point. The body, for Husserl, not only has an orientation in space, it also orients space around it. It is the 'bearer of the zero point (*Nullpunkt*) of orientation, the bearer of the here and now' (*Ideas* II § 18). Every space is experienced from the inescapable 'here' of my body: right and left, up and down, near and far. All orientation involves a body and all distances are marked off taking the body as the point of departure. Even if one is imagining something, e.g. a centaur, one imagines seeing it from a particular bodily perspective, facing towards or away from the imaginer; I can look over the body of the centaur and grasp its orientation; it is facing toward me or away from me. Husserl uses various variations on the concept of a 'zero point', e.g. the 'zero point of intensity' (DR Hua),XVI 87), or 'zero point of orientation (*Nullorientierung*, DR § 5); see also CM I 152; IV 56; and Hua VI 311, 426.

Bibliography

The literature on Husserl is vast, but see, in particular: Lapointe, François. *Edmund Husserl and His Critics. An International Bibliography (1894–1979)*. Bowling Green, Ohio: Philosophy Documentation Center, 1980. Spileers, Steven, ed. *The Husserl Bibliography*. Dordrecht: Kluwer, 1999.

i Works by Edmund Husserl in German

The critical edition of Husserl's works is: *Husserliana: Edmund Husserl – Gesammelte Werke*. Dordrecht: Springer, 1956. (See http://www.springer.com/series/6062.)

To date the following 40 volumes have been published in this series:

- Volume I: *Cartesianische Meditationen und Pariser Vorträge*. Hrsg. Stephan Strasser. The Hague: Nijhoff, 1950. Reprinted 1991.
- Volume II: *Die Idee der Phänomenologie. Fünf Vorlesungen*. Nachdruck der 2. erg. Auflage. Hrsg. W. Biemel. The Hague: Nijhoff, 1973.
- Volume III/1: *Ideen zu einer reinen Phänomenologie und phänomenologischen Philosophie*. Erstes Buch: *Allgemeine Einführung in die reine Phänomenologie* 1. Halbband: *Text der 1–3. Auflage*. Hrsg. K. Schuhmann. The Hague: Nijhoff, 1977.
- Volume III/2: *Ideen zu einer reinen Phänomenologie und phänomenologischen Philosophie*. Erstes Buch: *Allgemeine Einführung in die reine Phänomenologie*. 2. Halbband: *Ergänzende Texte (1912–1929)*. Hrsg. K. Schuhmann. The Hague: Nijhoff, 1977.
- Volume IV: *Ideen zu einer reinen Phänomenologie und phänomenologischen Philosophie*. Zweites Buch: *Phänomenologische Untersuchungen zur Konstitution*. Hrsg. Marly Biemel. The Hague: Nijhoff, 1952. Reprinted 1991.
- Volume V: *Ideen zu einer reinen Phänomenologie und phänomenologischen*

Philosophie. Drittes Buch: *Die Phänomenologie und die Fundamente der Wissenschaften*. Hrsg. Marly Biemel. The Hague: Nijhoff, 1952. Reprinted 1971.

- Volume VI: *Die Krisis der europäischen Wissenschaften und die transzendentale Phänomenologie. Eine Einleitung in die phänomenologische Philosophie*. Hrsg. W. Biemel. The Hague: Nijhoff, 1962. Reprinted 1976.
- Volume VII: *Erste Philosophie (1923/24)*. Erster Teil: *Kritische Ideengeschichte*. Hrsg. R. Boehm. The Hague: Nijhoff, 1965.
- Volume VIII: *Erste Philosophie (1923/24)*. Zweiter Teil: *Theorie der phänomenologischen Reduktion*. Hrsg. R. Boehm. The Hague: Nijhoff, 1965.
- Volume IX: *Phänomenologische Psychologie. Vorlesungen Sommersemester 1925*. Hrsg. W. Biemel. The Hague: Nijhoff, 1968.
- Volume X: *Zur Phänomenologie des inneren Zeitbewusstseins (1893–1917)*. Hrsg. R. Boehm. The Hague: Nijhoff, 1966. Second Edition 1969.
- Volume XI: *Analysen zur passiven Synthesis. Aus Vorlesungs- und Forschungsmanuskripten (1918–1926)*. Hrsg. M. Fleischer. Dordrecht: Kluwer, 1988.
- Volume XII: *Philosophie der Arithmetik. Mit ergänzenden Texten (1890–1901)*. Hrsg. L. Eley. The Hague: Nijhoff, 1970.
- Volume XIII: *Zur Phänomenologie der Intersubjektivität. Texte aus dem Nachlass. Erster Teil. 1905–1920*. Hrsg. I. Kern. The Hague: Nijhoff, 1973.
- Volume XIV: *Zur Phänomenologie der Intersubjektivität. Texte aus dem Nachlass. Zweiter Teil. 1921–1928*. Hrsg. I. Kern. The Hague: Nijhoff, 1973.
- Volume XV: *Zur Phänomenologie der Intersubjektivität. Texte aus dem Nachlass. Dritter Teil. 1929–1935*. Hrsg. I. Kern. The Hague: Nijhoff, 1973.
- Volume XVI: *Ding und Raum. Vorlesungen 1907*. Hrsg. U. Claesges. The Hague: Nijhoff, 1973.
- Volume XVII: *Formale und transzendentale Logik. Versuch einer Kritik der logischen Vernunft. Mit ergänzenden Texten*. Hrsg. Paul Janssen. The Hague: Nijhoff, 1974.
- Volume XVIII: *Logische Untersuchungen*. Erster Band: *Prolegomena zur reinen Logik*. Text der 1. und der 2. Auflage. Hrsg. E. Holenstein. 1975.
- Volume XIX: *Logische Untersuchungen*. Zweiter Band: *Untersuchungen zur Phänomenologie und Theorie der Erkenntnis*. In zwei Bänden. Hrsg. Ursula Panzer. Dordrecht: Kluwer, 1984.

- Volume XX/1: *Logische Untersuchungen. Ergänzungsband. Erster Teil. Entwürfe zur Umarbeitung der VI. Untersuchung und zur Vorrede für die Neuauflage der 'Logischen Untersuchungen' (Sommer 1913).* Hrsg. U. Melle. Dordrecht: Kluwer, 2002.
- Volume XXI: *Studien zur Arithmetik und Geometrie. Texte aus dem Nachlass (1886–1901).* Hrsg. I. Strohmeyer. 1983.
- Volume XXII: *Aufsätze und Rezensionen (1890–1910).* Hrsg. B. Rang. 1979.
- Volume XXIII: *Phantasie, Bildbewusstsein, Erinnerung. Zur Phänomenologie der anschaulichen Vergegenwärtigungen. Texte aus dem Nachlaß (1898–1925).* Hrsg. Eduard Marbach. 1980.
- Volume XXIV: *Einleitung in die Logik und Erkenntnistheorie. Vorlesungen 1906/07.* Hrsg. Ullrich Melle. Dordrecht: Kluwer, 1985.
- Volume XXV: *Aufsätze und Vorträge 1911–1921.* Hrsg. H.R. Sepp, Thomas Nenon. Dordrecht: Kluwer, 1986.
- Volume XXVI: *Vorlesungen über Bedeutungslehre. Sommersemester 1908.* Hrsg. Ursula Panzer. Dordrecht: Kluwer, 1986.
- Volume XXVII: *Aufsätze und Vorträge 1922–1937.* Hrsg. Thomas Nenon, H. R. Sepp. Dordrecht: Kluwer, 1989.
- Volume XXVIII: *Vorlesungen über Ethik und Wertlehre (1908–1914).* Hrsg. Ullrich Melle. Dordrecht: Kluwer, 1988.
- Volume XXIX: *Die Krisis der europäischen Wissenschaften und die transzendentale Phänomenologie. Ergänzungsband. Texte aus dem Nachlaß 1934–1937.* Hrsg. Reinhold N. Smid. Dordrecht: Kluwer, 1992.
- Volume XXX: *Logik und allgemeine Wissenschaftstheorie. Vorlesungen 1917/18, mit ergänzenden Texten aus der ersten Fassung 1910/11.* Hrsg. Ursula Panzer. Dordrecht: Kluwer, 1996.
- Volume XXXI: *Aktive Synthesen: Aus der Vorlesung 'Transzendentalen Logik' 1920/21.* Hrsg. Roland Breuer. Dordrecht: Kluwer, 2000.
- Volume XXXII: *Natur und Geist. Vorlesungen Sommersemester 1927.* Hrsg. Michael Weiler. Dordrecht: Kluwer, 2001
- Volume XXXIII: *Die 'Bernauer Manuskripte' über das Zeitbewußtsein (1917/18).* Hrsg. Rudolf Bernet & Dieter Lohmar. Dordrecht: Kluwer, 2001.
- Volume XXXIII: *Zur Phänomenologischen Reduktionen. Texte aus dem Nachlass (1926–1935).* Hrsg. Sebastian Luft. Dordrecht: Kluwer, 2002.

- Volume XXXV: *Einleitung in die Philosophie. Vorlesungen 1922/23.* Hrsg. Berndt Goossens. Dordrecht: Kluwer, 2002.
- Volume XXXVI: *Transzendentaler Idealismus. Texte aus dem Nachlass (1908–1921).* Hrsg. Robin Rollinger & Rochus Sowa. Dordrecht: Kluwer, 2003.
- Volume XXXVII. *Einleitung in die Ethik. Vorlesungen Sommersemester 1920 und 1924.* Hrsg. Henning Peucker. Dordrecht: Springer, 2004.
- Volume XXXVIII. *Wahrnehmung und Aufmerksamkeit. Texte aus dem Nachlass (1893–1912).* Hrsg. Thomas Vongehr und Regula Giuliani. Dordrecht: Springer, 2004.
- Volume XXXIX. *Die Lebenswelt: Auslegungen der Vorgegebenen Welt und ihrer Konstitution.* Hrsg. Rochus Sowa. Dordrecht: Springer, 2008.
- Volume XL. *Untersuchungen zur Urteilstheorie.* Ed. Rochus Sowa. Dordrecht: Springer, 2010.

ii Other editions and selections of Husserl's works

Husserl, Edmund. *Allgemeine Erkenntnistheorie 1902/03.* Hrsg. E. Schuhmann. *Materialenband*, Vol. 3. Dordrecht: Kluwer, 2001.

Husserl, Edmund. *Briefwechsel.* Ed. Karl Schuhmann in collaboration with Elizabeth Schuhmann. *Husserliana Dokumente*, 10 vols. Dordrecht: Kluwer, 1994.

Husserl, Edmund. *Einführung in die Phänomenologie der Erkenntnis. Vorlesung 1909.* Hrsg. Elizabeth Schuhmann. *Materialenbände*, Vol. 7. Dordrecht: Springer, 2005.

Husserl, Edmund. 'Entwurf einer 'Vorrede' zu den *Logischen Untersuchungen* (1913)'. Hrsg. Eugen Fink, *Tijdschrift voor Filosofie*, 1(1) (February 1939): 107–133; (2) (May 1939): 319–39.

Husserl, Edmund. *Erfahrung und Urteil. Untersuchungen zur Genealogie der Logik.* Redigiert und Hrsg. Ludwig Landgrebe. Prague: Academia-Verlag, 1938. 7. Aufl. Hamburg: Felix Meiner, 1999.

Husserl, Edmund. *Logik. Vorlesungen SS 1895 und SS 1896.* Hrsg. E. Schuhmann. *Materialenband*, Vol. 1. Dordrecht: Kluwer, 2001.

Husserl, Edmund. *Méditations cartésiennes: introduction à la phénoménologie.* Trans. G. Peiffer and E. Levinas. Paris: Almand Colin, 1931.

Husserl, Edmund. *Natur und Geist. Vorlesungen Sommersemester 1919.* Hrsg. M. Weiler. *Materialenband*, Vol. 4. Dordrecht: Kluwer, 2002.

Husserl, Edmund. *Späte Texte über Zeitkonstitution (1929–1934). Die C-Manuskripte.* Hrsg. Dieter Lohmar. *Materialenband*, Vol.8. Dordrecht: Springer, 2006.

Husserl, Edmund. *Urteilstheorie Vorlesung 1905.* Hrsg. E. Schuhmann. *Materialenband*, Vol. 5. Dordrecht: Kluwer, 2002.

Husserl, Edmund. *Vorlesungen WS 1902/03.* Hrsg. E. Schuhmann. *Materialenband*, Vol. 2. Dordrecht: Kluwer, 2001.

iii Works by Edmund Husserl in English translation

Husserl, Edmund. *Analyses Concerning Passive and Active Synthesis. Lectures on Transcendental Logic.* Trans. Anthony J. Steinbock. Husserl Collected Works, Volume IX. Dordrecht: Kluwer, 2001.

Husserl, Edmund. *The Basic Problems of Phenomenology. From the Lectures, Winter Semester, 1910–1911.* Trans. Ingo Farin and James G. Hart. Dordrecht: Springer, 2006.

Husserl, Edmund. *Cartesian Meditations.* Trans. D. Cairns. The Hague: Nijhoff, 1967.

Husserl, Edmund. *The Crisis of European Sciences and Transcendental Phenomenology. An Introduction to Phenomenological Philosophy.* Trans. David Carr. Evanston, IL: Northwestern University Press, 1970.

Husserl, Edmund. *Early Writings in the Philosophy of Logic and Mathematics.* Trans. Dallas Willard. Collected Works, Volume V. Dordrecht: Kluwer, 1994.

Husserl, Edmund. *Experience and Judgment: Investigations in a Genealogy of Logic.* Revised and Edited by L. Landgrebe. Trans. J. S. Churchill and K. Ameriks. London: Routledge & Kegan Paul, 1973.

Husserl, Edmund. 'Fichte's Ideal of Humanity [Three Lectures].' Trans. James G. Hart. *Husserl Studies* 12 (1995): 111–33.

Husserl, Edmund. *Formal and Transcendental Logic.* Trans. D. Cairns. The Hague: Nijhoff, 1969.

Husserl, Edmund. *Husserl. Shorter Works.* Trans. and Eds Frederick Elliston and Peter McCormick. Notre Dame, IN: University of Notre Dame Press, 1981.

Husserl, Edmund. *The Idea of Phenomenology.* Trans. Lee Hardy. Collected Works, Volume VIII. Dordrecht: Kluwer, 1999.

Husserl, Edmund. *Ideas pertaining to a Pure Phenomenology and to a Phenomenological Philosophy, First Book.* Trans. F. Kersten. Dordrecht: Kluwer, 1983.

Husserl, Edmund. *Ideas pertaining to a Pure Phenomenology and to a Phenomenological Philosophy, Second Book.* Trans. R. Rojcewicz and A. Schuwer. Collected Works, Volume III. Dordrecht: Kluwer, 1989.

Husserl, Edmund. *Ideas pertaining to a Pure Phenomenology and to a Phenomenological Philosophy, Third Book.* Trans. Ted E. Klein and W. E. Pohl. Collected Works, Volume I. The Hague: Nijhoff, 1980.

Husserl, Edmund. *Ideas. A General Introduction to Pure Phenomenology.* Trans. W. R. Boyce Gibson. London: Allen & Unwin, 1931.

Husserl, Edmund. *Introduction to the Logical Investigations. Draft of a Preface to the Logical Investigations.* Ed. E. Fink. Trans. P. J. Bossert and C. H. Peters. The Hague, Nijhoff, 1975.

Husserl, Edmund. 'Kant and the Idea of Transcendental Philosophy'. Trans. Ted E. Klein and William E. Pohl. *Southwestern Journal of Philosophy*, 5 (Fall 1974): 9–56.

Husserl, Edmund. *Logical Investigations*, 2 vols. Trans. J.N. Findlay. Ed. with a New Introduction by Dermot Moran and New Preface by Michael Dummett. London and New York: Routledge, 2001.

Husserl, Edmund. *The Paris Lectures.* Trans. P. Koestenaum. The Hague: Nijhoff, 1970.

Husserl, Edmund. *Phantasy, Image Consciousness and Memory (1895–1925)*. Trans. John Brough. Husserl Collected Works, Vol. XI. Dordrecht: Springer, 2005.

Husserl, Edmund. *Phenomenological Psychology. Lectures, Summer Semester 1925*. Trans. J. Scanlon. The Hague: Nijhoff, 1977.

Husserl, Edmund. *On the Phenomenology of the Consciousness of Internal Time*. Trans. J. B. Brough. Collected Works, Volume IV. Dordrecht: Kluwer, 1990.

Husserl, Edmund. *The Phenomenology of Internal Time Consciousness*. Ed. Heidegger, Martin. Trans. J. S. Churchill. London: Indiana University Press, 1964.

Husserl, Edmund. *Philosophy of Arithmetic. Psychological and Logical Investigations*. Trans. Dallas Willard. Husserl Collected Works, Volume X. Dordrecht: Kluwer, 2003.

Husserl, Edmund. *Philosophy as a Rigorous Science*, 1911, in Quentin Lauer. *Edmund Husserl. Phenomenology and the Crisis of Philosophy*. New York: Harper & Row, 1964.

Husserl, Edmund. 'Philosophy as Rigorous Science,' trans. Marcus Brainard, *The New Yearbook for Phenomenology and Phenomenological Philosophy*, 2 (2002): 249–95.

Husserl, Edmund. *Psychological and Transcendental Phenomenology and the Confrontation with Heidegger (1927–31), The Encyclopaedia Britannica Article, The Amsterdam Lectures 'Phenomenology and Anthropology' and Husserl's Marginal Note in Being and Time, and Kant on the Problem of Metaphysics*. Trans. T. Sheehan and R.E. Palmer. Collected Works, Volume VI. Dordrecht: Kluwer Academic Publishers, 1997.

Husserl, Edmund. 'Syllabus of a Course of Four Lectures on 'Phenomenological Method and Phenomenological Philosophy,' Delivered at University College, London June 6, 8, 9, 12, 1922,' *Journal of the British Society for Phenomenology*, 1 (1) (1970): 18–23.

Husserl, Edmund. *Thing and Space: Lectures of 1907*. Trans. R. Rojcewicz. Collected Works, Volume VII. Dordrecht: Kluwer, 1997.

Welton, Donn. Ed. *The Essential Husserl*. Bloomington: Indiana University Press, 1999.

iv Selected further reading

Bell, David. *Husserl*. London: Routledge, 1991.

Bernet, Rudolf, Iso Kern and Eduard Marbach. *An Introduction to Husserlian Phenomenology*. Evanston, IL: Northwestern University Press, 1993.

Biceaga, Victor. *The Concept of Passivity in Husserl's Phenomenology*. Contributions to Phenomenology, Vol. 60. Dordrecht: Springer, 2010.

Brainard, Marcus. *Belief and Its Neutralization. Husserl's System of Phenomenology in Ideas I*. Albany, NY: State University of New York Press, 2002.

Cairns, Dorion. *Guide for Translating Husserl*. The Hague: Nijhoff, 1973.

Carr, David. *Interpreting Husserl: Critical and Comparative Studies*. Dordrecht: Kluwer, 1987.

Carr, David. *The Paradox of Subjectivity. The Self in the Transcendental Tradition*. Oxford: Oxford University Press, 1999.

Cobb-Stevens, Richard. *Husserl and Analytic Philosophy.* Dordrecht: Kluwer, 1990.

Crowell, Steven Galt. *Husserl, Heidegger, and the Space of Meaning: Paths toward Transcendental Phenomenology.* Evanston, IL: Northwestern University Press, 2001.

DeBoer, Theodor. *The Development of Husserl's Thought.* The Hague: Nijhoff, 1978.

De Warren, Nicolas. *Husserl and the Promise of Time. Subjectivity in Transcendental Philosophy.* New York: Cambridge University Press, 2009.

Derrida, Jacques. *Speech and Phenomena and other Essays on Husserl's Theory of Signs.* Ed. and Trans. David Allison. Evanston, IL: Northwestern University Press, 1973.

Derrida, Jacques. *Edmund Husserl's Origin of Geometry. An Introduction.* Trans. J. P. Leavey and D. B. Allison. Sussex: Harvester Press, 1978.

Dodd, James. *Idealism and Corporeity: An Essay on the Problem of the Body in Husserl's Phenomenology.* Dordrecht: Kluwer Academic Publishers, 1997.

Dreyfus, Hubert L. Ed. *Husserl, Intentionality and Cognitive Science.* Cambridge, MA: MIT Press, 1982.

Drummond, John J. *Husserlian Intentionality and Non-Foundational Realism. Noema and Object.* Dordrecht: Kluwer, 1990.

Drummond, John J. *Historical Dictionary of Husserl's Philosophy.* Lanham, MD: Scarecrow Press, 2008.

Elliston, F. and P. McCormick. Ed. *Husserl. Expositions and Appraisals.* Notre Dame, IN: University of Notre Dame Press, 1977.

Elveton, R. O. Ed. *The Phenomenology of Edmund Husserl. Selected Critical Readings.* Chicago Quadrangle, 1970. 2nd edn. Seattle: Noesis Press, 2000.

English, Jacques. *Le Vocabulaire de Husserl.* Paris: Editions Ellipses, 2004.

Farber, Marvin. *The Foundation of Phenomenology.* Cambridge, MA: Harvard University Press, 1943.

Fisette, Denis. Ed. *Husserl's Logical Investigations Reconsidered.* Dordrecht: Kluwer, 2003.

Føllesdal, Dagfinn, 'Husserl's Notion of Noema,' *Journal of Philosophy*, 66 (1969): 680–87.

Gander, Hans-Helmuth. Ed. *Husserl-Lexikon.* Darmstadt: Wissenschaftliche Buchgesellschaft, 2010.

Hart, James G. *The Person and the Common Life. Studies in a Husserlian Social Ethics.* Dordrecht: Kluwer, 1992.

Heidegger, Martin, *Being and Time.* Trans. John Macquarrie and E. Robinson. New York: Harper & Row, 1962.

Hill, Claire Ortiz. *Word and Object in Husserl, Frege and Russell.* Athens, OH: Ohio University Press, 1991.

Hopkins, Burt C. Ed. *Husserl in Contemporary Context.* Dordrecht: Kluwer, 1997.

Hopkins, Burt C. Ed. *The Philosophy of Husserl.* Durham, NC: Acumen, 2011.

Ingarden, Roman. *On the Motives which led Husserl to Transcendental Idealism.* Trans. Arnór Hannibalsson. The Hague: Nijhoff, 1975.

Kohák, Erazim. *Idea and Experience. Edmund Husserl's Project of Phenomenology in Ideas II.* Chicago, IL: University of Chicago Press, 1978.

Landgrebe, Ludwig. *The Phenomenology of Edmund Husserl. Six Essays.* Ed. D. Welton. Ithaca, NY: Cornell University Press, 1981.

Levinas, Emannuel. *The Theory of Intuition in Husserl's Phenomenology.* Trans. A. Orianne. Evanston, IL: Northwestern University Press, 1973.

McKenna, William R., R. M. Harlan and L. E. Winters. Eds. *Apriori and World. European Contributions to Husserlian Phenomenology.* The Hague: Nijhoff, 1981.

McKenna, William R. *Husserl's 'Introductions' to Phenomenology. Interpretation and Critique.* Dordrecht: Kluwer, 1982.

Marion, Jean-Luc. *Reduction and Givenness. Investigations of Husserl, Heidegger, and Phenomenology.* Trans. Thomas A. Carlson. Evanston, IL: Northwestern University Press, 1998.

Mensch, James Richard. *Intersubjectivity and Transcendental Idealism.* Albany, NY: SUNY Press, 1988.

Mensch, James Richard. *Postfoundational Phenomenology. Husserlian Reflections on Presence and Embodiment.* University Park, PA: Pennsylvania State University Press, 2001.

Merleau-Ponty, M. *The Phenomenology of Perception.* Trans. C. Smith. London: Routledge & Kegan Paul, 1962.

Mohanty, J. N. *Edmund Husserl's Theory of Meaning.* The Hague: Martinus Nijhoff, 1976.

Mohanty, J. N. Ed. *Readings on Edmund Husserl's Logical Investigations.* The Hague: Nijhoff, 1977.

Mohanty, J. N. *Husserl and Frege.* Bloomington: Indiana University Press, 1982.

Mohanty, J. N. *The Philosophy of Edmund Husserl. A Historical Development.* New Haven: Yale University Press, 2008.

Mohanty, J. N. and William R. McKenna. Eds. *Husserl's Phenomenology: A Textbook.* Washington, DC: Center for Advanced Research in Phenomenology and University Press of America, 1989.

Moran, Dermot. *Introduction to Phenomenology.* London and New York: Routledge, 2000.

Moran, Dermot. *Edmund Husserl. Founder of Phenomenology.* Cambridge: Polity Press, 2005.

Osborn, Andrew. *The Philosophy of Edmund Husserl in its Development from his Mathematical Interests to his First Conception of Phenomenology in the Logical Investigations.* New York: International Press, 1934.

Patočka, Jan. *An Introduction to Husserl's Phenomenology.* Trans. Erazim Kohák. Chicago, IL: Open Court, 1996.

Ricoeur, Paul. *Husserl. An Analysis of his Philosophy.* Ebanston, IL: Northwestern University Press, 1967.

Rollinger, Robin. *Husserl's Position in the School of Brentano.* Utrecht: Dept of Philosophy, Utrecht University, 1996.

Schuhmann, Karl. *Husserl-Chronik. Denk- und Lebensweg Edmund Husserls.* The Hague: Nijhoff, 1977.

Seebohm Thomas and Joseph Kockelmans. Eds. *Kant and Phenomenology.* Washington, DC: Center for Advanced Research in Phenomenology, 1984.

Smith, A. D. *Husserl and The Cartesian Meditations.* London and New York: Routledge, 2003.

Smith, Barry and David Woodruff Smith. Eds. *The Cambridge Companion to Husserl.* Cambridge: Cambridge University Press, 1995.

Smith, David Woodruff. *Husserl.* London: Routledge, 2007.

Smith, David Woodruff and Ronald McIntyre. *Husserl and Intentionality. A Study of Mind, Meaning and Language.* Dordrecht: Reidel, 1982.

Sokolowski, Robert. *The Formation of Husserl's Concept of Constitution.* The Hague: Nijhoff, 1964.

Sokolowski, Robert. *Husserlian Meditations. How Words Present Things.* Evanston, IL: Northwestern University Press, 1974.

Sokolowski, Robert. *Introduction to Phenomenology.* New York: Cambridge University Press, 1999.

Spiegelberg, Herbert, with Karl Schuhmann. *The Phenomenological Movement. A Historical Introduction.* 3rd edn. Dordrecht: Kluwer, 1994.

Stein, Edith. *On the Problem of Empathy.* Trans. Waltraut Stein. Collected Works of Edith Stein, Vol. 3. Washington, DC: ICS Publications, 1989.

Steinbock, Anthony J. *Home and Beyond. Generative Phenomenology after Husserl.* Evanston, IL: Northwestern University Press, 1995.

Ströker, Elizabeth. *Husserl's Transcendental Phenomenology.* Stanford, CA: Stanford University Press, 1993.

Welton, Donn. *The Origins of Meaning. A Critical Study of the Thresholds of Husserlian Phenomenology.* The Hague; Nijhoff, 1983.

Welton, Donn. *The Other Husserl.* Bloomington, IN: Indiana University Press, 2001.

Wetter, Helmuth. Ed. *Wörterbuch der phänomenologischen Begriffe.* Hamburg: Felix Meiner, 2005.

Wiegand, Olav K., R. Dostal, J. N. Mohanty, and J. J. Kockelmans. Eds. *Phenomenology on Kant, German Idealism, Hermeneutics and Logic.* Dordrecht: Kluwer, 2000.

Willard, Dallas. *Logic and the Objectivity of Knowledge. A Study in Husserl's Early Philosophy.* Athens, OH: Ohio University Press, 1984.

Zahavi, Dan. *Self-Awareness and Alterity. A Phenomenological Investigation.* Evanston, IL: Northwestern, 1999.

Zahavi, Dan. *Husserl and Transcendental Intersubjectivity.* Trans. Elizabeth A. Behnke. Athens, OH: Ohio University Press, 2001.

Zahavi, Dan. *Husserl's Phenomenology.* Stanford, CA: Stanford University Press, 2003.

Zahavi, Dan and Frederick Stjernfelt. Eds. *One Hundred Years of Phenomenology. Husserl's Logical Investigations Revisited.* Dordrecht: Kluwer, 2002.

Zahavi, Dan and N. Depraz. Eds. *Alterity and Facticity: New Perspectives on Husserl.* Dordrecht: Kluwer, 1998.

Index

This thematic and nominal index provides a comprehensive set of references to the key philosophical terms in the Husserl Dictionary. It also references the central philosophers of the phenomenological tradition as well as those figures in the history of philosophy who influenced Husserl's writings and thought.

The bold numbers represent the pages of the specific entries for each term and person when applicable.

Works are italicized (and also referenced to their original language) and dated in accordance with the original date of publication.

Printed in Great Britain
by Amazon